*Limited Classical Reprint Library*

# THE BOOK OF JOB

WITH INTRODUCTION AND NOTES

BY

EDGAR C. S. GIBSON D.D.

VICAR OF LEEDS AND PREBENDARY OF WELLS

Klock & Klock Christian Publishers
2527 GIRARD AVE. N.
MINNEAPOLIS, MINNESOTA 55411

Originally published by
Nethuen & Co.
1899

ISBN: 0-86524-170-8

Printed by Klock & Klock in the U.S.A.
1983 Reprint

# FOREWORD

Suffering is something from which we instinctively shrink. It is natural for us to try and avoid those situations in life which cause us to experience anxiety or feel pain. However, because it is as natural for man to encounter trouble or misfortune as it is for the sparks of a fire to fly upwards (Job 5:7), we can all learn from Job's experience how to endure suffering with patience.

As the story of Job unfolds, we find that at one period of his life he was deprived of everything. The loss of his wealth reduced him to penury. The sudden death of his children caused him to feel the anguish of loneliness. Sickness robbed him of his health. Only his wife remained, and in the bitterness of her trials even she turned against him.

But the story of Job does not end in dispair. His reliance on the Lord demonstrates for us that adversity accepted produces patience, and that perseverance in doing what is right leads to eventual triumph.

Of the many writers who have published their insights on the Book of Job and the place of suffering in human experience, one of the finest is Edgar Charles Sumner Gibson (1848-1924). A graduate of Oxford University, and a lecturer at Cambridge, Dr. Gibson had a remarkable career as both teacher and preacher. He also wrote several books of which his study of Job is his most famous.

Dr. Gibson begins his commentary on the Book of Job with a fitting introduction. This is followed by his comments on the text. Each section, however, is prefaced with a clear explanation of the biblical writer's theme. The exegetical and expository notes which make up the bulk of his work demonstrate how painstaking study can enrich and enhance one's study of the Word of God.

Edgar Gibson's *Book of Job* is perceptive and edifying, and deserves a place alongside the renowned work of William Henry Green. It should be in every minister's library.

Cyril J. Barber

## PREFATORY NOTE BY THE GENERAL EDITOR

THE primary object of these Commentaries is to be exegetical, to interpret the meaning of each book of the Bible in the light of modern knowledge to English readers. The Editors will not deal, except subordinately, with questions of textual criticism or philology ; but taking the English text in the Revised Version as their basis, they will aim at combining a hearty acceptance of critical principles with loyalty to the Catholic Faith.

The series will be less elementary than the Cambridge Bible for Schools, less critical than the International Critical Commentary, less didactic than the Expositor's Bible ; and it is hoped that it may be of use both to theological students and to the clergy, as well as to the growing number of educated laymen and laywomen who wish to read the Bible intelligently and reverently.

Each commentary will therefore have

(i) An Introduction stating the bearing of modern criticism and research upon the historical character of the book, and drawing out the contribution which the book, as a whole, makes to the body of religious truth.

(ii) A careful paraphrase of the text with notes on the more difficult passages and, if need be, excursuses on any points of special importance either for doctrine, or ecclesiastical organization, or spiritual life.

But the books of the Bible are so varied in character that considerable latitude is needed, as to the proportion which the various parts should hold to each other. The General Editor will therefore only endeavour to secure a general uniformity in scope and character : but the exact method adopted in each case and the final responsibility for the statements made will rest with the individual contributors.

By permission of the Delegates of the Oxford University Press and of the Syndics of the Cambridge University Press the Text used in this Series of Commentaries is the Revised Version of the Holy Scriptures.

WALTER LOCK.

# INTRODUCTION

## I. The place of the book in the Canon.

The place which the Book of Job occupies in our English Bibles after the historical books and before the Psalms is that which it has always occupied in the Western Church, at least since the days of S. Jerome, in whose translation (the Vulgate) it is found in this position, in accordance with the arrangement of the books commonly (though not invariably) adopted in the Greek Bibles. But in the original Hebrew an entirely different arrangement is found. It there stands after the Psalms and Proverbs in the third of the three divisions (the Law, the Prophets, and the *Cethubhim* or 'writings') into which the Scriptures are divided by the Jews. It is rightly placed in close connexion with the Psalms and Proverbs, as being, like them, *poetical* in form ; and accordingly in the Hebrew there is a special system of accentuation peculiar to these three books. It has also close affinities in another way with Proverbs, as well as with Ecclesiastes, for these three books stand out as the representatives within the Canon of what may be termed the 'Wisdom' literature of the Hebrews. The word 'wisdom' (*Khochmah*, חָכְמָה) is often used in the Old Testament as a kind of technical term. The 'wise man' (הֶחָכָם) had a recognized position in the nation as the third along with the 'priest' and the 'prophet.' So in Jeremiah xviii. 18 we read 'the law (תּוֹרָה) shall not perish from the *priest*, nor counsel from the *wise* (חָכָם), nor the word from the *prophet*' (נָבִיא). Thus the priest had his 'law,' or express direction from Jehovah Himself, whose commandment it embodied ; the prophet declared the 'word of the LORD,' revealing His will in those crises in which the ordinary rules failed ; while the wise man, without (apparently) any express revelation to appeal to, sought to give 'counsel' on those subjects which were outside the sphere of law and prophecy, and busied himself with the perplexities and puzzles of natural life and the moral relations of man, almost, as we might say, with physics and ethics. The cultivation of this 'wisdom' was not peculiar to Israel. It was found also among other nations of the East, as the Egyptians (cf. Isaiah xix. 11, 12), and also the Edomites (see Jer. xlix. 7 ; Obad. 8). In Israel it apparently took its rise in the days of Solomon, whose 'wisdom excelled the wisdom of all the children of the East and all the wisdom of Egypt' (see 1 Kings iv. 29—34). And since it was neither peculiar to Israel, nor directly concerned with subjects proper to 'revelation,' it is not surprising to find that the 'wise man' looked at life from the standpoint not of the covenant nation but of *man* in general, and that the common characteristic of the Wisdom literature is the *human* standpoint, stripped of everything peculiarly Israelitish. Thus in Proverbs we have not only proverbs traditionally ascribed to Solomon, but those also of King Lemuel, and Agur the son of Jakeh, neither of whom were probably Israelites, nor does the name of the covenant people, *Israel*, occur except in the title of that book (Prov. i. 1). In Ecclesiastes the name of the covenant God, Jehovah, is nowhere found ; while in Job the whole scene of the drama, and all the characters introduced are non-Israelite.

[See on the 'Wisdom' of the Hebrews, Driver, *Introduction to the Literature of the Old Testament*, p. 392 (ed. 6); Delitzsch, *Commentary on Job*, vol. i. p. 5 ; and Oehler, *Theology of the Old Testament*, vol. ii. p. 432.]

## II. The contents, structure, and main divisions of the book.

The structure of the book is easily seen. It falls into five well-defined and clearly marked divisions, the first and the last of which are in ordinary prose, while the three between them (as may be seen from the arrangement of the text in parallel lines in the Revised Version) are in poetry.

Chapters i. and ii. form the prologue. In them we have a brief description of Job's position and prosperity ; the account of the first scene in heaven with Satan's suggestion that Job's piety is only a refined form of selfishness ; the permission to tempt him ; the fourfold trial under which he stands firm ; the second scene in heaven with Satan's second suggestion ; the renewed trial of Job ; and the visit of his friends. Thus the Prologue gives the outline of Job's history, and introduces the *dramatis personæ*.

The second part (chapters iii.—xxxi.) contains the debate between Job and his three friends, Eliphaz the Temanite, Bildad the Shuhite, and Zophar the Naamathite. It is a dialogue constructed with consummate skill, and exquisitely arranged. After Job's 'curse upon his day' in chapter iii. the speeches form three circles, each friend speaking in turn and receiving his answer from Job before the next one takes up the charge. So the debate moves forward with perfect regularity through two complete circles (chapters iv.—xiv. and xv.—xxi.). But in the third (chapters xxii.—xxvi.), the brevity of the speech of Bildad, the second speaker of the three, in chapter xxv., and the way in which he can do little more than stammer out a few things that have been already said by a previous speaker, warn us that the friends have well-nigh exhausted their stock of argument; and accordingly it is no surprise to find that Zophar considers discretion the better part of valour, and misses his turn altogether, leaving Job as master of the field, to continue his discourse in the form of a monologue (chapters xxvii.—xxxi.).

After this, in the third part, a new speaker, not previously mentioned, appears upon the scene in the person of Elihu. Dissatisfied with the arguments of the friends, and yet shocked at the utterances of Job, he intervenes by pointing out certain considerations with regard to suffering and its providential purpose which have apparently escaped the notice of both parties in the dialogue. This episode—whether it formed part of the original poem, or whether it is a subsequent addition by a later poet, we need not at this point stop to inquire—occupies chapters xxxii.—xxxvii.

And then in the fourth part (chapters xxxviii.—xlii. 6) God Himself interposes. Job's challenge to Him has been heard. The Almighty answers Job out of the whirlwind, and overwhelms him with question after question designed to bring home to him the impossibility of his arguing with God, or understanding the whole scheme of Divine providence. The result is that Job is completely humbled and abases himself before God. 'I had heard of Thee by the hearing of the ear; but now mine eye seeth Thee, wherefore I abhor myself, and repent in dust and ashes.'

Finally, in the epilogue (chapter xlii. 7—17), which like the prologue is in prose, the story is brought to an end by the Divine verdict upon the speakers in the dialogue, and the restoration of Job's prosperity. 'The Lord turned the captivity of Job, and gave him twice as much as he had before.'

Thus the divisions of the book stand out as follows :

I.  The prologue.  i. ii.

II.  The debate between Job and his friends.  iii.—xxxi.

III.  The speeches of Elihu.  xxxii.—xxxvii.

IV.  The answer of the Almighty out of the whirlwind.
xxxviii.—xlii. 6.

V.  The epilogue.  xlii. 7—17.

## III.  The object and character of the book.

The fact that the book is written in poetry, and that its
character is so beautifully symmetrical, the well-ordered arrangement of the speeches, their length and artistic character, show at
once that we are not dealing with literal history.  Even in the prose
narrative of the prologue and epilogue there are indications that it
is a work of art rather than an exact record of historical facts with
which we are concerned.  The symmetrical character of Job's fourfold
trial has often been noticed.  The exact reward meted out to him
at the close, the number of his flocks and herds being literally
doubled, and the precise number of children born to him after his
trial equalling those whom he had lost in it—all these features
point to the same conclusion.  The work as a whole is a poem, and
is meant to be regarded as such.  There may of course be some
historical basis, but, to put it at the very lowest, the same license
and freedom in dealing with his materials must be granted to the
author of Job that is conceded to other poets treating of historical
situations.  How much literal history may lie at the basis of the
narrative does not really greatly concern us.  That Job was a
historical character is probable from the allusion to him in Ezekiel
xiv. 14, 'Though these three men, Noah, Daniel, and Job, were in it,
they should deliver but their own souls by their righteousness, saith
the Lord God,' and had the narrative been entirely created for the
sake of the lessons it was intended to convey, we should have expected the names of the *dramatis personæ* to be significant, and tell
us something of their character or position; whereas it is difficult to
attach importance to any of them, and even in the case of Job
himself, the hero of the story, it is doubtful whether the name is
intended to be especially appropriate, or descriptive of his position
(see the note on i. 1).  The probability, then, is that there was some
ancient traditional story of which Job was the hero, which the writer

took as the basis of his poem, and made the vehicle of conveying to the minds of his contemporaries the religious lessons which he desired to impress upon them. It was probably written (see below, § IV.) in an age when troubles and calamities were falling thick upon the people, and the old doctrine of retribution was felt to be breaking down. In early days men were content with the simple view that suffering was in all cases the punishment of sin, and that long life and happiness were invariably the reward of virtue.

This theory, as the author of the book sees clearly enough, is fraught with difficulties. The problem of the mystery of pain and suffering weighed heavily upon his mind, and through the medium of the old patriarchal story he would set his thoughts upon it before his contemporaries. He has no complete and consistent theory himself to put in the place of the old one which he demolishes, but one thing he can see clearly enough, viz. that you have no right to argue back from suffering to sin, and this he is determined to make others see as well. Further, there are various considerations, each of which requires to be taken into account, which he brings forward in the several portions of the poem. It is in the second and longest section that the workings of his mind are most fully revealed, and in this the main interest of the book is centred. It must be remembered that the parties to the debate knew nothing whatever of the scene in heaven as described in the prologue. The author of the book by placing this in the forefront has admitted us behind the scenes, and let us into the secret of Job's sufferings. They formed, as so many sufferings form to-day, a God-permitted Satanic temptation, allowed in order to test the patriarch's faith, and try whether his goodness was genuine, or whether his piety was after all a subtle form of selfishness, a serving God for what he could get out of Him. But of this neither the friends nor Job himself were aware. They only knew what they could see with the eye of sense. Here was a man who had lived in great prosperity, honoured and respected of all men, suddenly overwhelmed with calamity after calamity— his flocks and his herds destroyed, his children dead, himself a victim of a most loathsome disease. What did it all mean? That was the problem before them. What had they got to say to it? Probably up to this time Job and his friends alike had acquiesced without much consideration in what we might fairly call the ortho- dox theology of the day. The theory of suffering which held the field in that ancient world to which the poem transports us was a strict doctrine of exact retribution. Suffering was penal : it was the consequence of sin. Not content with a general view which would link the suffering of the race more or less closely with the sin of the race, there was a tendency to argue that in any individual case suffering was exactly meted out in proportion to individual sin : and thus it was natural to argue back from the existence of so much suffering, and infer the existence of so much previous sin as its cause. A notable sufferer, men said, must be a notable sinner. Holding this doctrine Job's friends are suddenly confronted with his case. What are they to make of it? Job was undoubtedly a great sufferer. Of that there was overwhelming evidence. The only theory known to them which would account for it was that Job had been secretly guilty of some great sin for which he was now being chastised by God. True, his whole past life gave the lie to this notion. His goodness and uprightness had been a living 'epistle known and read of all men.' But still, rather than question their theory, rather than give up their 'short and easy method,' they will shut their eyes to facts. It is not that they cannot see—it is that they will not see. There is a difference of tone between them. One may be more courteous—more of a gentleman, another may be of a coarser type, but that is all. The main position taken by all three is identical. Suffering is the punishment of sin. Job is a great sufferer. Therefore Job is a great sinner. This argument underlies all their speeches : veiled at the outset, and only hinted at in the first circle, but at last stated nakedly, and applied to Job with relentless cruelty. In spite of all that Job has to urge against them, in spite of his appeal to facts, they cannot conceive that there are more things in heaven and earth than are dreamt of in their philosophy. They have their theory, and if facts do not square with it, then—so much the worse for facts. Nothing would induce them to admit that 'the bed was shorter than a man could stretch himself on it, and the covering narrower than he could wrap himself in it.' They will not see that their theory was totally inadequate to meet all the needs of the whole case. We, as we read the book, with the fuller knowledge that the ages have brought, and the deeper insight that comes from a larger revelation of God's mind and purpose, can see clearly enough that, though their theory contained much truth, yet as a theory it was utterly inadequate because it failed to cover the whole ground. True that *some* suffering is penal, and is the direct consequence of sin. We see it every day of our lives; but true too that this does not hold good of *all* suffering. Some, as the prologue to Job reminds us, is permitted by God to test us. Life, as Bishop Butler puts it, is 'a time of probation.' Some, as Elihu suggests in his speeches, is designed not only for probation, but—to use Butler's phraseology again—for 'moral discipline and improvement,' in order that man may be not only *proved*, but also *improved* by it. Some still remains mysterious and shrouded in darkness. Perhaps the whole mystery of suffering is insoluble by us in our present condition; and whatever advances we make in knowledge, there will still be much which, as the speeches of the Almighty out of the whirlwind tell us, we cannot hope to understand unless we can comprehend the whole mind of God. Some—and here the Book of Job prepares the way for Christianity by stopping short and containing no hint of this—is vicarious, as in the highest and most unique sense the sufferings of Him who gave His life on the Cross for us; Whose sufferings are to be in some sense repeated in His members, even as an Apostle could say that he 'filled up what was wanting of the afflictions of Christ in his flesh, for His body's sake, which is the Church' (Col. i. 24). But to all these further considerations Job's friends are blind. Nothing can shake their adherence to the theory with which they started. Here is the conclusion at which Eliphaz, the most thoughtful and the most considerate of the three, arrives, inventing crimes wholesale, and laying them to Job's account, as the true explanation of his misfortunes :

> 'Is not thy wickedness great?
> Neither is there any end to thine iniquities.
> For thou hast taken pledges of thy brother for nought,
> And stripped the naked of their clothing.
> Thou hast not given water to the weary to drink,
> And thou hast withholden bread from the hungry.
> . . . . . . . . .
> Thou hast sent widows away empty,
> And the arms of the fatherless have been broken.
> Therefore snares are round about thee,
> And sudden fear troubleth thee,
> Or darkness, that thou canst not see,
> And abundance of waters cover thee.'          xxii. 5—11.

Turning now to consider the position taken up by Job himself, it is to be remarked that we are evidently to conceive of him as having, up to the time when his troubles fell upon him, acquiesced

J.

c

(like his friends) in the orthodox doctrine of the day. It was a doctrine which did well enough for fine weather, and for other people. So long as he was prosperous himself he could lightly acquiesce in the view that the sufferings of others somehow stood to their sin in the relation of effect to cause. But now he himself is exposed to 'the pelting of the pitiless storm.' Stroke after stroke beats down remorselessly upon him; and he feels that the old doctrine of retribution has broken down hopelessly in his case. He is not an exceptionally great sinner, nor has he done anything to deserve exceptionally severe treatment as a punishment. On this point his conscience is perfectly clear. The old doctrine must go. It has broken down hopelessly. But he has nothing to set in its place. The old theory must go, but the pain and pathos of the situation is that he cannot explain the facts which are forced upon his notice. He knows for his own part that his suffering is not a consequence of his sin. He can point to evidences in the world around him, such as the misfortunes into which good men fall, and the prosperity of the violent and rapacious, which give the lie to his friends' explanation. They had maintained that

'The light of the wicked shall be put out.'  xviii. 5.

He turns on them with bitterness in his tone, and asks

'How oft is it that the lamp of the wicked is put out?
That their calamity cometh upon them?
That *God* distributeth sorrows in His anger?
That they are as stubble before the wind?
And as chaff that the storm carrieth away?  xxi. 17, 18.

. . . . . . . . . . .

Their seed is established with them in their sight,
And their offspring before their eyes.
Their houses are safe from fear,
Neither is the rod of God upon them.
Their bull gendereth, and faileth not;
Their cow calveth, and casteth not her calf.
They send forth their little ones like a flock,
And their children dance.  xxi. 8—11.

. . . . . . . . . . .

Have ye not asked them that go by the way?
And do ye not know their tokens?
That the evil man is spared in the day of calamity?
That they are led away in the day of wrath?'  xxi. 29, 30.

He can see now clearly enough that such facts are incompatible with the view that he has hitherto accepted. But beyond this, at first, he cannot go. He has nothing to set in the place of the old, inadequate theory. He knows no considerations that can help him to bear his sufferings patiently—and oh, the misery of his condition! God is treating him as His enemy, setting him up as a target for His arrows, and there is none to tell the reason why. What conception can he form of God but that He is aimlessly cruel, and wantonly capricious? And so the temptation comes home to him to which the Satan had suggested that he was sure to yield, and which his own wife had urged on him : 'renounce God and die.' 'Renounce God,' that is, Bid farewell to Him (i. 5, note), and have nothing more to say to Him at all. That was the temptation, and a sore one it was. But it was just here that Job stood firm. Appearances were against God, but Job would trust Him in spite of appearances, certain that there must be some explanation, if only he could find it. Whatever happened he would never bid farewell to Him : and it was this that brought him through the storm and stress. He might say wild and unjustifiable things about God, he might have hard thoughts concerning Him, but the one thing which he would not do was to 'renounce God' altogether. No, 'not even when the whirl was worst,' for through it all he feels that if he could only get at God Himself, if he could only come and speak with Him face to face and plead his cause and demand an answer, all would be well.

'Only do not two things unto me,
    Then will I not hide myself from Thy face :
Withdraw Thine hand far from me ;
    And let not Thy terror make me afraid.
Then call Thou, and I will answer ;
    Or let me speak, and answer Thou me.'        xiii. 20—22.

'Oh that I knew where I might find Him,
    That I might come even to His seat !
I would order my cause before Him,
    And fill my mouth with arguments.
I would know the words which He would answer me,
    And understand what He would say unto me.
Would He contend with me in the greatness of His power ?
    Nay ; but He would give heed unto me.
There the upright might reason with Him ;
    So should I be delivered for ever from my judge.'        xxiii. 3—7.

And so, as he clings to this, gradually one consideration after another breaks in upon him. There is borne into his soul the thought of a day when present inequalities shall hereafter be righted; and there comes home to him the certainty that 'at the last' God will 'stand up' as his 'vindicator,' and make his righteousness manifest, and that somehow or other, whether 'in the flesh,' or 'out of the flesh,' he shall gain the vision for which he yearns, and himself shall 'see God.' And these thoughts bring a calmer tone to his words. After the great climax in chapter xix. we feel that his passion has largely spent itself. Though to the last he has no 'cut and dried' theory of his own to put in the place of the old one which he has demolished by his appeal to facts, yet before the dialogue has ended the feeling of *soreness* has to a great extent passed away. In his later utterances we are conscious that the fury of the storm is over, even though he longs as wistfully as ever for God to manifest Himself and lift the veil that hangs over the enigmas of life; and thus

> 'He came at length
> To find a stronger faith his own;
> And Power was with him in the night,
> Which makes the darkness and the light,
> And dwells not in the light alone,
> But in the darkness and the cloud[1].'

It is through thus tracing out the thought of the dialogue that we are best able to see the real purpose of the book. Its main aim is undoubtedly, as Dr Driver points out, 'a *negative* one, to controvert the dominant theory that *all suffering proceeds from sin:* God's retributive justice is not the *only* principle by which men are governed[2].' But, as has been shown in the above sketch, there is also a considerable amount of positive teaching in it; and finally it has also probably a '*practical* aim, that of helping the author's contemporaries, who appear to have been in circumstances of national depression, to understand the situation in which they were placed, and of encouraging them to hope for a favourable issue[3].'

---

[1] *In Memoriam* xcv. It may be added that this poem is well worth study as a companion picture of a mind gradually righting itself in the face of a great problem of suffering.

[2] *Introduction to the Literature of the Old Testament*, p. 410.

[3] *Ibid.* p. 411. It is interesting to compare the Book of Job with the Greek tragedians, who were constantly dealing with the same theme and who advanced even nearer to its solution. They reject the crude idea that the suffering of the

## IV. The date of the book.

I. In considering the date of the book it must be borne in mind that there are two different questions which need to be kept entirely distinct from each other : (1) What is the date at which the scene of the story is laid ? and (2) At what period was the poem containing it written ?

With regard to the former of these questions, there can be no hesitation in answering that *the scene is laid in patriarchal times.* Everything points to this.

(1) The description of Job himself, his person and position, takes us back at once to the days of the patriarchs. The description of his wealth in i. 3, ' His substance was seven thousand sheep, and three thousand camels, and five hundred yoke of oxen, and five hundred she-asses, *and a very great household,*' is akin to the description of Isaac in Genesis xxvi. 14, ' he had possessions of flocks, and possessions of herds, *and a great household.*' The ' piece of money ' which each of his friends bring him (xlii. 11) is the same (קְשִׂיטָה) which appears also in the narrative of the transaction between Jacob and the sons of Hamor (Gen. xxxiii. 19, cf. Josh. xxiv. 32), and the word occurs nowhere else. The great age to which Job lived, ' an hundred and forty years ' after his restoration to prosperity (xlii. 16), points to the same period, as does also the position which he takes in his household, himself acting as a priest, ' sanctifying his sons, and offering burnt offerings for them lest they might have sinned ' (i. 5). Job was no son of Aaron to offer sacrifice. It is rather the position of the patriarchs Abraham, Isaac and Jacob that he fills. These too, as heads of their households, acted as priests, and offered burnt-offerings and peace-offerings.

(2) Next it is to be noted that throughout the book we seem to be *outside the sphere of the Mosaic law.* Thus, quite consistently with the age to which Job belongs, the offerings which he and his

innocent is due to a malignant jealousy on the part of the gods : they show that it is partly due to the guilt of some ancestor, entailing sorrow on his posterity : but also that, where this is not so, it serves either to discipline the character of the sufferer or to be a source of blessing for the family or country to which he belongs ; and that the free acceptance of such vicarious suffering is one of the truest marks of nobility of character. Compare *Hellenica*, Essay II. S. H. Butcher, *Some aspects of the Greek Genius*, pp. 102—129 : and for the Christian solution of the question, *Lux Mundi*, Essay III. *The Problem of Pain.* Ed.

friends are represented as offering for sin are not the technical 'sin-offerings' which were the creation of the Law, but the older 'burnt-offerings' of the patriarchal days (see i. 5 ; xlii. 8). When we are told in i. 5 that he 'sanctified' his sons the word employed is a general one, and the special technical term of the law for 'making atonement' (כִּפֶּר) seems to be expressly avoided. The very word for 'law' (tôrah, תּוֹרָה) only occurs once (xxii. 22), and then in the perfectly general sense of *instruction*, with no possible reference to the law of Moses. Again, the allusions to definite provisions of the Mosaic code are very scanty, and have to be searched for. It is possible to detect such here and there, viz. in xxii. 6, 7, and xxiv. 2, 3 (the law of pledges and of landmarks ; cf. Exod. xxii. 26 ; Deut. xix. 14; xxiv. 17); xxxi. 11 (cf. Lev. xviii. 17); xlii. 15 (the law of inheritance; cf. Numb. xxvii. 8), but none of these are prominent, or really distinctive. They allude rather to ancient institutions such as we find embodied in the Law, and are scarcely out of keeping with patriarchal days.

(3) The *historical* allusions introduced into the speeches all belong to the earliest possible period, and references to the later history of Israel are entirely wanting. Thus we have possible references to Adam in xxxi. 33 (see the note *in loc.*) ; in xxii. 15, 16 to the Deluge ; to the destruction of the cities of the plain in xviii. 15 ; and in xxxi. 32 to the incident described in the history of Lot in Gen. xix.

So also (4) *the names of God* in ordinary use in this book are the older ones belonging to the most ancient days. While the writer in his own poem freely uses the covenant name Jehovah or Jahveh (יהוה) in the narrative (*e.g.* i. 5, 7, 8, 9, 12 ; ii. 1—7 ; xxxviii. 1 ; xl. 1, 3, 6 ; xlii. 1, 7, 10, 11, 12) yet he very rarely allows it to escape from the lips of any of the speakers in the dialogue. It is put into the mouth of Job in i. 21, but elsewhere only in xii. 9, and possibly in xxviii. 28. The names commonly employed by the speakers are *Shaddai* (שַׁדַּי), the Almighty, the name by which God specially revealed Himself to the patriarchs (see Genesis xvii. 1 ; xxxv. 11) or *El* (אֵל) and *Eloah* (אֱלוֹהַּ), names which belong to quite primitive times.

II.   But while all these indications combine to point to an early date for the events narrated, there are equally conclusive reasons for assigning *a comparatively late date to the poem*. The Jewish

tradition embodied in the Talmud that Moses wrote Job as well as
'his own book' (*Baba Bathra*, 14) is absolutely worthless. The
whole passage in which the statement occurs is 'manifestly destitute
of historical value[1]' and the tradition may be safely disregarded.

(1) By various *incidental allusions* the writer betrays his own
position and date. The fact that probable indications of a knowledge of the Law occur in the book, and that the writer habitually
uses in his own person the covenant name Jehovah show that he is
removed by some distance of time from the date assigned to his
hero. So while he makes Job himself as head of the household
offer sacrifices, yet he suffers a mention of *priests* to escape his lips
in xii. 19, and, as we have seen, the covenant name Jehovah is not
quite rigidly excluded from his speeches. Again, the mention of
Ophir in xxii. 24, xxviii. 16 is hardly consistent with a date earlier
than Solomon's day. The references to serfdom and forced labour
in xxiv. 9 may be thought to imply a time after the Israelites had
reduced the Canaanites to a state of servitude, nor does the allusion
to the 'unclean' in xxxvi. 14 (see the R.V. marg. and the note *in
loc.*) favour an early date ; while the notices of the administration of
justice in the gate (xxix. 7; xxxi. 21), and the references to legal
procedure scattered about through the book imply an acquaintance
with a somewhat advanced state of civilization and settled society.
The reference to the temptation to worship the heavenly bodies (in
xxxi. 26) is best illustrated from 2 Kings xvii. 16 ; xxi. 3, 5, &c.,
and the mention of 'the Satan' finds its only parallel in Zech. iii. 1, 2 ;
1 Chr. xxi. 1, both late passages.

(2) Further, *the evidence of language* is in favour of a relatively
late date. On this it will be sufficient to cite Dr Driver, who says
that 'the syntax is extremely idiomatic ; but the vocabulary contains
a very noticeable admixture of Aramaic words, and (in a minor
degree) of words explicable only from the Arabic. This is an indication of a date more or less contemporary with 2nd Isaiah ; though
it appears that the author came more definitely within the range of
Aramaizing influences than the author of Isaiah xl.—lxvi., and
perhaps had his home in proximity to Aramaic- and Arabic-
speaking peoples[2].'

---

[1] Driver, *Introduction*, p. vii.
[2] *Introduction*, p. 434.

(3) *The character of the question discussed* perhaps points to the same period. The problem which pressed so heavily upon Job was the difficulty of reconciling his calamities with the orthodox doctrine of retribution. The simple teaching of early days concerning earthly prosperity as the reward of faithful service of God, and suffering as the penalty of sin, has broken down, and there is nothing to set in its place. The fact of itself probably indicates a comparatively late date, and best suits a time when calamity was overtaking God's people, and God's ancient promises might seem to be failing. The same kind of question is discussed in Psalms xlix. and lxxiii., both of which are probably late; and we see from Ezekiel and Jeremiah how heavily the very same problem weighed on the minds of devout Israelites during the closing years of the kingdom and at the date of the Babylonish Captivity; and it is hard to resist the conclusion that the Book of Job belongs to the same general period.

(4) To the same conclusion we are brought by yet another consideration. There are in the course of the book a number of *coincidences of language* with other books of the Old Testament sufficiently close to point with tolerable certainty to indebtedness on one side or the other. In many cases there is nothing to enable us to determine positively on which side the obligation lies, whether Job is the original that is cited elsewhere, or whether the author of this book is borrowing from the Psalms or Prophets, as the case may be. Of this sort are the coincidences between v. 16, xii. 21, 24, 25, and Ps. cvii. 4, 27, 40, 42; xi. 20 and Ps. cxlii. 4; xvii. 14 and Ps. lxxxviii. 18; xix. 20 and Ps. cii. 5; xxvii. 15 and Ps. lxxviii. 64; xxvii. 16 and Zech. ix. 3. But there remain a certain number of cases in which a careful comparison makes it almost if not quite certain that Job is *not* the original, but that he is borrowing from older Scriptures. It may perhaps be doubtful whether in the curse upon his day in chapter iii. Job is imitating Jeremiah xx. 14—18, or whether the reverse is the case. But vii. 17 appears distinctly to be suggested by Ps. viii. 4, which it almost *parodies* (see the note *in loc.*). Again, there are various coincidences with the book of Proverbs which repay careful study. Cf. v. 17 with Prov. iii. 11; xviii. 5, 6 with Prov. xiii. 9, xxiv. 20; xviii. 7 with Prov. iv. 12; xxi. 17 with Prov. xiii. 9; and chapter xxviii. with Prov. i. 7, iii. 7, xvi. 6. Now in the book of Proverbs the old doctrine of retribution is taught in its simplest form. Plainly it still holds the field. Thus we are told twice over in it that 'the lamp of the

wicked shall be put out' (xiii. 9 ; xxiv. 20). This is exactly the doctrine maintained throughout by Job's friends, and indeed Bildad uses the very same words to express it (xviii. 5, 6). *But this is just the position which Job impugns.* 'How oft,' he asks in scorn, 'is it that the lamp of the wicked is put out?' (xxi. 17). It is clear that he has the received doctrine as stated in Proverbs before him, and that he feels keenly the difficulty of adhering to it[1]. Similarly he questions the doctrine of retribution as it is stated in some of the Psalms, which spoke of the wicked being driven away as the chaff, or as stubble before the wind. See Pss. i. 4 ; xxxv. 5 ; lxxxiii. 13. But, asks Job, 'how often is it that they are as stubble before the wind, and as chaff that the storm carrieth away?' (xxi. 18). In these cases, it is thought, there can be no reasonable doubt that priority is not on the side of Job, but that the author is citing from earlier Scriptures, and is really concerned to point out the difficulty of accepting their statements without some qualification. Again the words of xiv. 11 are identical with Isaiah xix. 5, where by 'the sea' from which the waters are said to 'fail' is intended either the Nile or the shallow lakes of Egypt. The context makes this perfectly clear, and hence the statement where it stands in Isaiah is natural enough. But in Job the words appear as a wholly general statement, and yet to make them true they have to be *limited* by the same meaning being assigned to 'the sea' as it bears in Isaiah xix., for it is not the case broadly and without qualification that 'the waters fail from the sea.' Here then we seem to have an indication that Job is later than Isaiah.

Thus all things seem to combine to point to a comparatively late date for the poem, and the book suits no time better than that of the later years of the Kingdom or the Babylonish Captivity, with the confusion, disaster and hardship which that catastrophe brought with it. Indeed some have thought that Job is definitely intended to represent the nation, and that his calamities are introduced as a figure of those through which the nation actually passed at this time, while the perplexity and agony of mind into which he was cast by them are a reflection of the perplexity and agony which (as we see from Jeremiah and Ezekiel) so many of the Jews were feeling in consequence of the apparent desertion of His people by God ; and

[1] See Davidson, *The Book of Job*, p. lx., where it is pointed out that both the main divisions of Proverbs i.—ix. and x.—xxii. appear to be anterior to Job.

it has even been maintained that definite allusions to the captivity
and the restoration may be detected in xii. 18 and xlii. 10. This
does not however appear probable, as is shown in the notes on these
passages. Further, it would seem unlikely that Job is later than
Isaiah xl.—lxvi., if, as appears certain, this is to be considered as the
work not of Isaiah of Jerusalem but of a later prophet writing shortly
before the restoration and the close of the captivity. The central
figure in the pages of this prophet is the 'servant of Jehovah,' and
there are certainly striking resemblances between this figure and
that of Job. "Both are innocent sufferers—'my servant Job, a
perfect and upright man' (Job i. 8), 'my righteous servant' (Is. liii.
11); both are afflicted in a way that strikes horror into the beholders, and causes them to deem them smitten of God (Is. lii. 14; liii.
4, Job *passim*); both are forsaken of men and subjected to mockery
and spitting (Job xix. 4 *seq.*; xvi. 10; xxx. 9 *seq.*; Is. l. 6; liii. 3);
both are restored and glorified and receive 'double,' as they both
continued faithful, assured that He was near that should justify
them (Job xiii. 18; xvi. 19; xix. 25; Is. l. 8)[1]." But there is one
very striking difference. A leading thought in the latter part of
Isaiah is that of *redemption through suffering*—redemption not of the
'servant' himself, but of others whose 'iniquity' is 'laid upon Him.'
Now the author of the Book of Job, as we have already seen, is
deeply concerned with the theory of suffering; but of *vicarious*
suffering, and its redemptive power, as described in 2nd Isaiah, he
gives no hint whatever. Surely then it is a fair and reasonable
inference that he is writing before such noble expression had been
given to the grand thought by the great prophet of the Exile[2]. If
he had had the thought before him it is inconceivable that he should

[1] Davidson, p. lxvii.

[2] The only argument against this is the coincidence of language between
Job xii. 9 and Is. xli. 20, where it may be plausibly argued that Isaiah is the
original, because in the expression 'the hand of the LORD' the covenant name
is, contrary to custom, employed in Job. If the verse is a quotation from Isaiah,
a natural explanation of this is thereby furnished. But the argument is scarcely
conclusive, for (1) 'the hand of the LORD' is a sort of standing expression which
the author of the Book of Job might easily in a moment of inadvertence suffer
to escape from his lips; and (2) the reading is not certain. Possibly 'the hand
of God' is the original; see the note *in loc.*
Other coincidences of language between Job and 2nd Isaiah may be seen in
xvi. 17 (=Is. liii. 9); xiii. 19 (=Is. l. 8); and xxv. 12 (=Is. li. 15), but nothing
can be determined as to the priority of one or other writer from them.

have ignored it so completely as he has done. More than this we cannot say. It is needless to attempt to fix the date more precisely : and if this cannot be done, it is idle to guess at the author. Happily the interest and value of the book are absolutely independent of all questions of date and authorship. Such have an interest that is almost purely literary ; and no dogmatic considerations are affected, whatever may be the conclusion arrived at.

## V. The integrity of the book.

Considerable doubt has been often expressed whether the whole book is the work of a single hand. It does not appear to be necessary here to discuss the views of those critics who would break up the book into a number of *disjecta membra*, destroying its unity altogether. But there are certain portions of it in regard to which peculiar difficulty has been felt, on which something should be said. These are (1) parts of Job's first monologue in xxvii., xxviii. ; (2) the speeches of Elihu in xxxii.—xxxvii. ; and (3) the descriptions of behemoth and leviathan in xl., xli. The difficulties in connexion with the first and third of these sections are sufficiently considered in the notes on the text, to which the reader is referred, where it is shown that there need be no hesitation in accepting them as integral portions of the original work. But with the speeches of Elihu the case is different ; and it will be well to state in this place the reasons which have led the majority of modern critics to regard them as a later addition to the poem by a different hand.

They are the following :

(1) There is no mention whatever of Elihu in either the prologue or the epilogue. The omission of such mention in the prologue would not be difficult to account for. It might be fairly urged that there was no need to mention him there, and that he was not introduced until he was wanted. But the omission of any notice of him in the epilogue is not so easily explained. The judgment of the Almighty is there given upon all the other speakers, and we might surely have expected that something would be said on the utterances of Elihu, and that we should be told whether he had spoken that which was 'right' or no, had his speeches formed part of the original work.

(2) The words of the Almighty in chapter xxxviii. refer back to Job's last utterance at the close of xxxi. without the slightest allusion to the intervening speeches. It seems natural to render

them in such a way as to suggest an immediate reference to Job's words, as if he had scarcely ceased speaking when God interposed, 'Who then is darkening counsel by words without knowledge?' And even if this rendering is not necessitated it will still remain that the utterances of Elihu are entirely ignored, and that it is very difficult to think that the author of the book can have intended no fewer than six chapters to intervene between xxxviii. 2, 3, and the words to which they refer.

(3) The style and language of this section is very different from that of the rest of the book. As Renan truly says, 'in the other parts of the poem the obscurity arises from our own ignorance; here it arises from the style itself.' Elsewhere we meet with a number of rare words, the meaning of which it is often hard to discover. But when we have arrived at this and are able to translate the words, the author's meaning is generally tolerably clear. In Elihu's speeches, however, this is far from being the case. The words are frequently such as occur in common use with well ascertained meanings; but the difficulty is to know what we are intended to understand by the sentences which they make when put together: in other words it is *the author's meaning* which is hard to discover because of the obscurity of his style. Again, his vocabulary is to some extent different from that of the rest of the book: and though the careful scrutiny to which the language has been subjected by Budde[1] has revealed much greater similarity and many more coincidences than had previously been recognised, yet Budde himself is only able to maintain that the Elihu sections belong to the original poem by supposing that considerable interpolations have been made in it, and by excising a considerable number of passages as later additions[2].

A fourth argument has sometimes been added, viz. that Elihu adds nothing to the solution of the problem. But this, if true, would cut both ways, for it would remove all motive for the interpolation; whereas it is impossible to suppose that these chapters were inserted at a later date unless some definite reason for this insertion can be found. But, as a matter of fact, the assertion does not appear to be correct; for (as is shown in the notes introductory

[1] Budde, *Beiträge zur Kritik des Buches Hiob*, pp. 65—160. Cf. *Handkommentar*, p. 16.
[2] Cf. Driver, *Introduction to the Literature of the Old Testament*, p. 429.

to the chapters in question) Elihu *does* add what is practically a new thought, viz. that *suffering is designed for moral discipline and improvement*. Of this there is no trace whatever in the prologue ; and only faint indications in the dialogue between Job and his friends. In Elihu's speeches, however, it assumes a prominence which is wanting elsewhere in the poem. Here, then, is a reasonable motive for the addition of these utterances ; and the probability is that when the importance of this view as an element in the solution of the problem had been fully grasped some later writer added these chapters with the express purpose of giving adequate expression to it, and of supplying what was felt to be an omission in the original work. It may be added that no question of 'Canonicity' or 'Inspiration' is affected by our judgment on this matter. We accept the book as part of the Jewish Canon. It has come to us *as a whole* from the Jewish Church ; and as such we accept it. But it does not follow that it all comes from the same period, or that it is the work of a single hand. There are clear indications in the Psalms and the Prophets that among Hebrew writers it was not uncommon for later ones freely to use, reedit, alter, and add to their predecessors' work ; and if on critical grounds it is made to appear probable that something of the kind has happened here, there will be nothing to surprise us, or make us hesitate in admitting the conclusion to which the evidence points. The inspiration of the unknown later poet will be precisely the same as that of the unknown author of the original poem.

## VI.  Versions.

The oldest translation of the book that exists is the Greek version known as the Septuagint, dating probably from the second century B.C. The most remarkable feature of this is its extreme brevity as compared with the Hebrew text. The fact was noted in ancient days by Origen[1], and later on by S. Jerome, who says that no fewer than 700 or 800 'verses' were wanting in the LXX.[2]. These missing portions were added by Origen in his Hexapla from the version of Theodotion and other sources, with an asterisk to indicate that they were additions, and not part of the true LXX. text. Unfortunately the column was ordinarily copied without the distinguishing marks, and it is only of late years that the true text of

---

[1] Ep. ad Africanum, *Opera*, Vol. i. p. 15.          [2] Præf. in Iobum.

the LXX. has been freed from interpolations[1]. There is, however, no doubt about it at the present time. It is shorter by about 400 lines than the Hebrew, and the only question is which text should be preferred. That the claims of the LXX. to represent the original text of the book are greater than those of the received Hebrew (the so-called 'Massoretic' text) has been maintained by Hatch[2], Bickell, and others; and Bickell has gone so far as to publish a revised text of the book based upon the LXX.[3]. His treatment of the text is, however, often arbitrary, nor has it commended itself to the majority of scholars. The discovery of a portion of the original Hebrew of the book of Ecclesiasticus has recently revealed to us another instance of a discrepancy between the Greek and Hebrew which is analogous to that which meets us in Job, for there also a considerable number of clauses found in the Hebrew are wanting in the Greek. But in this case no attempt has been made to claim greater originality for the Greek: and in Job also it may, we think, be taken as practically certain that it is the Greek text which is at fault, and that no hesitation need be felt in accepting those clauses which are wanting in it.

Of the remaining Greek versions, viz. those of Aquila, Symmachus, and Theodotion (none of them older than the first century A.D.), only scanty fragments are in existence. These may be found in Field's edition of Origen's Hexapla.

The oldest Syriac Version, the Peschitto, dates probably from the second century of the Christian era. It is a literal translation of the Hebrew, and is thought to have been made for Jews or Jewish Christians[4]. It must be carefully distinguished from the 'Hexaplar Syriac' which is a direct translation from the LXX. made by Paul, bishop of Tella, in 616—618[5].

It would appear from the Talmud that a written *Targum*, or Aramaic paraphrase, on the Book of Job was extant so early as the

---

[1] The Sahidic (Coptic) Version was made from the LXX. text as it existed before Origen's time, and is thus free from the interpolations found elsewhere. See Hatch, *Essays in Biblical Greek*, p. 215 seq.

[2] *Op. cit.*

[3] *Das Buch Job nach Anleitung der Strophik und der Septuaginta auf seine ursprüngliche Form zurückgeführt und im Versmasse des Urtextes übersetzt.* See also Dillon, *The Sceptics of the Old Testament*, where an English translation of Bickell's work may be found.

[4] See Driver, *Notes on the Hebrew Text of the Book of Samuel*, p. xlii.

[5] C. H. H. Wright, *Introduction to the Old Testament*, p. 51.

first century A.D., and according to the opinion of some scholars it was actually the earliest Targum to be committed to writing. Unfortunately it is no longer in existence, for (if the Talmud is to be relied on) owing to the objections to it raised by Gamaliel it was suppressed by being buried in the ground according to a regular Jewish practice in such cases[1]. There is, however, *a* Targum on this book which still exists. It was probably formed in Syria, and is strictly a *compilation*, containing 'relics of different authors of different times,' and in the form in which it has come down to us it must be the work of some centuries later than that which Gamaliel suppressed[2].

Of the Latin versions, the earliest, that known as the 'Old Latin,' was made from the unrevised LXX.; this was revised by S. Jerome towards the close of the fourth century, so as to make it correspond more closely with the Greek, with which in his revision it agrees very exactly. But later on Jerome proceeded to form a new translation of this, as of the other books of the Old Testament, *from the original Hebrew.* And it is this translation which is now found in the Vulgate. Of Jerome's struggles with the Book of Job he has left us an amusing account[3]. He found it of excessive difficulty. It was 'slippery as an eel.' Accordingly he engaged at no small cost a Jewish teacher from Lydda, who had a great reputation, but who failed to throw much light on the book, for Jerome confesses sadly that after he had gone through it with him he was no wiser than before ! In spite of this, however, no student of the book can venture to ignore his work, for his translation is 'far before its age' and is often of great service to the expositor.

Of the English versions prior to 1611 nothing need here be said. The Authorized Version of King James's reign represents very fairly the Hebrew scholarship of the age, but it cannot be said that it is always intelligible. Even, however, where its readings are demonstrably wrong it will often be found that the translators were following Jewish authority for the renderings which they adopted. But it must be confessed that to the English reader in general the book remained hopelessly obscure until the publication of the Revised Version in 1884. Perhaps there is no part of the Old Testament in which the gain is greater. Difficult the book must

---

[1] Talmud, *Shabbath* (115 a), cf. Wright, *op. cit.*, p. 42.
[2] See Deutsch, in Smith's *Dictionary of the Bible*, Vol. IV. p. 1662.
[3] Præf. in Librum Iob.

always remain, but it is no longer unintelligible ; and it may be well to point out to the reader that he should on no account neglect the *marginal renderings* of the R.V. It must be remembered that one of the rules which governed the revisers was that no change should be introduced into the text of the A.V. unless by the vote of a two-thirds majority of the company present and voting. This rule, it is known, operated in many cases to exclude from the *text* and relegate to the *margin*, renderings which commended themselves to an actual majority of the revisers present and voting. It may fairly be presumed that in this majority were often to be found the best Hebrew scholars ; and certainly it appears to the present writer that in a large number of instances the marginal renderings deserve to be adopted in preference to those which have been assigned the position of honour in the text.

## VII. Commentaries.

A full account of commentaries and treatises on the book may be found in Wright's *Introduction to the Old Testament*, p. 151, and Driver's *Introduction to the Literature of the Old Testament*, p. 408 (ed. 6). Here it is sufficient to mention a few which the reader may find specially helpful. Dillmann's *Hiob* (*Kurzgefasstes exegetisches Handbuch*) is perhaps the most important, and it is hoped that an English translation of this will shortly be published. The *Commentaries* of Delitzsch and Ewald have already been translated, and are published in the 'Foreign Theological Library,' and 'Theological Translation Fund Library,' respectively. A. B. Davidson's little volume in *The Cambridge Bible for Schools and Colleges* is in every way admirable, and S. Cox's *Commentary on the Book of Job* is an original and often suggestive work. Mention may also be made of Dean Bradley's *Lectures on the Book of Job*, of Cheyne's *Job and Solomon*, and of the studies of the book to be found in J. B. Mozley's *Essays*, vol. II., and J. A. Froude's *Short Studies on Great Subjects*, vol. I.

On all questions connected with the state of the text and the renderings of the ancient versions, Beer's *Text des Buches Hiob* is most useful ; and attempted reconstructions of the Hebrew text may be found in Merx, *Das Gedicht von Hiob*, Siegfried, *The Book of Job* (in P. Haupt's *Sacred Books of the Old Testament*), and Bickell, *Das Buch Job*. But they are all more or less arbitrary and unsatisfactory.

# THE BOOK OF JOB.

## PART I. THE PROLOGUE. CHAPTERS I. AND II.

THIS portion of the work falls into six well-defined sections.

**I.** 1 There was a man in the land of Uz, whose name was

**I. 1—5. Description of Job and his prosperity.** The man himself (1), his family (2), his wealth (3), and the proof of his piety (4, 5). This description makes it at once clear that the scene of the story is laid in patriarchal times. The character of Job's wealth (*v.* 3), and the way in which he offers *burnt* offerings (not *sin* offerings) for the sin of his sons are of themselves indications of this. See above in the Introduction, p. xix.

1. *the land of Uz.* The LXX. has *in the land of Ausitis,* and in some curious additions appended at the close of the book further describes it as *on the borders of Edom and Arabia.* These additions,

which are based on the notices in Gen. xxxvi. 31—35, give the genealogy of Job, identifying him with Jobab, the son of Zerah, king of Edom (Gen. xxxvi. 33), and making him out as 'the fifth from Abraham.' The identification of the two names Job and Jobab is philologically impossible, and the additions, as a whole, are worthless; but the specification of the region in which the land of Uz is to be looked for seems to be tolerably correct, for in Lam. iv. 21 the land of Uz is connected with Edom, and Uz appears as a descendant of Seir in Gen. xxxvi. 28 (though a different account of the origin of the nation is given in Gen. xxii. 21, where Uz appears as

¹Job ; and that man was perfect and upright, and one that feared God, and eschewed evil.  2 And there were born unto him seven sons and three daughters.  3 His ²substance also was seven thousand sheep, and three thousand camels, and five hundred yoke of oxen, and five hundred she-asses, and a

¹ Heb. *Iyob.*                        ² Or, *cattle*

a descendant of Nahor, while in Gen. x. 23 Uz is simply a son of Aram). With this agree the indications in the book of Job itself, e.g. the quarter from which the attacks upon his flocks came, viz. Chaldæa and Arabia, the proximity of the wilderness (i. 19), and the fact that of his three friends one came from Edom (Eliphaz the Temanite), and another was a Shuhite, i.e. a descendant of Shuah, a son of A-braham by Keturah (Gen. xxv. 2). In all probability, then, we should locate 'the land of Uz' somewhere on the east of the Jordan, north of Edom, towards the Arabian desert.

*whose name was Job.*  The name occurs nowhere else in the O. T. except in this book and in the reference to its hero in Ezek. xiv. 14, 20. Its meaning is uncertain ; 'the persecuted,' 'the pious,' and 'the penitent' have all been suggested as possible meanings, but it is probable that it is simply the name which tradition had handed down of the hero of the story on which the inspired author founded his poem. None of the other names in the book appear to be of any special significance, and there is no need to think that we are intended to discover any connexion between the name of the hero and his circumstances. It is interesting to find that the very similar form Ayab is found on one of the Tel el-Amarna tablets (Winckler, no. 237).

*perfect and upright, and one that feared God, and eschewed evil.* These expressions are evidently intended to insist strongly on Job's moral integrity, but it would be a mistake to press them as if they denoted absolute freedom from sin. Compare the somewhat similar description of Zacharias and Elisabeth in the New Testament. 'They were both righteous before God, walking in all the commandments and ordinances of the Lord blameless.' S. Luke i. 6.

2. *seven sons and three daughters.* Since these numbers *seven* and *three* are sacred ones, it is commonly thought that here they are symbolical. But there appears to be no good reason why they should be so regarded. They may well have been the numbers handed down by tradition.

3. *His substance also was seven thousand sheep &c.* Cf. the description given of Isaac's wealth in Gen. xxvi. 14, 'he had possessions of flocks, and possessions of herds, and *a great household,*' the last words being identical with those here used. In connexion with the author's description of his hero we should read the account which Job himself is made to give of his life in the days of his prosperity (see xxix.), which implies more of a settled life and less of the nomad character than we might have imagined from the passage before us.

very great household ; so that this man was the greatest of all the children of the east. 4 And his sons went and held a feast in the house of each one upon his day ; and they sent and called for their three sisters to eat and to drink with them. 5 And it was so, when the days of their feasting were gone about, that Job sent and sanctified them, and rose up early in the morning, and offered burnt offerings according to the number of them all : for Job said, It may be that my sons have sinned, and ¹renounced God in their hearts. Thus did Job continually.

¹ Or, *blasphemed*  So ver. 11, ch. ii. 5, 9.

*children of the east.* A general term frequently used for the inhabitants of the region which stretches eastward from Palestine to the Euphrates. See Gen. xxix. 1 ; Judg. vi. 3, and other passages.

4. *upon his day.* For *day* used of a 'festival day,' cf. Hos. vii. 5, 'the day of our king'; ii. 13, 'the days of the Baalim.' The expression here may either refer to the birthdays of Job's sons, or may imply that each of them had one day in each week on which he entertained his brothers and sisters. The fact is mentioned to explain the presence of all the family together in the eldest brother's house in verse 13.

5. *sanctified them...and offered burnt offerings.* Attention has been drawn in the Introduction to these phrases, see p. xix. The writer seems of set purpose to avoid the technical expressions of the Mosaic law, and to use only such general terms as would be appropriate to a non-Israelite.

*renounced,* better than 'cursed' of the A.V. The word is the same as that found in verse 11, and in ii. 5 and 9, where it is also rendered *renounce* in the R.V. and *curse* in the A.V. It is the ordinary word for

'to bless' in Hebrew, *barach* (בָּרַךְ). Such a meaning is, however, manifestly inappropriate in these passages in Job, as well as in 1 Kings xxi. 10, nor does it suit well in Ps. x. 3. It is possible that in all these passages it is merely a euphemism for 'to curse'; indeed it has been suggested that the text has been altered, and that the word now read in it is a correction due to religious reasons ; but it is more probable that the word *barach* has the definite meaning of 'renounce,' which may easily be arrived at from the general sense of the benediction employed in salutations at parting. So our own 'Farewell,' or 'Good-bye,' may be used to indicate the idea of renunciation; cf. Wolsey's 'Farewell, a long farewell to all my greatness.' Job feared lest in the midst of their prosperity and well-being his sons might have forgotten God altogether, and practically bidden farewell to Him. Similarly, in his own case the temptation which pressed upon him with such awful force, the temptation to which Satan suggested he was certain to yield, was that of *renouncing* God altogether, of bidding good-bye to Him, and having nothing more to do with Him. This,

1—2

6 Now there was a day when the sons of God came to present themselves before the LORD, and ¹Satan came also among them. 7 And the LORD said unto Satan, Whence comest thou? Then Satan answered the LORD, and said, From going to and fro in the earth, and from walking up and

¹ That is, *the Adversary.*

however, was exactly what Job never would do. Hard, wild words he uses about God, but he never said good-bye to Him. Contrast what he says of the wicked in xxi. 14, and for his own position all through 'even while the whirl was worst' see xxiii.

**6—12. The first scene in Heaven.** The Almighty holds His court in heaven, and among the sons of God the Satan presents himself (6). The colloquy between him and the Almighty with regard to the character of Job's piety (7—11) and the permission to try him within certain limits (12).

6. *the sons of God,* lit. *sons of the Elohim.* LXX. οἱ ἄγγελοι τοῦ Θεοῦ, 'the angels of God' (similarly the Targum), undoubtedly correct as an *interpretation,* though not literal as a translation. An almost identical expression occurs in xxxviii. 7, 'When the morning stars sang together, and all the sons of God (sons of Elohim) shouted for joy,' and similar phrases are found in Ps. xxix. 1; lxxxix. 7, 'sons of the mighty' (Heb. 'sons of Elim'). Cf. also Dan. iii. 25, where 'a son of the gods' is parallel with, and explained by, 'his angel' in ver. 28. The only other passage in which the expression 'sons of the Elohim' occurs is Gen. vi. 4, and here also it is probable that the angels are referred to.

*to present themselves.* The same word is used in Zech. vi. 5, of the

'spirits, which go forth from *presenting themselves* before the Lord of all the earth.' See R.V. marg. Cf. S. Luke i. 19, 'I am Gabriel, that *stand* (ὁ παρεστηκὼς) in the presence of God.' The word is used of courtiers presenting themselves before kings in Prov. xxii. 29.

*and Satan came also among them,* lit. 'the Satan' (LXX. ὁ διάβολος, Vulg. Satan). In itself the Hebrew word *satan* merely means *an adversary,* and as such is not unfrequently used of a human enemy. See 1 Sam. xxix. 4, where it is used by the Philistines of David, 1 Kings v. 4; xi. 14, 23, 25, of the 'adversaries' or 'satans' whom the LORD stirred up against Solomon. So in Ps. cix. 6, where the A.V. and P.B.V. have 'let Satan stand at his right hand,' we should read 'let an adversary stand at his right hand.' In Numb. xxii. 22 it is used of the angel of the LORD, who 'placed himself in the way for an adversary' (Heb. *for a satan*) to Balaam. In three passages only in the O.T. is the word appropriated as a title of the arch-enemy of mankind, the evil spirit known to theology as 'the devil' and 'Satan,' viz. the passage before us, Zech. iii. 1 (where, as here, the word has the article), and 1 Chr. xxi. 1.

7. *From going to and fro in the earth, and from walking up and down in it.* In Zech. i. 10 the riders seen in the prophet's vision

down in it.  8 And the LORD said unto Satan, Hast thou considered my servant Job? ¹for there is none like him in the
earth, a perfect and an upright man, one that feareth God,
and escheweth evil.  9 Then Satan answered the LORD, and
said, Doth Job fear God for nought? 10 Hast not thou
made an hedge about him, and about his house, and about all
that he hath, on every side? thou hast blessed the work
of his hands, and his ²substance is increased in the land.
11 But put forth thine hand now, and touch all that he hath,
and he will renounce thee to thy face.  12 And the LORD said
unto Satan, Behold, all that he hath is in thy ³power ; only
upon himself put not forth thine hand.  So Satan went forth
from the presence of the LORD.

¹ Or, *that*      ² Or, *cattle*      ³ Heb. *hand.*

are spoken of as those 'whom the
LORD hath sent *to walk to and fro
through the earth.*' We may suppose
therefore that the Satan, like the
other sons of the Elohim, was com-
missioned by the Almighty to inspect
and report upon the affairs of earth,
but that he abused his mission and
converted it into an opportunity of
'*walking about,* as a roaring lion,
seeking whom he may devour,' 1 Pet.
v. 8.

9.  *Doth Job fear God for
nought?* Satan's suggestion is that
after all Job's piety is only a well-
calculated selfishness.  He does not
serve God freely (LXX. δωρεάν, *gratis*),
but only because it 'pays' him to do
so.

11.  *renounce.* See the note on
verse 5.

12.  Permission is given to
the Satan to test Job, and try
whether his suggestion is correct,
the only limitation set to the trial
being this, that he is not to 'put
forth his hand' upon the man himself.

A few words must here be added

on the questions, how is the scene
here described to be understood?
and what light does it throw on the
Scriptural doctrine of the devil?
As Delitzsch points out, 'from the
writer assigning the earthly measure
of time to the place of God and
spirits we see that celestial things
are represented by him parabolically.'
The account is clearly not intended
to be taken as literal history.  The
description is drawn from the
court of an earthly monarch, whose
courtiers have access to his throne,
and present themselves before him,
much as in the not dissimilar repre-
sentations with regard to the spirit
world in 1 Kings xxii. 19—22 and
Zech. iii., which should be compared
with this narrative. 'The earthly
elements of time, space, and dialogue
belong to the poetic drapery'
(Delitzsch) ; but, though the whole
scene must be regarded as a poetic
and parabolic representation, yet
there are clearly certain facts concerning the invisible world which
are intended to be taught by it.  It
will be noted that both here and in

THE BOOK OF JOB [I. 13

13 And it fell on a day when his sons and his daughters were eating and drinking wine in their eldest brother's house,

Zech. iii. (and cf. 1 Kings xxii. 21) Satan appears as admitted into the presence of God (like a Judas among the Twelve) and that he is still regarded as one of the sons of the Elohim. It is in complete harmony with this that we find indications in the New Testament that it is only through the victory won by the Incarnation and Passion of the Redeemer that 'the accuser of our brethren is cast down, which accused them before our God night and day,' Rev. xii. 10; cf. S. Luke x. 18, 'I beheld Satan as lightning fall from heaven,' and S. John xii. 31, 'Now shall the prince of this world be cast out.' Not till the end will he be cast into the lake of fire, Rev. xx. 10. Thus as Martensen says in regard to the passage before us: 'He is not yet the Satan of the New Testament who is driven from the presence of God because he wills evil as such: but he takes a malicious pleasure in undermining and deceiving human virtue. His joy consists in spying out the weaknesses and sins of men, and in bringing men by his temptations to manifest these; and then he returns back to the Lord as the accusing angel to prove the untrustworthiness of human virtue' (*Christian Dogmatics*, p. 194). The whole subject of the fall of Satan is confessedly obscure, and perhaps all that we can say is that there are intimations in Scripture, both here and elsewhere, that so long as Satan is not finally vanquished and condemned we ought to regard him as having in some sort access to God, by whom his temptations of men are permitted, though a limit is put to them, for 'He will not suffer you to be tempted above that ye are able' (1 Cor. x. 13): and it may well be thought that so much is implied by our Lord's words in S. Luke xxii. 31, 'Simon, Simon, behold Satan *asked* [or even *obtained you by asking*, R.V. marg.] to have you, that he might sift you as wheat: but I made supplication for thee that thy faith fail not.' It is a similar fact in the invisible world which lies at the basis of the scene before us, expressed as it is in the imagery of this world.

See further on the doctrine of Satan in the Old Testament, Oehler's *Theology of the Old Testament*, vol. II. p. 288; and note the *reserve* of the Old Testament upon the subject. It is in striking contrast with the fuller revelation made in the New Testament, with the frequent allusions to 'Satan' or 'the devil' there; and (like this) is markedly different from the grotesque beliefs of the later Jews as shown in the book of Tobit and Rabbinical writings, which (rather than the Canonical Scriptures) are really responsible for the forms which popular superstitions have taken among Christians in various ages.

13—22. **The first (fourfold) trial of Job.** Successive messages brought to Job telling him of the attack of the Sabeans upon the oxen and asses and those attending them (13—15); the destruction of the sheep and servants by the lightning (16); the attack of the Chaldæans upon the camels and servants

14 that there came a messenger unto Job, and said, The oxen
were plowing, and the asses feeding beside them : 15 and ¹the
Sabeans fell *upon them*, and took them away ; yea, they have
slain the ²servants with the edge of the sword ; and I only
am escaped alone to tell thee. 16 While he was yet speaking,
there came also another, and said, The fire of God is fallen
from heaven, and hath burned up the sheep, and the ²servants, and consumed them ; and I only am escaped alone to
tell thee. 17 While he was yet speaking, there came also
another, and said, The Chaldeans made three bands, and ³fell
upon the camels, and have taken them away, yea, and slain
the ²servants with the edge of the sword ; and I only am
escaped alone to tell thee. 18 While he was yet speaking,
there came also another, and said, Thy sons and thy daughters
were eating and drinking wine in their eldest brother's house:
19 and, behold, there came a great wind ⁴from the wilderness,
and smote the four corners of the house, and it fell upon the

---

¹ Heb. *Sheba*.    ² Heb. *young men*    ³ Or, *made a raid*    ⁴ Or, *over*

---

(17); and the destruction of Job's
children by the great wind from the
desert (18, 19). Job's behaviour on
the receipt of the news (20—22).

The symmetrical character of the
trials here described has been
thought to be an indication that we
are not dealing with literal history.
The first and the third, it will be
noticed, are from *men*, while the
second and fourth are due to the
forces of nature. Thus 'while heaven
and men alternate their strokes upon
him, these strokes follow one another
with increasing severity, and in each
case only one escapes to bring the
grievous tidings.' Davidson.

13. The presence of all the
sons and daughters 'in their eldest
brother's house' is accounted for
by the custom mentioned in ver. 4.
The catastrophe would be the more
tragic, because it occurred at the

commencement of a new cycle of
feasting, just after Job's sacrifices
at the close of a previous one in
order to avert the wrath of heaven.

15. *the Sabeans*, i.e. the A-
rabians, mentioned again in vi. 19,
and frequently referred to in the
Old Testament, e.g., 1 Kings x. 1 ;
Is. lx. 6 ; Ezek. xxvii. 22 ; Ps. lxxii.
10. According to Gen. x. 28, Sheba
was a son of Joktan, the progenitor
of many of the Arabian tribes.

16. *the fire of God*, i.e. the
lightning, so called also in 1 Kings
xviii. 38 ; 2 Kings i. 12 ; and cf.
Exodus ix. 23, 'The LORD sent
thunder and hail, and fire ran down
unto the earth.' This seems better
than to take it of the hot Samûm
wind of the desert.

17. *three bands*, a common mili-
tary disposition. See Judg. vii. 16 ;
ix. 43 ; 1 Sam. xi. 11.

young men, and they are dead ; and I only am escaped alone
to tell thee. 20 Then Job arose, and rent his mantle, and
shaved his head, and fell down upon the ground, and worshipped ; 21 and he said, Naked came I out of my mother's
womb, and naked shall I return thither : the LORD gave, and
the LORD hath taken away; blessed be the name of the
LORD. 22 In all this Job sinned not, nor charged God with
foolishness.

**II.** 1 Again there was a day when the sons of God came
to present themselves before the LORD, and Satan came also
among them to present himself before the LORD. 2 And the

20, 21. The effect of the tidings
upon Job. *He rent his mantle,
and shaved his head,* these actions
being the ordinary signs of grief.
See Gen. xxxvii. 29, 34; xliv. 13 ;
2 Sam. xiii. 31; 2 Kings xviii. 37,
for the rending of the garments,
and Micah i. 16, for the shaving of
the head. But not content with
this, he *fell down upon the ground
and worshipped,* i.e. he abased himself before God and acquiesced in
the dispensations of His providence.
21. *Naked came I out of my
mother's womb, and naked shall
I return thither.* ' Thither,' i.e. to
the womb of the earth ' the mother
of all things,' as the phrase is ex-
panded in Ecclus. xl. 1, ' from the
day that they go out of their mother's
womb till the day that they return
to the mother of all things.' The
idea which underlies the expression
here put into the mouth of Job is
that the creation of Adam from the
dust of the earth is in some sort
repeated at the creation of all the
sons of men. Cf. Ps. cxxxix. 15.
Job's words anticipate S. Paul's ' we
brought nothing into the world, for
neither can we carry anything out,'
1 Tim. vi. 7.
*the Lord.* Heb. יהוה Jehovah.

The writer here, contrary to his
almost invariable custom, puts the
sacred Covenant Name into the
mouth of the patriarch. See above,
Introduction, p. xx.
22. *In all this Job sinned
not.* The writer's verdict, showing
that Satan has failed in his first
assault.
*nor charged God with foolish-
ness,* better than A.V. ' charged God
foolishly ' ; for the writer means to
say that in spite of the severity of
the trial, and its apparently arbitrary
character, Job did not attribute to
God anything *unsavoury* in His conduct towards him. The word
(*tiphlah*) occurs again in xxiv. 12,
in the complaint that God regards
not the cruelties inflicted by tyrants,
and does not attribute *unsavouriness* to them, as well as in Jer. xxiii.
13, where God is said to have 'seen
*unsavouriness*' in the false prophets
of Samaria. A kindred word is
found in vi. 6, of the insipidity of
that which is ' eaten without salt.'

**II. 1—6. The second scene
in Heaven.** The Almighty holds
His court again, and once more the
Satan presents himself among the
sons of God (1). A second colloquy

THE BOOK OF JOB

LORD said unto Satan, From whence comest thou? And Satan answered the LORD, and said, From going to and fro in the earth, and from walking up and down in it. 3 And the LORD said unto Satan, Hast thou considered my servant Job? [1]for there is none like him in the earth, a perfect and an upright man, one that feareth God, and escheweth evil: and he still holdeth fast his integrity, although thou movedst me against him, [2]to destroy him without cause. 4 And Satan answered the LORD, and said, Skin for skin, yea, all that a man hath will he give for his life. 5 But put forth thine hand now, and touch his bone and his flesh, and he will renounce thee to thy face. 6 And the LORD said unto Satan, Behold, he is in thine hand ; only spare his life. 7 So Satan

[1] Or, *that*          [2] Heb. *to swallow him up.*

takes place with regard to Job in which the Satan suggests the reason of the failure of the first trial, and insinuates that under one which touches him *personally* Job will yield (2—5). Permission is granted to make such trial (6). The narrative of this audience is given as far as possible in the exact words of the previous one. The changes begin in verse 3, where the Almighty adds in His words to the Satan the pointed reference to the fact that Job *still holdeth fast his integrity, although thou movedst me against him, to destroy him without cause.*

4, 5. Satan's reply is to the effect that the trial was not sufficiently severe to test Job thoroughly. It had not touched his person. Let God *put forth his hand and touch his bone and his flesh,* and the result will be very different.

*Skin for skin.* The expression is evidently proverbial; but it is difficult to say precisely what is the conception in which the proverb (which is found nowhere else) origi-

nated. The second clause may either be (1) parallel with the first, and repeat the same idea—so Ewald and Davidson, 'Like for like, so all that a man hath etc.'— or it may be (2) an advance upon it, forming a sort of climax. So Delitzsch, 'One gives up one's skin to preserve one's skin ; one endures pain on a sickly part to preserve the whole skin : but for his life, i.e. his highest good, man willingly gives up everything that can be given up.' Neither explanation seems thoroughly satisfactory. The origin of the proverbs of one nation is not seldom unintelligible to those of another, so we may well be content to leave 'Satan's old saw' in its obscurity, for the general drift of his remark is clear enough. He reiterates his former sentiments, and maintains that Job's piety is purely selfish, a sort of bargain with God.

6. Permission is granted for personal affliction, but a limit is put to it, *only spare his life.*

went forth from the presence of the LORD, and smote Job
with sore boils from the sole of his foot unto his crown.
8 And he took him a potsherd to scrape himself withal ; and
he sat among the ashes. 9 Then said his wife unto him, Dost
thou still hold fast thine integrity? renounce God, and die.
10 But he said unto her, Thou speakest as one of the ¹foolish
women speaketh. What? shall we receive good at the hand

¹ Or, *impious*

7—10. **The second trial of
Job.** Job is smitten with the leprosy (7). His behaviour under it (8).
The suggestion of his wife, and his
repudiation of it (9, 10).

7. *with sore boils from the
sole of his foot unto his crown.*
The very same words are found in
the denunciatory passage in Deut.
xxviii. 35, 'The LORD shall *smite
thee* in the knees, and in the legs,
*with a sore boil*, whereof thou canst
not be healed, *from the sole of thy
foot unto the crown of thy head*,'
the '*boil* of Egypt' having been
mentioned above in verse 27; cf.
Exod. ix. 9, 11, where the same word
is used in the account of the plague
of boils. Boils are also mentioned
among the preliminary symptoms of
leprosy in Lev. xiii. 18—23, the
only other place where the word
here employed is found in the Old
Testament ; and there is a general
agreement among scholars that in
the disease from which Job suffered
we are intended to see the so-called
black leprosy or elephantiasis.

8. *to scrape himself withal*,
because of the intolerable itching
which accompanies the disease.
*and he sat.* Better *while* or *as
he sat among the ashes.* By *the
ashes* we are probably intended to
understand the dung heap outside
the gate, where all the refuse of an

Arab city is thrown. So the LXX.
and the Vulgate, *in sterquilinio*;
whence the conventional representation of Job on his dunghill. A
vivid description of such a *Mezbele*
is given by Consul Wetzstein in
Delitzsch's Commentary on Job, vol.
II. p. 152, a portion of which may be
cited here as showing how true to
life the poem is : 'There all day
long the children play about; there
the outcast, who has been stricken
with some loathsome malady, and is
not allowed to enter the dwellings
of men, lays himself down, begging
an alms of the passers-by by day,
and by night sheltering himself
among the ashes which the heat of
the sun has warmed. There too lie
the village dogs, perhaps gnawing a
fallen carcase, which is often flung
there.' Cf. the description which
Job himself gives of his condition in
xxx. 9. Job's temptation becomes
sorer as his wife turns against him,
and becomes (as Augustine calls
her) *diaboli adjutrix*.

10. *one of the foolish women* :
cf. 2 Sam. xiii. 13, where a similar expression occurs. The word
for foolish ('nabal') is regularly used
in the Old Testament with the idea
of something more than what we
term 'folly.' It suggests *impiety*
rather than stupidity, and sometimes almost Atheism, as when 'the

of God, and shall we not receive evil? In all this did not Job sin with his lips.

11 Now when Job's three friends heard of all this evil that was come upon him, they came every one from his own place; Eliphaz the Temanite, and Bildad the Shuhite, and Zophar the Naamathite: and they made an appointment together to come to bemoan him and to comfort him. 12 And when they lifted up their eyes afar off, and knew him not, they lifted up their voice, and wept; and they rent every one his mantle, and sprinkled dust upon their heads toward

fool' says in his heart 'there is no God.' Ps. xiv. 1. Hence the margin of the R.V. 'as one of the *impious* women speaketh.'

*Shall we receive good...and shall we not receive evil?* Job's attitude is still that of absolute submission and acquiescence in the will of God, an attitude which he did not maintain throughout, but to which he is brought back by the intervention of the Almighty at the close of the book.

**11—13. Introduction of Job's three friends.** His three friends come to bemoan him (11). Their consternation at the sight of him, and speechless grief (12, 13).

*Eliphaz the Temanite.* The name Eliphaz appears in Gen. xxxvi. 4 as that of a son of Esau; and Teman is frequently connected with Esau or Edom, and was a district famous for the wisdom of its inhabitants. Thus Teman is a grandson of Esau according to Gen. xxxvi. 11, 15, and the name is found in the closest connexion with Edom in Jer. xlix. 20; cf. Obad. 9; Ezek. xxv. 13; Hab. iii. 3.

*Bildad the Shuhite.* The name Bildad does not occur elsewhere. 'Shuhite,' probably a descendant of Shuah, a son of Abraham by

Keturah, see Gen. xxv. 2. The land of 'Suhu' is mentioned in several Eastern inscriptions, and apparently lay 'between the mouths of the Belich and the Khabur, confluents of the Euphrates.' Cheyne, *Job and Solomon,* p. 15.

*Zophar the Naamathite.* Zophar is not found elsewhere, unless it be the same as Zepho or Zephi, a grandson of Esau, mentioned in Gen. xxxvi. 11; 1 Chr. i. 36 (so LXX. Σωφάρ in all three passages). The locality of Naamah is unknown. It must have been somewhere on the east of Jordan, and cannot be the same place as the Naamah, a town of Judah, mentioned in Josh. xv. 41. The LXX. implies a different reading, and makes Zophar 'king of the *Minœans*,' as it also makes Eliphaz 'king of the Temanites,' and Bildad 'tyrant of the Shuhites.' These statements are repeated at the close of the book in the worthless additions already alluded to.

12. *and knew him not,* such was the disfigurement caused by the ravages of the disease.

*they rent every one his mantle,* as Job had done on the receipt of the news of his first calamities, i. 20.

*and sprinkled dust upon their heads toward heaven,* another com-

heaven.   13 So they sat down with him upon the ground
seven days and seven nights, and none spake a word unto
him : for they saw that his ¹grief was very great.

¹ Or, *pain*

mon sign of grief among Easterns,
cf. Josh. vii. 6 ; 1 Sam. iv. 12 ; Lam.
ii. 10.

13. *So they sat down...upon
the ground*, a customary attitude
for mourners. See the whole description in Lam. ii. 10, which
admirably illustrates the conduct
of Job's friends : 'The elders of
the daughter of Zion *sit upon the
ground, they keep silence; they
have cast up dust upon their heads;*
they have girded themselves with
sackcloth'; cf. 2 Sam. xii. 16. Similarly in Shakespeare

'For God's sake, let us *sit upon*
   *the ground*
And tell sad stories of the death
   of kings.'
         *Richard II.* Act III. Sc. 2.

*seven days and seven nights*,
the time during which Ezekiel 'sat
astonied,' before God opened his
mouth, when he 'came to them of
the captivity at Tel-abib,' Ezek. iii.
15. So Joseph 'made a mourning
for his father seven days,' Gen. l.
10; and when the men of Jabesh
Gilead buried the bones of Saul
they 'fasted seven days,' 1 Sam.
xxxi. 13.

With the introduction of the
three friends the prose narrative
of the prologue is brought to a
close. Its purpose has not been
merely to introduce the *dramatis*

*personæ* in the dialogue which
follows, or to explain the position
of affairs which is there assumed.
Over and above these objects it has
an independent value of its own,
and makes its own special contribution to the permanent teaching
of the book. It is obviously intended
to enforce two main lessons : (1) By
the steadfast submission of Job
under the severest of trials there is
established the fact that all piety is
*not* necessarily a refined form of
selfishness and the result of a
calculation of advantages, but that
*man is capable of disinterested
goodness, and of serving God without any thought of the material
benefits which may thereby accrue
to him;* while (2) by drawing back
the veil and admitting us to scenes
which belong to the invisible
world, the writer discloses the fact,
which, however familiar it may be
to us, once came as a revelation to
men, that one purpose for which
suffering is permitted by God is to
*test* men, i.e. in Bishop Butler's
words, *this life is a time of probation.* See the *Analogy*, Part I.
c. iii. This fact, it is obvious, has
an important bearing on all dis-
cussions concerning the mystery of
pain, beyond the merely negative
value of breaking down the theory
that all suffering is penal, and the
consequence of sin.

## PART II. THE DEBATE BETWEEN JOB AND HIS FRIENDS. CHAPTERS III.—XXXI.

With Chapter iii. we enter on the second of the main sections of the book, containing the account of the debate between Job and his three friends, who have just been introduced. Before, however, the actual discussion commences Job 'opened his mouth and cursed his day.' He is the first to break the seven days' silence, and this curse of his upon the day of his birth with its implied reproach against God forms as it were the text of the discussion which follows, and explains the position taken up by his friends.

The chapter falls into three well-defined divisions, and contains a threefold 'curse':

(1) *The wish that he had never been born at all.*   1—10.
(2) *The wish that he had died at his birth.*   11—19.
(3) *The wish that he might die now.*   20—26.

With the main thought of the Chapter cf. Sophocles, *Œd. Col.* 1225 (quoted by Cox),

> 'Happiest beyond compare
> Never to taste of life;
> Happiest in order next,
> Being born, with quickest speed
> Thither again to turn
> From whence we came.'

> PLUMPTRE's Translation, p. 105.

A comparison of the curse with that to which Jeremiah gave utterance (Jer. xx. 14—18) shows clearly that the two passages are not independent of each other, but that one writer is consciously or unconsciously borrowing from the other : but there is nothing to indicate precisely which of the two is the original of the other. This must be decided on more general grounds. See above, Introduction, p. xxii.

**III.** 1 After this opened Job his mouth, and cursed his day. 2 And Job answered and said :

III. 1—10. **The wish that he had never been born at all.** Job begins with an imprecation on the whole period of twenty-four hours (the day and night) in which he was born, invoking destruction upon it (1—3); and he follows this up in detail by the wish (*a*) that the *day* might be turned into darkness (4, 5), and (*b*) that the *night* might be

3 Let the day perish wherein I was born,
And the night which said, There is a man child conceived.
4 Let that day be darkness ;
Let not God ¹regard it from above,
Neither let the light shine upon it.
5 Let darkness and ²the shadow of death claim it for their
own ;
Let a cloud dwell upon it ;
Let all that maketh black the day terrify it.
6 As for that night, let thick darkness seize upon it :
Let it not ³rejoice among the days of the year ;
Let it not come into the number of the months.
7 Lo, let that night be ⁴barren ;
Let no joyful voice come therein.

¹ Or, *inquire after*    ² Or, *deep darkness* (and so elsewhere)
³ Some ancient versions read, *be joined unto.*    ⁴ Or, *solitary*

blotted out altogether (6—9), ending with the reason for this imprecation (10).

3. *And the night which said.* The night is personified and regarded as proclaiming the news of his birth. This seems better than the tamer rendering of the A.V. 'the night in which it was said,' which has, however, the authority of the LXX. and Vulgate.

5. *the shadow of death.* This is a single word in the original. The rendering of the text follows the Massoretic pointing, and has the support of the LXX. and other early versions. If it is correct, the word must be regarded as a compound one ; but it is now commonly held by scholars that the pointing is wrong, and that the word merely means *deep darkness*; so R.V. marg.

*claim it for their own.* This translation is certainly correct, LXX. ἐκλάβοι : the A.V. *stain it* is wrong.

The word (*gaal*) is a special one, meaning 'to redeem,' and the participle, Goêl, became a technical term under the Mosaic law for the nearest blood relation, who had the right of redemption of property (cf. Lev. xxv. 25 ; Ruth iv. 4, 6), and the duty of avenging bloodshed (cf. Numb. xxxv. 12). We shall meet with it again in xix. 25, where see note. Here the meaning may be : Let darkness and deep darkness *redeem it*, i.e. *retake possession of it*, so that day shall be swallowed up in night, or it may be merely 'Let them claim it as akin to them.'

*all that maketh black the day,* viz. eclipses, and other supposed supernatural obscurations of the light.

6. *rejoice.* Better than the A.V. 'be joined unto,' which is possible, but requires different vowel points. It has, however, the support of the LXX. and Vulg.

8 Let them curse it that curse the day,
    Who are ¹ready to rouse up leviathan.
9 Let the stars of the twilight thereof be dark :
    Let it look for light, but have none ;
    Neither let it behold the eyelids of the morning :

¹ Or, *skilful*

8. *Who are ready* (marg. *skil-ful*) *to rouse up leviathan.* There is no room for doubt about the correctness of the translation, what-ever meaning is to be extracted from it. The A.V. 'their mourning' rests on a confusion with a late Rabbinic word which is quite out of place here. The word 'leviathan' is clear enough, being the same word which occurs in c. xli. 1 [Heb. xl. 25] as the name of the crocodile of the Nile, as well as in Pss. lxxiv. 14; civ. 26; and Is. xxvii. 1. So the LXX. and Vulgate : 'Qui parati sunt suscitare Leviathan.' The verse then can only be explained as an allusion to an ancient my-thological notion (found also among the Indians), according to which eclipses were produced by a myth-ical dragon or monster of the sky which swallowed up the sun or moon, and so created the darkness. The belief in this strange notion still exists among the peasants of Pales-tine, for in May 1891 Professor G. A. Smith 'witnessed at Hasbeya, on the western skirts of Hermon, an eclipse of the moon. When the shadow began to creep across her disc, there rose from the village a hideous din of drums, metal pots and planks of wood beaten to-gether; guns were fired, and there was much shouting.' And he was 'told that *this was done to terri-fy the great fish which was swallowing the moon, and to make*

*him disgorge her.' Book of the Twelve Prophets*, vol. II. p. 524. The same custom, according to Delitzsch, is found among the Chinese and the Algerians. Thus the whole verse invokes the aid of those who are skilled in enchant-ments so as to be able to overwhelm days with misfortune, and plunge them into the deepest darkness by stirring up the dragon and inciting him to devour the sun and moon. There is nothing in such a mytho-logical allusion which need surprise us or cause us any difficulty, as if it were out of place in inspired Scripture. We shall meet with others in ix. 13 ; xxvi. 13, and possibly in xxix. 18. There is no need to raise the question whether the writer believed the fable which he makes use of. The book is a poem, and it would be absurd to make a poet responsible for hold-ing as literal every such allusion which he may introduce into his work.

9. *the eyelids of the morning.* It is a distinct gain to have the beautiful figure of the original, which occurs again in xli. 18 (Heb. 10), introduced into the R.V. in the place of the tamer paraphrase of the A.V. 'the dawning of the day.' Cf. Sophocles, *Antigone*, l. 103, χρυ-σέας ἁμέρας βλέφαρον, and Milton, 'the opening eyelids of the morn,' *Lycidas*, l. 26.

10 Because it shut not up the doors of my *mother's* womb,
   Nor hid trouble from mine eyes.
11 Why died I not from the womb?
   Why did I not give up the ghost when I came out of the
      belly?
12 Why did the knees receive me?
   Or why the breasts, that I should suck?
13 For now should I have lien down and been quiet;
   I should have slept; then had I been at rest:
14 With kings and counsellors of the earth,
   Which ¹built up waste places for themselves;
15 Or with princes that had gold,
   Who filled their houses with silver:

¹ Or, *built solitary piles*

**11—19. The wish that he had died at his birth.** Having given utterance to the vain wish that the day of his birth might be blotted out so that he might never have been born at all, Job next passes on to wish that, if that were impossible, he might either have died immediately at his birth (11—15), or even have been born dead (16—19). In either case he would have been spared his present misery and been at rest in the shadowy under-world. To the Hebrews death always appeared as in itself an evil, and what was beyond it was merely a shadowy, cheerless existence, not worthy to be called 'life.' It shows, then, the depth of Job's agony that even this state appeared to him far preferable to his present condition of misery, so that as he speaks of it his words grow calmer, and he lingers over the description of the release which he expects, and paints its freedom from suffering in words which Christians have often made their own, and employed to describe the rest of Paradise.

14. It is worth noticing that no difference of conditions in the grave is contemplated: rather it is assumed that the lot of all will be alike there. There are to be found kings, counsellors and princes, and there also are those who were oppressed in this life, prisoners and servants.

*built up waste places*, marg. *solitary piles*, lit. *ruins* (Vulg. *solitudines*, Heb. חׇרָבוֹת). The expression is a difficult one in this connexion. The same phrase occurs several times in the Prophets (Is. lviii. 12; lxi. 4; Ezek. xxxvi. 10, 33; Mal. i. 4) of the anticipated restoration of the *places which had been ruined* and left desolate by the conquerors; but this sense is not suitable here. Consequently it has been thought that the word 'ruins' is used proleptically, and that the writer means to speak of those who have built up for themselves edifices which presently become ruinous heaps. This, however, seems rather forced, and it is tempting if unsafe to adopt Ewald's suggestion, and

16 Or as an hidden untimely birth I had not been ;
   As infants which never saw light.
17 There the wicked cease from [1]troubling ;
   And there the weary be at rest.
18 There the prisoners are at ease together ;
   They hear not the voice of the taskmaster.
19 The small and great are there ;
   And the servant is free from his master.
20 Wherefore is light given to him that is in misery,
   And life unto the bitter in soul ;
21 Which [2]long for death, but it cometh not ;
   And dig for it more than for hid treasures ;
22 Which rejoice [3]exceedingly,   2 Sam. 18[17]. Isah. 7[26]
   And are glad, when they can find the grave ?
23 *Why is light given* to a man whose way is hid,   19[6]
   And whom God hath hedged in ?

---

[1] Or, *raging*        [2] Heb. *wait*.        [3] Or, *unto exultation*

see in the word an allusion to the *Pyramids*, as the Hebrew letters might conceivably be intended to represent the Egyptian word for these mighty piles. Such an allusion would be quite natural here, as in several other places an Egyptian colouring is manifest in this book, and the writer was certainly acquainted with that country. Many moderns, however, think that there must be some error in the text.

16. Cf. Ps. lviii. 8.

20—26. **The wish that he might die now.** Since it is now an impossibility that he should never have been born, or that he should nave died immediately at his birth, one thing alone remains for Job to wish for, viz. that death might now be granted to him as speedily as possible : hence the complaint in this third part of the 'curse,' that life and light are given to the man who is longing for death (20—23),

whose tears are his meat (24), and who is overwhelmed with terrors (25, 26).

21. *Which long for death &c.* Cf. Rev. ix. 6. *And dig for it more than for hid treasures.* Cf. S. Matt. xiii. 44. To an Eastern this would be the most forcible expression possible to denote the eager, restless seeking for death, with which Job was possessed. See Thomson, *The Land and the Book*, p. 135 : 'There is not another comparison within the whole compass of human actions so vivid as this. I have heard of diggers actually fainting when they have come upon even a single coin. They become positively frantic, dig all night with desperate earnestness, and continue to work till utterly exhausted. There are, at this hour, hundreds of persons thus engaged all over the country.'

23. *a man whose way is hid, and whom God hath hedged in.*

J.                                                      2

24 For my sighing cometh [1]before I eat,   *1 Sam.* 1[16]
   And my roarings are poured out like water.
25 For [2]the thing which I fear cometh upon me,
   And that which I am afraid of cometh unto me.
26 [3]I am not at ease, neither am I quiet, neither have I rest ;
   But trouble cometh.

[1] Or, *like my meat*      [2] Or, *the thing which I feared is come &c.*
[3] Or, *I was not at ease...yet trouble came*

With these words Job comes directly to his own case. In the previous verses (20—22) he has been speaking generally, and has avoided mentioning God as the author of the misery of those who long for death but find it not. Now he speaks plainly of himself as 'a man whose way is hid,' so that he can see no clear path before him, and one 'whom God hath hedged in,' so that he can find no outlet from his calamities. In this last phrase we note the first indication of the tendency to regard God as his enemy, which is so strongly marked later on.

24. *before I eat.* Better, as the marginal rendering : *like my meat.* Cf. Ps. xlii. 3, 'my tears have been my meat day and night.'

25, 26. *For the thing which I fear cometh upon me &c.* or (as

R. V. marg.) *the thing which I feared is come.* The reference is certainly not to his past condition, as A.V., but to his present state. His present condition of disquiet and fear of worse evils is the ground for his longing for death.

Looking back over the chapter as a whole, it is easy to see that Job's words are already rash and wild ; but it must be remembered that the reason why Job thus bitterly curses the day of his birth is that he feels forsaken by God, and therefore he wishes that he had never been born ; and, wild as his words are, there is beneath them the truth that in the case of a man who is *really*, and not only in appearance, cast off by God 'it were good for that man if he had not been born.' (S. Matt. xxvi. 24.)

**IV., V.** Chapter iv. commences the first circle of speeches in the discussion which is now entered upon, and which occupies the longest section in the book. This first circle lasts to ch. xiv. The debate is conducted with scrupulous regularity. Each of the three friends is allowed to have his say, and is answered in due course by Job. No one ever interrupts another, and nobody speaks out of his turn. The order followed in this first circle is continued in the two following ones, except that in the third circle Zophar misses his turn altogether. Thus we have

(1)  The first speech of Eliphaz, iv. v.   with Job's answer, vi. vii.
(2)  The first speech of Bildad, viii.      with Job's answer, ix. x.
(3)  The first speech of Zophar, xi.        with Job's answer, xii—xiv.

For the position of the three friends as the representatives of the orthodox theology of the day, and for their theory of a strict system of retribution as carried out in the visible government of this world, which underlies all their arguments, see the Introduction, p. xiii.  Briefly the theory amounts to this : suffering is the punishment of sin.  Holding this, they are confronted with the case of Job.  Here is manifestly a great sufferer : *therefore*, so runs their argument, he is a great sinner.  In this first debate all three speakers speak in the main in general terms, and content themselves with stating their theory broadly, only hinting at its definite application to the case of Job, as explaining his miserable plight. They *assume* rather than state that Job must be guilty, and that his troubles are the consequence of his sin, and each of them holds out the promise of a bright future as in store for him on his repentance: Eliphaz in v. 17—27 ; Bildad in viii. 6, 7 and 21 ; and Zophar in xi. 13—19.

This first speech of Eliphaz in chapters iv. and v. falls into three parts, and may be analysed as follows :

(1) *Introduction, and statement of the doctrine of retribution.* iv. 1—11.

(2) *A revelation which had been made to the speaker.  Man cannot be righteous before God.  Hence it is folly and wickedness for man to complain of God, as the result in the life of the wicked shows.* iv. 12—v. 7.

(3) *It is man's wisdom to submit to God, as the result in the life of the righteous shows: practical application of this to Job's case.* v. 8—27.

**IV.** 1 Then answered Eliphaz the Temanite, and said,
2 If one assay to commune with thee, wilt thou be grieved ?
But who can withhold himself from speaking ?
3 Behold, thou hast instructed many,
And thou hast strengthened the weak hands.
4 Thy words have upholden him that was falling,
And thou hast confirmed the ¹feeble knees.

¹ Heb. *bowing.*

IV. 1—11. Introduction, and statement of the doctrine of retribution.  Job's curse upon his day moves Eliphaz to speak.  He begins in a tone of courtesy, with a half-apology for presuming to instruct one who has in his time been a support and teacher of others in trouble, but who, now that trouble comes upon himself, appears to be overwhelmed by it (1—5).  He next proceeds to suggest a thought which may help the sufferer.  His 'integrity' and 'fear of God' should surely uphold him, because, if he is really innocent, God will never allow him to *perish*, for (and here Eliphaz anticipates S. Paul) 'whatsoever a man soweth, that shall he also reap' (6—8) ; and then, changing his metaphor, he describes the retribution which overtakes the wicked under the figure of the destruction and breaking up of a lion's den (10—11).

3, 4. *thou hast strengthened the weak hands...the feeble knees.*

2—2

5 But now it is come unto thee, and thou [1]faintest ;
  It toucheth thee, and thou art troubled.
6 Is not thy fear *of God* thy confidence,
  *And* thy hope the integrity of thy ways ?
7 Remember, I pray thee, who *ever* perished, being innocent?
  Or where were the upright cut off?
8 According as I have seen, they that plow iniquity,
  And sow [2]trouble, reap the same.
9 By the breath of God they perish,
  And by the blast of his anger are they consumed.
10 The roaring of the lion, and the voice of the fierce lion,
   And the teeth of the young lions, are broken.
11 The old lion perisheth for lack of prey,
   And the whelps of the lioness are scattered abroad.

---

[1] Or, *art grieved*          [2] Or, *mischief*

The same vivid figures for helplessness are found in Isaiah xxxv. 3. (Cf. Heb. xii. 12.) That Eliphaz was justified in speaking in such terms of the support which in former days Job had given to the weak and helpless is shown by Job's own description of his life in the days of his prosperity, when he was 'eyes to the blind, and feet to the lame.' See xxix. 12—17.

5. *But now it is come unto thee.* 'It,' viz. trouble, but there is no need to insert the word, as the LXX. does. Rather, it would appear that Eliphaz purposely avoids specifying what 'it' is.

6. *Is not thy fear of God thy confidence.* This rendering of the R.V. makes the meaning clear. Eliphaz suggests that Job may find consolation and support in his *mens conscia recti*. If he is really conscious of integrity, and of the 'fear of God' (i.e. piety, cf. xv. 4), there is no cause for despondency.

7. Cf. Ps. xxxvii. 25 seq.

8. For similar figures expressing the inevitable result of an evil life see Prov. xxii. 8; Hos. viii. 7; x. 13; and especially Gal. vi. 7, 8; but notice how the apostle looks beyond this life in considering the 'harvest.'

9 is closely connected with the preceding, and describes the judgment which overtakes the wicked, under the figure of the fiery breath of God (as in 2 Thess. ii. 8), which scorches and withers up the grass of the field. Cf. Is. xl. 7; Amos i. 2; S. James i. 11.

10, 11. Eliphaz appends a second picture of the discomfiture of the wicked. The impious man may be mighty as a lion, but his home shall be suddenly broken up, and his children be vagabonds, just as the den of the fierce lion is destroyed and his whelps scattered abroad. For the lion as a figure of the wicked oppressor cf. Ps. xxii. 13, xxxv. 17. The Hebrew language is peculiarly rich in names for lions,

12 Now a thing was [1]secretly brought to me,
   And mine ear received a whisper thereof.
13 In thoughts from the visions of the night,
   When deep sleep falleth on men,
14 Fear came upon me, and trembling,
   Which made all my bones to shake.

[1] Heb. *brought by stealth.*

no fewer than *five* different ones being used in these verses, besides the word for 'whelps' (*Gûr*), which is not confined to the whelps of the lion. See Lam. iv. 3. (1) *Aryeh :* the general name for 'lion'; (2) *Shakhal,* 'the fierce lion'; either the roaring lion, or possibly the black lion; (3) *C'phîrim,* 'the young lions,' no longer mere 'whelps,' but already weaned, and having begun to ravin : see Ezek. xix. 2, 3; Ps. civ. 21; (4) *Layish,* 'the old lion,' perhaps 'the strong lion,' but the word is a rare one, only found here and Is. xxx. 6; Prov. xxx. 30; (5) *Labhî,* possibly 'the lioness.'

iv. 12—v. 7. **A revelation which had been made to the speaker. Man cannot be righteous before God. Hence it is folly and wickedness for man to complain of God, as the result in the life of the wicked shows.** This section begins with a very striking and impressive account of a vision which had been granted to the speaker in the night. A spiritual manifestation was made to him, and the silence was broken by a voice proclaiming the impossibility of man being 'just before God,' or 'pure before his Maker.' Even the angels are not clean before Him. How much less can frail man be free from sin (12—21)? Eliphaz next challenges Job to appeal to the

angels and see whether there is any of them who will espouse his cause (v. 1). Then by a sudden turn, he lays down the principle that it is only the 'foolish man' or the 'silly one' who allows himself to complain of God, following this up with a description drawn from life of the destruction which overtakes one who is so foolish as to resent God's dispensations (3—5), and ending by 'condensing into a vivid aphorism his teaching in this section' (Davidson). The misfortune that overtakes the fool is nothing to be surprised at. It might have been foreseen all along, for 'affliction' is no chance weed that springs up haphazard, but 'man is born to trouble as the sparks fly upward' (6, 7).

This appears to be the general drift of the passage, but it must be confessed that the intention of the opening verses of chapter v. is somewhat obscure; and it is possible that there has been some corruption of the text (Siegfried rejects verse 1 altogether).

12—16. *The vision.* A wonderfully graphic description of the manifestation and the terror which it excited. In verse 15 it is doubtful whether the meaning is *then a spirit passed before my face,* or (as R.V. marg.) *then a breath passed over my face.* The latter is perhaps the more probable rendering.

15 Then ¹a spirit passed before my face ;
   The hair of my flesh stood up.
16 It stood still, but I could not discern the appearance
      thereof;
   A form was before mine eyes :
   ²*There was* silence, and I heard a voice, *saying,*
17 Shall mortal man ³be more just than God?
   Shall a man ⁴be more pure than his Maker?
18 Behold, he putteth no trust in his servants ;
   And his angels he chargeth with folly :

¹ Or, *a breath passed over*
³ Or, *be just before God*

² Or, *I heard a still voice*
⁴ Or, *be pure before his Maker*

It was the feeling of this mysterious breath upon him that caused his horror. And then in verse 16 he describes what he saw. *It stood still.* 'It,' i.e. the mysterious 'form' of which he could not discern 'the appearance.' Cox aptly quotes, as probably suggested by this, one of the finest passages in Milton's description of Death.

'If shape it might be called that shape had none
Distinguishable in member, joints, or limb ;
Or substance might be called that shadow seemed.'
                    *Paradise Lost*, ii. 666.

*There was silence, and I heard a voice,* or possibly, with R.V. marg., *I heard a still voice.* Cf. 1 Kings xix. 12, where the words in the original are almost the same.

17. *Shall mortal man...be more pure than his Maker?* As far as the grammar is concerned this translation is perfectly natural : but such a sentiment seems unnecessary and out of place here, as there was no question of Job setting himself up to be more righteous or pure than God. Hence there is

little doubt that the margin of the R.V. gives the correct rendering :

Shall mortal man be just before God?
Shall a man be pure before his Maker ?

(1) This translation is equally possible grammatically (cf. Numb. xxxii. 22, where the same construction is found); (2) it has the support of the LXX.; (3) it gives a meaning which is thoroughly in place in the argument of Eliphaz, who is here showing that the sufferings of the ungodly are the result of their sins ; and (4) it is supported by the very similar passages in xv. 14–16, and xxv. 4–6, where it is the only meaning possible.

18. *folly.* The Hebrew word occurs nowhere else, and though a possible root has been suggested for it, which would give the meaning of 'error' rather than folly, it is noteworthy that the change of a single letter would give in its place the word *unsavouriness*, which we have already met with in i. 22, and which is used with the same verb as here in xxiv. 12.

19 How much more them that dwell in houses of clay,
　Whose foundation is in the dust,
　Which are crushed ¹before the moth !
20 ²Betwixt morning and evening they are ³destroyed :
　They perish for ever without any regarding it.
21 ⁴Is not their tent-cord plucked up within them ?
　They die, and that without wisdom.

---

¹ Or, *like*　　² Or, *From morning to evening*　　³ Heb. *broken in pieces.*
⁴ Or, *Is not their excellency which is in them removed ?*

---

**19.** *them that dwell in houses of clay &c.* i.e. men who are 'formed out of the clay' (xxxiii. 6), and made 'of the dust of the ground' (Gen. ii. 7). Cf. S. Paul's phrase 'our earthly house of this tabernacle,' 2 Cor. v. 1, where the 'house,' as here, refers to the body.

*Which are crushed before the moth.* Better, *like the moth.* So the margin of the R.V. after the LXX.; the Hebrew word *before* is the same as that found in iii. 24, where see note.

**20.** *Betwixt morning and evening they are destroyed,* i.e. they are as shortlived as the moth, the creature of a day, and are as little regarded. Cf. the similar expression, '*From day even unto night* wilt thou make an end of me' in Is. xxxviii. 12, where the meaning is 'in the course of a single day.'

**21.** *Is not their tent-cord plucked up within them ?* The verse is very obscure, but by adopting this rendering of the R.V. a good sense may be obtained.

The tent is a figure for the 'earthly house of this tabernacle' (2 Cor. v. 1, where S. Paul *combines* the two figures of verses 19 and 21), and the plucking up of the tent-cord leading to the collapse of the tent forcibly expresses the sudden death of its inhabitant. Cf. again Is. xxxviii. 12, 'Mine age (*marg.* habitation) is removed, and is carried away from me as a shepherd's tent.' It is difficult to extract any intelligible meaning out of the A.V.

*They die, and that without wisdom.* A touch which heightens the tragedy of man's fate : he dies before he has ever attained unto wisdom.

Davidson rightly lays stress on the *considerateness* of all this part of the speech of Eliphaz. ' He does not touch Job's murmurs directly, but seeks to reach them by suggesting other thoughts to Job. First, he speaks of the exalted purity of God, to awaken reverence in Job's mind. Then he descends to the creatures and seeks to look at them as they appear unto God. In His eyes, so sublime is He in holiness, all creatures, angels and men, are erring. Thus Eliphaz makes Job cease to be an exception, and renders it more easy for him to reconcile himself to his history and acknowledge the true cause of it. He is but one where all are the same. There is nothing strange in his having sinned (v. 6, 7). Neither, therefore, are his afflictions strange. But it will be something strange if he murmurs against God.'

**V.** 1 Call now ; is there any that will answer thee ?
And to which of the [1]holy ones wilt thou turn ?
2 [1]For vexation killeth the foolish man,
And [2]jealousy slayeth the silly one.
3 I have seen the foolish taking root :
But suddenly I cursed his habitation.
4 His children are far from safety,
And they are crushed in the gate,
Neither is there any to deliver them.

[1] See ch. xv. 15.      [2] Or, *indignation*

**V. 1.** *which of the holy ones.* The interpretation of the LXX., *the holy angels,* is undoubtedly correct. See xv. 15, where the same word, *the holy ones,* is used in a verse which is parallel with iv. 18, *angels.* The word is also used of the angels in Ps. lxxxix. 7, and probably in Zech. xiv. 5 ; cf. also Dan. viii. 13.

**2.** *For vexation killeth the foolish man &c.* It is idle for Job to complain of his hapless plight to the angels. None of them would regard his complaint. Rather let him remember that such 'vexation' and 'jealousy' as he shows with regard to God's treatment of him, brings down in due time a judgment on the man who is so foolish as to give way to it. The word for 'foolish' is a different one from that used in ii. 10, but like it, it often denotes one who is morally bad, see Prov. i. 7, xiv. 9, xv. 5.

**3—5.** Eliphaz recalls an instance to illustrate the thought to which he has just given expression, and describes the case of a man whom he had seen apparently prosperous and taking root, when suddenly his prosperity was at an end and he and his children were involved in ruin.

**3.** *I cursed his habitation.* This can only mean 'I pronounced his habitation accursed,' as if Eliphaz foresaw the ruin that was coming, and so declared that the household was accursed. But the expression is certainly a strange one, and it is possible that the text is corrupt. The LXX. have 'and suddenly his house was consumed,' which gives an excellent sense but implies a different reading (possibly the same word that is found in Prov. x. 7; Is. xl. 20).

**4.** *they are crushed in the gate.* 'The gate' here, as so often, means the open space at the gate of the city where judgment was given. Cf. xxix. 7, xxxi. 21 ; Deut. xxv. 7 ; Prov. xxii. 22 ; Is. xxix. 21 ; Amos v. 10. Consequently the thought here is that the sons, after the overthrow of their father, are unable to obtain justice, and thus are 'crushed,' there being 'none to deliver them,' no powerful champion able to bribe or overawe the judge. Contrast Ps. cxxvii. 5, where the children are 'not ashamed, when they speak with their enemies in the gate.'

5　Whose harvest the hungry eateth up,
　　And taketh it even out of the thorns.
　　And [1]the snare gapeth for their substance.
6　For [2]affliction cometh not forth of the dust,
　　Neither doth trouble spring out of the ground ;
7　But man is born unto trouble,
　　As [3]the sparks fly upward.
8　But as for me, I would seek unto God,
　　And unto God would I commit my cause :

---

[1] According to many ancient versions, *the thirsty swallow up.*
[2] Or, *iniquity* See ch. iv. 8.　　　[3] Heb. *the sons of flame* or *of lightning.*

5.　So complete is their ruin that the hungry marauder fears not to break through the hedge of 'thorns' surrounding the homestead, in order to rob and carry off the harvest.

*and the snare gapeth for their substance.* 'The snare.' If the text is correct, this is the only translation possible. 'Robber' of the A.V., which comes from the Targum, has no real authority. The word is only found again in xviii. 9, where it certainly has the meaning of 'snare.' Thus Eliphaz means to say that the wealth and property of the fool disappears 'as though some huge trap which had long gaped for it, had swallowed it in an instant' (Cox). It will be seen, however, that the margin of the R.V. suggests an alternative rendering, '*the thirsty swallow up their substance,* according to many ancient versions.' This gives an excellent sense, and the allusion to 'the thirsty' forms a natural parallel to the previous clause speaking of 'the hungry.' The change required for this reading is only one of punctuation, and as it has the support of the versions of Aquila and Symmachus as well as the Vulg. it certainly deserves consideration.

6, 7.　'Affliction' and 'trouble' are not really necessitated by man's environment : they come 'not forth of the dust,' and do not 'spring out of the ground'; but man brings them quite naturally upon himself through his sinful nature, from which evil rises up as naturally 'as the sparks fly upward.'

**8—27. It is man's wisdom to submit to God, as the result in the life of the righteous shows : practical application of this to Job's case.**

Having now shown in general the consequences of sin in the life of the wicked, Eliphaz turns to Job and tells him (as it is so easy for a prosperous man to do) what he himself would do if he were in the sufferer's place. He would commit his case unreservedly to God, Who is so great and so good (8—11), Who exercises judgment upon the wicked, and saves the poor and needy (12—16). Let Job, then, consider himself happy in being corrected by God, for He Who makes sore will also bind up (17, 18), and will deliver His afflicted and humble servant and restore him to all, and more than all, his former prosperity (19—27).

9 Which doeth great things and unsearchable ;
  Marvellous things without number :
10 Who giveth rain upon the earth,
  And sendeth waters upon the fields :
11 So that he setteth up on high those that be low ;
  And those which mourn are exalted to safety.
12 He frustrateth the devices of the crafty,
  So that their hands [1]cannot perform their enterprise.
13 He taketh the wise in their own craftiness :
  And the counsel of the froward is carried headlong.
14 They meet with darkness in the day-time,
  And grope at noonday as in the night.
15 But he saveth from the sword [2]of their mouth,
  Even the needy from the hand of the mighty.
16 So the poor hath hope,
  And iniquity stoppeth her mouth.

[1] Or, *can perform nothing of worth*    [2] Heb. *out of their mouth.*

**10.** *Who giveth rain upon the earth.* The gracious rain is here mentioned, as often elsewhere, as an instance of God's beneficence. Cf. Ps. lxv. 9; lxviii. 9; civ. 13; cxlvii. 8.

**11.** *So that he setteth up on high those that be low.* These words, among many other passages of the Old Testament, appear to have been in the mind of the Blessed Virgin when she gave utterance to the Magnificat. Cf. S. Luke i. 52, where the first clause is apparently suggested by Job xii. 19, and the second (ὕψωσεν ταπεινούς) by the line before us (LXX. τὸν ποιοῦντα ταπεινοὺς εἰς ὕψος). Cf. also 1 Sam. ii. 7 seq.

**13.** *He taketh the wise in their own craftiness.* These words are quoted by S. Paul in 1 Cor. iii. 19 as Scripture, being introduced by the formula 'it is written.' This is the only formal and acknowledged quotation from the book in the New Testament. But there is also the historical allusion to Job in S. James v. 11, and there are a few other passages besides that just noted above in which recollections of this book have apparently influenced the language of the New Testament, e.g. Westcott and Hort mark Phil. i. 19 as a citation of Job xiii. 16, and note the coincidence of phrase between 1 Thess. v. 22 and Job i. 1, ii. 3; 2 Thess. ii. 8 and Job iv. 9; and Rev. ix. 6 and Job iii. 21 ; while Rom. xi. 35 is a reminiscence of Job xli. 11.

*is carried headlong,* i.e. being hastily conceived and executed it is frustrated.

**15.** *from the sword of their mouth.* As the margin of the R.V. notes, the Hebrew has 'out of their mouth'; and the text is open to suspicion of incorrectness, but the general sense is clear enough.

**16.** *And iniquity stoppeth her*

17 Behold, happy is the man whom God [1]correcteth :
   Therefore despise not thou the chastening of the Almighty.
18 For he maketh sore, and bindeth up ;
   He woundeth, and his hands make whole.
19 He shall deliver thee in six troubles ;
   Yea, in seven there shall no evil touch thee.
20 In famine he shall redeem thee from death ;
   And in war from the power of the sword.
21 Thou shalt be hid from the scourge of the tongue ;
   Neither shalt thou be afraid of destruction when it cometh.
22 At destruction and dearth thou shalt laugh;
   Neither shalt thou be afraid of the beasts of the earth.
23 For thou shalt be in league with the stones of the field ;
   And the beasts of the field shall be at peace with thee.
24 And thou shalt know that thy tent is in peace ;
   And thou shalt visit thy [2]fold, and [3]shalt miss nothing.

---

[1] Or, *reproveth*    [2] Or, *habitation*    [3] Or, *shalt not err*

*mouth.* These words occur again in Ps. cvii. 42, a Psalm which has other coincidences with Job; cf. verse 40 with chapter xii. 21, 24.

17. *Behold, happy is the man &c.* These words seem to be borrowed from Prov. iii. 11 seq. (on the relation that exists between Job and Proverbs see Introd. p. xxii), which are quoted in the New Testament in Hebrews xii. 5. It is almost unnecessary to call attention to the beauty of the passage which begins with this verse, and the lovely picture which it sets before us. Even the most careless reader cannot be insensible to it.

19. *He shall deliver thee in six troubles; yea, in seven &c.* ' Six, yea seven.' This is an instance of what is called the 'ascending enumeration' in Hebrew, whereby the speaker after mentioning one number adds a still higher one, to denote *emphasis and completeness.* Almost any number will do. Thus we have 'one and two' in xxxiii. 14; Ps. lxii. 11 ; 'two and three' in Ecclus. xxiii. 16, xxvi. 28, l. 25; 'three and four' in Ecclus. xxvi. 5, Amos i. 3 seq. ; Prov. xxx. 15 seq. ; 'six and seven ' in the passage before us; 'seven and eight' in Micah v. 5 ; Eccles. xi. 2 ; and 'nine and ten' in Ecclus. xxv. 7.

21. *the scourge of the tongue,* a very vigorous phrase for the sin of calumny, detraction, and defamation, which the Psalmists so smarted under.

22, 23. All nature is at peace with the man whose heart is at peace with God. See Hosea ii. 18, and cf. Horace, *Odes,* I. xxii.

24. *thou shalt visit thy fold, and shalt miss nothing.* The changes in the R.V. make the meaning of this verse clear to the English reader. *tent* is much more natural than *tabernacle* in the first clause ; *fold* expresses the meaning more accurately than the colourless *habi-*

25 Thou shalt know also that thy seed shall be great,
    And thine offspring as the grass of the earth.
26 Thou shalt come to thy grave in a full age,
    Like as a shock of corn cometh in in its season.

*tation*; and *shalt miss nothing* indicates the general idea of the verse—that of the Eastern farmer overlooking his homestead, and finding all secure, and not one lacking.

26. The crowning blessing of the Old Covenant shall be his, viz. long life, so that he shall die 'in a good old age,' and be carried to his grave as the sheaf of ripe corn is carried in at the harvest-home. Almost all commentators quote as illustrative of this verse Milton's noble lines:

So may'st thou live, till, like ripe fruit, thou drop
Into thy mother's lap; or be with ease
Gathered, not harshly plucked; for death mature.
            *Paradise Lost*, xi. l. 537–39.

It is universally admitted that this speech of Eliphaz is 'one of the masterpieces of the book' (Davidson), and that there are few more exquisite passages anywhere in it than the closing verses of chapter v. And yet it is not difficult to see why it fails to bring comfort to Job. It fails in two ways: (1) although almost everything that Eliphaz says is true, *it is not the whole truth.* Underlying his whole argument is the assumption that *all* suffering is the punishment of sin, even if designed to be corrective, and not simply vindictive. Hence, true as his reflections are with regard to much of the suffering in this world, *they do not touch the case of Job at all*, for of his sickness we may say that it was 'sent unto him,' not 'to correct and amend in him whatso-

ever did offend the eyes of his heavenly Father,' but rather 'to try his patience for the example of others, and that his faith might be found in the day of the Lord laudable, glorious, and honourable, to the increase of glory and endless felicity.' See the exhortation to the sick person in the 'Order for the Visitation of the Sick' in the Book of Common Prayer, and remark how in it the *one-sided* and narrow view of Eliphaz as to the purpose of suffering is avoided. (2) A second reason why Eliphaz fails to help Job is that throughout he adopts the tone of the moralist or lecturer rather than that of the sympathetic friend who 'weeps with those that weep.' What Job needed was sympathy: what he met with was moralizing. Hence his friend's words only embittered him. They brought him no more help than the well-meant consolations of his friends brought to Tennyson, according to the well-known lines:

One writes that 'Other friends remain,'
    That 'Loss is common to the race'—
And common is the commonplace,
    And vacant chaff well meant for grain.

That loss is common would not make
    My own less bitter, rather more:
Too common! Never morning wore
    To evening, but some heart did break.
            *In Memoriam*, vi.

27 Lo this, we have searched it, so it is ;
   Hear it, and know thou it ¹for thy good.

¹ Heb. *for thyself.*

**VI., VII.** Chapters vi. and vii. contain Job's reply. The moralizing of Eliphaz has only irritated him. It has not helped him to bear his misery patiently by throwing any light upon the true account of it, or by revealing its cause, for Job, who up to this time has evidently acquiesced, like his friends, in the orthodox theory of suffering, is conscious that he has done nothing to deserve this exceptionally severe treatment at the hand of God as a punishment. Hence he can but renew the complaint to which he had already given utterance in his curse upon his day, and describe once more his hapless plight. His speech falls into two main divisions, the first (vi) addressed to his friends; the second (vii) addressed to God, and each of these may be further subdivided, so that the analysis of the whole speech may be given as follows.

(1)  *The answer to his friends.*  vi.

  (*a*)  renewal and defence of his former complaints, 1—13.

  (*b*)  the failure of his friends to help him, 14—30.

(2)  *The appeal to God.*  vii.

  (*a*)  description of his hapless, hopeless condition, 1—10.

  (*b*)  expostulation with God for His inexplicable treatment of him, 11—21.

**VI.**  1 Then Job answered and said,
   2 Oh that my vexation were but weighed,
      And my calamity laid in the balances together !

**VI. The answer to his friends.**
1—13. **Renewal and defence of his former complaints.** Eliphaz had reproved him for his 'vexation' (v. 2). Job, accordingly, begins by taking up this word, and wishing that his 'vexation' could be weighed against his calamity. The result would be the explanation and justification of his wild words (1—4). He next points out that there must be *some* ground for his complaints, as his friends might well have perceived (5—7); and then, overcome by his misery, he breaks out suddenly into a passionate cry for death, which he would gladly welcome (8—10), and shows how utterly impossible it is for him to endure patiently (11—13).

2.  *Oh that my vexation were but weighed &c.* Apparently what Job wishes is that his *vexation* (cf. v. 1) or the resentment to which he has given expression, might be weighed against his *calamity*, or the misery which he has to endure.

3 For now it would be heavier than the sand of the seas :
  Therefore have my words been rash.
4 For the arrows of the Almighty are within me,
  The poison whereof my spirit drinketh up :
  The terrors of God do set themselves in array against me.
5 Doth the wild ass bray when he hath grass?
  Or loweth the ox over his fodder?
6 Can that which hath no savour be eaten without salt?
  Or is there any taste in ¹the white of an egg?
7 ²My soul refuseth to touch *them* ;
  They are as loathsome meat to me.

¹ Or, *the juice of purslain*
² Or, What things *my soul refused to touch, these are as my loathsome meat*

3. *For now it would be heavier &c. it*, viz. the 'calamity,' the weight of which would far outweigh any resentful utterances of his.

*Therefore have my words been rash*, a far more probable rendering than that of the A.V. *are swallowed up.*

4. *the arrows of the Almighty*, the origin of S. Gregory's name for sufferings, 'the bitter arrows in the hand of God'; and cf. Shakespeare's 'the slings and arrows of outrageous fortune.' *Hamlet*, Act III. Sc. 1.

5. *Doth the wild ass bray when he hath grass?* Job evidently means by these questions to ask whether there is no cause for his complaint. Asses do not bray, nor oxen low, when they have food sufficient: and neither would he make so much noise unless he had a sense of want.

6. A further defence of his complaints. Can he be expected to enjoy his afflictions any more than unsavoury food?

*the white of an egg.* Of the two words here used the latter is not found again in Scripture and its meaning must be more or less conjectural. The former occurs elsewhere only in 1 Sam. xxi. 13, where it is used of the spittle or slime which David let fall upon his beard; and so it might conceivably be used of the slimy 'white' of an egg. This rendering, which is that of both A.V. and R.V., is already found in the Targum. But the Syriac Version gives another translation which is adopted in the margin of the R.V. Taking the second word, which is found nowhere else, not as 'an egg,' but as the name of a plant, 'purslain,' and supposing that the first word refers to the slime or juice of this, it renders the words *broth* (or *juice*) *of purslain*, a beverage which evidently stood to the translator as the type of insipidity. Either translation seems possible.

7. *My soul refuseth to touch them. them*, and *they* in the next clause, are evidently his sufferings, which he shrinks from naming. Cf. iii. 24, where he has said that they are 'like my meat.'

8  Oh that I might have my request ;
 And that God would grant *me* the thing that I long for !
9  Even that it would please God to crush me ;
 That he would let loose his hand, and cut me off !
10  Then should I yet have comfort ;
 [1]Yea, I would [2]exult in pain [3]that spareth not :
 [4]For I have not [5]denied the words of the Holy One.
11  What is my strength, that I should wait ?
 And what is mine end, that I should be patient ?
12  Is my strength the strength of stones ?
 Or is my flesh of brass ?
13  Is it not that I have no help in me,
 And that [6]effectual working is driven quite from me ?
14  To him that is ready to faint kindness *should be shewed*
  from his friend ;
 [7]Even to him that forsaketh the fear of the Almighty.

[1] Or, *Though I shrink back*  [2] Or, *harden myself*
[3] Or, *though he spare not*  [4] Or, *That*  [5] Or, *concealed*
[6] Or, *sound wisdom*  [7] Or, *Else might he forsake* Or, *But he forsaketh*

8—10. The one thing for which he longs is death, which by releasing him from his agony would bring him *comfort*; and he feels that he could face the pains of death gladly, yea exultingly, because supported by the consciousness of his integrity.

10. The text of the R.V. *I would exult* is to be preferred to the marginal renderings *though I shrink back*, or *harden myself* (cf. A.V.), and similarly it is better to connect the last words of this line, *that spareth not*, closely with the foregoing (pain), than to take them as a separate clause referring to God, *though he spare not*, R.V. marg., or *let him not spare*, A.V.

11—13. Death is the only 'end' to his afflictions. Why then should it be postponed? He is not made of stone or brass, so that he is capable of bearing anything without feeling, and all his resources are exhausted.

13. *effectual working*. Margin, *sound wisdom*. The Hebrew word, which occurs several times in this book (v. 12; vi. 13; xi. 6; xii. 16; xxvi. 3), and Proverbs (ii. 7; iii. 21; viii. 14; xviii. 1), and is very rare elsewhere (only Is. xxviii. 29; Micah vi. 9), is a very difficult one to translate satisfactorily. It appears to be a technical term of the Hebrew 'wisdom' or philosophy. It seems to mean primarily *sound* or *efficient wisdom*, and secondly, as the result or effect of this, *abiding success*, which is perhaps the meaning here. *Abiding success is driven from me*. See the new Hebrew Lexicon (Clarendon Press) *sub voce*.

14—30. **The failure of his friends to help him.** So far in his answer Job has been defending and

15 My brethren have dealt deceitfully as a brook,
   As the channel of brooks that pass away ;
16 Which are black by reason of the ice,
   *And* wherein the snow hideth itself :
17 What time they [1]wax warm, they vanish :
   When it is hot, they are consumed out of their place.
18 [2]The caravans *that travel* by the way of them turn aside ;
   They go up into the waste, and perish.

[1] Or, *shrink*        [2] Or, *The paths of their way are turned aside*

accounting for his own attitude. He now turns upon his friends, and upbraids them with their failure to help him and their cruelty towards him (14). They are like the torrent in the desert, which is dried up in the summer and fails the thirsty traveller just when he needs it most (15—21). Then in a tone of bitter irony he reminds them that it was not much which he had asked from them. He had looked for no material succour, and had never invited them to rescue him from his oppressors (22, 23). Let them only give him some real instruction, and he will gladly hold his peace : but such arguments as theirs are really worthless, and their treatment of him betrays a spirit which would lead them on to inhuman cruelties (24—27); and finally, in a somewhat calmer tone, he challenges them to look on him without prejudice and say whether he is capable of injustice and of lying to their faces (28—30).

15—21. The simile of the deceitful brook is worked out with great elaborateness and beauty. In winter it is turbid (*black*) and swollen with ice and snow, and then when summer comes it is dried up and vanishes away.

18. *The caravans.* The word is the same one which occurs in the next verse, where it undoubtedly means 'caravans.' Hence the R.V., taking this verse as describing in general terms what is more fully elaborated immediately afterwards. The caravans that travel by the way of the dried-up stream *turn aside,* i.e. make a wide detour in search of water, wander away into the desert *waste,* and finally perish of thirst. To this Davidson objects that 'it is not usual for caravans to leave the route and "turn aside" in search of water, a route is selected and formed rather because water is found on it.' But the whole point of the illustration seems to be that water *was* expected to be found ; and if the expected supply had failed what could the caravan do but *turn aside*? Thus the R.V. may well be supported, and it seems to yield a preferable sense to the marginal rendering (which agrees with the A.V.), which is open to the objection that it takes the same word in two completely different senses in two consecutive verses. *The paths of their way are turned aside.* This makes *the streams* the subject of the verse, which is supposed to be descriptive of the manner in which the brook winds its way into the desert and is lost in the sand.

19 The caravans of Tema looked,
   The companies of Sheba waited for them.
20 They were ashamed because they had hoped ;
   They came thither, and were confounded.
21 For now ye ¹are nothing ;
   Ye see a terror, and are afraid.
22 Did I say, Give unto me ?
   Or, Offer a present for me of your substance ?
23 Or, Deliver me from the adversary's hand ?
   Or, Redeem me from the hand of the oppressors ?
24 Teach me, and I will hold my peace :
   And cause me to understand wherein I have erred.

¹ Another reading is, *are like thereto*.

19. *Tema,* a district in the northern part of Arabia, mentioned (in connexion with the caravans of Dedan) in Is. xxi. 14; and Jer. xxv. 23. For *Sheba* see on i. 15, 'Sabeans.'

20. *They were ashamed,* i.e. they were disappointed. In Hebrew 'people are often said to be "a-shamed" when the help or support upon which they rely fails them.' Driver on Joel i. 11. Cf. Is. i. 29; xx. 5; xxx. 5; and contrast Rom. v. 5.

21. *For now ye are nothing.* This follows the *marginal* reading of the Massoretic text. The word rendered 'nothing' is *lo* (לֹא), the ordinary adverb of negation, which is never elsewhere used as a substantive, and it is very doubtful whether it can be so employed. Further, the negative, though found in the Targum, is not recognized here either in the LXX. or Vulgate, and the Massoretic *text* (as distinct from the margin) reads in its place another word of similar sound, but different spelling, *lo* (לֹו), which gives the meaning adopted in the margin of the R.V. *for now ye are*

like *thereto*: literally *ye are become it,* as if Job said to his friends 'That's what you are like.' This yields an excellent sense and should probably be adopted.

It may be added that some commentators, as Ewald and Siegfried, think that neither reading is original, and would alter the text, so as to read, ' *Thus* have ye now become *to me*' לִי; but this seems unnecessary.

[The two words לֹא, *not* and לֹו *to it* or *him,* are several times confused in the text of the Old Testament. According to the Massorah, לֹא is written for לֹו fifteen times (there seem, however, to be at least *eighteen* instances), two of which occur in the Book of Job, xiii. 15 (where see note) and xli. 4 [E.V. 12]; while לֹו *to it,* is said to be written three times for לֹא the negative ; viz. here and in 1 Sam. ii. 16; xx. 2.]

*Ye see a terror,* i.e. the sight of Job himself in his misery.

22, 23. It was only sympathy that he had asked for from them : no gift of a costly present, no sum of money that might ransom a captive.

24. He demands to be shown

25 How forcible are words of uprightness !
   But what doth your arguing reprove ?
26 Do ye imagine to reprove words ?
   Seeing that the speeches of one that is desperate are ¹as
     wind.
27 Yea, ye would cast *lots* upon the fatherless,
   And make merchandise of your friend.
28 Now therefore be pleased to look upon me ;
   ²For surely I shall not lie to your face.
29 Return, I pray you, let there be no injustice ;
   Yea, return again, ³my cause is righteous.
30 Is there injustice on my tongue ?
   Cannot my taste discern mischievous things ?

¹ Or, *for the wind*
² Or, *And it will be evident unto you if I lie*
³ Heb. *my righteousness is in it.*

what the sin is of which he has been guilty.

25. *words of uprightness*, i.e. straightforward dealings, he can appreciate : they are *forcible*, or, possibly, *sweet* (if, as some think, the word found here is only another form of that which occurs in Ps. cxix. 103, 'How *sweet* are thy words unto my taste'), but what is he the better for the kind of arguments which his friends give him ?

26. Are they imagining that they are reproving the words of his curse upon his day ? Why, the words of a desperate man, such as he is, are idle as the wind !

27. *Yea, ye would cast* lots *upon the fatherless.* The A.V. *ye over-whelm* is impossible with the present text, and, though the ellipse of the word for 'lots' is rather violent, yet it finds a parallel in 1 Sam. xiv. 42. The R.V. is, therefore, probably correct.

*make merchandise of.* The same

word occurs in this sense in xli. 6 (Heb. xl. 30) *make traffic of.*

28. He challenges the friends to look him straight in the face, and judge by his bearing whether he would claim to be innocent if he were really guilty. *Surely,* he says, *I shall not lie to your face ;* or (as the margin of R.V. with A.V.), *it will be evident unto you if I lie.*

29. Though the general sense is sufficiently clear, the exact meaning is uncertain. Either (1) ' let them renew their investigations again and again, and they will still find his cause is righteous,' lit. *my righteousness is in it ;* or (2) 'let them *turn*' (not *return*), i.e. 'let them adopt another course, seek another cause for his sufferings, and not accuse him unjustly ; and they will find that he has right on his side.'

30. Do they really imagine that his moral sense—his *taste*—is so perverted, that he can no longer

**VII.**   1  Is there not a ¹warfare to man upon earth?
And are not his days like the days of an hireling?

2  As a servant that earnestly desireth the shadow,
And as an hireling that looketh for his wages:

3  So am I made to possess months of vanity,
And wearisome nights are appointed to me.

4  When I lie down, I say,
²When shall I arise? but the night is long;
And I am full of tossings to and fro unto the dawning of
the day.

5  My flesh is clothed with worms and clods of dust;
My skin ³closeth up and breaketh out afresh.

6  My days are swifter than a weaver's shuttle,
And are spent without hope.

¹ Or, *time of service*      ² Or, *When shall I arise, and the night be gone?*
³ Or, *is broken and become loathsome*

discern right from wrong? With these words Job turns away from his friends, despairing of being understood by them, and makes his appeal to God.

**VII. 1—10. Description of his hapless, hopeless condition.** In these verses Job first describes his lot as the hard labour to which the mercenary or the hireling is condemned (1—3). From this he passes to a more detailed description of the nature of his sufferings and the symptoms of his disease (4—6); and appeals to God to remember that his life is but a mere breath which passes away, for there is no hope for him in the grave (7—10).

1. *a warfare.* Rather *a time of service*, R.V. marg. It is the hárd service of the hired soldier to which Job compares his life. The word is used in the same sense in xiv. 14.

2. *that earnestly desireth the shadow.* The slave forced to bear the burden and heat of the day pants for the shades of evening: and the hireling looks forward to the same hour, when he shall receive his wages; cf. S. Matt. xx. 8.

3. Like these, Job is forced to endure and labour, until the appointed hour for his discharge comes; though meanwhile he may have to endure *months of vanity* and *wearisome nights*.

4. Cf. Deut. xxviii. 67.

5. A vivid description of his sufferings from the leprosy. Ulcers broke out upon his body and bred worms: the *clods of dust* are the crust of his sores, which kept forming and discharging. This, which is the meaning of the R.V. (*closeth up and breaketh out afresh*), is probably correct.

6. He now laments the shortness of his life, though only a little while before he had longed for death. Such inconsistencies are perfectly natural, and are only what we should expect under the circumstances.

3—2

7 Oh remember that my life is wind :
  Mine eye shall no more see good.
8 The eye of him that seeth me shall behold me no more :
  Thine eyes shall be upon me, but I shall not be.
9 As the cloud is consumed and vanisheth away,
  So he that goeth down to ¹Sheol shall come up no more.
10 He shall return no mo ɔ to his house,
  Neither shall his place know him any more.
11 Therefore I will not refrain my mouth ;
  I will speak in the anguish of my spirit ;
  I will complain in the bitterness of my soul.

¹ Or, *the grave*

8—10. These verses, in which Job contemplates the approach of death, are noteworthy as showing that at this stage he had no hope or even thought of a resurrection. Such a thing does not seem to have occurred to him, for nothing can be stronger than the language which he uses to denote the finality of his condition in the grave. See further on xiv. 7 seq., where a change may be noted.

8. *Thine eyes shall be upon me,* perhaps '*against* me,' as in Amos ix. 8, God's eyes are said to be 'against the sinful kingdom,' the preposition being the same.

*I shall not be.* This does not mean that he will be *annihilated* by death, but simply that he will not be found in the land of the living. Death was never regarded by the Hebrews as extinction or annihilation. A shadowy existence of some sort, joyless and not worthy to be called 'life,' was always assumed to be the lot of the departed.

9. This verse was appealed to in after days as illustrating the teaching of the Sadducees, who denied the possibility of the resurrection. See

J. Lightfoot's *Horæ Hebraicæ*, on S. Matt. xxii. 23.

*he that goeth down to Sheol.* The substitution of the Hebrew word 'Sheol' for 'the grave' in a large number of passages in the O.T. is one of the great gains for English readers from the Revised Version. (See the remarks on it in the Revisers' preface.) The word is never used simply for the place of burial, but is the regular name employed among the Hebrews for the abode of departed spirits, like the Greek Hades.

11—21. **Expostulation with God for His inexplicable treatment of him.** The thought of the shortness of his time and the approach of death makes Job feel that he can no longer refrain himself, but that he must speak out his complaint (11). He wants to know *why* it is that God is treating him in this way, and boldly puts three questions : (1) Is he so dangerous that God feels bound to set a watch over him ; is it for this that just when he is hoping for some refreshing sleep God terrifies him with such horrible dreams and visions

12 Am I a sea, or a sea-monster,
   That thou settest a watch over me?
13 When I say, My bed shall comfort me,
   My couch shall ease my complaint;
14 Then thou scarest me with dreams,
   And terrifiest me through visions:
15 So that my soul chooseth strangling,
   And death rather than *these* my bones.
16 ¹I loathe *my life*; I ²would not live alway:
   Let me alone; for my days are ³vanity.
17 What is man, that thou shouldest magnify him,
   And that thou shouldest set thine heart upon him,
18 And that thou shouldest visit him every morning,
   And try him every moment?
19 How long wilt thou not look away from me,
   Nor let me alone till I swallow down my spittle?

---

¹ Or, *I waste away*        ² Or, *shall*        ³ Or, *as a breath*

---

that he would rather die than endure them any longer (12—16)? (2) What, after all, is man? Is he of sufficient importance for God to consider him, and try him so? Cannot He be content to let him alone even for a moment (17—19)? and (3) Even supposing he *has* sinned, what does it really matter to God? why cannot He pardon him and have done with it, instead of making him an encumbrance and a burden to himself (20, 21)?

12. *Am I a sea, or a sea-monster?* Some have seen in these words an allusion to the Nile, and to the fact that watches are set to keep it in proper channels as soon as it breaks forth. This, however, is very improbable, though the Nile is apparently termed 'the sea' in Is. xviii. 2; xix. 5; Nahum iii. 8. More probably there is a half-mythological allusion to the dragon or sea-monster as the representative and embodiment of the sea itself, which is regarded as a restless, dangerous creature which needs to be carefully watched lest it should do some serious injury. Am I such a creature as this? Job seems to say.

14. Hideous dreams are said to be among the miseries of the disease of elephantiasis from which Job was suffering.

15. *strangling*, or rather, *suffocation*, in which the disease is said often to terminate.

*rather than* these *my bones*. His flesh has wasted away, so that he can only speak of himself as a skeleton, almost 'a bag of bones.'

17, 18. Here Job, in his agony, takes up the words of Ps. viii and parodies them, turning the question which the Psalmist asked in awe and wonder into one of bitter sarcasm.

19. *till I swallow down my*

20 If I have sinned, what ¹do I unto thee, O thou ²watcher
  of men?
  Why hast thou set me as a mark for thee,
  So that I am a burden to myself?
21 And why dost thou not pardon my transgression, and take
  away mine iniquity?
  For now shall I lie down in the dust;
  And thou shalt seek me diligently, but I shall not be.

---

¹ Or, *can I do*          ² Or, *preserver*

*spittle*, a phrase, found also in Arabic, equivalent to 'in the twinkling of an eye.'

20. *O thou watcher of men.* Not, as A.V., *preserver.* The term is evidently one of reproach—almost 'O thou *spy* of men'; so Renan, 'O espion de l'homme.'

*as a mark for thee.* A different word for 'mark' is used in xvi. 12, where the thought is that Job is made a target for God's arrows. Here the meaning is 'that Job is a block or obstacle in the way so that God was always stumbling over him' (Cox).

*a burden to myself.* According to the Jews this passage contains one of the eighteen *tikkunê Sopherim* or 'corrections of the scribes.' It is said that the original reading was 'a burden to thee'; but that this was considered too bold (though it is hard to see how it is bolder than the previous expression 'a mark for thee'), and that therefore it was altered by the scribes to 'a burden to myself.' The reading 'to thee' is found in the LXX., Symmachus, and a few Hebrew MSS., and is accepted by many moderns; but both the Targum and the Vulgate have 'to myself.' (For a list of the *tikkunê Sopherim* see Buxtorf's Lexicon, col. 2631. The only other one in this book is in xxxii. 3.)

21. *seek me diligently*, in the original a single word, which means to seek earnestly, and has nothing to do with a word of similar sound meaning 'morning.' The mistaken idea that the two words were connected has led to the A.V. 'seek in the morning' here, and to similar renderings in other passages; as viii. 5; xxiv. 5; Prov. viii. 17, &c.

**VIII.   First speech of Bildad.**

Job had expostulated with God for His treatment of him, and by rejecting the various solutions of it propounded in vii. 12 seq., had implied that it was inexplicable, and had practically accused God of a lack of discrimination and of injustice in His dealings with men.   To this Bildad directs his answer, which consists of three parts:

  (1) *Introductory statement of the doctrine of retribution: God does discriminate.* 1—7.
  (2) *The doctrine supported by the wisdom of the ancients.* 8—19.
  (3) *Conclusion with reference to Job.* 20—22.

The position which he takes up is really identical with that maintained by Eliphaz, though there is a marked difference of *tone* between the two speakers. Eliphaz had urged his point with consideration, in a dignified, grave and self-restrained manner, and had spoken with great beauty and pathos of the bright future that might yet be in store for Job. Bildad does not ignore this possibility, but touches lightly on it, and is much less careful of the feelings of his friend, taking no pains to avoid what must have bitterly hurt him, viz., the unkind allusion to the supposed sin of his children in verse 4. It is interesting also to note that whereas Eliphaz supported his doctrine by a Divine revelation made to him in a vision, Bildad falls back, in a thoroughly Eastern manner, upon the teaching of the ancients, and quotes a piece of the proverbial wisdom of antiquity almost as an end of controversy.

**VIII.**　1 Then answered Bildad the Shuhite, and said,

2 How long wilt thou speak these things?

And *how long* shall the words of thy mouth be *like* a mighty wind?

3 Doth God pervert judgement?

Or doth the Almighty pervert justice?

4 [1]If thy children have sinned against him,

And he have delivered them into the hand of their transgression:

5 If thou wouldest seek diligently unto God,

And make thy supplication to the Almighty;

---

[1] Or, *If thy children sinned...he delivered &c.*

---

**1—7. Introductory statement of the doctrine of retribution. God does discriminate.** Bildad begins with a rebuke to Job for his stormy words, and for daring to imagine that God can pervert justice (1—3). Suppose his children have sinned, they have only received the due reward of their transgression (4); and if Job himself would only turn to God, and show himself pure and upright, he would find God ready to bless him abundantly (5—7).

4. Render (with the margin of the R.V.) *If thy children have sinned against Him, He delivered them into the hand of their transgression.* It seems best to make this verse a distinct sentence by itself, and to take 5 and 6 by themselves as containing another sentence, rather than with R.V. to take the three verses as but one sentence with a triple protasis. 'If thy children...If thou wouldest seek...If thou wert pure...' cf. Driver, Tenses of the Hebrew Verb, § 127 (γ) and 142 (where see note).

5. *seek diligently*: the same word as in vii. 21, where see note.

6 If thou wert pure and upright ;
 Surely now he would awake for thee,
 And make the habitation of thy righteousness prosperous.
7 And though thy beginning was small,
 Yet thy latter end should greatly increase.
8 For inquire, I pray thee, of the former age,
 And apply thyself to that which their fathers have searched
  out :
9 (For we are but of yesterday, and know nothing,
 Because our days upon earth are a shadow :)
10 Shall not they teach thee, and tell thee,
 And utter words out of their heart?
11 Can the ¹rush grow up without mire?
 Can the ²flag grow without water?
12 Whilst it is yet in its greenness, *and* not cut down,
 It withereth before any *other* herb.

¹ Or, *papyrus*      ² Or, *reed-grass*

**8—19. The doctrine supported by the wisdom of the ancients.** Distrusting his own judgment as 'a man of yesterday,' Bildad now appeals to Job to consider the traditional wisdom of former days (8—10). He will there find proverbs that teach him that, as the luxuriant water-plant perishes without water, so does the wicked man when the favour of God is withdrawn (11—13). His confidence is shortlived as the threads of gossamer (14, 15), one day he may be like a flourishing plant in the garden, and apparently firmly rooted, but, if God destroys him, so completely is every vestige of him swept away that even the very place where he was denies that it ever knew him (16—19).

11. These proverbial sayings are evidently Egyptian in their origin. The *rush* (a rare word, possibly Coptic in origin) is really the *papyrus* of the Nile (so R.V. marg. after the LXX.): the word occurs again in Exod. ii. 3, of the ark of 'bulrushes,' and twice in Isaiah, xviii. 2 and xxxv. 7 ; and *flag* is the *reed grass*, mentioned only here and in Gen. xli. 2, 18, in Pharaoh's dream (possibly also it should be read in Hos. xiii. 15). The word is apparently Egyptian in its origin, and comes from no known Semitic root.

*mire.* The word occurs again in xl. 21, of the mire, or 'fen,' where the hippopotamus lies. Elsewhere only in Ezek. xlvii. 11.

12. *Whilst it is yet in its greenness,* i.e. before it is really ripe and ready to be cut down. It is worth noticing in passing that the R.V. substitutes 'its' for 'his' of the A.V.; 'its' for the neuter of the possessive never occurring in the seventeenth century version.

13 So are the paths of all that forget God ;
　And the hope of the godless man shall perish :
14 Whose confidence shall [1]break in sunder,
　And whose trust is a spider's [2]web.
15 He shall lean upon his house, but it shall not stand :
　He shall hold fast thereby, but it shall not endure.
16 He is green before the sun,
　And his shoots go forth over his garden.
17 His roots are wrapped [3]about the heap,
　He beholdeth the place of stones.
18 If he be destroyed from his place,
　Then it shall deny him, *saying*, I have not seen thee.
19 Behold, this is the joy of his way,
　And out of the [4]earth shall others spring.

---

[1] Or, *be cut off*　　[2] Heb. *house.*　　[3] Or, *beside the spring*　　[4] Or, *dust*

**13.** The application of the simile. *the godless man,* better than *the hypocrite* of the A.V., the word occurs again in xiii. 16, xv. 34, xvii. 8, xx. 5, xxvii. 8, xxxiv. 30, xxxvi. 13, but outside this book is very rare.

**14.** *whose trust is a spider's web,* literally *house.* Davidson and Cox aptly quote in illustration of this the saying in the Koran, 'The likeness of those who take to themselves patrons beside God is as the likeness of a spider who taketh to herself a house; and verily the frailest of houses is the spider's house, if they did but know' (Kor. xxix. 40). The flimsiness of the works of the wicked is compared to spiders' webs in Is. lix. 5, 6.

**16.** Another figure, of a luxuriant garden-plant, *green before the sun,* i.e. probably under the fostering care of the sun (Davidson).

**17.** *His roots are wrapped about the heap.* This must mean that his roots strike down and entwine themselves firmly round 'the heap' of stones, giving him a secure hold of his position (so LXX. and Vulg.). But the word rendered ' heap ' has apparently the meaning of a 'spring' or 'fountain' in Cant. iv. 12 (if the text there be correct). Hence the alternative suggested in the margin of the R.V. *beside the spring.*

*He beholdeth the place of stones.* A difficult phrase to explain exactly, but it is just possible that the word for *behold* is used (as it is said to be in the dialect of the Hauran) in the sense of *divide* or *separate.* This would require us to amend the text and read 'between (*ben* בֵּין) the stones,' for 'the place (lit. ' house,' *beth* בֵּית) of stones.' ' He *pierces* between the stones.' A still further alteration of the text adopted by Siegfried has some support from the LXX., ' He remains alive, is preserved, among the stones.'

**19.** *Behold, this is the joy of his way.* The clause is of course ironical. The second clause, *and out of*

20 Behold, God will not cast away a perfect man,
   Neither will he uphold the evil-doers.
21 ¹He will yet fill thy mouth with laughter,
   And thy lips with shouting.
22 They that hate thee shall be clothed with shame ;
   And the tent of the wicked shall be no more.

¹ Or, *Till he fill*

*the earth shall others spring*, means that his place is taken by others, just as if he had never been at all.

**20—22. Conclusion with reference to Job.** Bildad ends by pointing out that since God *does* discriminate, and neither casts away a perfect man, nor (as he has just fully demonstrated) upholds an evil-doer (20), therefore Job may yet find a joyous future in store for him, and may see the discomfiture of those that hate him (21, 22).

20. *a perfect man.* The word that had been used to describe Job himself in the Prologue, not only by the writer of the book (i. 1), but also by God Himself (i. 8).

21. The R.V. is probably correct, *He will yet fill thy mouth &c.* With this verse cf. Ps. cxxvi. 2, and with ver. 22 a cf. Ps. xxxv. 26.

**IX., X.** Job's second speech, in reply to Bildad. Bildad had declared that a moral principle might be discerned in the government of this world, that the good were rewarded and the wicked punished. This Job altogether rejects. God's government, he says, is arbitrary and capricious. But his speech is intended even more as an answer to Eliphaz, from whose words in iv. 17 he takes his text. Of course, he says, man cannot be righteous before God. It is absurd to suppose that he can ; because God is so great and so mighty that man never has a chance of making good his position before Him. This he illustrates fully, and with appalling boldness, from his own case, shrinking not from charging God with deliberate cruelty and unfairness in His treatment of him. It seems to him that *the dice are loaded*, and that it is hopeless for him to contend against God. Nowhere in the whole book are his words wilder and more reckless than in these two chapters, *Nihil asperius in libro*, says Jerome. No wonder that they have shocked and puzzled Christian commentators. But yet in spite of his hopeless misery, and his hard thoughts of God, he never goes so far as to bid goodbye to God altogether. He is sure that if only he could 'get at' God, and come face to face with Him, all would be well.

The speech is a peculiarly difficult one to analyse satisfactorily, but perhaps the following attempt may assist the reader to discover the main lines of thought in it.

(1) *Description of God's majesty and might.* ix. 1—10.

(2) *Impossibility for man to stand up to Him.* 11—24.

(3) *Description of God's treatment of Job himself, and expression of a longing for some umpire to intervene between them.* 25 35.

(4) *Expostulation with God for His treatment of him.* x. 1—7.

(5) *God's gracious dealings with him in the past in forming him.*
8—12.

(6) *Contradiction between this and His present treatment of him.*
13—17.

(7) *Cries of despair: Why was he ever born? and why will not
God leave him alone now?* 18—22.

**IX.**　1 Then Job answered and said,
2 Of a truth I know that it is so:
　¹But how can man be just ²with God?
3 ³If he be pleased to contend with him,
　He cannot answer him one of a thousand.
4 *He is* wise in heart, and mighty in strength:
　Who hath hardened himself against him, and prospered?
5 Which removeth the mountains, and they know it not,
　When he overturneth them in his anger.

---

¹ Or, *For*　　　² Or, *before*
³ Or, *If one should desire...he could not &c.*

---

**IX. 1—10. Description of God's
majesty and might.** Job starts
by admitting the truth of what has
been said. *Of course* man cannot
be just before God (1, 2), because
God is so mighty that if He chooses
to enter the lists against man, man
must be overwhelmed at once (3, 4).
Why, if He pleases, God can overturn the mountains (5), or shake the
earth to pieces (6), or prevent the
sun from shining and the stars from
giving their light (7), since it is He
to whom the heavens and the heavenly bodies owe their existence (8,
9). What He does is utterly beyond
man's capacity to comprehend (10).

2. *Of a truth I know that it is
so.* It is not quite clear whether
(1) Job means to assent to the last
remarks of Bildad; or whether (2)
he is already thinking of the words
of Eliphaz to which he refers in the
next clause. If the former view be
adopted the conjunction with which
clause 2 begins should be rendered
'But.' If the latter, 'For.' It is
capable of being used in either sense.

*How can man be just &c.*, see iv.
17.

3. *If he be pleased to contend with
him.* It is doubtful if we should
take 'God' or 'man' as the subject.
Either yields an excellent sense. In
the second clause, of course, *man*
must be the subject. He cannot
answer one out of a thousand questions God may put to him; and
then in ver. 4, *God* is again the
subject.

5. *and they know it not*, i.e.
'unawares' and so 'suddenly'; cf.
Jer. l. 24, where the phrase has
the same meaning.

6 Which shaketh the earth out of her place,
And the pillars thereof tremble.

7 Which commandeth the sun, and it riseth not ;
And sealeth up the stars.

8 Which alone stretcheth out the heavens,
And treadeth upon the [1] waves of the sea.

9 Which maketh the Bear, Orion, and the Pleiades,
And the chambers of the south.

10 Which doeth great things past finding out ;
Yea, marvellous things without number.

11 Lo, he goeth by me, and I see him not :
He passeth on also, but I perceive him not.

[1] Heb. *high places.*

**6.** *Which shaketh the earth.* The reference is to earthquakes or great convulsions of nature.

*And the pillars thereof tremble.* For the 'pillars' of the earth cf. Ps. lxxv. 3. The idea is of the earth as a solid mass upborne on pillars. The same conception is applied to the heavens, the 'pillars' of which are also said to 'tremble' at the reproof of God, in xxvi. 11.

**8.** *Which alone stretcheth out the heavens,* cf. Ps. civ. 2, 'Who stretcheth out the heavens like a curtain.'

*And treadeth upon the waves of the sea,* lit. 'the *high places* of the sea.' Cf. Amos iv. 13, and Micah i. 3, where God is said to 'tread upon the high places of the earth.' This seems a more natural expression than the one before us, which can only refer to the waves of the sea running mountains high in the storm.

**9.** *Which maketh the Bear, Orion, and the Pleiades.* All these three constellations are mentioned again in xxxviii. 31. The early translators were not at one in their identification of them. The LXX. has here Πλειάδα καὶ Ἕσπερον καὶ Ἀρκτοῦρον, but in xxxviii. 31 it takes the Pleiades for the *last* of the three here mentioned (Heb. *Kîmah*); Orion, for the second (*K'sîl*); and Hesperus for the first (*Âsh* or *Âyish*). The Vulgate has *Arcturus et Oriona et Hyadas.* The Syriac : *The Pleiades, Arcturus, and the Giant.* The Targum leaves Âsh and Kîmah (the first and third) untranslated, but renders K'sîl, the second, by a word for giant. It is now generally agreed that *Âsh* or *Âyish* means the Great Bear ; *K'sîl*, or 'the fool,' Orion ; *Kîmah*, the Pleiades. The last two are mentioned again in Amos v. 8.

*And the chambers of the south* : apparently the vast spaces of the southern hemisphere.

**10.** Job concludes this description of the mighty power of God by citing the words which had been previously used by Eliphaz in v. 9, with which this verse agrees almost word for word.

**11—24. Impossibility for man to stand up to God.** If God is so

12 Behold, he seizeth *the prey*, who can [1]hinder him?
　Who will say unto him, What doest thou?
13 God will not withdraw his anger;
　The helpers of [2]Rahab [3]do stoop under him.

[1] Or, *turn him back*　　[2] Or, *arrogancy*　See Is. xxx. 7.　　[3] Or, *did*

great and incomprehensible, says Job, how can I expect to discover Him or to call Him to account for His ways (11, 12)? The haughty defiers of heaven in days of old were cowed before Him, and far less can I venture to stand up before Him (13, 14). Even if innocent, my only course is to appeal to His mercy, even supposing that He be willing to listen to my plea, which it is vain to think He would do (15, 16), for He shows Himself determined to crush me without giving me a chance, and to prove me in the wrong (17—20). Yet I will maintain my innocence, though it cost me my life, for His treatment of me is only of a piece with His treatment of others. No moral rule can be discerned in the government of the world, and if God is not the author of confusion, who is (21—24)?

11 forms the transition from the incomprehensibility of God's ways to their irresponsible character.

13. *the helpers of Rahab.* A literal translation, but one which requires a good deal of explanation. The word 'Rahab' according to its etymology means *pride*, or *arrogancy* (see the margin of R.V.), and hence the A.V., paraphrasing 'helpers of pride,' by *proud helpers*. But in Is. xxx. 7; li. 9; Ps. lxxxvii. 4; lxxxix. 10, 'Rahab' is for some reason or other taken as a symbolical name for Egypt. Accordingly some have thought of an allusion of an historical character here, perhaps

to the destruction of the Egyptians at the Red Sea, *the helpers of Rahab* being a poetical way of speaking of the Egyptians and their allies. This, however, is improbable, for two reasons, (1) though historical allusions are not entirely wanting in this book, yet they are *all* to still earlier days, the scene of the book itself being laid in patriarchal days before the Exodus. An allusion to the destruction of the Egyptians would therefore be an anachronism which the writer would not be likely to put into the mouth of Job. (2) Such reference does not fit xxvi. 12, where Rahab is mentioned again, and where the allusion must be mythological not historical. The allusion, then, here also is probably mythological, and may be explained in this way: Rahab was apparently taken as the symbolical name for Egypt from its native monster, the crocodile, which was probably termed Rahab (as well as Leviathan) as 'king over all the children of pride' (cf. xli. 34, where, however, the word is not 'Rahab'). It will be noticed that in Ps. lxxxix. 10 'Rahab' is parallel with 'Leviathan,' and in Is. li. 9 with 'the dragon.' Hence we may take it that Rahab was originally the name for some sea-monster or dragon; and we may well suppose an allusion here to some primitive myth in which the stormy sea was personified under the figure of its native monster, and regarded as assaulting heaven with

14 How much less shall I answer him,
   And choose out my words *to reason* with him?
15 Whom, though I were righteous, yet would I not answer;
   I would make supplication to ¹mine adversary.
16 If I had called, and he had answered me;
   Yet would I not believe that he hearkened unto my voice.
17 ²For he breaketh me with a tempest,
   And multiplieth my wounds without cause.
18 He will not suffer me to take my breath,
   But filleth me with bitterness.
19 ³If *we speak* of the strength of the mighty, ⁴lo, *he is
   there*!
   And if of judgement, who will appoint me a time?

---

¹ Or, *him that would judge me*        ² Heb. *He who*
³ Or, *If* we speak *of strength, lo, he is* mighty
⁴ Or, *Lo,* here am I, saith he; *and if of judgement, Who &c.*

---

its waves. Thus the quelling of the storm is supposed to be the bowing down of the haughty defiers of the power of heaven. If such powers as these, says Job, are forced to bow down before God, how much less can I expect to stand up against Him! The translators of the LXX., κήτη τὰ ὑπ' οὐρανόν, probably saw in the words some similar allusion to an ancient myth or 'tradition according to which a monster which had once with its allies been overcome by God, was by way of example fastened as a constellation in the heavens, where it now shines for ever proclaiming to the world its vain resistance of God. Similar things are told of several constellations, of Orion also; and as just before, ver. 9, other constellations were mentioned, it was natural to refer here to something of the kind.' Ewald. Possibly something of the same sort underlies the rendering of the Vulgate 'qui portant orbem.'

15. *mine adversary*: more accu-

rate than *my judge* of the A.V. The thought is of pleadings in a court, but God is regarded not as the judge but as the opponent or adversary in the case, whom Job is called on to ' answer.'

16. The case is now reversed, and Job here supposes that *he* cites God to appear. In such a case, he says, even if God appeared to answer, I could never believe that He would really listen to my plea.

17, 18. Probably the verbs should be rendered (as in ver. 16) as hypothetical, *He would break me...and multiply....He would not suffer: but would fill me.*

19. We should probably follow the margin of the R.V. here. The passage is one of extreme boldness. God is supposed to break in upon Job's proposal and interrupt him. *If we speak of the strength of the mighty ' Lo, here am I,'* saith He, *and if of judgment—' Who will set me a time?'*

20 Though I be righteous, mine own mouth shall condemn
    me :
    Though I be perfect, [1]it shall prove me perverse.
21 [2]I am [3]perfect ; I regard not myself ;
    I despise my life.
22 It is all one ; therefore I say,
    He destroyeth the perfect and the wicked.
23 If the scourge slay suddenly,
    He will mock at the [4]trial of the innocent.
24 The earth is given into the hand of the wicked :
    He covereth the faces of the judges thereof ;
    If *it be* not *he*, who then is it ?
25 Now my days are swifter than a [5]post :
    They flee away, they see no good.

[1] Or, *he*    [2] Or, *Though I be perfect, I will not regard &c.*
[3] See ch. i. 1    [4] Or, *calamity*    [5] Or, *runner*

20. Job supposes that he will be so overwhelmed and confused in the presence of his mighty Adversary, that in spite of knowing that he is really innocent, he will be ready to confess to anything.

21. An abrupt and broken utterance in which Job practically defies his Adversary and becomes reckless and careless of consequences. *I am innocent,* he declares, using the very word *perfect* which had been applied to him in i. 1, *I regard not myself,* lit. *I know not my soul.* Nay, *I despise my life.*

22. *It is all one,* i.e. it is a matter of indifference whether I live or die.

24. *He covereth the faces of the judges,* i.e. He veils their eyes so that they cannot see to discern between good and evil. We should note that in these last verses, 22–24, Job for the first time touches on the principle on which his friends had been arguing, and shows that it does not hold good in the government of the world. He only *touches* on it, however, as he is still too much concerned with his own personal case to consider the general principle at all fully or calmly. See further on xxi.

25—35. Description of God's treatment of Job himself, and expression of a longing for some umpire to intervene between them. Job has scarcely touched on the general question of God's government of the world before he reverts to his own case, and is once more overwhelmed by the contemplation of his misery. My life, he says, is drawing all too swiftly and gloomily to its end (25, 26). I may try to forget my misery, but it is useless (27—29). I may strive my utmost to cleanse myself, but to what purpose is it, when God will at once plunge me into some foul ditch, and make me filthier than ever (30—31)? If He were only a man, like myself, then I might meet Him on equal terms

26 They are passed away as the ¹swift ships :
   As the eagle that swoopeth on the prey.
27 If I say, I will forget my complaint,
   I will put off my *sad* countenance, and ²be of good cheer:
28 I am afraid of all my sorrows,
   I know that thou wilt not hold me innocent.
29 I shall be condemned ;
   Why then do I labour in vain ?
30 If I wash myself ³with snow water,
   And ⁴make my hands never so clean :
31 Yet wilt thou plunge me in the ditch,
   And mine own clothes shall abhor me.

---

¹ Heb. *ships of reed*
³ Another reading is, *with snow*

² Heb. *brighten up.*
⁴ Heb. *cleanse my hands with lye.*

(32); or would that there were some umpire to intervene and decide the matter between us (33)! or it would be enough if God would but cease from overwhelming me by manifesting His power. Content with this, I would fearlessly speak up, and state my case (34, 35).

25. *a post*, i.e. a courier or runner.

26. *swift ships*. This translation (R.V. and A.V.) follows the Syriac and the version of Symmachus ; but the margin of the R.V. is probably correct *ships of reed*. The word rendered *reed* occurs nowhere else and is of uncertain origin, but perhaps means papyrus, out of which the lightest and swiftest boats on the Nile were made. Cf. Is. xviii. 2, where 'vessels of papyrus' are mentioned. Davidson quotes Pliny, *H. N.* xiii. 11, 'ex ipso quidem papyro navigia texunt'; and Lucan, *Pharsalia*, iv. 36, 'conseritur bibula Memphitis cymba papyro.' The rendering of the Vulgate (which agrees with the

Targum) is a curiosity, and comes from a false etymology, 'poma portantes.'

*the eagle*, or more accurately *the vulture*, see the note on xxxix. 27.

27. *be of good cheer*. Lit. *brighten up*, or almost *smile*. The word occurs again in x. 20, as well as Ps. xxxix. 13 (probably a reminiscence of the last-named passage), and Amos v. 9, where see Driver's note in the *Cambridge Bible for Schools*.

30. *with snow water*. This follows the marginal reading of the Hebrew Bible, but the *margin* of R.V. follows the reading found in the text of the Hebrew, which also has the support of the LXX., *with snow*. This is far more natural, for as Davidson notes, 'snow-water is turbid and foul, vi. 16; snow is the symbol of the most perfect purity, Is. i. 18; Ps. li. 7.'

*And make my hands never so clean*, lit. *cleanse my hands with lye*, or potash.

32 For he is not a man, as I am, that I should answer him,
   That we should come together in judgement.
33 There is no ¹daysman betwixt us,
   That might lay his hand upon us both.

¹ Or, *umpire*

33. *There is no.* The Hebrew is exceptional, and a very slight change (*lû* for *lô*, for which cf. 2 Sam. xviii. 12) would enable us to follow the LXX. and read *Oh that there were.*

*daysman,* or *umpire;* the Hebrew word is the participle of a verb which is found in Gen. xxxi. 37, for 'to act as an arbiter,' R.V. *judge betwixt us two.* This explains its meaning here. The English word *daysman* (found here in Coverdale's version 1535) is an old word for arbitrator. The verb to 'day,' is used for 'submit to arbitration,' and the substantive is used in 1 Sam. ii. 25, in the version of 1551, 'If one man synne agaynst another *dayesmen* may make hys peace; but yf a man sinne agaynst the Lord, who can be hys dayesman?' The expression is generally thought to be connected with the Latin *diem dicere.*

What Job here expresses is a longing for someone to intervene as an umpire and arbitrate between him and God. It must be remembered that throughout he is regarding God as his persistent enemy who is determined to destroy him. The controversy between them is utterly unequal, because one of the parties is so powerful and uses his power without scruple against his weaker antagonist. 'He is not a man,' he exclaims, 'so that I can meet him on equal terms; and oh

that there were some umpire who could intervene and "lay his hand on both,"' i.e. impose his authority on us both, and do justice between us. It is only natural that this famous passage should frequently have been taken as a prophecy of the Incarnation of the 'one mediator (the LXX. actually translates by μεσίτης) between God and man'; but before it can be regarded as such it must be remembered that (1) at best it is only a *longing* for such a mediator, and according to the Massoretic text it is even a denial that one exists; and (2) the conception which was in the mind of Job when he uttered the words is very far from being the Christian conception of the mediator between God and man. Job wants someone to interpose between him and the seemingly arbitrary and cruel treatment of God, Who is regarded as his 'enemy.' The Catholic doctrine of the Mediation of Christ declines altogether to accept as anything but a caricature that which has sometimes been presented in its place, viz. the theory of an angry Father, vindictive and longing to punish, from whose wrath we are saved by the intervention of a Mediator, Who is all mercy and love. Rather, it sees in the Incarnation and Atonement a proof of the love of the Eternal Father equally with that of the Eternal Son, in that 'God *spared not* His

34 Let him take his rod away from me,
   And let not his terror make me afraid :
35 Then would I speak, and not fear him ;
   For I am not so in myself.
   **X.**  1 My soul is weary of my life ;
   I will give free course to my complaint ;
   I will speak in the bitterness of my soul.

own Son,' and that ' God so *loved* the world that He *gave* His only begotten Son.' Thus much it seemed necessary to say to avoid misconception and exaggeration. But after all deductions are made on these accounts, it remains that there is a real element of truth in the old view which regarded Job's words as a prophecy. Crude and mistaken as were his notions of the relations between God and man, yet through them all he sees a real need on the part of mankind, the need for one who shall intervene as a mediator, and who shall in a far deeper sense than Job conceived 'lay his hand on both'; and the fact that his words give voice and utterance to the deep craving and longing that rises up in the heart of man for reconciliation with God, and the necessity of an intervention of some sort if this is to be brought about, give it a claim to be regarded as the expression of a need which is only satisfied in the Incarnation. 'The idea of a days-man,' says Dr Watson, ' although the possibility of such a friendly helper is denied, is a new mark of boldness in the thought of the drama. In that one word the in-spired writer strikes the note of a Divine purpose which he does not yet foresee. We must not say that we have here the prediction of a Redeemer at once God and man.

The author has no such affirmation to make. But very remarkably the desires of Job are led forth in that direction in which the advent and work of Christ have fulfilled the decree of grace. There can be no doubt of the inspiration of a writer who thus strikes into the current of the Divine will and revelation. Not obscurely is it implied in this Book of Job that, however earnest man may be in religion, however upright and faithful (for all this Job was), there are mysteries of fear and sorrow connected with his life in this world which can be solved only by One who brings the light of Eternity into the range of time, Who is at once " very God and very man," Whose overcoming demands and encourages our faith.' The Book of Job in *The Expositor's Bible*, p. 147.

35. *For I am not so in myself*, i.e. in himself there is no reason why he should fear God. The clause seems to mean much the same as S. Paul's words in 1 Cor. iv. 4, ' I know nothing against myself.'

**X. 1—7. Expostulation with God for His treatment of him.** Job now takes his courage in his hands, and ventures to expostulate with God for His treatment of him, appealing to Him to show him *why* it is (1, 2), and suggesting (only to reject as impossible) three con-

2 I will say unto God, Do not condemn me ;
　Shew me wherefore thou contendest with me.
3 Is it good unto thee that thou shouldest oppress,
　That thou shouldest despise the ¹work of thine hands,
　And shine upon the counsel of the wicked ?
4 Hast thou eyes of flesh,
　Or seest thou as man seeth ?
5 Are thy days as the days of man,
　Or thy years as man's days,
6 That thou inquirest after mine iniquity,
　And searchest after my sin,
7 Although thou knowest that I am not wicked ;
　And there is none that can deliver out of thine hand ?
8 Thine hands have framed me and fashioned me
　Together round about ; yet thou dost destroy me.

¹ Heb. *labour.*

ceivable hypotheses to explain it.
(1) Is it any pleasure to God to
treat His own creation in this contemptuous and arbitrary fashion
(3)? (2) Does God look on things
with mortal eyes, that are often
subject to illusion (4)? (3) Is God's
life so short that He is obliged to
employ the inquisition lest His
victim (whom He knows to be innocent) should escape Him altogether (5—7)?

These three hypotheses should be
compared with those thrown out in
a similar way in vii. 12 seq. But
there is a difference of character
between them. In the earlier passage Job was looking at *man* to see
whether he could find in *him* any
reason to account for God's treatment of him. Here he is looking
at *God Himself*, and asking whether
there is anything *in the Divine
nature* that will explain it.

3. *Is it good unto thee*, i.e. Is
it any pleasure to thee ? Cf. the

use of the words in Deut. xxiii. 16
(Heb. 17). The more usual phrase
is 'good in the eyes of' anyone.
See Gen. xvi. 6; Deut. vi. 18; or the
words may possibly mean, Is it *becoming* or befitting to Thee ?

4. *eyes of flesh*, i.e. mortal eyes,
which are subject to illusion, 'for
man looketh on the outward appearance, but the Lord looketh on
the heart.' 1 Sam. xvi. 7.

8—12. **God's gracious dealings
with him in the past in forming
him.** He now prepares the way
for a keener reproach than any
which he has yet uttered by reminding God of the gracious care
which He had bestowed on his
creation in the past, when He had
fashioned him in the womb (8—10),
clothed him with flesh and bones
(11), and granted him life and favour
(12). He has just previously spoken
of man as 'the work of God's hands'
in verse 3 ; and it is probably this
expression which suggests to him

4—2

9 Remember, I beseech thee, that thou hast fashioned me
  as clay;
  And wilt thou bring me into dust again?
10 Hast thou not poured me out as milk,
  And curdled me like cheese?
11 Thou hast clothed me with skin and flesh,
  And knit me together with bones and sinews.
12 Thou hast granted me life and favour,
  And thy ¹visitation hath preserved my spirit.
13 Yet these things thou didst hide in thine heart;
  I know that this *is* with thee:
14 If I sin, then thou markest me,
  And thou wilt not acquit me from mine iniquity.
15 If I be wicked, woe unto me;
  And if I be righteous, yet shall I not lift up my head;

¹ Or, *care*

the thoughts of the wonderful love and care which had been shown in his creation and preservation in the past, which render it inconceivable that God can now be determined to destroy him, and bring him into dust again. The whole passage gives a wonderfully vivid description of the formation and growth of the embryo, the only parallel to which in the Old Testament is to be found in Ps. cxxxix. 13 seq.: and for the awe with which the Hebrews contemplated the mystery of conception and birth see Eccl.xi.5.

9. *wilt thou bring me into dust again?* lit. *cause me to return.* The words seem like a reminiscence of Gen. iii. 19, 'unto dust thou shalt return.'

10. The words are intended to describe the generation and formation of the embryo. *Cruddled* in the A.V. is only the old form of *curdled*, which has been substituted for it in modern editions since 1762.

13—17. **Contradiction between this and His present treatment of him.** All the while that God was lavishing such tender care upon him, there was another purpose in His heart, and it was only to lead up to this (13), viz. to a condition of things in which, if he sinned, God would mete out the severest punishment to him, and, if he were righteous, God would not suffer him to raise his head (14, 15), but would spring on him, as a lion on his prey, with ever increasing fury (16, 17).

13. *these things*, viz. the purpose to destroy Job.

*I know that this* is *with thee*: better *was with thee.*

14. *If I sin*, i.e. If I am guilty of slight offences, even these God will note and will not pardon.

15. *If I be wicked*, i.e. If I am guilty of great sins, then *woe is me!* the consequences are too terrible to be expressed.

*if I be righteous, yet shall I not*

[1]Being filled with ignominy
And looking upon mine affliction.

16 And if *my head* exalt itself, thou huntest me as a lion :
And again thou shewest thyself marvellous upon me.

17 Thou renewest thy witnesses against me,
And increasest thine indignation upon me ;
[2]Changes and warfare are with me.

18 Wherefore then hast thou brought me forth out of the
womb?
I had given up the ghost, and no eye had seen me.

19 I should have been as though I had not been ;
I should have been carried from the womb to the grave.

20 Are not my days few? [3]cease then,
And let me alone, that I may [4]take comfort a little,

---

[1] Or, *I am filled with ignominy, but look thou...for it increaseth: thou &c.*
[2] Or, *Host after host is against me*
[3] Another reading is, *let him cease, and leave me alone.*  [4] Heb. *brighten up.*

*lift up my head*, i.e. I must appear with the downcast look of guilt, and not dare to raise my head with the glad confidence of rectitude. Cf. the use of the phrase 'to lift up the face' in xi. 15. In the latter part of this verse and the beginning of the next the R.V. is almost certainly correct, as against both A.V. and R.V. marg.

16. *thou huntest me as a lion*, cf. xvi. 9.

17. *Thou renewest thy witnesses against me*: the expression is best explained by means of xvi. 8, 'And thou hast laid fast hold on me, which is a witness against me : and my leanness riseth up against me, it testifieth to my face.' The 'witnesses' are the marks of suffering which Job is called on to endure.

*Changes and warfare are with me*: probably the words mean hosts fight against me, continuously succeeding one another. See the margin of R.V., *host after host is against me*.

'When sorrows come, they come not single spies,
But in battalions.'  (*Hamlet*, IV. 5.)

18—22. **Cries of despair: Why was he ever born? and why will not God leave him alone now?** Once more he recurs to the thought to which he had first given utterance in his curse upon his day in chapter iii. Why was he ever born at all? and on that he might have been carried straight from the womb to the grave (18, 19)! and now, as his time on earth is so brief, why will not God give him a little respite, so that he may smile once more, before he passes away into the gloom and darkness of Sheol (20—22)?

18, 19. Cf. iii. 11.

20. *Are not my days few?* cf. vii. 6, 7.

*take comfort*: rather *brighten up*, or *smile*. It is the same word that was used in ix. 27, where see note.

21  Before I go whence I shall not return,
      *Even* to the land of darkness and of the shadow of death ;
22  A land of thick darkness, as darkness *itself* ;
      A *land* of the shadow of death, without any order,
      And where the light is as darkness.

21, 22.  The intense gloom of these verses is very noticeable. Job heaps together almost all the words in the Hebrew language for darkness, in order to describe the blackness of the night which awaits him in Sheol. He evidently contemplates his condition there as a final one. It is not only that he denies the possibility of a 'return' from it, but that he gives no hint of the possibility of anything beyond it, of any 'morning' beyond the 'night.'

*the shadow of death.* See the note on this word on iii. 5.

22.  *thick darkness.* The word is apparently the same as that found in Amos iv. 13. It does not occur elsewhere. *Darkness itself* is the word rendered *thick darkness* in iii. 6.

*without any order*, the abode of Chaos.

*And where the light is as darkness*, imitated by Milton: 'No light, but rather darkness visible,' *Paradise Lost*, I. l. 63.

**XI.**  The first speech of Zophar, the roughest and least considerate of the three friends. Job in his last speech had (1) more than once insisted on his innocence (ix. 21; x. 7), thereby flatly contradicting the 'orthodox' doctrine of retribution, according to which he *must* be a grievous sinner *because* he is such a grievous sufferer; and (2) besides this, he had boldly expostulated with God for His treatment of him, and expressed his desire to meet Him face to face and reason it out with Him. To these two points Zophar directs his reply. He is deeply shocked at Job's 'boastings,' and wishes that God would meet him as he had desired, and teach him wisdom. Job had imagined that he could 'find out' God by searching. Zophar can teach him, however, that the Divine Wisdom is really inscrutable, and that it is presumption for man to think that he can call God to account for His actions. But, like his friends, Zophar ends by holding out to Job a promise of restoration to prosperity on his repentance.

The speech is perhaps best divided into four parts :

(1)  *Introductory rebuke of Job for his boastings.*  1—4.

(2)  *Wish that God would appear and teach Job wisdom.*  5, 6.

(3)  *The greatness of the Divine Wisdom, and the impossibility of 'finding out' God, or calling Him to account.*  7—12.

(4)  *Exhortation to Job to repent, and promise of a bright future if he does so; with a final word of warning.*  13—20.

**XI.** 1 Then answered Zophar the Naamathite, and said,
2 Should not the multitude of words be answered?
　And should a man full of talk be justified?
3 Should thy boastings make men hold their peace?
　And when thou mockest, shall no man make thee
　　ashamed?
4 For thou sayest, My doctrine is pure,
　And I am clean in thine eyes.
5 But Oh that God would speak,
　And open his lips against thee;
6 And that he would shew thee the secrets of wisdom,
　[1]That it is manifold in effectual working!

[1] Or, *For sound wisdom is manifold*

**1—4. Introductory rebuke of Job for his boastings.** Zophar begins with a half-apology for saying anything, as if Job's talk and boastings had compelled him to speak (1—3), for he had actually dared to maintain his innocence (4).

**3.** *boastings,* not as the A.V. *lies.* It is probably Job's protestations of innocence to which Zophar refers. Cf. the use of the word in Is. xvi. 6; xliv. 25; Jer. xlviii. 30; l. 36.

**4.** *For thou sayest.* Zophar does not quote Job's exact words, but gives what he supposes to be the drift of them.

*My doctrine is pure.* The reference is probably to the position which Job took up as to his own rectitude. He had asserted all through that he was right, and this is the 'doctrine' which he maintained to be 'pure.'

*I am clean in thine eyes.* 'Thine eyes' must be God's eyes. So the LXX., either paraphrasing or following a different reading: 'before *Him.*' Job had maintained that God knew him to be innocent all the time (x. 7), and Zophar may refer to this.

**5, 6. Wish that God would appear and teach Job wisdom.** If only God would take Job at his word and appear and answer him! How different the result would be from what Job anticipated! He would indeed learn something of the Divine Wisdom, and would discover how mercifully he had been dealt with.

**6.** *it is manifold in effectual working.* A most perplexing expression, no explanation of which appears to be entirely satisfactory.

*effectual working* is the word which we have already met with in v. 12; vi. 13, where see note. *Manifold* is literally *double.* According to some, the whole phrase should be rendered *there are double folds to His counsel,* i.e. it is complicated, inexplicable. Davidson renders, 'It (wisdom) is double in (true) understanding,' explaining this to mean that God's wisdom is twofold what Job conceived of it, in other words that, in regard to its true insight, it far exceeded all conception. The R.V. gives a good sense but it is hard to wring it out of the Hebrew

Know therefore that God [1] exacteth of thee less than thine
iniquity deserveth.

7 [2] Canst thou by searching find out God?
Canst thou find out the Almighty unto perfection?

---

[1] Or, *remitteth* (Heb. *causeth to be forgotten*) *unto thee of thine iniquity*
[2] Or, *Canst thou find out the deep things of God?*

---

words, and Cheyne suggests a slight alteration of the text (which obtains some support from Is. xxviii. 29 Heb.) and renders '*wondrous are they in perfection.*' (*Job and Solomon*, p. 26.)

*Know therefore.* This is not so much an admonition on the part of Zophar as the consequence of God's supposed revelation, as if Zophar said, 'So shalt thou know.'

*exacteth of thee less than thine iniquity deserveth.* This rendering, which is that of the A.V. as well as of the R.V., comes from the Vulgate: '*intelligeres quod multo minora exigaris ab eo quam meretur iniquitas tua.*' As a *translation* it can scarcely be defended, for it rests on a confusion between two Hebrew words, but it probably gives with sufficient accuracy the thought of the original, of which a literal rendering is given in the margin of the R.V., *causeth to be forgotten unto thee of thine iniquity*, i.e. God 'remembers not' all Job's sins. Zophar is of course taking for granted his doctrine of retribution, and so he means to say that if only God *did* reveal Himself, Job would discover that so far was God from dealing cruelly and harshly with him, that He had actually caused some of his sins not to be remembered before Him. The cruelty of such a suggestion is obvious. It far surpasses anything that we have

met with from either of the other speakers. It should, however, be mentioned that the LXX. avoids this cruellest touch of all, rendering 'and then thou shouldest know that thou hast received from the Lord thy deserts for thine iniquities.' This must imply a different reading from that found in the Massoretic text, which is accordingly altered by Bickell and Cheyne.

**7—12. The greatness of the Divine Wisdom, and the impossibility of 'finding out' God, or calling Him to account.** Does Job really think that the most careful search will enable him to 'find out' God, i.e. to comprehend His wisdom (7)? Why, the length and breadth and depth and height of it are simply incomprehensible (8, 9). If God chooses to enter into judgment with man, no one can call Him to account or withstand Him for He knows who are the wicked, and His eyes can discern their iniquity (10, 11). But it is hopeless to expect a 'vain man' to understand this (12)!

7. *Canst thou by searching find out God?* or perhaps (with the margin of the R.V.), *Canst thou find out the deep things of God?* (lit. that which *has to be searched out* in God). The word is the same as that translated '*recesses* of the sea' in xxxviii. 16.

8 ¹It is high as heaven ; what canst thou do ?
　Deeper than ²Sheol ; what canst thou know ?
9 The measure thereof is longer than the earth,
　And broader than the sea.
10 If he pass through, and shut up,
　And ³call unto judgement, then who can hinder him ?
11 For he knoweth vain men :
　He seeth iniquity also, ⁴even though he consider it not.
12 ⁵But vain man is void of understanding,
　Yea, man is born *as* a wild ass's colt.

---

¹ Heb. *The heights of heaven.*　　　² Or, *the grave*
³ Heb. *call an assembly.*　　⁴ Or, *and him that considereth not*
⁵ Or, *But an empty man will get understanding, when a wild ass's colt is born a man*

8. This verse may be rendered literally :

Heights of heaven! What canst thou do?
Deeper than Sheol! What canst thou know?

Was this passage in which the length and breadth and depth and height of the Divine Wisdom, or the 'deep things' of God, are said to be incomprehensible by man in S. Paul's mind when he uttered the wish in Eph. iii. 18, 'that ye may be strong to apprehend with all the saints what is the breadth and length and height and depth, and to know the love of Christ which passeth knowledge' ?

10. The words refer back directly to what Job had said in his last speech ; *pass through* is the same word rendered *passeth on* in ix. 11; *who can hinder him* is a quotation from ix. 12, and *if he call to judgement* seems to allude to ix. 32. *Shut up* means *arrest* or *imprison*.

11. *even though he consider it not.* Apparently this means that God's eyes are quick to perceive iniquity, *without His having any*

need to consider it carefully. This seems better than the margin of the R.V., which takes it as an addition to the word iniquity : *and him that considereth not.*

12. A verse that is the despair of commentators. The words taken singly are easy enough to translate. There is only one in the whole verse, of the meaning of which there is room for any reasonable doubt, viz. the verb rendered *is void of understanding* in the R.V. This more probably means *will get understanding*, as R.V. marg. So A.V. *would be wise.* But when the words are combined together and an attempt is made to extract sense from them they baffle us entirely, and the ancient versions yield no help. Of the various suggestions which have been made, the one for which there is most to be said *as a translation* is the extraordinary one found in the margin of the R.V. *But an empty man will get understanding, when a wild ass's colt is born a man!* If this be adopted, it will be evident that Zophar means it to be a cut at

13 If thou set thine heart aright,
    And stretch out thine hands toward him ;
14 If iniquity be in thine hand, put it far away,
    And let not unrighteousness dwell in thy tents ;
15 Surely then shalt thou lift up thy face without spot ;
    Yea, thou shalt be stedfast, and shalt not fear :
16 For thou shalt forget thy misery ;
    Thou shalt remember it as waters that are passed away :
17 And *thy* life shall ¹be clearer than the noonday ;
    Though there be darkness, it shall be as the morning.
18 And thou shalt be secure, because there is hope ;
    Yea, thou shalt search *about thee,* and shalt take thy rest
     in safety.
19 Also thou shalt lie down, and none shall make thee afraid;
    Yea, many shall make suit unto thee.

¹ Or, *arise above*

Job himself, as if he said, in despair of teaching Job, 'I would as soon expect to see a wild ass bring forth a man as look for any sense proceeding from an empty man like you!' But coarse and unfeeling as Zophar is undoubtedly intended to be, it is difficult to believe that the author of the poem can really have meant to make him say this; and on the whole it is best to suppose that in the words there is embodied some ancient proverb, the key to the interpretation of which is now lost.

**13—20. Exhortation to Job to repent, and promise of a bright future if he does so; with a final word of warning.** If, however, Job will only repent and put away his sin, then he need not fear to lift up his face as an innocent man (13—15), and even the recollection of his sorrows will pass out of his mind (16). Once more his life shall be bright, and he shall be able to sleep securely (17—19). But still, let him

remember the fate in store for the wicked (20).

13. *set thine heart aright*: the same phrase as in Ps. lxxviii. 8, and cf. 1 Sam. vii. 3; 1 Chr. xxix. 18; 2 Chr. xx. 33.

*stretch out thine hands toward him,* viz. in prayer, see Exod. ix. 29, 33; 1 Kings viii. 38; Ps. xliv. 20.

14. *If iniquity be in thine hand,* i.e. if thou hast been guilty of *personal* sin, *put it far from thee.*

*And let not unrighteousness dwell in thy tents,* i.e. put away the sin of thy *household* and *family,* cf. i. 5.

15. *lift up thy face*: an allusion to Job's declaration that even if he were righteous, he would not venture to 'lift up his head'; x. 15.

17. Contrast Job's words in x. 21, 22, which are evidently in Zophar's mind. Even if 'darkness' should come, it will be only for a moment. It will soon be 'morning' again.

18. *thou shalt search* about thee: i.e. he shall look carefully round to

20 But the eyes of the wicked shall fail,
  And ¹they shall have no way to flee,
  And their hope shall be the giving up of the ghost.

¹ Heb. *refuge is perished from them.*

see that all is secure and safe from robbers; and then shall be able to *take his rest in safety.*

20. *they shall have no way to flee,* literally, *refuge is perished from them.* The same words are found in Ps. cxlii. 4, with the exception of *from me,* instead of *from them.*

This verse seems to be intended as a warning to Job of what is in store for him if he does *not* repent.

Ewald notices how 'even the closing word promising hope in the speeches of the friends gets gradually more and more ambiguous: Eliphaz appends scarcely a slight warning, v. 27 ; Bildad already briefly introduces into it the opposite of hope, viii. 20 b, 22 b; Zophar appends a word, verse 20, which already appears as an outpost of the host of similar hard, threatening words, xv, xviii, xx.'

**XII.—XIV.**   Job's third speech, in reply to Zophar.

Zophar's speech has, perhaps not unnaturally, embittered Job more than anything that has yet been said, for not only has his guilt been assumed, as by the other speakers, but he has actually been told that he has come off better than he deserved.   Hence in this next speech of his he turns upon his friends and pours scorn and sarcasm upon them.   Their vaunted wisdom, of which they are so proud, is nothing more than the brute beasts could teach them.   He himself knows everything that they have tried to tell him.   They are 'forgers of lies,' and 'physicians of no value,' and had better hold their peace altogether.   Then turning away from them, he determines at all costs to make his appeal to God and plead his cause before Him, either as defendant or plaintiff, he cares not which; and so, as if rehearsing his intended speech, he pleads his cause, once more expostulating with God for His treatment of him, complaining of the hopelessness of his condition, and contrasting his hapless fate with that of the trees of the forest.   These, even when cut down, have something like a future life in store for them, for the young shoots spring up from their stock.   If only there were anything like this for *him,* he could wait and be patient.   But, as it is, he can have no hope, and thus falls back into despair.

The speech is not easy to analyse satisfactorily.   On the whole it is best to make two main divisions, and subdivide, as follows.

(1)  *Scornful repudiation of his friends' superior knowledge.*   xii.— xiii. 12.

(*a*)  Sarcastic introduction.   xii. 1—6.

(*b*) This knowledge of which Zophar is so proud might be learnt from the brute creation, or from any old man, 7—12.

(*c*) Description of God's absolute power, to match Zophar's picture of the Divine wisdom, 13—25.

(*d*) Utter failure of his friends to help him, and falsehood of their *a priori* reasonings. xiii. 1—12.

(2) *Determination to turn away from man and appeal to God.* xiii. 13—xiv. 22.

(*a*) The determination, and the challenge to God. xiii. 13—22.

(*b*) The appeal to God. xiii. 23—xiv. 22.

and herein : i. expostulation (xiii. 23—28); ii. contrast of the hopelessness of man's fate with the hope there is for a tree (xiv. 1—12); iii. longing for a 'hereafter' for man (13—15); iv. closing complaints of present misery and hopelessness (16—22).

**XII.** 1 Then Job answered and said,

2 No doubt but ye are the people,
And wisdom shall die with you.

3 But I have understanding as well as you ;
I am not inferior to you :
Yea, who knoweth not such things as these ?

4 I am as one that is a laughing-stock to his neighbour,
*A man* that called upon God, and he answered him :
The just, the perfect man is a laughing-stock.

5 In the thought of him that is at ease there is contempt for misfortune ;
It is ready for them whose foot slippeth.

**XII.—XIII. 12. Scornful repudiation of his friends' superior knowledge.**

**XII. 1—6. Sarcastic introduction.** No doubt his friends think that they have a monopoly of wisdom (1, 2), but as a matter of fact, he himself is quite their equal (3); yes, even he who, in spite of his piety, is now made a laughing-stock to men (4)! Those who are happy and prosperous may well be contemptuous of the misfortune which dogs the footsteps of others, while the wicked seem secure from all evil (5, 6).

3. *I have understanding,* literally *heart.* The verb akin to this is used in xi. 12, 'an empty man will *get understanding*' (or *heart*). Hence some think that Job is referring back to Zophar's words there.

*I am not inferior to you.* An unusual phrase in the original, repeated in xiii. 2, and found nowhere else.

5. *In the thought of him that is at ease there is contempt for misfortune; It is ready for them whose foot slippeth.* This translation is undoubtedly correct. The

6 The tents of robbers prosper,
  And they that provoke God are secure ;
  ¹Into whose hand God bringeth *abundantly*.
7 But ask now the beasts, and they shall teach thee ;
  And the fowls of the air, and they shall tell thee :
8 Or speak to the earth, and it shall teach thee ;
  And the fishes of the sea shall declare unto thee.
9 Who knoweth not ²in all these,
  That the hand of the LORD hath wrought this ?
10 In whose hand is the soul of every living thing,
  And the ³breath of all mankind.
11 Doth not the ear try words,
  Even as the palate tasteth its meat ?

¹ Or, *That bring* their *god in their hand*      ² Or, *by*      ³ Or, *spirit*

A.V. is curious, *He that is ready to slip with his feet is as a lamp despised in the thought of him that is at ease.* This is suggested by the Vulgate. 'Lampas contempta apud cogitationes divitum, parata ad tempus statutum.' But the word rendered *lamp* is really a substantive meaning *misfortune* (occurring again in xxx. 24 and xxxi. 29) with a preposition and the article before it.

6. *Into whose hand God bringeth* abundantly. Or, possibly, as the margin of the R.V. renders it : *that bring* their *god in their hand,* i.e. whose strength is their god, as in Hab. i. 11.

7—12. **This knowledge of which Zophar is so proud might be learnt from the brute creation, or from any old man.** Let Zophar interrogate the beasts of the earth, or the fowls of the air, or even the fishes of the sea, and he will learn from any of these lessons of God's wisdom and absolute sway (7—10); or let him listen to the voice of

experience, and he will find that any old man could tell him the same (11, 12).

8. *speak to the earth,* 'the earth' here must mean the small creeping things upon the earth.

9. *the hand of the Lord hath wrought this,* i.e. all things are to be traced to God, who rules with absolute sway, and holds all creatures in the hollow of His hand.

It should be noticed that if the text is correct here, as in i. 21, the poet allows the sacred name Jehovah to escape from Job's lips. But some MSS. read '*the hand of God*' (Eloah), which is perhaps original. Cf. the Introduction, p. xx.

11, 12. Apparently this means 'that the ear (as well as the eye, 7—10) is a channel of sound information.' Davidson. By listening to the talk of old men (12) he might learn the same lesson which observation of the brute creation could teach him on the works of God. Or possibly the margin of the R.V. may be correct, *With aged men,*

12 ¹With aged men is wisdom,
   And in length of days understanding.
13 With him is wisdom and might ;
   He hath counsel and understanding.
14 Behold, he breaketh down, and it cannot be built again ;
   He shutteth up a man, and there can be no opening.
15 Behold, he withholdeth the waters, and they dry up ;
   Again, he sendeth them out, and they overturn the earth.
16 With him is strength and ²effectual working ;
   The deceived and the deceiver are his.
17 He leadeth counsellors away spoiled,
   And judges maketh he fools.
18 He looseth the bond of kings,
   And bindeth their loins with a girdle.

---

¹ Or, *With aged men*, ye say, *is wisdom*          ² Or, *sound wisdom*

---

ye say, *is wisdom &c*. It is true that these words have nowhere occurred in the speeches of the friends but they might be taken to refer to Bildad's words in viii. 8. In this case there would be a contrast between verses 12 and 13, Job replying that with *God* alone, not men, is wisdom and understanding (both words occur again in 13).

**13—25. Description of God's absolute power, to match Zophar's picture of the Divine Wisdom.** Zophar has described the character of the Divine Wisdom, and has asserted that a moral principle underlies its action (xi. 7—12). Is it so? asks Job. God is great as well as wise, and it is rather the action of Absolute Power that is to be seen in all the great catastrophes which overtake men. It is He who breaks down and shuts up (14)— Who at one time withholds, and at another sends forth the waters (15) —Who is Lord of all men, and treats all classes as He will (16—21) —Who discovers things hidden in darkness (22), and deals with nations as He does with men (23—25).

14. *he breaketh down*, whether walls, or houses, or cities.

*He shutteth up a man* in prison. Lit. shuts (the door) *over* a man—as if he were in some underground dungeon. Cf. Jer. xxxvii. 16 marg. 'the house of the pit'; and xxxviii. 6.

15 refers to droughts and floods.

17. *spoiled*, or *stripped*, as the same word is rendered in Micah i. 8.

18. *looseth the bond of kings*, i.e. the bond imposed by kings, and so dissolves their authority. This requires a slight change in the pointing of the Hebrew word for *correction* (מוּסָר), in order to read the similar word for bonds (מוֹסֵר). Their authority being dissolved, they are themselves bound with the girdle of service, or possibly the cord of the captive.

19 He leadeth priests away spoiled,
   And overthroweth the mighty.
20 He removeth the speech of the trusty,
   And taketh away the understanding of the elders.
21 He poureth contempt upon princes,
   And looseth the belt of the strong.
22 He discovereth deep things out of darkness,
   And bringeth out to light the shadow of death.
23 He increaseth the nations, and destroyeth them :
   He spreadeth the nations abroad, and ¹bringeth them in.
24 He taketh away the heart of the chiefs of the people of
      the ²earth,
   And causeth them to wander in a wilderness where there
      is no way.
25 They grope in the dark without light,
   And he maketh them to ³stagger like a drunken man.
   **XIII.**   1 Lo, mine eye hath seen all *this*,
   Mine ear hath heard and understood it.

---

¹ Or, *leadeth them away*      ² Or, *land*      ³ Heb. *wander.*

19. *priests.* It is curious that the author allows Job to speak of 'priests,' though the scene of the book is laid in patriarchal times, and Job himself as head of the family acted as priest in his own household (i. 5). Of course such passages as Gen. xiv. 18 and Exod. ii. 16 show the existence of priest-hood in these early days, and it is possible that Job may be alluding to such cases : but the probability is that it is through a momentary forgetfulness of his position that the writer allows him to use the word. Cf. above on ver. 9 and see the Introduction, p. xxi. There is no doubt about the meaning of the word, which *always* signifies *priests*, although the A.V. here (*princes*) and in 2 Sam. viii. 18 ; xx. 26 ; 1 Kings iv. 5 (*chief rulers*), shrinks from so rendering it.

21. *He poureth contempt upon princes.* The same words occur in Ps. cvii. 40, the latter half of which is found below in verse 24, while verse 27 of the same Psalm affords a parallel with verse 25 of the chapter before us. See v. 16 for other parallels between this Psalm and Job.

*looseth the belt of the strong.* Cf. Is. v. 27, 'neither shall the girdle of their loins be loosed,' where much the same figure for relaxing effort is used. The paraphrase of the A.V. *weakeneth the strength of the mighty* is suggested by the Targum.

XIII. 1—12. Utter failure of Job's friends to help him ; and the falsehood of their a priori

2 What ye know, *the same* do I know also :
    I am not inferior unto you.
3 Surely I would speak to the Almighty,
    And I desire to reason with God.
4 But ye are forgers of lies,
    Ye are all physicians of no value.
5 Oh that ye would altogether hold your peace !
    And it should be your wisdom.
6 Hear now my reasoning,
    And hearken to the pleadings of my lips.
7 Will ye speak unrighteously for God,
    And talk deceitfully for him ?
8 Will ye [1]respect his person ?
    Will ye contend for God ?
9 Is it good that he should search you out ?
    Or as one [2]deceiveth a man, will ye [3]deceive him ?

---

[1] Or, *shew him favour*      [2] Or, *mocketh*      [3] Or, *mock*

---

**reasonings.** All this absolute power of God Job knows quite as well as his friends (1, 2), and he longs to reason it all out with God (3). His friends are utterly incapable of helping him, and have shown themselves wanting in straightforwardness (4), and if they value their reputation, they will be wise to hold their tongues altogether (5). Let them attend to his rebuke for the way in which they have lied on behalf of God (6—8), Who will certainly reject their advocacy and punish them (9—11). Why, even their best utterances are 'proverbs of ashes,' and their arguments crumble to pieces (12).

4. *physicians of no value.* Cf. the expression '*the worthless* (the same word as here) shepherd' in Zech. xi. 17.

5. Cf. Prov. xvii. 28, 'Even a fool when he holdeth his peace is counted wise : when he shutteth

his lips he is esteemed prudent.' Davidson adds, 'Si tacuisses, philosophus mansisses.'

6. The *reasoning* and *pleadings of the lips* in this verse do not refer to the pleading of Job's cause before God, but to the rebuke which he is prepared to offer to his friends.

7, 8. The friends had *spoken unrighteously for God* and *talked deceitfully* for Him, because they had refused to look facts in the face and twisted them so as to suit their theory of retribution. They had *respected the person of God* by showing partiality for Him, in jumping to the conclusion that Job *must* have been a sinner, because God was afflicting him so grievously.

9. How will they like it, if God searches them out and probes them to the uttermost ? they will find that they cannot deceive Him as they might hope to deceive a mere man.

10 He will surely reprove you,
　If ye do secretly ¹respect persons.
11 Shall not his excellency make you afraid,
　And his dread fall upon you?
12 Your memorable sayings *are* proverbs of ashes,
　Your defences *are* defences of clay.
13 Hold your peace, let me alone, that I may speak,
　And let come on me what will.
14 ²Wherefore should I take my flesh in my teeth,
　And put my life in mine hand?

¹ Or, *shew favour*　　　² Or, *At all adventures I will take &c.*

10. God will reject favouritism, even when shown on His behalf.

11. His Majesty will overawe them and strike terror into their hearts.

12. *Your memorable sayings* are *proverbs of ashes.* The *memorable sayings,* literally 'memorials,' are the maxims and apophthegms which they have uttered in the course of the argument, such as Bildad's quotations of the proverbial wisdom of the ancients in viii. 11. These are but 'proverbs of ashes,' i.e. light and fallacious. Cf. the expression, 'he feedeth on ashes' in Is. xliv. 20.

*Your defences* are *defences of clay.* The word rendered *defences* means properly 'the back.' Hence the A.V. *bodies,* as if the part was put for the whole, after the Targum, LXX., and Vulgate. But the word is used for the boss of a buckler in xv. 26, and so it may perhaps be used of a *defence* or shield; and thus, in this passage, of the defence which the friends have constructed for God, the arguments by which they have supported His cause.

XIII. 13—XIV. 22. Determination to turn away from man and appeal to God.

13—22. **The determination, and the challenge to God.** Job now sharply enjoins his friends to hold their peace and let him speak out at all costs (13): He will take his life in his hand, and wait till God answers him, even though he die for it; and will maintain his cause before Him, secure in this, that no ungodly person would venture into His presence (14—16). Let them listen to this: he has prepared his case: he *knows* that he has right on his side. Nay, so sure of this is he that he would cheerfully keep silence and submit to death, could anyone prove him guilty (17—19). Two conditions only he asks for from God: (1) that He would grant him a cessation of his troubles, and (2) that He would not overwhelm him with His Majesty (20, 21). These granted, he is prepared to take his place either as defendant or appellant, he cares not which (22).

14. *Wherefore.* The general sense of this verse is clear, and it must be intended to express Job's determination to risk everything; but if so, it is unnatural that it should be put in the form of a

15 ¹Though he slay me, yet will I wait for him :
Nevertheless I will ²maintain my ways before him.

¹ Or, *Behold, he will slay me; I wait for him* or, according to another reading,
*I will not wait* or, *I have no hope*          ² Heb. *argue.*

question: and it seems best to
adopt the marginal rendering of
the R.V. and instead of *Wherefore*,
translate *At all adventures, I will
take &c.*, which seems to be a possible rendering. There is another
alternative, however, for which a
good deal may be said, viz. to ex-
punge the word *Wherefore* altogether. It is not recognized in the
LXX. and may easily have crept into
the text through the accidental
repetition of the four last letters of
the previous verse.

*take my flesh in my teeth, and
put my life in mine hand.* The first
of these expressions occurs nowhere
else, but it is evidently intended to
be a synonymous parallel with the
second, which is a standing phrase
for incurring extreme risk. (See
Judges xii. 3; 1 Sam. xix. 5; xxviii.
21; and cf. Ps. cxix. 109.) Shakespeare seems to imitate it, when he
speaks of men
          Compelled by hunger
And lack of other means, *in desperate manner
Daring the event to the teeth.*
          *Henry VIII.* Act i. Sc. ii.
          (Quoted by Cox).

15. *Though he slay me, yet will
I wait for him.* The various suggestions to be found in the margin
of the R.V. show the uncertainty
which hangs over this famous verse.
To begin with, the *text* is doubtful,
as there is here a confusion between
the two Hebrew words *lo'* and *lo,*
similar to that with which we have
already met in vi. 21, except that

*here* the Hebrew has the negative
(*lo'*) in the text, and the preposition
with the pronoun (*lo,* 'for him') in
the margin. This marginal reading
of the Hebrew is strongly supported
by the authority of the ancient
versions (with the doubtful exception of the LXX.), the Targum,
Syriac, Aquila, and the Vulgate; and
from the last-mentioned 'Etiam si
occiderit me, in Ipso sperabo' comes
the familiar and noble rendering of
the A.V., *Though he slay me, yet will
I trust in him,* a rendering which
one is most unwilling to surrender.
But it must be confessed that it is a
translation which it is impossible to
defend, for the verb in the latter
half of the clause does not mean
*trust,* but rather *wait* for something
or someone. See the use of it in
the following passages of our book,
vi. 11; xiv. 14; xxix. 21, 23; xxx.
26. In all these passages the R.V.
renders it *wait,* and quite consistently adopts the same rendering
here, giving us, however, two alternatives to choose between. *Though
he slay me, yet will I wait for him,*
in the text; and *Behold, he will
slay me; I wait for him* in the
margin. Of these alternatives, the
first approaches nearest to the A.V.,
but it is not clear how the Revisers
would have us interpret it. It might
be taken as the expression of Job's
willingness to 'wait' for a manifestation of God after he had been
slain, and thus as a splendid affirmation of his belief in a future life
(cf. xiv. 14, where the verb occurs

16 ¹This also shall be my salvation ;
   ²For a godless man shall not come before him.
17 Hear diligently my speech,
   And let my declaration be in your ears.
18 Behold now, I have ordered my cause ;
   I know that I ³am righteous.
19 Who is he that will contend with me ?
   For now ⁴shall I hold my peace and give up the ghost.
20 Only do not two things unto me,
   Then will I not hide myself from thy face :

¹ Or, *He*      ² Or, *That*      ³ Or, *shall be justified*
⁴ Or, *if I hold my peace, I shall give up &c.*

again). But such an affirmation would be out of place at so early a stage (see the notes on xiv. 13 seq., and xix. 25 seq.), and the *nevertheless* of the following clause is against it. There is much more to be said in favour of the margin, which, on the whole, appears to be the most probable of the various renderings suggested. Job has just expressed his sense of the extreme risk he was running in approaching God, and it is only natural that he should advance a step further, and say straight out, *Behold, he will slay me; I wait for him,* i.e. 'I wait what He will do,' and then proceed *nevertheless I will maintain my ways before Him.*

There remains, however, the possibility that, in spite of the versions, the Hebrew *text* may be correct, and that we ought to read the negative *not* instead of *for him.* Adopting this, the margin of the R.V. again gives us two alternatives, *I will not wait,* or *I have no hope.* The former of these is the more natural, and gives its proper force to the verb. It may well mean 'wait for a change for the better'; and so (practically) 'be patient.' Cf. vi. 11, and see Cheyne, *Job and Solomon,* p. 28.

16. *For a godless man.* Better (with the margin) *that* a godless man. Job means to say that his security lies in the fact that no one with a guilty conscience would thus venture into the presence of God.

18. *I have ordered my cause,* cf. xxiii. 4.

19. *Who is he that will contend with me?* Cf. Is. l. 8, where almost identical words occur. They are there the expression of a confidence that no one will be found so to contend; and must have the same meaning here. If, says Job, anyone were found able to rise up and convict me, I would cheerfully accept my fate, *hold my peace and give up the ghost.*

20. *Only do not two things unto me.* The 'two things' are specified in the following verse : (1) Let God give him a little respite from his suffering, and (2) Let Him not overwhelm him with the terror of His appearance.

5—2

21 Withdraw thine hand far from me ;
   And let not thy terror make me afraid.
22 Then call thou, and I will answer ;
   Or let me speak, and answer thou me.
23 How many are mine iniquities and sins ?
   Make me to know my transgression and my sin.
24 Wherefore hidest thou thy face,
   And holdest me for thine enemy ?
25 Wilt thou harass a driven leaf ?
   And wilt thou pursue the dry stubble ?
26 For thou writest bitter things against me,
   And makest me to inherit the iniquities of my youth :
27 Thou puttest my feet also in the stocks, and markest all
       my paths ;
   Thou drawest thee a line about the soles of my feet :

**XIII. 23—XIV. 22. The appeal to God.**

23—28. **Expostulation with God for His treatment of him.** Job now makes his appeal to God, or rather, since it is evident that we are not to suppose any appearance of God in answer to the challenge in 20—22, he as it were *rehearses* what he would say if God were to take him at his word. He begins, then, by expostulating with Him much as he had done before in chapters vii. and x. Will not God tell him straight out what his sin is (23), and why He has turned from him and treats him as His enemy (24) ? Is it worth while, for the sins of his boyhood, to treat him like a dangerous criminal to be put in the stocks and carefully watched, feeble and worn out as he is (25—28) ?

23. *How many are mine iniquities and sins?* It must always be remembered that in spite of his protestations of innocence, Job nowhere means to claim absolute immunity from sin. Like his friends, he has always accepted the 'orthodox' doctrine of retribution, and has supposed that suffering is the consequence of sin. But his conscience is clear of any sins that might account for the exceptional treatment he is receiving from God. Hence the present appeal. What *are* the sins for which I am being punished ?

25 is in close connexion with what follows. Is he worth the effort which his punishment must cost God, when He prescribes such bitter penalties for boyish sins (the only ones of which he is conscious) ?

26. *thou writest bitter things against me,* i.e. *thou decreest.* Cf. the use of the word *write* in Is. lxv. 6 ; Hos. viii. 12.

27. *in the stocks.* For this punishment cf. Jer. xx. 2 ; xxix. 26 (though the word for *stocks* in the original is different), and in the N.T. Acts xvi. 24. The whole of the first half of this verse is quoted by Elihu in xxxiii. 11.

*Thou drawest thee a line about*

28 [1]Though I am like a rotten thing that consumeth,
Like a garment that is moth-eaten.
**XIV.** 1 Man that is born of a woman
Is of few days, and full of trouble.
2 He cometh forth like a flower, and [2]is cut down :
He fleeth also as a shadow, and continueth not.
3 And dost thou open thine eyes upon such an one,
And bringest me into judgement with thee?
4 [3]Who can bring a clean thing out of an unclean? not one.
5 Seeing his days are determined, the number of his months
is with thee,
And thou hast appointed his bounds that he cannot pass ;

---

[1] Heb. *And he is like.*    [2] Or, *withereth*
[3] Or, *Oh that a clean thing could come out of an unclean! not one* can

---

*the soles of my feet.* Job means that God carefully marks out for him a line beyond which he may not pass. Cf. Solomon's treatment of Shimei in 1 Kings ii. 36, 37.

28. *a rotten thing,* cf. Hos. v. 12, where the same word occurs parallel with the mention of 'a moth.'

**XIV.** 1—12. Contrast of the hopelessness of man's fate with the hope that there is for a tree. Leaving for the moment his own individual case, Job now thinks of the common lot of men, and of the way in which their days are few and evil, their life brief as the life of a flower, and passing away like a shadow (1, 2) ; and yet God is a rigorous judge of such frail creatures (3)! Moreover man starts with a taint in his blood, and is not master of his fate. Why, then, will not God take His eyes off him, and give him a little respite (4—6)? Even a tree is better off than he is, for there is hope for it, even after it is cut down, since fresh shoots may spring up from the dry

stock (7—9). But man has no such hope. For him death is final. He lies down and rises no more (10—12).

2. *He cometh forth like a flower, and is cut down.* Cf. the same figure in Ps. xc. 5, 6 ; Is. xl. 6—8.

3. *dost thou open thine eyes upon such an one?* i.e. dost thou observe him so diligently and carefully? Cf. xiii. 27, 'and markest all my paths.'

4. The first clause is really in form a wish (as R.V. marg.). *Oh that a clean thing could come out of an unclean! not one can.* But practically it becomes an affirmation of universal depravity, such as is found also in other parts of the Old Testament, e.g. Gen. vi. 5 ; Ps. li. 5. It would be too much to say that in such passages we have the Church's doctrine of original sin declared; but at least there may be found in them the basis and preparation for the doctrine as developed in S. Paul's teaching in the Epistle to the Romans and formulated by the Church.

6 Look away from him, that he may ¹rest,
  Till he shall ²accomplish, as an hireling, his day.
7 For there is hope of a tree, if it be cut down, that it will
  sprout again,
  And that the tender branch thereof will not cease.
8 Though the root thereof wax old in the earth,
  And the stock thereof die in the ground ;
9 Yet through the scent of water it will bud,
  And put forth boughs like a plant.
10 But man dieth, and ³wasteth away :
  Yea, man giveth up the ghost, and where is he ?
11 ⁴*As* the waters ⁵fail from the sea,
  And the river decayeth and drieth up ;

¹ Heb. *cease.*    ² Or, *have pleasure in*
³ Or, *lieth low*    ⁴ See Is. xix. 5.    ⁵ Heb. *are gone.*

6. *Look away from him.* Cf. vii. 19.

*Till he shall accomplish.* The meaning is slightly doubtful. The rendering of the English versions may perhaps be defended, but the natural meaning of the verb is *to have pleasure in* or *enjoy*, and this is adopted by most commentators here : that he may have such poor enjoyment as the hireling has, who sustains himself through the long hours of the day's toil with the thought of evening and what it brings.

7—9. With this allusion to the sprouting of the tree that has been cut down cf. the similar references in Isaiah vi. 13 ; xi. 1.

10—12. The contrast for man. For the tree there is the hope of a future : for man there is none. It is interesting to contrast with the view of the respective portions of the man and the tree here given by Job, the lesson drawn by the Christian poet from the falling leaves of autumn :

How like decaying life they seem to
  glide !
And yet no second life have they in
  store,
But where they fall, forgotten to
  abide
Is all their portion : and they ask
  no more.
Man's portion is to die and rise
  again :
Yet he complains : while these, un-
  murmuring, part
With their sweet lives, as pure from
  sin and stain
As his, when Eden held his virgin
  heart.

Keble, *The Christian Year*, xxiii Sunday after Trinity.

11. *As the waters fail from the sea &c.* The whole of this verse occurs again almost word for word in Isaiah xix. 5, in 'the burden of Egypt.' 'The river' there is certainly the Nile, and 'the sea' is the inland pool or lake which is to be dried up, and to suffer from its waters failing. This explains the passage before us. Cf. Introduction, p. xxiii.

12 So man lieth down and riseth not :
  Till the heavens be no more, they shall not awake,
  Nor be roused out of their sleep.
13 Oh that thou wouldest hide me in ¹Sheol,
  That thou wouldest keep me secret, until thy wrath be
    past,
  That thou wouldest appoint me a set time, and remember
    me !
14 If a man die, shall he live *again*?
  All the days of my warfare ²would I wait,
  Till my ³release should come.

---

¹ Or, *the grave*       ² Or, *will...shall come*       ³ Or, *change*

---

**12.** *Till the heavens be no more,* that is *for ever,* the 'heavens' being here regarded as eternal as in Ps. lxxxix. 29. It would be entirely out of place to read into this verse the thought of the extinction of the heavens spoken of in Isaiah li. 6, and to imagine that Job was teaching that man actually would rise again, but not till this took place. This has indeed been the view of many commentators since the days of Gregory the Great. But nothing can be clearer than the fact that Job here definitely denies any resurrection (cf. vii. 8—10). But he has scarcely uttered the words before a *longing* for one seizes him, suggested by the thought of the future in store for a tree; and to this he gives utterance in the following verses.

**13—15.** **Expression of a longing for a 'hereafter' for man.** He has just declared that for man death is final. But at once the thought occurs : what if it should prove *not* to be so ? What if God would keep him only for a time in Sheol, and appoint a day in the distant future when He would remember him (13) ? How gladly would he endure, and how patiently would he wait for his discharge if this could be (14)! God would then lovingly remember the work of His hands and summon him forth, and he would at once answer (15).

It is thus that the thought of a future life, and even more, of a resurrection struggles forth from Job's heart as an intense desire and longing, as a thought which, *if he could only believe it,* would not indeed solve the enigmas of life, but help him to 'bear the burden of the mystery, the heavy and the weary weight of all this unintelligible world.' At present it is no more than this. It is not belief, it is only desire. But even this is a great advance on his previous condition, when 'Sheol' with its gloomy shadowy existence bounded his horizon, and he conceived of nothing beyond. The thought and longing having once occurred to him, he can never quite let go of them ; and they will lead in time to something more than desire, viz. to belief and conviction (see the note on xix. 25 seq.).

**14.** *warfare,* the same word as

15 ¹Thou shouldest call, and I would answer thee :
   Thou wouldest have a desire to the work of thine hands.
16 But now thou numberest my steps :
   Dost thou not watch over my sin ?
17 My transgression is sealed up in a bag,
   And thou fastenest up mine iniquity.
18 And surely the mountain falling ²cometh to nought,
   And the rock is removed out of its place ;
19 The waters wear the stones ;
   The overflowings thereof wash away the dust of the
   earth :
   And thou destroyest the hope of man.
20 Thou prevailest for ever against him, and he passeth ;
   Thou changest his countenance, and sendest him away.
21 His sons come to honour, and he knoweth it not ;
   And they are brought low, but he perceiveth it not of
   them.

---

¹ Or, *Thou shalt call, and I will &c.*          ² Heb. *fadeth away.*

---

in vii. 1. The change of mood in the R.V. in this and the following verse *would* I wait (instead of *will* I wait, A.V.) makes the meaning quite clear.

16—22. **Closing complaints of present misery and hopelessness.** The thought, however, seems too good to be true, for, as it is, God is on the watch, and notes and treasures up his sins, so as to visit them all upon him (16, 17). And just as the mountain crumbles away at last, or as the persistent falling of water will wear away the hardest rock, so God's unrelenting treatment *must* destroy man (18—20). His children may come to honour or meet with disgrace. But in the darkness of the grave, he will know nothing of it. Nothing can affect him there but his own pain and sorrow (21, 22).

16. Cf. x. 6, 14 ; and xiii. 27.

17. The meaning of this verse is that God carefully treasures up Job's sins (fastens them up in a bag and seals them for security) in order to visit them upon him.

18, 19. Did these verses suggest the lines ?

The sturdy rock for all his strength
  By raging seas is rent in twain,
The marble stone is pierced at length
  By little drops of rain.

With 19 cf. Lucretius I. 313
'Stilicidi casus lapidem cavat.'

21. Cf. Eccl. ix. 5, 6. 'The dead know not anything, neither have they any more a reward ; for the memory of them is forgotten. As well their love, as their hatred and their envy, is now perished ; neither have they any more a portion for ever in anything that is done under the sun.'

22 ¹But his flesh upon him hath pain,
   And his soul within him mourneth.

¹ Or, *Only for himself his flesh hath pain, and for himself his soul mourneth*

22. It is perhaps best to follow the margin of the R.V. and render, *only for himself his flesh hath pain, and for himself his soul mourneth.* The idea is that in the grave man has no concern beyond his own suffering. If it should seem strange that Job should speak of the dead man's *flesh* still having pain, it should be remembered that similar language is found in our Lord's parable of Dives and Lazarus. 'Send Lazarus that he may dip the tip of his finger in water, and cool *my tongue*; for I am in anguish in this flame.' S. Luke xvi. 24.

With this the first debate or circle of speeches is brought to a close. To sum up the result so far: the friends have broadly stated their position, and their theory of suffering, hinting with more or less clearness at its application to the case of Job, and to the lesson which he is to draw from it. Job, on the other hand, though nowhere fairly grappling with their theory, has shown plainly enough that he is utterly unable to accept it as explaining his own case. His conscience assures him that he is not an exceptional sinner; and yet he is being apparently treated as if he were one. Knowing no other theory of suffering than that which his friends have urged, God's treatment of him is hopelessly inexplicable. It looks like injustice on the part of God. And yet so sure is he that God, if He be God, is righteous that he appeals boldly to Him to allow him to plead his cause before Him, sure that if he could only do this, he *must* be righted. One more thought has come to him in his agony, for finally there has arisen within him a great longing for a resurrection to a life after death, and his heart goes out towards this, as the one thing which, could he but believe it, would enable him to bear patiently all his present distress.

WITH CHAPTER XV. begins the second debate or circle of speeches. This lasts to Chapter xxi., and the order in which the several speakers are brought before us is identical with that in the previous debate.
Thus we have

(1)  The second speech of Eliphaz, xv.      with Job's answer, xvi., xvii.

(2)  The second speech of Bildad, xviii.    with Job's answer, xix.

(3)  The second speech of Zophar, xx.       with Job's answer, xxi.

In this second discussion the friends in reality make no advance whatever upon their previous position. They can only restate the old doctrine of retribution, though they approach it rather differently, dwelling less on the character of God, and more upon His manifested government of the world; describing more fully the fate of the wicked; and hinting with

increasing clearness at its application to the case of Job, and dropping out
of sight all thought of his repentance and restoration, which each of them
had contemplated as a possibility in the first circle, but to which no one of
them makes the slightest reference in this.   (Contrast the close of xv. with
v. 17 seq. ; of xviii. with viii. 20, 21 ; and of xx. with xi. 13—19.)

Much, if not all, that they say of the ungodly and their fate is true.
It is only false (1) if regarded as an *universal* truth, and as being the
whole account of suffering, and (2) in its application to the case of Job.
' De te fabula narratur' is evidently what they intend to suggest.   This is
especially manifest in the speech of Bildad in xviii. where the details of
the picture are seemingly selected with reference to Job's own case (see
the notes on 12 seq.).   It should be noticed also that the character of the
friends is skilfully maintained.   The grave Eliphaz is still the most gentle-
manly of the three with his appeal to authority and dignified rebuke of
Job in xv.   Again, we see the cruelty of Bildad in xviii.; while the
coarseness of Zophar is once more very apparent in xx.   (See the note on
ver. 12.)

Turning now to the speeches of Job we see that while his friends make
no advance, he on the contrary does make a very real one, and this in two
ways : (1) the longing for a future life and for God's vindication of him,
which was manifested at the close of the first circle, becomes in this a
*certainty*; and (2) he ends by demolishing the arguments of his friends
(which he scarcely grapples with in the earlier debate) by a powerful
appeal to the logic of facts.   But before he reaches these two assured
positions there is still a sore struggle.   Only ' through much tribulation '
can he enter into the fresh provinces in the kingdom of God's truth ; and
in all his earlier utterances, in the answer to Eliphaz (xvi., xvii.) and in
the greater part of his reply to Bildad (xix.) we cannot fail to notice the
increasing bitterness of his words, and the passion of his utterances as he
describes God's treatment of him (xvi. and xix.), or anticipates death and
darkness as awaiting him (xvii. 10—16), or appeals in his agony to earth to
cover not his blood (xvi. 18), and to his friends for pity and compassion
(xix. 21).

**XV.**   The second speech of Eliphaz.   The manner in which Job has
practically charged God with injustice appears not unnaturally to Eliphaz
to do away with religion altogether.   Consequently he commences his next
speech by a rebuke to Job for his arrogance and impiety.   He then passes
on to give a wonderfully powerful picture of the evil conscience of the
wicked man, showing how 'Conscience makes cowards of us all,' and
describing the righteous retribution which falls upon the wrong-doer : the
object of it all evidently being to 'awaken Job's conscience, and to induce
him to see himself reflected in the mirror thus held up before him'
(Driver).   The speech falls into two main divisions as follows :

(1)   *The rebuke of Job.*   1—16.

(2)   *Restatement of the doctrine of retribution with the description of
the fate of the wicked.*   17—35.

**XV.** 1 Then answered Eliphaz the Temanite, and said,
2 Should a wise man make answer with ¹vain knowledge,
  And fill his belly with the east wind?
3 Should he reason with unprofitable talk,
  Or with speeches wherewith he can do no good?
4 Yea, thou doest away with fear,
  And ²restrainest ³devŏtion before God.
5 For ⁴thine iniquity teacheth thy mouth,
  And thou choosest the tongue of the crafty.
6 Thine own mouth condemneth thee, and not I;
  Yea, thine own lips testify against thee.
7 Art thou the first man that was born?
  Or wast thou brought forth before the hills?

¹ Heb. *knowledge of wind.*          ² Heb. *diminishest.*
³ Or, *meditation.*      ⁴ Or, *thy mouth teacheth thine iniquity*

1—16. **The rebuke of Job.** Eliphaz here begins with a threefold reproof of Job: i. for his *empty and unprofitable speeches* (1—3), which are utterly incompatible with reverence and religious feeling (4), are dictated by impiety (5), and are in themselves the best proof of his guilt (6). ii. He then brings against him a charge of *arrogance*, as if he had assumed that he was endowed with superior wisdom, and in a position to be specially favoured with a knowledge of God beyond that possessed by others (7—10); and had thus ignored as beneath his notice the consolations which God provided for him (11). iii. Finally he rebukes him for his *lack of restraint* (12, 13), and repeats, with a darker touch than before, his former teaching on the impossibility of man being righteous before God (14—16).

2. *Should a wise man &c.* Job had expressly laid claim to a wisdom not less than that of his friends (see xii. 3; xiii. 2). If he were

really wise, would his words be so windy and vain?

*the east wind*, a figure of what is vain and pernicious, as in Hos. xii. 1.

4. *fear*, not 'terror,' but 'the fear of the Lord,' i.e. reverence.

*devotion.* Literally *meditation*, almost *reverent thoughtfulness* (Cox); the actual word only occurs again in Ps. cxix. 97, 99, but cf. Ps. cii. title; and cxlii. 2.

5. *thine iniquity teacheth thy mouth.* This rendering is preferable to that of the margin, or of the A.V. Eliphaz means to say that his words were dictated by his guilt or sin.

*thou choosest the tongue of the crafty*, i.e. all Job's protestations of innocence were only cunning devices to conceal his guilt.

7. The sarcastic question in this verse assumes that the first created man as coming fresh from the hand of God had a more direct and profound insight into the mysteries of the world which was only then

8  ¹Hast thou heard the secret counsel of God?
   And dost thou restrain wisdom to thyself?

9  What knowest thou, that we know not?
   What understandest thou, which is not in us?

10 With us are both the grayheaded and the very aged men,
   Much elder than thy father.

11 Are the consolations of God too small for thee,
   ²And the word *that dealeth* gently with thee?

12 Why doth thine heart carry thee away?
   And why do thine eyes wink?

13 That thou turnest thy spirit against God,
   And lettest *such* words go out of thy mouth.

14 What is man, that he should be clean?
   And he which is born of a woman, that he should be
     righteous?

15 Behold, he putteth no trust in his holy ones;
   Yea, the heavens are not clean in his sight.

16 How much less ³one that is abominable and corrupt,
   A man that drinketh iniquity like water!

---

¹ Or, *Dost thou hearken in the council*
² Or, *Or is there any secret thing with thee?*          ³ Or, *that which is*

coming into existence (cf. Delitzsch *in loc.*). Most commentators since Schlottmann (1851) quote the Hindu proverb, 'Yes, indeed, he is the first man—no wonder that he is so wise!'

8. Another sarcastic suggestion to account for his wisdom. Has he been admitted to the council chamber of God, and has he a monopoly of wisdom? Cf. S. Paul's question to the Corinthians; 1 Cor. xiv. 36.

10. This is generally taken as a claim on the part of Eliphaz to have the verdict of old experience on his side. But Davidson thinks that in the words *grayheaded* and '*aged*' (both of which in the original are in the singular) he is indirectly alluding to himself.

11. *the consolations of God*, viz.

the considerations which Eliphaz and his friends have been offering. Hence Job's reply in xvi. 2, *Miserable comforters* (or *consolers*, from the same root as the word here) *are ye all.*

14—16. Cf. iv. 17—19, which is practically repeated here.

15. *holy ones*, viz. the angels. See the note on v. 1.

16. In his earlier speech, in speaking of man as unclean in the sight of God Eliphaz had touched chiefly on his frailty. Here he lays stress on his corruption, and the avidity with which he seizes evil, drinking it in like water. The language is of course perfectly general, but Job may apply it to himself if he pleases.

17 I will shew thee, hear thou me ;
   And that which I have seen I will declare :
18 (Which wise men have told
   From their fathers, and have not hid it ;
19 Unto whom alone the land was given,
   And no stranger passed among them :)
20 The wicked man travaileth with pain all his days,
   ¹Even the number of years that are laid up for the oppressor.
21 A sound of terrors is in his ears ;
   In prosperity the spoiler shall come upon him :

¹ Or, *And years that are numbered are laid up &c.*

**17—35. Restatement of the doctrine of retribution with the description of the fate of the wicked.** Eliphaz here makes a special appeal for Job's attention, claiming for the doctrine, which he is about to assert, that it rests upon a pure tradition which has come down to him (17—19). He then gives a vivid description of the misery and terror in which an evil conscience involves a man who is ever haunted by presentiments and the dread of coming calamities (20 —24) : these terrors that haunt his imagination being due to his arrogant opposition to God (25, 26), and his coarse satisfaction in enriching himself upon the ruins of another's prosperity (27, 28). To this he adds a description of his fate, prophesying for the sinner himself poverty and ruin in the place of his prosperity, and for his family a speedy and complete extinction (29—35). Thus the whole passage falls into four well-defined sections : (i) the introduction, 17—19 ; (ii) the evil conscience of the sinner, 20—24 ; (iii) the cause of this, 25—28 ; and (iv) his fate 29—35.

**17—19.** Just as in his first speech Eliphaz had fortified his position by an appeal to a Divine oracle (iv. 12 seq.), so here also he relies not on his own authority, but supports himself by an appeal to the traditions of the wise.

**19.** *Unto whom alone the land was given &c.* Eliphaz means that since these wise men to whom he refers lived in the land of their birth and did not mingle themselves with strangers, they have therefore been able to preserve their traditions pure, and unalloyed by foreign admixture.

**20—24.** 'The picture of the evil conscience is drawn here with great force and is without a parallel in the Old Testament' (Driver). For the sense of conscience among the Hebrews cf. however Ps. cxxxix. and Prov. xxviii. 1.

**20.** *Even the number of years &c.* This clause is simply a further definition of 'all his days.' *laid up for* (not *hidden to*, as A.V.), i.e. destined or appointed for. Cf. the use of the same word in xxi. 19.

**21.** *the spoiler shall come upon him*, i.e. he is always in terror of this happening.

22 He believeth not that he shall return out of darkness,
   And he is waited for of the sword :
23 He wandereth abroad for bread, *saying*, Where is it?
   He knoweth that the day of darkness is ready at his
      hand :
24 Distress and anguish make him afraid ;
   They prevail against him, as a king ready to the battle :
25 Because he hath stretched out his hand against God,
   And ¹behaveth himself proudly against the Almighty ;
26 He runneth upon him with a *stiff* neck,
   ²With the thick bosses of his bucklers :
27 Because he hath covered his face with his fatness,
   And made collops of fat on his flanks ;
28 And he hath dwelt in ³desolate cities,
   In houses which no man ⁴inhabited,
   Which were ready to become heaps.

---

¹ Or, *biddeth defiance to*      ² Or, *Upon*
³ Heb. *cut off.*      ⁴ Or, *would inhabit*

---

**22.** *He believeth not that he shall return out of darkness*, viz. the darkness (cf. 23) or night of calamity, which he expects to overwhelm him in total ruin.

*he is waited for of the sword:* almost *he is destined for.* The *sword* is the sword of God, the punishment of which *wrath bringeth.* Cf. xix. 29, and Zech. xiii. 7.

**23.** *He wandereth abroad for bread.* A very graphic description of his dread of want and famine. He pictures himself as already a famished wanderer upon the face of the earth ; so sure is he that *the day of darkness is ready at his hand.*

**25—28.** Now follow the two reasons for this state of haunting fears, each introduced by the same word *because:* the first is the insolent arrogance with which he set himself up against God, and practically defied Him.

**26.** The wicked man is still the subject, the description of his behaviour towards God being here continued.

*with a stiff neck.* Cf. Ps. lxxv. 5.

**27.** The second reason for his presentiments of evil: he has gorged himself upon the ruins of the prosperity of others.

**28.** The idea of this verse is that the man is so abandoned as actually to settle in those places upon which God's curse rested, places which had been banned for the wickedness of their inhabitants, such as Jericho. See the doom pronounced upon the man who should rebuild it, Josh. vi. 26, and its fulfilment in 1 Kings xvi. 34, and cf. Deut. xiii. 12—18.

29 He shall not be rich, neither shall his substance continue,
   Neither shall ¹their produce bend to the earth.
30 He shall not depart out of darkness ;
   The flame shall dry up his branches,
   And by the breath of his mouth shall he go away.
31 Let him not trust in vanity, deceiving himself :
   For vanity shall be his recompence.
32 It shall be ²accomplished before his time,
   And his branch shall not be green.
33 He shall shake off his unripe grape as the vine,
   And shall cast off his flower as the olive.
34 For the company of the godless shall be barren,
   And fire shall consume the tents of bribery.
35 They conceive mischief, and bring forth iniquity,
   And their belly prepareth deceit.

¹ Or, *their possessions be extended on the earth*    ² Or, *paid in full*

29—35. The fate of the sinner.

29. *Neither shall their produce bend to the earth.* (Correct the A.V., which is quite wrong.) The figure is that of heavy grain bending beneath its own weight. Such, says Eliphaz, shall *not* be the harvest of the wicked. But the word rendered *produce* is uncertain. It occurs nowhere else, and possibly the text is corrupt. One MS. actually reads *their flocks,* and if this were adopted we might perhaps render *their flocks shall not spread themselves out on the land.* The ancient versions are obscure and give us no help.

30. *the breath of his mouth,* i.e. God's mouth, cf. iv. 9. 'By the breath of God they perish.'

32. The wicked man is cut off in the midst of his days, cf. Ps. lv. 23.

33. *He shall shake off his unripe grape as the vine.* But, as Davidson points out, the vine does *not* shake off its unripe grapes, and as the word properly means *to wrong* it may be used figuratively for *fail to nourish.*

*And shall cast off his flower as the olive.* 'The olive is the most prodigal of all fruit-bearing trees in flowers. It literally bends under the load of them. But then not one in a hundred comes to maturity. *The tree casts them off by millions, as if they were of no more value than flakes of snow, which they closely resemble.*' Thomson, *The Land and the Book,* p. 54.

34. *godless,* the same word as in viii. 13, where see note.

*barren* : better than *desolate* of the A.V. See iii. 7, where the word is also found.

35. Cf. Ps. vii. 14 ; Is. xxxiii. 11.

**XVI, XVII.** Job's answer to Eliphaz. These chapters contain one of the most striking speeches in the whole book, bringing us almost to the climax of Job's misery. Eliphaz had reproved him for disregarding the 'consolations of God, and the word that dealt gently' with him, and had held up to him the fate of the wicked as supporting his doctrine of retribution. But his words brought him no help, for conscious as he is of innocence, he cannot accept the explanation of his affliction which they suggest. Accordingly his agony and perplexity are as sore as ever; and after a few words of scornful repudiation of his friend's 'consolation,' he once more describes, and in even more daring language than that which he had previously employed, the relentless manner in which God is persecuting him. And yet, arbitrary and cruel as this treatment of him appears to be, so certain is he that if he could only gain a hearing from Him and state his case, he *must* be righted, that he boldly appeals *from* God *to* God, and in fullest expectation that his sufferings can only end in death, calls on Him to avenge the blood that has been unjustly shed.

The speech falls into four tolerably clearly marked divisions:

(1) *Scornful introduction with direct reference to the words of Eliphaz.* xvi. 1—5.

(2) *Description of God's treatment of him, and its inexplicable character.* xvi. 6—17.

(3) *Passionate cries and longing to come face to face with God.* xvi. 18—xvii. 9.

(4) *Folly of his friends' promise of a bright future: nothing remains for him but death.* xvii. 10—16.

**XVI.** 1 Then Job answered and said,
2 I have heard many such things:
¹Miserable comforters are ye all.
3 Shall ²vain words have an end?
Or what provoketh thee that thou answerest?

¹ Or, *Wearisome*     ² Heb. *words of wind.*

**XVI. 1—5. Scornful introduction with direct reference to the words of Eliphaz.** He begins by reminding Eliphaz that he has heard all that he has got to say before; and that his words are 'words of wind' (1—3); and then sarcastically remarks that, if only their positions were reversed, he could give them just the same kind of consolation which they are offering him—the same arguments, the same solemn reproofs, and the same sort of solace (4, 5).

2. *Miserable comforters,* or *consolers*: with direct reference to the words of Eliphaz in xv. 11, the 'consolations' of God.

3. *Shall vain words* (lit. *words of wind*) *have an end?* Another reference to the very words which Eliphaz had used, see xv. 2, 'knowledge of *wind.*' Is there no end, he asks, to his friends' empty and

4 I also could speak as ye do ;
  If your soul were in my soul's stead,
  I could join words together against you,
  And shake mine head at you.
5 *But* I would strengthen you with my mouth,
  And the solace of my lips should assuage *your grief.*
6 Though I speak, my grief is not assuaged :
  And though I forbear, ¹what am I eased?
7 But now he hath made me weary :
  Thou hast made desolate all my company.
8 And thou hast ²laid fast hold on me, *which* is a witness
  *against me* :
  And my leanness riseth up against me, it testifieth to my
  face.

---

¹ Heb. *what departeth from me ?*　　　² Or, *shrivelled me up*

windy utterances, and what is it which provokes them so that they keep on answering him ?

4. *And shake mine head at you.* The gesture of one who is shocked and surprised at what he sees, as well as of scornful mockery. Cf. Ps. xxii. 7, 8 ; Isaiah xxxvii. 22.

5. But *I would strengthen you.* The *but* of the R.V. as well as the A.V. should be omitted. The verse clearly carries on the thoughts of the previous one. Job is still ironically describing how he could act just as his friends are doing, if he were in their place. *I could strengthen you &c.*

6—17. **Description of God's treatment of him and its inexplicable character.** He hardly knows whether to speak or keep silence : in either case he is equally miserable (6). But unable to restrain himself he bursts forth into a description of the way in which God is afflicting him, and his bodily sufferings tell their tale and witness against him (7, 8). God has attack-

ed him like some fierce beast of prey (9) ; and men too have followed with their base mockery, as God has given him over into their hands (10, 11). Nay, when he was in peace and security, God suddenly seized upon him and destroyed him—set him up as a target for his arrows— battered him about as some mighty giant might have done, let him humble himself as he would (12—16); and all this in spite of his innocence in word and deed (17).

7. Both clauses refer to God, who is spoken of in the third person in clause *a,* and then immediately afterwards addressed in the second person in 7*b* and 8. Such rapid changes are not uncommon in Hebrew.

*Thou hast made desolate all my company.* This must mean that God has broken up his domestic circle, and bereft him of his friends. The word for *company* is the same that was used by Eliphaz for 'the *company* of the godless' in xv. 34.

8. *thou hast laid fast hold on me.* This is probably the meaning of

J.　　　　　　　　　　　　　　　　　　　　6

9 He hath torn me in his wrath, and ¹persecuted me ;
  He hath gnashed upon me with his teeth :
  Mine adversary sharpeneth his eyes upon me.
10 They have gaped upon me with their mouth ;
  They have smitten me upon the cheek reproachfully :
  They gather themselves together against me.
11 God delivereth me to the ungodly,
  And casteth me into the hands of the wicked.
12 I was at ease, and he brake me asunder ;
  Yea, he hath taken me by the neck, and dashed me to
    pieces :
  He hath also set me up for his mark.

---

¹ Or, *hated*

the word which only occurs again in xxii. 16. The A.V. *thou hast filled me with wrinkles* (cf. R.V. marg.) seems to have been suggested by the Latin. Job means to say that the fact that God has thus laid His hand upon him and afflicted him is the visible proof to men that He is holding him guilty. His miserable emaciated state is the best evidence of this.

9. He is still speaking of God, and the way in which He is treating him. It is *God* Who has *gnashed upon him with his teeth*, and Who is his *adversary* Who *sharpeneth his eyes* upon him. The figure is that of some fierce beast, tearing his prey. 'Gnashing the teeth' is elsewhere used as a figure of rage. Pss. xxxv. 16; xxxvii. 12; cxii. 10 (disappointed rage); Lam. ii. 16: the other expression, to *sharpen the eyes*, occurs here only. It indicates the flashing eyes of the savage beast who will not let go his prey. For the comparison of God to the beasts of prey, as He executes His judgments upon men, see Hosea xiii. 7, 8, 'Therefore I am unto them as a

lion ; as a leopard will I watch by the way : I will meet them as a bear that is bereaved of her whelps, and will rend the caul of their heart ; and there will I devour them like a lion ; the wild beast shall tear them.' Appalling as Job's language appears to us in its boldness, it is after all only drawing out in full what is implied in such a passage as this, and applying it personally.

10, 11. A description of those who are ever ready to turn upon one that is down. The enmity of God is reflected in the conduct of men. He is not speaking here of his friends, but rather of the 'rabble' whom he describes so graphically in xxx. 'Gaping with the mouth,' and 'smiting upon the cheek' are common terms for insult and scorn. Cf. Micah v. 1 (Heb. iv. 14) ; 1 Kings xxii. 24 ; Ps. xxii. 13.

12. Again God is the subject ; but the figure is changed. The thought is no longer of the beast of prey, but rather of some mighty giant, who seizes on a lesser man unawares—lifts him up by the scruff

13 His ¹archers compass me round about,
   He cleaveth my reins asunder, and doth not spare ;
   He poureth out my gall upon the ground.
14 He breaketh me with breach upon breach ;
   He runneth upon me like a ²giant.
15 I have sewed sackcloth upon my skin,
   And have ³laid my horn in the dust.
16 My face is ⁴foul with weeping,
   And on my eyelids is the shadow of death ;
17 Although there is no violence in mine hands,
   And my prayer is pure.
18 O earth, cover not thou my blood,
   And let my cry ⁵have no *resting* place.

---

¹ Or, *arrows*   Or, *mighty ones*      ² Or, *mighty man*         ³ Or, *defiled*
              ⁴ Or, *red*         ⁵ Or, *have no more place*

---

of his neck and dashes him down in his fury. In the last clause there is a further change, and a fresh metaphor is introduced, that of an archer aiming at a mark. Job is now the target for the arrows of God. For the word for mark cf. 1 Sam. xx. 20, and see the note on vii. 20. Job has already spoken of his sufferings as inflicted by *the arrows of the Almighty*, vi. 4, and cf. Lam. iii. 12, 'He hath bent His bow, and set me as a mark for the arrow.'

13. *His archers*: better (with the margin of R.V. after all the ancient versions) *his arrows. He poureth out my gall upon the ground.* 'The Oriental speaks of the gall and the gall-bladder where we might refer to the blood and the heart.' Davidson.

14. Yet another figure : that of some fortress, in the wall of which God makes 'breach upon breach.' Cf. for a similar figure xxx. 14.

15, 16. These verses may be intended simply to describe the

result of all this treatment, or they may be taken as describing the condition caused by suffering, which, it might have been thought, would appeal for pity.

*sackcloth*, the garb of mourners. See Gen. xxxvii. 34 for its use in patriarchal days.

*my horn*, a frequent image of power : to 'exalt the horn' is to increase the power. Cf. 1 Sam. ii. 10. Similarly to 'lay the horn in the dust,' signifies that his power and glory is brought low.

17. *Although there is no violence in mine hands.* The very same words are used of the suffering 'servant of Jehovah' in Isaiah liii. 9 ; and it is possible that they are there borrowed from the passage before us. See the Introduction, p. xxiv.

**XVI. 18—XVII. 9. Passionate cries, and longing to come face to face with God.** The thought that, notwithstanding his innocence, he is thus being pitilessly destroyed,

19 Even now, behold, my witness is in heaven,
   And he that voucheth for me is on high.

leads Job now to break forth into a passionate cry to the earth not to 'cover his blood,' but to let it still cry to God for vengeance (18); and he follows this up by the startling affirmation that, in spite of all God's treatment of him here, there is One above Who will witness and vouch for him (19). Men may scorn him, but he will still cry to God to maintain his right with Himself (20). Death is coming speedily upon him, and he will soon be in his grave (xvii. 1), for the hopes and promises held out to him are provoking and delusive mockeries (2); and therefore, since there is none else to stand bail for him, he will boldly appeal to God—to God Who is his opponent—to be also his surety (3, 4). There follows a bitter word against his friends (5). But he has scarcely uttered it before his thoughts are again concentrated on his own forlorn condition, as a by-word among the people, a mere shadow (6, 7), a spectacle at which good men might well stand aghast, and which might stir the innocent against the godless (8). But in spite of it all, and through it all, the righteous will undisturbed 'hold on his way,' and will even 'wax stronger and stronger' (9).

In this wonderful utterance Job's agitation reaches its height. But out of it all there emerges a new thought, and one of amazing boldness. The idea that, innocent though he knows himself to be, he yet must die by the visitation of God is intolerable to him. It seems to be the height of injustice, a thing which God, *if He be God*, cannot allow to pass and remain for ever

unrighted. And thus there is borne in upon him the conception of a double Personality as it were in God : there is the *seeming* God of the present, who is his relentless enemy, and there is the *real* God of the future, a God of justice and love. From the former of these, the seeming God of cruelty, he turns away, and cries out to the real God of love, and appeals to Him to right him. But such a vindication as that for which he looks can only come after death (for the whole passage would be unmeaning unless he contemplated his speedy death under a cloud), and thus there is a real advance upon the longing for a future life expressed in xiv., and he is led a step further in the direction of the great declaration and certain conviction of xix. (where see note).

18. *O earth, cover not thou my blood.* The idea is that blood, unjustly shed, cries to God for vengeance so long as it remains upon the face of the ground. Cf. Gen. iv. 10, 'The voice of thy brother's blood crieth unto me from the ground'; and the remarkable passage in Ezek. xxiv. 7, 8, 'For her blood is in the midst of her; she set it upon the bare rock; she poured it not upon the ground, to cover it with dust; that it might cause fury to come up to take vengeance, I have set her blood upon the bare rock, that it should not be covered.' Cf. also Is. xxvi. 21, and see Robertson Smith, *Religion of the Semites*, p. 397.

*let my cry have no* resting *place,* i.e. let it ring on and sound through the courts of heaven.

19. *my witness is in heaven.*

20 My friends scorn me :
   *But* mine eye poureth out tears unto God ;
21 ¹That he would maintain the right of a man with God,
   And of a son of man with his neighbour !
22 For when a few years are come,
   I shall go the way whence I shall not return.
   **XVII.**   1 My spirit is consumed, my days are extinct,
   The grave is *ready* for me.
2 Surely there are ²mockers with me,
   And mine eye abideth in their provocation.
3 Give now a pledge, be surety for me with thyself ;
   Who is there that will strike hands with me ?

¹ Or, *That one might plead for a man with God, as a son of man* pleadeth *for his neighbour*   ² Heb. *mockery.*

The 'witness' is the real God of love and justice Who will testify to his innocence, of whom Job by a stupendous effort of faith now conceives, and to whom he turns.

*he that voucheth for me*: again it is God of whom he speaks, and Whom he now regards as one who will stand sponsor for him (the Hebrew word here used *Sahădi* recalls the Aramaic name given by Laban to the *heap of witness* (Galeed) in Gen. xxxi. 47, 'And Laban called it *Jegar-sahadutha*').

20. *My friends scorn me.* The text of this verse cannot be considered altogether certain. The form of the word for 'scorn me' occurs nowhere else with this meaning, and the LXX. apparently had a different reading, for they render *Oh that my prayer might come before God.*

21. The A.V. here is entirely wrong, and there is no doubt that the verse is, as the R.V. takes it, the expression of Job's longing that God would maintain his right before

Himself as well as men. Cheyne aptly quotes 'the fine words of the Koran' that *there is no refuge from God but unto Him* (Surah ix. 119).

*son of man*, i.e. simply a man. So regularly in the O.T., as e.g. Ps. viii. 4.

22—**XVII. 2.** These verses give the reason for this appeal, viz. the immediate approach of death.

2. A difficult verse, but probably the R.V. gives the true sense. The thought of his approaching death reminds him of the bright promises held out to him by his friends on his repentance, and these he seems to say are a delusive mockery, which can only embitter him. *Surely there are mockers with me, mine eye must rest on their provocation.* His eye must rest on it, i.e. he cannot shut his eyes to it.

3. *Give now a pledge, be surety for me with thyself.* Once more he turns to God, and in his agony at the thought of dying without having his innocence recognized appeals to

4 For thou hast hid their heart from understanding :
  Therefore shalt thou not exalt *them.*
5 He that denounceth his friends for a ¹prey,
  Even the eyes of his children shall fail.
6 He hath made me also a byword of the people ;
  And I am become ²an open abhorring.

---

¹ Heb. *portion.*          ² Or, *one in whose face they spit*

---

him to *give a pledge,* to deposit something, as it were, as a guarantee that his name shall be cleared ; and to *stand as surety for him with Himself.* Again we notice the idea of a double personality in God. It is God Who requires the surety, and yet the appeal is made to Him Himself to act as one. A similar appeal is made in Isaiah xxxviii. 14 where the very same word *be surety for me* is found, but the idea of the double personality is not emphasised there, as it is here by the pointed addition of the words *with thyself.*

*Who is there that will strike hands with me ?* The *form* of the question in the original is identical with that in xiii. 19, and cf. iv. 7. Job means to say that he appeals to God in this way to be surety for him, because there is no one else who can be found to *strike hands* with him, in token that he would undertake this office for him. For the action of 'striking hands' in becoming surety see Proverbs xvii. 18, 'A man void of understanding striketh hands, and becometh surety in the presence of his neighbour,' cf. also Prov. vi. 1 ; xi. 15 ; xxii. 26.

4. The alienation of men is traced to the action of God. It is because He has *hid their heart from understanding,* that they have thus turned away from him ; and since they are

thus blinded, God will *not exalt them,* i.e. give them the victory, as it were, over Job in the debate.

5. Another very difficult verse ; and it seems almost certain that there must be some corruption or mutilation of the text. The A.V. *he that speaketh flattery to his friends,* is certainly wrong ; and it is hard to extract the meaning given by the R.V. *he that denounceth his friends for a prey* (as the margin notes, Hebrew *portion*) out of the three words which form this clause in the original. The first word *for a portion,* though used elsewhere for a *share* of the spoil or booty, is never used absolutely for a *prey* ; nor is there any real justification for taking the Hebrew verb *to sell,* in the sense of *denounce* or *betray.* It is best perhaps to admit that as they stand the words are untranslatable.

6. *He hath made me also a byword of the people.* For the phrase 'to become a byword' cf. Deut. xxviii. 37 ; 1 Kings ix. 7 ; 2 Chr. vii. 20 ; Ps. lxix. 11 ; Jer. xxiv. 9.

*And I am become an open abhorring.* The curious rendering of the A.V. *Aforetime I was as a tabret* is due to a misunderstanding of the Hebrew word. The translators took the word *topheth* as equivalent to *toph,* a timbrel or tabret. But it pro-

7 Mine eye also is dim by reason of sorrow,
  And all my members are as a shadow.
8 Upright men shall be astonied at this,
  And the innocent shall stir up himself against the godless.
9 Yet shall the righteous hold on his way,
  And he that hath clean hands shall wax stronger and
    stronger.
10 But return ye, all of you, and come now :
  ¹And I shall not find a wise man among you.
11 My days are past, my purposes are broken off,
  Even the ²thoughts of my heart.

----

¹ Or, *For I find not*          ² Heb. *possessions.*

----

bably means *spittle*, and hence the paraphrase of the R.V. (which follows the LXX.) is perfectly justifiable. Cf. xxx. 10 and Isaiah l. 6.

8, 9 describe the effect of this upon 'the upright.' They are dumbfounded at the sight, and their indignation is roused against the ungodly. But, in spite of it all, the righteous will *hold on his way*, i.e. continue steadily and unmoved in the right course, and the man whose hands are clean will even *wax stronger and stronger*. The language is quite general, but there can be little doubt that Job is thinking of himself, and that the words amount almost to a declaration that in spite of all the apparently unjust treatment which he has received, nothing can shake him from his determination to keep the right way. Thus he 'shakes himself free from complete despair just when it threatened to overpower him' (Ewald). It is a noble utterance and shows how he is advancing on towards the climax which is reached in the great outburst of faith in xix.

10—16. **Folly of his friends'**

promise of a bright future : **nothing remains for him but death.** Once more, after this mighty effort of faith, there comes a reaction, and he sinks back into a condition bordering upon utter despair. Again he taunts his friends with the failure of their vaunted wisdom (10). He feels that his day is over, and that he has no longer anything to live for (11); but still they keep on urging that 'when night is darkest, dawn is nearest' (12). Yet all the while he knows so well that there is no home for him but the darkness of Sheol, and that the only friends that are left to him are corruption and worms, that he can have no earthly hope whatever, and can look for no rest, but in the dust (13—15).

10. A scornful challenge to his friends to renew the debate. In the second clause it is perhaps best to translate the verb as a present tense (so R.V.), *I find not a wise man among you.*

11. All his plans and purposes for the future seem to be broken to pieces, and the thoughts (lit. *possessions*) of his heart fail, so that he feels that his day is over.

12 They change the night into day :
   The light, *say they*, is near ¹unto the darkness.
13 ²If I look for ³Sheol as mine house ;
   If I have spread my couch in the darkness ;
14 If I have said to ⁴corruption, Thou art my father ;
   To the worm, *Thou art* my mother, and my sister ;
15 Where then is my hope ?
   And as for my hope, who shall see it ?
16 It shall go down to the bars of ³Sheol,
   When once there is rest in the dust.

¹ Or, *because of*      ² Or, *If I hope, Sheol is mine house ; I have spread...I have said...and where now is my hope ?*      ³ Or, *the grave*      ⁴ Or, *the pit*

12. A difficult verse : but the probability is that the R.V. gives the sense. In the first clause, *they change the night into day*, he apparently intends to describe how his friends are always promising him a bright future, thus as it were turning the darkness of the present into the dawn of a new day. Cf. xi. 17, where Zophar says, 'Thy life shall be clearer than the noonday ; though there be darkness, it shall be as the morning.' The second clause must be intended to be a quotation of their very words, and to make this clear the R.V. ventures to insert in italics, *they say*. 'The light, *they say*, is near unto darkness.' Cf. the saying 'When night is darkest, dawn is nearest.' The rendering of the A.V. 'the light is *short* because of darkness' is certainly wrong, and is difficult to explain or account for.

13 seq. In contrast to the hopes held out by his friends of restoration in this life, he insists with all the emphasis he can command that his

only hope is in the grave.
   *spread my couch.* Cf. Ps. cxxxix. 8, 'If I make my bed in Sheol.'
14. He claims as akin to him the denizens of the gloomy world of Hades, *corruption* (or *the pit*) and *worms* (cf. xxi. 26). The thought seems to be imitated in Ps. lxxxviii. 18, where the Psalmist says 'Lover and friend hast thou put far from me, and *mine acquaintance are darkness*' (R.V. marg.), i.e. darkness is the only friend left to him.
15. If the text of this verse be correct, which is doubtful, it must be rendered as in the R.V. *It*, viz. my hope, *shall go down to the bars of Sheol*, when once *there is rest in the dust. bars of Sheol*, because Sheol is conceived of as a fortress with its gates and bolts and bars. Cf. xxxviii. 17, 'gates of death'; Pss. ix. 13; cvii. 18; and Isaiah xxxviii. 10. But the irregular grammar and the rendering of the LXX. both seem to indicate that the text is corrupt.

**XVIII.** The second speech of Bildad.
   Job's contemptuous remarks concerning his friends (xvi. 2—5, xvii. 10) have sorely stung Bildad, and he replies in an angrier tone than has previously been adopted by any of the speakers, rebuking Job severely for

the line which he has taken and then restating with great energy his doctrine of retribution, describing very fully the punishment that overtakes the wicked, with no hint of any possible bright future to relieve the darkness of the picture which he paints, but, with characteristic want of feeling, putting into the sketch a number of details which can only have been intended to suggest to Job the application to his own case. See the description of the ravages of disease in verses 12 and 13 ; the allusion to brimstone scattered upon his habitation (in verse 15), which could hardly fail to recall to the sufferer the thought of the 'fire of God' which had burnt up his sheep, and consumed his servants ; and—cruellest touch of all, to a man whose children had just been slain—the reminder that the wicked shall have 'neither son nor son's son' to succeed him (19). Altogether it is the hardest and most unfeeling speech that we have yet met with. In this hardness of tone it is characteristic of Bildad (see the notes on viii.), and in style as well as tone the character of the speaker is well maintained, as a comparison of this speech with his earlier one may show. There he had appealed to the wisdom of the ancients, and had quoted various proverbial maxims and pithy sayings. Here he not only begins in the very same way that he did there, with an indignant *Quousque tandem,* how long? (cf. xviii. 2 with viii. 2) but the whole speech like the former one is 'full of wise saws,' and contains similar allusions to proverbial philosophy.

It admits of an easy division into two parts :

(i) *An indignant expostulation with Job for his unbecoming language.* 1—4.

(ii) *Description of the fate of the wicked to illustrate the doctrine of retribution.* 5—21.

**XVIII.**　1 Then answered Bildad the Shuhite, and said,
2 How long will ye lay snares for words?
Consider, and afterwards we will speak.

1—4. **An indignant expostulation with Job for his unbecoming language.** Bildad begins by asking Job how long he means to go on using such clap-trap arguments (2), and why he is treating his friends with such contempt (3). How absurd it is, he adds, for a man who is simply destroying himself by his passion, to expect that the order of nature should be interfered with on his account (4)!

These verses are full of allusions to Job's words in the speech that he had just made. He had implied that his hands were clean (xvii. 9), and had thus hinted that his friends were *unclean.* He had said of God, (xvi. 9) that He had *torn* him *in His wrath.* Bildad replies *You are tearing yourself in your wrath.* He had appealed to the earth not to cover his blood (xvi. 18). Is the order of nature to be interfered with for this? asks Bildad.

2. *How long will ye lay snares for words?* The rendering of the A.V. *How long will it be ere ye make an end of words?* is based on that of the LXX. and Vulg. But the

3 Wherefore are we counted as beasts,
  *And* are become unclean in your sight?
4 Thou that tearest thyself in thine anger,
  Shall the earth be forsaken for thee?
  Or shall the rock be removed out of its place?
5 Yea, the light of the wicked shall be put out,
  And the ¹spark of his fire shall not shine.
6 The light shall be dark in his tent,
  And his lamp ²above him shall be put out.
7 The steps of his strength shall be straitened,
  And his own counsel shall cast him down.
8 For he is cast into a net by his own feet,
  And he walketh upon the toils.

---

¹ Or, *flame*          ² Or, *beside*

R.V. is probably correct, though the word translated *snares* is found nowhere else. To *lay snares for words* seems to mean to 'catch at clap-trap arguments.'

4. Is the order of nature and the world to be interfered with for his sake? The law of retribution is fixed by God. Job may rage and tear himself as he will, but this law will remain powerful to rule over the evil-doer.

**5—21. Description of the fate of the wicked to illustrate the doctrine of retribution.** Bildad now illustrates his teaching on the fixity of God's law by describing the fate which overtakes the sinner. His light is put out (5, 6). He is entangled in his own devices, and entrapped in his own meshes (7—10). Terrors dog his footsteps (11). The ravages of disease do their worst upon him (12, 13), and bring him to death (14). His home is waste and desolate (15): his family extinct; and his very name forgotten (16—19). The only memory remaining will be

horror at his fate (20). Such, says Bildad, is the portion of the evil-doer (21).

5, 6. The doctrine of these verses is identical with that of the book of Proverbs, from which they are apparently drawn (see the Introduction, p. xxii). Indeed Bildad's words *the light of the wicked shall be put out... his lamp above him shall be put out* may be said to be a direct quotation from Prov. xiii. 9; xxiv. 20. *The lamp of the wicked shall be put out.* The putting out of the lamp in the tent forms a natural figure for the extinction of the family, just as the kindling or keeping alive the lamp denotes the continuance and preservation of the house. See 1 Kings xi. 36; xv. 4; 2 Kings viii. 19.

7. *The steps of his strength shall be straitened.* Another allusion to Proverbs. See iv. 12 (of him who is taught by Wisdom), 'When thou goest *thy steps shall not be straitened.*'

8—10. Bildad here heaps together every word he can find for *nets* or

9 A gin shall take *him* by the heel,
  *And* a snare shall lay hold on him.
10 A noose is hid for him in the ground,
  And a trap for him in the way.
11 Terrors shall make him afraid on every side,
  And shall chase him at his heels.
12 His strength shall be hungerbitten,
  And calamity shall be ready ¹for his halting.
13 It shall devour the ²members of his body,
  *Yea*, the firstborn of death shall devour his members.
14 He shall be rooted out of his tent wherein he trusteth ;
  And ³he shall be brought to the king of terrors.

¹ Or, *at his side*    ² Heb. *bars of his skin.*
³ Heb. *it shall* (or *thou shalt*) *bring him.*

*snares* to describe the manner in which the wicked man is taken in his own devices, as (to use Shakespeare's phrase) ' an engineer hoist with his own petard.'

9. *gin.* So modern editions of the A.V., but the standard edition of 1611 and subsequent ones up to 1762 give the form *grinne* or grin, which is said to be a form frequently found in old writers.

*snare.* The same word as that used in v. 5, where see note. The A.V. *robber* is certainly wrong.

11. This verse seems hardly to refer to the fears of the evil conscience, so vividly described by Eliphaz (xv. 20 seq.): but rather to the terror of the man when involved in one trouble after another.

12, 13. Descriptive of the ravages of disease.

*hungerbitten,* i.e. famished, cf. Holinshed, *Chronicle* (ed. 1586), III. p. 616, ' The poore distressed people that were *hunger bitten,* made them brede of ferne roots,'

quoted in Wright's *Bible Word-Book,* p. 327.

*calamity shall be ready for his halting.* The revisers take the last word to be the same as that used in Ps. xxxv. 15, *When I halted* (lit. *at my halting*) *they rejoiced,* cf. xxxviii. 17, *I am ready to halt.* The margin, however, gives the rendering of the A.V. *at his side,* taking it from a much commoner word ; and this seems to yield an equally good sense.

13. *the members of his body,* literally *the bars of his skin.* The Hebrew word for ' bars ' is used in xli. 12 (*Heb.* 4) of the members (R.V. *limbs*) of the crocodile.

*the firstborn of death,* i.e. deadly disease.

14. *the king of terrors,* death, which is here personified as the ruler in the grave. See Ps. xlix. 14, ' They are appointed as a flock for Sheol : *death shall be their shepherd* (i.e. shall rule them like a king).' Cf. Rev. ix. 11.

15 ¹There shall dwell in his tent that which is none of his :
　Brimstone shall be scattered upon his habitation.
16 His roots shall be dried up beneath,
　And above shall his branch ²be cut off.
17 His remembrance shall perish from the earth,
　And he shall have no name in the street.
18 He shall be driven from light into darkness,
　And chased out of the world.
19 He shall have neither son nor son's son among his people,
　Nor any remaining where he sojourned.

¹ Or, *It shall dwell in his tent, that it be no more his* or, *because it is none of his*
² Or, *wither*

15. *There shall dwell in his tent that which is none of his.* The general sense is clear, but the construction of the clause is very difficult. The R.V. however is grammatically defensible, and seems better than the A.V. which supposes that 'terror' is still referred to. Taking the R.V. the meaning would be that his home is desolate, and given up to *that which is none of his*, i.e. satyrs and night monsters such as those referred to in Isaiah xxxiv. 11—15, as inhabiting the desolate land of Edom, which lies under God's curse, and 'the dust thereof is turned into brimstone' Is. xxxiv. 9. So in the next clause of the verse before us Bildad says *brimstone shall be scattered upon his habitation*, alluding probably to the fate of Sodom and Gomorrah, so often held up as a warning: cf. Gen. xix. 24.

16. *His roots...and...his branch.* The entire extinction of his family 'root and branch.' This allusion is characteristic in the mouth of Bildad. See viii. 16, 17, where the sinner in the days of his prosperity is compared to a tree, whose '*branch* shooteth forth in his garden,' and whose '*roots* are wrapped about the heap.' Cf. also for similar figures xxix. 19; Is. xxxvii. 31; Amos ii. 9. Driver on the last mentioned passage quotes a striking illustration from the epitaph on Eshmunazar, king of Sidon, invoking a curse on anyone who violates the tomb: 'may he have no root beneath, or fruit above, or any beauty among the living under the sun.'

19. *neither son nor son's son*: the two Hebrew words occur together also in Gen. xxi. 23, and Isaiah xiv. 22, but are found nowhere else. Here and in the passage in Isaiah the A.V. translates the second of them by the word *nephew*; taking this word in its ancient sense of *grandson* (Lat. nepos). The word *nephew* also stands for *grandson* (not son of a brother or sister) where it occurs in the A.V. in Judg. xii. 14; 1 Tim. v. 4; and the usage of the word in this sense is common in Old English.

20 ¹They that come after shall be astonied at his day,
   As they that went before ²were affrighted.
21 Surely such are the dwellings of the unrighteous,
   And this is the place of him that knoweth not God.

¹ Or, *They that dwell in the west are...as they that dwell in the east are &c.*
² Heb. *laid hold on horror.*

**20.** *They that come after shall be astonied at his day, as they that went before were affrighted.* If this rendering be correct the words mean that the horror at the fate of the sinner will last to times far distant; *later* as well as *earlier* generations shall feel it. But many Commentators prefer the rendering given in the margin of the R.V. *They that dwell in the west are astonied at his day, as they that dwell in the east are affrighted,* a rendering which expresses the *universality* of the horror felt.

*his day,* i.e. the day of disaster or death, as in Ezek. xxi. 25 (*Heb.* 30); Ps. xxxvii. 13.

**XIX.** Job's answer to Bildad.

It is no wonder that Job is more than ever hurt and embittered by this last speech of Bildad with its cruel suggestions and scarcely veiled innuendoes. It shows him, as nothing else could do, how completely *isolated* he is. To Bildad's '*how long* will ye lay snares for words' he retorts '*how long will ye vex my soul?*' and adds bitter words on the hard treatment which his friends are meting out to him. He repudiates altogether the explanation which Bildad had suggested of his sufferings, and insists once more that they are simply due to *God*, Who is counting him as one of His adversaries. In pathetic terms he describes his helpless condition, the seemingly cruel treatment to which he is subjected, and the manner in which it is imitated by men—even those nearest and dearest to him having turned against him. Then the recollection of all that he has to endure wrings from him an agonizing cry for pity, when suddenly the thought which has long been struggling for utterance finds expression, and the hope of a vindication after death, for which he had already shown his intense yearning, bursts forth, as no longer only a hope or desire, but as a sure conviction that in the end he will be righted, and that, after the powers of death have done their worst upon his bodily frame, he will yet himself in his own person 'see God.' Thus, as Ewald says, 'this profoundly pathetic speech combines the lowest human humiliation, and the highest divine exaltation, the utmost despair and the most enthusiastic hope and most enraptured certainty. It occupies...the highest central point of the contention and of the action of the whole drama...The spark of the eternal hope that is raised above all time and vicissitudes of time, which at first faintly glimmered, xiv., then sprang forth more brightly, xvi., xvii., here bursts into a clear fire, warming and sustaining the man who would otherwise have now perished in the ancient superstition and in the dark abyss of unbelief.'

In analysing this speech the following divisions may be made :

(i) *Introductory rebuke of his friends and repudiation of their doctrine.* 1—6.

(ii) *Description of God's treatment of him, and of the way in which it is reflected in the conduct of men.* 7—20.

(iii) *Passionate cry for pity and longing to have his protestations indelibly engraven.* 21—24.

(iv) *The strong conviction that after death he shall be righted, and shall himself see his Vindicator.* 25—27.

(v) *Closing threat to his friends.* 28, 29.

**XIX.** 1 Then Job answered and said,

2 How long will ye vex my soul,
   And break me in pieces with words?

3 These ten times have ye reproached me :
   Ye are not ashamed that ye deal hardly with me.

4 And be it indeed that I have erred,
   Mine error remaineth with myself.

5 ¹If indeed ye will magnify yourselves against me,
   And plead against me my reproach :

---

¹ Or, *Will ye indeed...reproach!*

---

**1—6. Introductory rebuke of his friends and repudiation of their doctrine.** How long, Job asks, do his friends mean to go on with their cruel suggestions? Why should they thus remorselessly reproach him (1—3)? Grant that he has been in the wrong, yet this concerns him alone (4). If, however, they insist on setting themselves against him, and reproaching him with his condition, let them know that it is entirely God's doing, and that He alone is responsible for it (5, 6).

3. *These ten times* : ten is used as a round number just as in Gen. xxxi. 7 ; Numb. xiv. 22.

*deal hardly.* The Hebrew word

occurs here only, and the meaning is somewhat uncertain ; but the A.V. *make yourselves strange*, is certainly wrong. The R.V. follows the LXX. ἐπίκεισθε, and Vulg. *opprimentes*, and is probably correct.

4. The meaning of this verse is doubtful. *Mine error remaineth with myself* may mean either 'it is my concern,' and nothing to you ; or possibly, 'I have to pay the penalty of it.'

5. The verse is best taken as a question (as R.V. marg.). *Will ye indeed magnify yourselves against me, and plead against me my reproach?* For *magnify yourselves* cf. Pss. xxxv. 26; xxxviii. 16; lv. 12.

6 Know now that God hath ¹subverted me *in my cause,*
  And hath compassed me with his net.

7 Behold, I ²cry out of wrong, but I am not heard:
  I cry for help, but there is no judgement.

8 He hath fenced up my way that I cannot pass,
  And hath set darkness in my paths.

9 He hath stripped me of my glory,
  And taken the crown from my head.

10 He hath broken me down on every side, and I am gone:
   And mine hope hath he plucked up like a tree.

11 He hath also kindled his wrath against me,
   And he counteth me unto him as *one of* his adversaries.

12 His troops come on together, and cast up their way
       against me,
   And encamp round about my tent.

13 He hath put my brethren far from me,
   And mine acquaintance are wholly estranged from me.

---

¹ Or, *overthrown me*            ² Or, *cry out, Violence!*

6.   Bildad had said, with an evident reference to Job, *he is cast into a net by his own feet.* To this Job retorts, It is all God's doing. It is He who *hath compassed me with his net.*

7—20.  **Description of God's treatment of him, and of the way in which it is reflected in the conduct of men.**  Having asserted that his suffering is due to God's action, he now proceeds to describe at length what he has to suffer from Him : his cries for help are unavailing (7). God has hedged him in, and shut him up in the dark ; stripped him of his glory ; broken him down, driven him to despair (8—10). In His wrath He has declared war against him, summoned His troops against him, and isolated him from his friends (11—13). His nearest and dearest have turned against him, his ser-

vants, his brethren, his wife herself. Even young children mock him ; such a living skeleton is he reduced to (14—20).

7.   The margin of the R.V. gives a vigorous rendering : '*Behold, I cry out, Violence* ; but I am not heard.' He is like a man shouting, Murder! Similar expressions occur in Jer. xx. 8 ; Hab. i. 2, and should be translated in the same way.

*judgement,* i.e. justice.

8.   *He hath fenced up my way.* The same figure for obstructing the path of life occurs in Hos. ii. 6 (*Heb.* 8) ; Lam. iii. 7, 9.

12.   The figure is that of an army casting up a way to the beleaguered city over against which they have encamped.

13.   *mine acquaintance are wholly estranged from me.* It has been thought that the words *are wholly estranged* (אַךְ זָרוּ) are used

14 My kinsfolk have failed,
  And my familiar friends have forgotten me.
15 They that ¹dwell in mine house, and my maids, count me
    for a stranger :
  I am an alien in their sight.
16 I call unto my servant, and he giveth me no answer,
  *Though* I intreat him with my mouth.
17 My breath is strange to my wife,
  And ²my supplication to the children ³of my *mother's*
    womb.
18 Even young children despise me ;
  If I arise, they speak against me.
19 All ⁴my inward friends abhor me :
  And they whom I loved are turned against me.

---

¹ Or, *sojourn*    ² Or, *I make supplication*   Or, *I am loathsome*
    ³ Or, *of my body*    ⁴ Heb. *the men of my council.*

---

with an intentional play upon the word for *cruel* (אַכְזָר). With the thought of this verse cf. Ps. lxxxviii. 18, 'Lover and friend hast thou put far from me.'

14. His friends and relations seem to have forgotten his existence.

15, 16. His household servants ignore him, and pay no heed to his appeals.

17. Even his wife and those nearest to him are turned against him.

*And my supplication to the children of my* mother's *womb.* While the general sense of the whole passage is clear enough, the exact meaning of this clause is doubtful, though the A.V. (*though I entreated for the children's sake of my own body*) is indefensible. The word rendered in R.V. *my supplication* is uncertain. It may be a substantive with this meaning, but it is more probably a verb (as

R.V. marg. 2) *I am loathsome.* Again, the exact meaning of the following words is difficult to determine. Literally they are *children of my womb.* This may mean (1) *my sons,* i.e. children of my body (cf. Deut. vii. 13, xxviii. 4, *fruit of thy body,* where the same word is used, and the pronoun is masculine). But according to i. it would appear that all Job's children were slain ; and it is unnatural to introduce the thought of children of concubines, as the LXX. does. More probably the phrase means (2) *my brothers,* i.e. children of my mother's womb, or, of the womb that bare me. Cf. iii. 10, where the words are literally 'it shut not up the doors of *my womb.*' Others, as Dillmann, think that the reference is to *grandchildren.* So Symmachus (υἱοὺς παίδων μου). But this seems less probable than the explanation just given.

20 My bone cleaveth to my skin and to my flesh,
   And I am escaped with the skin of my teeth.
21 Have pity upon me, have pity upon me, O ye my friends ;
   For the hand of God hath touched me.
22 Why do ye persecute me as God,
   And are not satisfied with my flesh ?
23 Oh that my words were now written !
   Oh that they were inscribed in a book !

20. *My bone cleaveth &c.* Cf. Ps. cii. 5, where much the same words occur, *My bones cleave to my flesh,* and Lam. iv. 8, *Their skin sticketh* (a different verb) *to their bones.* The allusion in the passage before us is of course to the emaciation which is said to accompany the disease of elephantiasis from which Job suffered.

*I am escaped with the skin of my teeth.* The expression is evidently a proverbial one, though found nowhere else in the O.T. The meaning is that there is hardly a sound place in his body, nothing but 'the skin of his teeth.'

21—24. **Passionate cry for pity, and longing to have his protestations indelibly engraven.** There now escapes Job's lips a passionate cry for pity from his friends. God has turned against him, and they have gone with Him, and are copying His treatment of him. There is no end to their malicious charges (21, 22). Would that his protestations of innocence might not merely be written in the pages of a book that is soon destroyed, but placarded in imperishable characters cut into the solid rock so that future generations might read them (23, 24)!

This exclamation follows naturally on what has gone before. He has described fully God's persecution of him (7—13) and the way it is reflected in the conduct of men (14—20). Hence this cry with its reproach : *Why do ye persecute me as God ?*

*And are not satisfied with my flesh.* 'To eat the flesh' of anyone in Hebrew is equivalent to 'to slanderously or maliciously accuse anyone.' Cf. Ps. xxvii. 2, 'evildoers came upon me to eat up my flesh,' and Dan. iii. 8, vi. 24 (*Heb.* 25), where 'accused' is literally 'ate the parts of.' Hence Job means to reproach his friends with their cruel and malicious charges, showing once more that he sees clearly enough the application which they intend him to make of their words.

23. *Oh that my words were now written !* What are the words which Job wishes to have thus inscribed? Two views have been taken : (1) that the wish is introductory to what follows, and that the actual 'inscription' is contained in verses 25—27. There is something very attractive about this view, and if (with LXX., Vulg. and A.V.) we could translate the first word of verse 25 as *for,* there would be no reason to question it. But such a translation is not the natural one : the Hebrew is much more naturally rendered *But* or

24 That with an iron pen and lead
   They were graven in the rock for ever !

*Yet I know* (cf. Ps. ii. 6, *Yet I have
set my king*, where the form of the
sentence is exactly the same). And
if it is so translated as to indicate
a contrast between what goes before
and what follows, it is clear that
verses 25—27 are not the inscription. We are driven then to hold
(2) that what Job desires to have
thus inscribed is the assertion of his
innocence which he has so frequently
made. This is to be engraven in
the rock so that after his death
future generations may read it as a
record of a man who was unjustly
slain. It thus becomes a sort of
appeal to posterity.

*in a book.* The Hebrew has the
definite article, *in the book.* But
no particular book is meant. It is
one of those cases where the Hebrews used the definite article because the thing spoken of 'appeared
definite to the imagination of the
speaker.' Cf. Exod. xvii. 14 ; 1 Sam.
x. 25 ; Jer. xxxii. 10. In such
cases the English idiom requires
the indefinite article. See Davidson's *Hebrew Syntax*, § 21 c.

24. *That with an iron pen and
lead they were graven in the rock
for ever.* The 'book' would be
liable to perish, and therefore Job
would have his words cut in the
solid rock, with lead run into the
incisions, so as to give them a
permanent and indelible character
that they might remain as a testimony for all generations. For the
*iron pen* cf. Jer. xvii. 1, where the
same phrase is used figuratively.

*for ever.* The version of Theodotion has *for a testimony*, which

only requires a change of the vowel-
points. This gives a good sense ;
cf. Gen. xxxi. 44, and Deut. xxx. 19,
but the correction is not necessary.
The LXX. (Cod. B) has εἰς τὸν αἰῶνα,
and so the Targum takes the word.

With the rendering of the Vulgate a curious question is connected.
In the printed texts the verse stands
as follows, 'Quis mihi tribuat ut
scribantur sermones mei ? quis
mihi det ut exarentur in libro stylo
ferreo, et plumbi lamina, *vel celte*
sculpantur in silice ?' Here the
words *vel celte*, 'or with a flint
instrument' (what antiquarians now
call a 'celt'), represent the Hebrew
of '*for ever.*' It is needless to say
that *as a translation* this is impossible, and there seems to be
little doubt that what Jerome really
wrote was not *vel celte* but *vel certe*,
a reading which is found in all the
earlier MSS. of the Vulgate. Thus
the word *celtes* or *celte* would here
be merely a clerical error. But, although the word has now become
firmly established as the technical
name for a flint instrument, it is
remarkable that apart from this
passage independent evidence for
the existence of such a word is very
slender and on the whole it would
seem probable that the word actually
originated in a clerical error, and
that as a Latin word it has no real
existence. 'The word was assumed
on the authority of the Vulgate to
be a genuine word, and as such the
term was admitted into the technical vocabulary of archæology about
1700.' No wonder then that it has
always been a puzzle how to ex-

25 ¹But I know that my ²redeemer liveth,
And that he shall stand up at the last upon the ³earth :

¹ Or, *For*    ² Or, *vindicator* Heb. *goel.*    ³ Heb. *dust.*

plain it, or discover a derivation for
it! See Murray's *New English
Dictionary, sub voce.*

**25—27. The strong conviction
that after death he shall be
righted, and shall himself see his
vindicator.** But, after all, the
fact that his protestations thus remained would profit him but little.
It is a thought in which he cannot
find repose; and thus he rises to
something higher, and declares his
conviction that God will be his
Vindicator, and will manifest Himself in the end (25); and after his
body has been dissolved in death,
he shall yet somehow 'from his
flesh' himself see God—a thought
the greatness of which so overwhelms him that he cries out like
one ready to faint (26, 27).

**25.** *But I know that my redeemer liveth.* On the opening
word 'but' instead of 'for' (of the
A.V.) see above, p. 97. The A.V. in
this clause exactly follows the Vulgate *Scio enim quod redemptor
meus vivit.* But the word *redeemer*
does not express the meaning of the
original so accurately as the *Vindicator* of the margin of R.V. The
word used is *Goêl*, the participle of
a verb which signifies to 'procure
compensation for the down-trodden
and unjustly oppressed,' and so to
'rescue.' It is often applied to
God as the deliverer of His people
out of captivity, especially in the
latter part of Isaiah, e.g. xliii. 1;
xliv. 22, 23. Under the Mosaic
system the participle *Goêl* (the form
used here) was the technical term
for the nearest blood relation, who

had both the right of redemption of
property (see Lev. xxv. 25; Ruth
iv. 4) and also the duty of avenging
bloodshed (see Numb. xxxv. 19, 21).
By Job's assertion, therefore, that
his *Goêl liveth* he declares his
conviction that in spite of all, God
(for 26, 27 make it clear that it is
to Him he refers) will rescue him,
and vindicate him from the unjust
and cruel imputations under which
he lies.

*And that he shall stand up at the
last upon the earth.* The English
versions here rightly desert the
Vulgate, which mistranslates the
clause and finds in it an affirmation
of Job's own expected resurrection.
*Et in novissimo die de terra sur-
recturus sum,* though *in novissimo
die* probably suggested *at the latter
day* of the A.V. The Hebrew word
so rendered is really an adjective
meaning *coming after* or *behind.*
It occurs in Isaiah xli. 4 for *the
last* as opposed to *the first.* The
English versions both understand
it to be used here adverbially, as
*afterwards* or *at the last.* But it
is more probable that it is a second-
ary predicate, and that the clause
should be translated 'and *as one
coming after me* he shall stand up
upon the earth' or rather *the dust.*

*The dust* (R.V. marg.) in which
Job himself is so soon to be laid.
The word is almost equivalent to
*the grave* (see xvii. 16; xx. 11; xxi.
26) upon which the Vindicator shall
take his stand, *as an after man,*
to vindicate and establish the innocence of the sufferer who has passed
away.

7—2

26 ¹And after my skin hath been thus destroyed,
   Yet ²from my flesh shall I see God :

¹ Or, *And after my skin hath been destroyed, this* shall be, *even from &c.*
   Or, *And* though *after my skin this* body *be destroyed, yet from &c.*
                    ² Or, *without*

26. *And after my skin hath been thus destroyed.* Up to this point the meaning is tolerably clear, and the differences of interpretation are comparatively unimportant. The real difficulty of the passage begins with the words now before us. The LXX. is very obscure and gives no help, while the Vulgate is altogether wrong in seeing in words which can only speak of the destruction of the body, a definite reference to its resurrection : *Et rursum circumdabor pelle mea.* The A.V. endeavours to get over the difficulty of the words by boldly inserting 'worms' and 'body,' '*And* though *after my skin* worms *destroy this* body'; insertions which cannot be defended. Many modern writers give up the text as corrupt, and take refuge in conjectural emendations. Taking it, however, as it stands, the sense of the words seems to be fairly represented in the R.V. Literally they run as follows, ' And after my skin they have destroyed, this.' The verb is in the active : but the 'indefinite subject' is often employed in Hebrew where we should use the passive voice (cf. vii. 3, ' wearisome nights *are appointed* to me,' lit. '*they have appointed* to me.' See Davidson's *Hebrew Syntax*, § 108, 2, rem. 2). The meaning of the verb is shown by Is. x. 34, where it is used of cutting off the branches of a tree : and the word ' this' at the end of the clause is used δεικτίκως, as if Job pointed to his emaciated frame, all skin and bone ; and the whole clause will be an emphatic expression of the fact that what he hopes for in the following clause can only take place, *after this my skin has been hacked to pieces.*

*Yet from my flesh shall I see God.* The R.V. translates literally, *from my flesh*, and does not remove the ambiguity of the Hebrew. Grammatically two interpretations are possible: (1) 'from my flesh,' i.e. ' looking out from my flesh,' and so as A.V. after the Vulgate 'in carne mea,' *in my flesh* ; (2) 'apart from' or '*without* my flesh' (cf. xi. 15, '*without* spot,' where the preposition is the same ; and see other examples of this *privative* sense of the preposition in Davidson's *Hebrew Syntax*, § 101, *rem.* c). Of these alternatives the latter is the more probable. Such a definite statement of the resurrection of not merely ' the body,' but ' the flesh' as the former involves would be most startling in the mouth of Job, whereas the conviction that 'without his flesh,' i.e. after his flesh has been destroyed, he may still survive and ' see God' forms the natural climax to the longing which has been struggling upwards in his heart ever since xiv. 13.

27 Whom I shall see ¹for myself,
   And mine eyes shall behold, and not ²another.
   My reins are consumed within me.

¹ Or, *on my side*          ² Or, as *a stranger*

**27.** *Whom I shall see for myself,* or (as R.V. marg.) *on my side.*

*and not another.* It is better to take these words as referring not to Job but to God and render (with R.V. marg.) *and not as a stranger.* God had been treating him as His enemy, and had become estranged from him; hereafter, Job declares, he will see God 'on his side,' and no longer 'estranged' (it is another part of the same verb that is used in verse 13, 'mine acquaintance are wholly estranged').

*My reins are consumed within me.* The thought is so overpowering that Job is ready to faint from his agitation. The words form an exclamation, almost equivalent to 'my heart faints.' For the verb *are consumed* cf. Pss. lxxxiv. 2, cxix. 81, in both of which passages it is translated *faint.* The *reins* or kidneys stand in Hebrew for the affections, and are often used where we should speak of 'the heart,' cf. Prov. xxiii. 16.

If the interpretation of the several clauses that has now been given is correct the passage as a whole affords distinct evidence that Job has fought his way to a new belief, and has reached the conviction that after death he shall be granted a vision of God. Against this interpretation two objections are sometimes brought.

(1) It is said that it contradicts Job's earlier utterances. This objection, however, does not appear to be a formidable one. It may be freely granted that this passage is very different from some earlier ones, and does contradict the statements of vii. 7—10, and xiv. 7—12. It is clear that at the outset, when his troubles first fell upon him Job did not believe in any future life: the very idea of it as a possibility does not seem to have occurred to him. It evidently formed no part of his creed and was no article of faith in the days in which the scene of the story is laid. But the book shows us very carefully exactly how he arrived at the belief: it was only at the close of a prolonged struggle, the stages of which are clearly marked, that he came to accept it. Two distinct lines of thought meet in the passage before us. (*a*) The thought that God, *if He be God,* must ultimately manifest Himself as the Vindicator of the innocent sufferer. In preparation for this we have had in ix. 33 the expression of Job's earnest desire for a 'daysman' or arbiter, and in xvi. 19—xvii. 3, the appeal to God to maintain his right with Himself, and to stand surety for him. But (*b*) since death is all along contemplated as the issue of his sufferings, this interposition and manifestation can only take place after death, and therefore there *must* be a future life. To this he has come at last; beginning in vii. 7—10 with absolute disbelief, he has worked his way to it, through the great longing for it suggested to him in xiv. 7—15 by the contemplation of the facts in the natural

world which point in this direction. He feels then that, *if he could only accept it*, it would enable him to bear his intolerable sufferings with patience : and, the thought and longing having thus occurred to him, it is but natural that in time they should give birth to conviction. This first objection, therefore, based on the contradiction between this passage and earlier utterances, falls to the ground.

But (2) a second objection is raised to which more weight must be attached. It is said that if Job has really reached this assured position it is inconceivable that this solution of his difficulties should never again be alluded to in the book by Job himself, or by any of the other speakers. The fact that there *is* no further reference to it is certainly strange, and difficult to account for : but the force of the objection is considerably weakened when it is noticed what a real effect the conviction, to which Job here gives expression, has upon his subsequent utterances. In all that follows there is a far calmer tone, and much less of the passion with which he has flung out his charges against God ; and further it is only after this that he is able to pay any attention to his friends' argument, and bring forward his refutation of it (see below on xxi.). This can only result from his having reached such an assured position as the interpretation given above assumes ; and though the absence of any further reference to his conviction is admitted to be remarkable, yet it would be far more remarkable and perplexing if the longing and struggle upwards of xiv. 7—15, and xvi. 19—xvii. 3, did *not* issue at length in a 'sure and certain hope.'

Two other explanations ought to be mentioned, to show the reader what the alternatives are if the interpretation adopted above be abandoned.

(1) *Job expects his vindication before death.* According to those who hold this view we must either alter the text of verse 26, or translate it in some such way as this : 'behind my skin, which has been thus mangled, yea, out of my flesh shall I see God.' But the objections to this view appear to be overwhelming. (*a*) It would involve a startling contradiction of everything that Job has already said. Nothing can be clearer than the fact that all through he is expecting to die under his afflictions with his innocence unrecognized. ' He invariably repels the idea, whenever his friends present it to him, of any improvement in his condition in this world as plainly impossible.' (*b*) For him to accept the view that he will be vindicated in this life, and restored to prosperity would be not only to abandon the position which he has taken up, but to *adopt the very view of his friends.* See Green, *Argument of Job*, pp. 204, 5.

(2) The other alternative is that though the vindication of his innocence which Job expects is to take place after his death, yet when he speaks of his vision of it, he is referring to a spiritual vision which he already enjoys as he looks forward and anticipates the future. This would require us to translate the verbs in 26, 27 as presents. *I see*, not *I shall see.* But such an interpretation appears very forced, and it is anything but natural to think that Job would be satisfied with such a spiritual vision, or emphasize his conviction of it so forcibly. If

28 If ye say, How we will persecute him !
  ¹Seeing that the root of the matter is found in ²me ;
29 Be ye afraid of the sword :
  For ³wrath *bringeth* the punishments of the sword,
  That ye may know there is a judgement.

---

¹ Or, *And that*      ² Many ancient authorities read, *him.*      ³ Or, *wrathful are*

he is to die with his innocence unrecognized, it can be no satisfaction to him to anticipate the fact that hereafter it *will* be recognized, for the benefit of posterity, if for him there is no future life in which he will see it; 'for,' as he says himself later on, ' what pleasure has he in his house after him, when the number of his months is cut off ? '

On the whole, then, it is believed that nothing but the belief in a future life satisfies the requirements of the words used. No interpretation is free from difficulty : but this labours under fewer objections than any other. It is not improbable that there may be some corruption of the text in the first clause of verse 26, where the Hebrew is obscure, but there seems to be no justification for attempts to amend the text elsewhere ; and the LXX. translators, who may have had a different reading before them in this clause, still found in the passage the doctrine of a future life ; while, among moderns, Siegfried, who alters the text with great daring, is nevertheless constrained to admit that it gives expression to this belief, though he arbitrarily removes it from the text as an interpolation, and writes of it as follows : ' we look upon the whole passage as a later gloss in which the resurrection of the just is regarded as a possibility (cf. Dan. xii. 13 ; 2 Macc. vii. 9, 11), contrary to the opinion put

forth in the book of Job with regard to Sheol (iii. &c.).'

**28, 29. Closing threat to his friends.** If, after this, Job's friends continue to persecute him, and to insist that the real cause of his misery lies in himself (28), let them dread the punishment of God's wrath which awaits them (29).

**28.** *If ye say, How we will persecute him !* The A.V. is quite wrong in the turn which it gives to this. *But ye should say, why persecute we him.* Job is not advising them what they ought to say, but is warning them against the consequences (stated in verse 29) of their language.

*Seeing that the root of the matter is found in me.* For *in me* a considerable number of Hebrew MSS. read *in him* and this reading has the support of the LXX., Vulgate and Targum and is probably correct. The clause forms part of the supposed utterance of the friends, whom Job imagines to say that the real cause of his misfortunes (*the root of the matter*) is to be found in himself, i.e. in his own sinful conduct.

**29.** *wrath.* It is God's wrath that is spoken of : but probably the word is the predicate and the substantive is used, as often in Hebrew, where we should use an adjective, and instead of *wrath* bringeth *the punishments of the sword,* we should render *wrathful* are *the punishments of the sword.* So

**XX.** Second speech of Zophar.

Zophar, as has already been pointed out, is the roughest and coarsest of the three friends. He now shows himself the densest: for though Job has just given expression to the grand conviction that his Vindicator lives and will right him hereafter, yet Zophar is totally incapable of entering into the thought, and is simply indignant that Job should dare to threaten them as he did in his last words. Hence, after a few words expressing his impatience with his friend, he reiterates the old doctrine of retribution, describing once more the fate which falls upon the wicked, and insisting on the *brevity* of his triumph, and the *speedy* character of the judgment which overtakes him. It is this reference alone which distinguishes his speech from the last one of Bildad, whose general line he follows closely; and of course, like Bildad, he means Job to read between the lines, and to discover in the picture held up to him a portrait of himself.

The chapter is best divided into four sections :

(i)   *Introductory acknowledgment of his impatience.* 1—3.

(ii)   *Description of the transitory character of the prosperity of the wicked.* 4—11.

(iii)   *Sin and its retribution.* 12—22.

(iv)   *God's wrath and vengeance upon the sinner.* 23—29.

**XX.** 1 Then answered Zophar the Naamathite, and said,

2 Therefore do my thoughts give answer to me,
   ¹Even by reason of my haste that is in me.

3 I have heard the reproof which putteth me to shame,
   ²And the spirit of my understanding answereth me.

¹ Or, *And by reason of* this *my haste is within me*
² Or, *But out of my understanding* my *spirit answereth me*

R.V. marg. *The sword* is the Divine Sword, cf. xv. 22 ; xxvii. 14.

*That ye may know there is a judgement.* The last word of this verse is almost certainly corrupt. The simplest change would give as the rendering *that ye may know the Almighty*, but the corruption is perhaps too deeply seated for the original text to be restored with certainty.

1—3. **Introductory acknowledgment of his impatience.** Zophar here asserts that in his impatience and excitement his thoughts

have already suggested the answer he wishes to make (2). He has listened to Job's reproaches which were intended to make him ashamed, but his understanding has already supplied his spirit with the reply to them (3).

2. *by reason of my haste,* i.e. impatience or inward excitement.

3. *the reproof which putteth me to shame,* viz. that contained in xix. 28, 29. The R.V. is clearer than the A.V., *the check of my reproach*, which, however, means the same, 'check' being used in

4 Knowest thou *not* this of old time,
　　Since man was placed upon earth,
5 That the triumphing of the wicked is short,
　　And the joy of the godless but for a moment?
6 Though his excellency mount up to the heavens,
　　And his head reach unto the clouds;
7 Yet he shall perish for ever like his own dung:
　　They which have seen him shall say, Where is he?
8 He shall fly away as a dream, and shall not be found:
　　Yea, he shall be chased away as a vision of the night.
9 The eye which saw him shall see him no more;
　　Neither shall his place any more behold him.
10 ¹His children shall seek the favour of the poor,
　　And his hands shall give back his wealth.

¹ Or, as otherwise read, *The poor shall oppress his children*

the old sense of 'reproof' or 're-buke'; as in Shakespeare, 'I never knew yet but rebuke and *check* was the reward of valour,' *Henry IV.*, Pt. II., Act IV., Sc. 3.

The second clause is best taken as in R.V. marg., *But out of my understanding my spirit answer-eth me.*

**4—11. Description of the tran-sitory character of the prosperity of the wicked.** Is not Job aware, he now asks in scorn, of the univer-sal truth (which is as old as the hills) that the prosperity of the wicked is only for a moment (4, 5): he may be exalted to the skies, but his destruction is complete (6, 7): he passes away like a dream, and his place knows him no more (8, 9). His children are at the mercy of others, and his ill-gotten wealth he is made to restore (10). Lusty and vigorous as he may seem, yet in his full strength he is brought down to the grave (11).

5. *That the triumphing of the wicked is short.* Zophar's solution of the difficulty is that which was adopted by the author of Ps. xxxvii. 'They shall soon be cut down like the grass.'...'Yet a little while, and the wicked shall not be: yea, thou shalt diligently consider his place and he shall not be.' It is true, but not, as Zophar implied, a *universal* truth; and in regard to Job's case the assertion was not pertinent.

7. *like his own dung*: the coarse-ness is characteristic of Zophar.
　*Where is he?* Cf. xiv. 10.

8. *He shall fly away as a dream.* Cf. Ps. lxxiii. 20, 'As a dream when one awaketh; so, O Lord, when thou awakest, thou shalt despise their image.'

9. Cf. Job's own words in vii. 8—10.

10. *His children shall seek the favour of the poor.* The trans-lation is not certain. The margin of the R.V. notes 'as otherwise read, *the poor shall oppress his children.'* The verb may be read in two different ways and this

11 His bones are full of his youth,
   But it shall lie down with him in the dust.
12 Though wickedness be sweet in his mouth,
   Though he hide it under his tongue ;
13 Though he spare it, and will not let it go,
   But keep it still within his mouth ;
14 Yet his meat in his bowels is turned,
   It is the gall of asps within him.

marginal rendering has the support of the LXX. and the Targum, but on the whole the rendering of the R.V. (text) is the more natural.

*his hands shall give back his wealth,* i.e. the man has to disgorge his ill-gotten goods.

11. *His bones are full of his youth.* The A.V. 'his bones are full of *the sin of* his youth' is suggested by the Vulgate 'Ossa ejus implebuntur vitiis adolescentiae ejus'; but there is no authority for this insertion of *sin* (vitiis). *Youth* is used for 'youthful vigour,' cf. xxxiii. 25; and it is this 'youthful vigour' which is poetically represented in the next clause as 'lying down with him in the dust,' i.e. The wicked man shall die in his full strength. Cf. Ps. lv. 23, 'Bloodthirsty and deceitful men shall not live out half their days.'

12—22. **Sin and its retribution.** Having thus described the fate of the wicked, Zophar now proceeds to show that it is due to his sin, which brings its own punishment. The man may revel in his wickedness and gloat over it, as an epicure over some dainty morsel (12, 13), but he will find that it turns to poison within (14). He will have to disgorge the wealth he has swallowed down, and what he has been consuming so greedily shall prove

to be the deadliest of poisons (15, 16). He shall not live to enjoy days of plenty and prosperity (17); but must give up all that he has amassed so painfully (18): and all this, because he was so cruel an oppressor of the poor, so restless and greedy a tyrant (20, 21). In the midst of plenty he shall come to penury, and even the very abjects shall turn against him (22).

The thought of the whole passage is the same as that of Shakespeare :
'The Gods are just, and of our
   pleasant vices
Make instruments to plague us.'
          *King Lear*, Act v. Sc. 3.
Cf. also Wisd. xi. 16.

12, 13. Sin is here compared to some rich delicacy which the epicure rolls under his tongue, and gloats over, unwilling to swallow it down, and let it go. The coarseness of the description is characteristic of Zophar; cf. verse 7.

14. *the gall of asps.* The word for *gall* occurs again in verse 25. It is probably the same as that which is found in xvi. 13, though pointed differently. The poison of serpents was erroneously believed by the ancients to reside in the gall or bile; hence the expression. Cf. Pliny, *N. H.* xi. 37, 'No one would be astonished that it is the gall which constitutes the poison of serpents.'

15 He hath swallowed down riches, and he shall vomit them
    up again :
    God shall cast them out of his belly.

16 He shall suck the poison of asps :
    The viper's tongue shall slay him.

17 He shall not look upon the rivers,
    The flowing streams of honey and butter.

18 That which he laboured for shall he restore, and shall not
    swallow it down ;
    According to the substance ¹that he hath gotten, he shall
    not rejoice.

19 For he hath oppressed and forsaken the poor ;
    He hath violently taken away an house, ²and he shall not
    build it up.

20 Because he knew no quietness ³within him,
    He shall not save aught of that wherein he delighteth.

¹ Heb. *of his exchange.*    ² Or, *which he builded not*
³ Or, *in his greed* Heb. *in his belly.*

For *asps* cf. Is. xi. 8; Pss. lviii. 4; xci. 13. Tristram identifies the Biblical asp with the hooded cobra of Egypt. See *Natural History of the Bible*, p. 270.

16. *the poison of asps.* Cf. Deut. xxxii. 33, where the same words occur.

*The viper's tongue.* For *viper* cf. Is. xxx. 6; lix. 5 : identified by Tristram with the highly poisonous sand viper. See *Natural History of the Bible*, p. 276. The verse is only a figurative way of saying that his meat turns to poison within him, i.e. his ill-gotten wealth works his ruin.

17. *the rivers, the flowing streams of honey and butter :* frequent images of plenty and prosperity. For *butter* cf. xxix. 6.

18. The verse is somewhat obscure, and possibly the text is corrupt (the LXX. apparently follows a different reading), but the R.V. appears to give the general sense correctly. Zophar means to say that the sinner is forced to restore what he has appropriated before he has thoroughly assumed possession of it, and that he gets no pleasure out of his acquisitions.

19. The reason why this retribution falls upon him.

*He hath violently taken away an house, and he shall not build it up* : i.e. the house which he has taken violent possession of (for the verb cf. Gen. xxi. 25) shall not be established and extended.

20. *within him.* The Hebrew is literally (as A.V.) *in his belly.* This may mean either (1) his innermost part, i.e. *his inmost soul,* as in Prov. xviii. 8; xxvi. 22; or (2) as R.V. marg. *in his greed,* the belly being regarded as the seat of gluttonous appetite.

21  There was nothing left that he devoured not ;
    Therefore his prosperity shall not endure.
22  In the fulness of his sufficiency he shall be in straits :
    The hand of every one that is in misery shall come upon
        him.
23  ¹When he is about to fill his belly,
    *God* shall cast the fierceness of his wrath upon him,
    And shall rain it upon him ²while he is eating.
24  He shall flee from the iron weapon,
    And the bow of brass shall strike him through.
25  He draweth it forth, and it cometh out of his body :
    Yea, the glittering point cometh out of his gall ;
    Terrors are upon him.

¹ Or, *Let it be for the filling of his belly that* God *shall cast &c.*
² Or, *as his food*

22. *The hand of every one that is in misery shall come upon him.* Cf. the description which Job himself gives of the way in which the miserable rabble have turned against him in xxx. 1—16.

23—29. **God's wrath and vengeance upon the sinner.** Just as the man is gorging himself with his ill-gotten wealth God's judgment overtakes him (23). He is struck down in the very act of fleeing from vengeance (24) ; the fatal weapon pierces him through, and has to be drawn forth from the wound (25). Terror and darkness are his portion. He and all his are consumed by a fire of no earthly kindling (26). Heaven and earth combine to declare against him (27), and in the day of God's wrath his prosperity is swept away as by a flood (28). Such is God's judgment upon the sinner (29).

23. *And shall rain it upon him.* See the same figure in Ps. xi. 6, ' Upon the wicked He shall rain snares : fire and brimstone and burning wind shall be the portion of their cup.'

*while he is eating* : better, as R.V. marg. *as his food*.

24. *the bow of brass* (cf. Ps. xviii. 34) *shall strike him through.* The verb is used again in this sense in Judg. v. 26, of Jael *striking through* Sisera's temples.

25. There is very probably some corruption in the text of this verse, which, as it now stands, can only be rendered as in the R.V. ; but it is certainly very tame and prosaic to say that he draws forth the arrow, and it comes out of his body ! The versions are very obscure, and it seems impossible to suggest any satisfactory emendation of the text.

*the glittering point.* The word properly means *lightning*, and elsewhere is used for the *flash* of weapons, e.g. thy *flashing* sword, Deut. xxxii. 41 ; the *flashing* spear, Nah. iii. 3 ; Hab. iii. 11, but in these other instances the weapon is named,

26 All darkness is laid up for his treasures :
   A fire not blown *by man* shall devour him ;
   ¹It shall consume that which is left in his tent.
27 The heavens shall reveal his iniquity,
   And the earth shall rise up against him.
28 The increase of his house shall depart,
   *His goods* shall flow away in the day of his wrath.
29 This is the portion of a wicked man from God,
   And the heritage appointed unto him by God.

¹ Or, *It shall go ill with him that is left*

whereas here there is no word in the original representing *point*. It is simply '*the flash* cometh out of his gall,' an almost impossible expression, which again seems to indicate that the text is corrupt.

*Terrors.* The same word as in ix. 34, xiii. 21, used also elsewhere (Exod. xv. 16 ; xxiii. 27 ; Deut. xxxii. 25 ; Ps. lxxxviii. 16) for terrors inspired by God.

26. *All darkness is laid up for his treasures.* This rendering is better than that of the A.V., *All darkness shall be hid in his secret places.* The words mean that all calamities are held in reserve for the treasures which the wicked man has amassed.

*A fire not blown* by man : either (1) kindled by God in His wrath ; or possibly (2) self-kindled. For the figure cf. xv. 34, and Is. xxxiii. 11— 14. There is probably in Zophar's

mind an allusion to the 'fire of God' which burnt up Job's sheep and servants, i. 16.

27. *The heavens shall reveal his iniquity, and the earth shall rise up against him.* A cruel retort after Job's appeal to heaven and earth to witness for him in xvi. 18, 19.

28. *The increase of his house shall depart.* A change of pointing in the verb would give the same word as that in Amos v. 24, 'Let judgment *roll down* as waters' ; and this suits well with the following clause, though the change is perhaps not necessary. Cf. for the word found in the Massoretic text 1 Sam. iv. 21 ; Is. xxiv. 11.

*in the day of his wrath*, i.e. God's wrath.

29. A copy of Bildad's closing words in his last speech ; see xviii. 21.

**XXI.**   Job's answer to Zophar.

At the close of his last speech Job had reached a sure conviction that in spite of all God would somehow vindicate him and manifest Himself on his side hereafter. The result of his having reached this position is very manifest in this his next utterance. It is not merely that his words take a calmer tone, but it is even more that he is now, and for the first time, able fairly to face the arguments of his friends. All through the debate they have been asserting in one form or another their theory of retribution, and their argument admits of being put in a syllogistic form after this fashion.

> All suffering is the punishment of sin:
> Job is a great sufferer:
> *Therefore* Job is a great sinner.

Till now Job has been occupied almost exclusively with the conclusion. He has passionately repudiated the notion that he is an exceptionally great sinner, and that he has done anything to deserve to be singled out for exceptionally severe treatment. But he has nowhere fully dealt with the premises on which the conclusion rests. They are only just touched upon in ix. 23, 24, and xii. 6. Now, however, that he has reached an assured position, and is convinced that though in his death he may appear to men to be a sinner, yet hereafter he will be righted and his innocence acknowledged, he is able to consider the argument as a whole and to show where the fallacy lies. His answer to the syllogism of his friends is this: *Nego majorem*. Granted their premises, the conclusion inevitably follows. But by a powerful appeal to the logic of facts Job shows that their major premise does not hold good. There is not the close and necessary connexion between suffering and sin which they assumed. If suffering be always the punishment of sin, how is it that the wicked live and prosper? They had maintained that 'the lamp of the wicked shall be put out.' *How often is it*, asks Job, *that this really happens?* As a matter of fact it is the wicked man who is spared in the day of calamity, who is exceptionally prosperous in life, and is honoured in his death. While, however, he breaks down in this way the argument of his friends, and shows where the fallacy in it lies, it must be remembered that he has no theory of his own to set in its place. He can only acquiesce in the mystery, as others have done since. His words only establish the fact that God's moral government here is *not* perfect (the admission with which Butler starts in his famous chapter on Moral Government, *Analogy*, Part I. c. iii.). This however is much to have done, for so long as men acquiesced in the old doctrine of retribution, there could be no advance, no deeper insight into the mystery of suffering. The old doctrine must be shown to be inadequate, or men will never seek to penetrate deeper into the problem. Thus the establishment of the fact that moral government as exhibited on earth is not perfect, that there is no necessary connexion between the individual's suffering and the individual's sin, is a real advance, a step forward, because it teaches men to look for some further object in suffering than mere punishment: it prepares the way for the deeper teaching on the subject of pain which is elsewhere revealed. And how necessary it was that the old doctrine should be broken down, and that Scripture should furnish a striking example of its inadequacy is shown by the constant recurrence of it, and the inveterate tendency in the minds of men to argue as Job's friends argued. It was centuries later that we read that 'there were some present which told Him of the Galileans whose blood Pilate had mingled with their sacrifices,' and who were met with the rebuke: 'Think ye that these Galileans were sinners above all the Galileans because they suffered these things? I tell you, nay: but except ye repent, ye shall all in like manner perish' (S. Luke xiii. 1—3). And even the Apostles could ask, 'Master, Who did sin, this man or his parents, that he should be born blind?' (S. John ix. 2).

The analysis of the chapter is not difficult; it falls into five divisions:

(1) *Brief introduction, claiming a hearing.* 1—6.

(2) *Description of the prosperity of the wicked.* 7—15.

(3) *Rarity of troubles overwhelming them.* 16—21.

(4) *Perplexity of the problem.* 22—26.

(5) *Folly and ignorance of the friends in their application of their doctrine to the case of Job himself.* 27—34.

**XXI.** 1 Then Job answered and said,

2 Hear diligently my speech;
And let this be your consolations.

3 Suffer me, and I also will speak;
And after that I have spoken, [1]mock on.

4 As for me, is my complaint [2]to man?
And why should I not be impatient?

5 [3]Mark me, and be astonished,
And lay your hand upon your mouth.

[1] Or, *thou shalt mock*    [2] Or, *of*    [3] Heb. *Look unto me.*

1—6. **Brief introduction, claiming a hearing.** Job here begins by appealing to his friends to hear him patiently, after which they may mock on, if they please (1—3). It is not of *man's* conduct that he is complaining, and he has good cause for the impatience which he shows (4). Let them listen in silent astonishment, for the problem is one which he himself cannot think upon without agitation (5, 6).

2. *let this be your consolations.* Eliphaz had hinted that the arguments advanced by himself and his friends were *the consolations of God* to Job (xv. 11). Job retorts that the only 'consolation' which he asks from his friends is the consolation afforded by a good listener.

3. *mock on.* In the Massoretic text this word is in the singular, as if it was addressed to Zophar in particular. But the Versions (LXX., Symmachus, Syriac, Vulg.) all translate as if they read the word in the plural, which is actually found in one Hebrew MS.

4. *is my complaint to man?* Better, *of man*, as R.V. marg. Job means that it is not concerning man, but rather concerning God, that he feels he has ground of complaint.

5. *lay your hand upon your mouth.* See the use of similar phrases as indicating the silence of awe and astonishment in xl. 4 and Micah vii. 16.

6  Even when I remember I am troubled,
   And horror taketh hold on my flesh.
7  Wherefore do the wicked live,
   Become old, yea, wax mighty in power?
8  Their seed is established with them in their sight,
   And their offspring before their eyes.
9  Their houses are ¹safe from fear,
   Neither is the rod of God upon them.
10  Their bull gendereth, and faileth not ;
   Their cow calveth, and casteth not her calf.
11  They send forth their little ones like a flock,
   And their children dance.
12  They ²sing to the timbrel and harp,
   And rejoice at the sound of the pipe.

---

¹ Or, *in peace, without fear*          ² Heb. *lift up* the voice.

---

**6.** *when I remember*, i.e. when I think or reflect upon : cf. the use of the word *remember* in xli. 8 (*Heb.* xl. 32). The object of his reflection, though not yet stated, is clearly the prosperity of the wicked, of which he proceeds to speak in the following verses.

**7—15. Description of the prosperity of the wicked.** The problem is now stated. Why is it, Job asks, that the wicked thrive ? (7). They are blessed with children : their houses are secure : their cattle increase : their lives are full of mirth and merriment, and their death preceded by no painful and lingering illness (8—13). Yet these are the very men who have bidden good-bye to God, and have refused altogether to render homage to Him (14, 15)!

**8.** *Their seed is established with them in their sight.* Job is evidently thinking of the mournful contrast to this afforded by his own case. Cf. i. 19.

**9.** *the rod of God.* Cf. ix. 34, and xxxvii. 13 where 'correction' is literally 'a rod.'

**11.** *They send forth their little ones like a flock.* The same comparison is found in Ps. cvii. 41, 'maketh him families *like a flock*.'

**12.** *They sing*, literally *lift up* (the voice). Other instances of the verb being used absolutely without the word *voice* expressed are Numb. xiv. 1; Is. iii. 7; xlii. 2, 11.

*the timbrel*, or tambourine, chiefly used by women as an accompaniment to dancing. See Exod. xv. 20; Judg. xi. 34; Jer. xxxi. 4.

*the pipe*, better than *the organ* of the A.V. which follows the Vulgate. It is the simplest of wind instruments, mentioned elsewhere in Gen. iv. 21; Ps. cl. 4, and in c. xxx. 31, where the harp and pipe are the symbols of mirth and merriment.

13 They spend their days in prosperity,
    And in a moment they go down to ¹Sheol.
14 Yet they said unto God, Depart from us ;
    For we desire not the knowledge of thy ways.
15 What is the Almighty, that we should serve him?
    And what profit should we have, if we pray unto him?
16` ²Lo, their prosperity is not in their hand :
    The counsel of the wicked is far from me.

---

¹ Or, *the grave*          ² Or, Ye say, *Lo &c.*

**13.** *in prosperity*, better than the *wealth* of the A.V. since this word is now restricted to the meaning of riches. In the sixteenth and seventeenth centuries it had the wider sense of weal or well-being generally, as it is used in the Book of Common Prayer, e.g. in the Litany : 'in all time of our tribulation, in all time of our *wealth*,' and in the Collect for the sovereign 'Grant her in health and *wealth* long to live.'

*in a moment they go down to Sheol.* Cf. Ps. lxxiii. 4, 'There are no bands (or *pangs*) in their death.' From the purely animal point of view sudden death may be much to be desired (cf. a striking passage in the *Life of Bishop Dupanloup*, Vol. I. p. 182); nevertheless the Christian prays against it, asking by his prayer 'that death when it cometh may give us some convenient respite, or secondly, if that be denied us of God, that we may have wisdom to provide always beforehand that those evils overtake us not which death unexpected doth use to bring upon careless men, and that although it be sudden in itself, nevertheless in regard of our prepared minds it may not be sudden.' Hooker, *E. P.* Bk. v. c. xlvi.

**14.** Yet these men, who are thus exceptionally prosperous in life and death, did just what Satan with all his trials was unable to induce Job to do, viz. *bid good-bye to God.* Cf. on i. 11.

**16—21. Rarity of troubles overwhelming the wicked.** The friends may say that the wicked have no secure tenure of their prosperity, and may piously exclaim that they will have none of the counsel of the ungodly (16), but Job retorts with the query how often is it that darkness and calamity really overtake the sinner, and that God's vengeance falls upon him (17, 18). Again, the friends may suggest that the judgment is inflicted upon the children, on whom the father's sins are visited. It ought rather, says Job, to fall upon the sinner himself, for how does the fate of his children affect him when once he is in his grave (19—21)?

**16.** *Lo, their prosperity is not in their hand.* A difficult verse. According to one view the first clause of the verse is closely joined with the preceding account of the sinner's prosperity : Job means to say that sinners do not create their own fortune : it comes from God ; and yet he himself in spite of his misery repudiates their principles,

17 ¹'How oft is it that the lamp of the wicked is put out?
   That their calamity cometh upon them?
   That *God* distributeth sorrows in his anger?
18 That they are as stubble before the wind,
   And as chaff that the storm carrieth away?
19 ²*Ye say,* God layeth up his iniquity for his children.
   Let him recompense it unto himself, that he may know it.

¹ Or, *How oft is the lamp of the wicked put out, and* how oft *cometh their calamity upon them!* God *distributeth sorrows in his anger. They are as stubble ...away.*   ² Or, *God layeth up his iniquity for his children: he rewardeth him, and he shall know it. His eyes shall see his destruction, and he shall drink &c.*

and exclaims *the counsel of the wicked be far from me!* But on the whole it seems better to suppose that the verse is intended to be put, as it were, into the mouth of the friends as their account of the matter. So the margin of the R.V. Ye say, Lo, *their prosperity is not in their hand,* i.e. they have no sure grasp, no certain tenure of it; to which Job replies with the question in ver. 17. According to this view ver. 16 corresponds exactly with ver. 19, where another explanation of the supposed case is similarly put into the mouth of the friends, and immediately answered by Job.

*The counsel of the wicked is far from me.* The words are actually used by Eliphaz in the next chapter, xxii. 18.

17. Bildad had maintained the orthodox doctrine declaring (after Proverbs xiii. 9; xxiv. 20) that 'the light of the wicked shall be put out...and his lamp above him shall be put out.' To this Job refers, and turns upon him with the four-fold question, *How oft is it that the lamp of the wicked is put out? that their calamity cometh upon them? that God distributeth sorrows in his anger? that they are*

*as stubble before the wind?* It is obvious that the answer expected is 'seldom or never'; and the A.V. by turning the sentence into an exclamation *How oft is the candle of the wicked put out!* entirely alters the meaning.

18. *That they are as stubble before the wind, and as chaff that the storm carrieth away.* Frequent figures expressive of God's vengeance upon sinners. See e.g. Pss. i. 4; xxxv. 5, and lxxxiii. 13. Thus Job's words are evidently intended to call in question the 'orthodox' doctrine of retribution, and to suggest that facts do not bear it out.

19. The first clause must certainly be taken (as in R.V.) as put into the mouth of the friends, being their suggestion in order to explain the apparent failure of the doctrine. The man himself may escape, but *God,* Who 'visiteth the sins of the fathers upon the children,' *layeth up his iniquity for his children.* To this Job replies that the sinner himself *ought* to bear the punishment of his own sin. When he is dead and gone, the fate of his children can be no concern of his. Thus he again arraigns the popular

20 Let his own eyes see his destruction,
And let him drink of the wrath of the Almighty.
21 For what pleasure hath he in his house after him,
When the number of his months is cut off in the midst?
22 Shall any teach God knowledge?
Seeing he judgeth those that are high.
23 One dieth in his full strength,
Being wholly at ease and quiet:
24 His ¹breasts are full of milk,
And the marrow of his bones is moistened.

¹ Or, *milk pails*

doctrine, and shows its unsatisfactory character, when taken too broadly, and applied as the explanation of the facts of life generally. Cf. Ezek. xviii., which shows how the doctrine that God visiteth the sins of the fathers upon the children was attracting attention and causing perplexity to thoughtful minds at the time of the Babylonish captivity.

*that he may know it*, i.e. *experience*, or *feel* it. Cf. Is. ix. 9; Hos. ix. 7.

20. *let him drink of the wrath of the Almighty.* For the figure of the cup of the wrath of the Lord cf. Pss. xi. 6; lxxv. 8; Jer. xxv. 15.

22—26. **Perplexity of the problem.** Job now asks with a touch of scorn, Is it for man to instruct God and to teach Him how to rule the world (22)? Plainly the method of His government is inscrutable by us. Here are the facts. To one man death comes after a vigorous life, spent in the enjoyment of ease and prosperity (23, 24). To another it is the close of a life of wretchedness and misery (25). Their lots in life are very different: and the only thing that they have in common is death (26).

The problem how to account for this still remains to perplex men as it did in Job's day.

'Who knows the inscrutable design?
Blessed be He Who took and gave:
Why should your mother, Charles, not mine,
Be weeping at her darling's grave?
We bow to heaven that will'd it so.
That darkly rules the fate of all,
That sends the respite or the blow,
That's free to give or to recall.

This crowns his feast with wine and wit:
Who brought him to that mirth and state?
His betters, see, below him sit,
Or hunger hopeless at the gate.
Who bade the mud from Dives' wheel
To spurn the rags of Lazarus?
Come, brother, in that dust we'll kneel,
Confessing heaven that ruled it thus.'
(*W. M. Thackeray.*)

22. *Seeing he judgeth those that are high.* The last word *those that are high* is used in 2 Sam. xxii. 28, for the haughty and proud possessors of power; and these may be referred to here. Or we may take it of the heavens and the dwellers in them. (Cf. Ps. lxxviii. 69, where the word is used of the heights of heaven.) If God judge these, shall man presume to instruct Him?

24. *His breasts*, a word of very doubtful meaning which occurs no-

25 And another dieth in bitterness of soul,
   And never tasteth of good.
26 They lie down alike in the dust,
   And the worm covereth them.
27 Behold, I know your thoughts,
   And the devices which ye wrongfully imagine against me.
28 For ye say, Where is the house of the prince?
   And where is the tent wherein the wicked dwelt?
29 Have ye not asked them that go by the way?
   And do ye not know their tokens?
30 That the evil man is ¹reserved to the day of calamity?
   That they are ²led forth to the day of wrath?

¹ Or, *spared in &c.*            ² Or, *led away in &c.*

where else. The LXX., Vulg. and Syriac take it of a man's *inward parts*, and hence the rendering of A.V. and R.V. The marginal rendering of R.V. *milk pails* is due to the Targum and Aben Ezra. In any case the general sense of the verse is clear enough.

25. Wise and foolish, strong and weak, are alike in death, 'one event happeneth to them all.' Cf. Eccl. ii. 14—16.

27—34. **Folly of the friends in their application of their doctrine to the case of Job himself.** He now turns on his friends and tells them plainly that he is perfectly aware of the way in which they mean their descriptions of the fate of the wicked to apply to him (27, 28). But anyone who had ever gone outside his own gate could point out to them instances which prove the falsity of their inferences (29); and could have shown them examples of sinners spared in the day of calamity (30); of wrongdoers who come off apparently scotfree (31); who die in the odour of sanctity, and find numberless admirers and imitators (32, 33). No wonder, then, that their 'consolations' have proved as vain as they are false (34)!

28. *the house of the prince.* Zophar had compared Job to some petty tyrant, who had violently oppressed the poor. See xx. 19. To this Job perhaps alludes, and the word for *prince* may possibly be taken in a bad sense, almost as *tyrant.*

29. *them that go by the way.* The same phrase is found in Pss. lxxx. 12; lxxxix. 41, where it means *passers by.* Here, however, it must be taken rather in the sense of *travellers*, to whose wide experience appeal is made.

*their tokens.* This must mean the signs, instances, or proofs which they bring forward as the ground of their assurances.

30. The margin of the R.V. gives what is apparently the true rendering of the verse: *that the evil man is spared in the day of calamity? that they are led away in the day of wrath?* The experience of travellers does not confirm the asser-

31 Who shall declare his way to his face?
   And who shall repay him what he hath done?
32 ¹Yet shall he be borne to the grave,
   And ²shall keep watch over the tomb.
33 The clods of the valley shall be sweet unto him,
   And all men shall draw after him,
   As there were innumerable before him.

¹ Or, *Moreover he is borne to the grave, and keepeth watch over his tomb.*
*The clods of the valley are sweet unto him; and all men draw &c.*
² Or, *they shall keep*

tion of the friends that sinners always meet with retribution. Rather it points to instances in which they are *spared* when calamity overwhelms others, and *led away* in safety, like just Lot, when some manifestation of God's wrath falls upon a guilty city. *Spared* : for the use of the word in this sense see 2 Kings v. 20, and (possibly) 2 Sam. xviii. 16. *Led away*. Cf. the use of the word in Is. lv. 12. The A.V. and R.V. (text), in taking the words as pointing to the fate which ultimately overtakes the sinner, follow in the main the LXX., Vulg. and Targ., but can hardly be correct.

31. *Who shall declare his way to his face? and who shall repay him what he hath done?* Two interpretations of these words are possible. (1) They may refer to the 'evil man' spoken of in the previous verse, the question being intended to imply that there is no one who dares to tell him his misdeeds to his face, or who can pay him back in his own coin. Or (2) they may refer to God, as if Job said almost parenthetically, 'Who can rise up against God, even when incomprehensible things happen?' But the former interpretation is preferable. Since the evil man is the subject

not only of verse 30 but also of verse 32, it is unnatural to take the intermediate verse of God.

32. The sinner who thus escapes the vengeance due to his sins in this life, is accorded an honourable funeral after his death. *He shall be borne to the grave*, and his tomb remains inviolate.

*And shall keep watch over the tomb.* The subject may be the indefinite 'one,' i.e. 'men shall keep watch,' in order to preserve it from desecration. Or the words may refer to the effigy of the deceased, carved on his sarcophagus, and regarded as thus keeping watch over his grave. The word for *tomb* occurs nowhere else in this sense (elsewhere the same form is used of a stack of sheaves, v. 26; Exod. xxii. 5; Judg. xv. 5), but the meaning may be supported from the Arabic.

33. *The clods of the valley shall be sweet unto him.* Davidson appropriately quotes Euripides, *Alcestis*, l. 462, κοῦφα σοι χθὼν ἐπάνω πέσειε γύναι, and the Latin, *Sit tibi terra levis*, 'Light fall the dust upon thee.'

*And all men shall draw after him, as there were innumerable before him*, i.e. the evil man shall

34  How then comfort ye me ¹in vain,
    Seeing in your answers there remaineth *only* ²falsehood?

¹ Or, *with vanity*                    ² Or, *faithlessness*

have countless followers and imitators, as he himself was only following the example of innumerable
predecessors in wickedness.    Cf.
Eccl. iv. 15, 16.

34.  *Seeing in your answers
there remaineth* only *falsehood,* i.e.
this is all that is left when the
truths which Job has stated so
vigorously have been subtracted.

Chapter **XXII.** begins the third debate or circle of speeches.  As in
the previous one Eliphaz begins, and the order of the speakers is as
follows :

(1)  Third speech of Eliphaz, xxii., with Job's answer, xxiii., xxiv.

(2)  Third speech of Bildad, xxv., with Job's answer, xxvi.

(3)  Twofold monologue of Job, in xxvii.—xxxi.

It will be seen from this that the third speech of Zophar is wanting.
Nor is this altogether surprising.  The friends have never been able to
make any advance upon the position which they took up in the first
instance.  This position Job has in the second debate completely demolished.  Not only has he risen to convictions which materially help him to
endure his hapless plight, but he has further destroyed the conclusion of
his friends, by showing that one of the premises on which it rested was
false.  Consequently in this third circle we are called to notice how the
friends are gradually silenced.  Eliphaz begins by charging Job with the
most terrible guilt, and by insisting once more that his calamities prove
that he *must* be a sinner.  To this Job replies by drawing a powerful
picture of the confusions of this world, and the misery and wrong-doing
which is allowed to continue without any interference on God's part.  In
answer to this Bildad can only stammer out a few words (xxv.), containing
nothing new, and merely repeating what Eliphaz has already said more
than once ; and then, after Job's brief reply (xxvi.), Zophar evidently has
nothing whatever to say, and, considering discretion to be the better part
of valour, he wisely holds his tongue, and leaves Job master of the field
to continue his utterance in the form of a monologue.

The debate really reached its climax in the second circle of speeches ;
and it must be admitted that as an ethical and psychological study this
third circle has less of interest.  Job's passion has largely spent itself, and
the assured position which he reached in xix. gives his words a calmer
tone, so that his *longing to find God* in xxiii. is expressed with great
pathos and tenderness, but with infinitely less of the vehemence and
tremendous force which we have noticed in his earlier utterances.  But if
the psychological interest is diminished, yet Job's greater calmness enables
him to give increased *artistic finish* to his utterances ; and in this third
circle of speeches we meet for the first time with elaborately worked up
pictures, exquisitely finished in every minute detail, like some old Flemish

painting, which from this time onward form a prominent feature of the
book.

**XXII.**  Third speech of Eliphaz.

Job at the close of the previous debate had openly arraigned the
doctrine of God's providence, and had brought forward the stubborn
evidence of facts to support his view that no system of perfect moral
government can be traced in the ordering of this world.  Eliphaz ignores
altogether this disproof of the theory which he and his friends have
advanced, and after an attempt to prove from the doctrine of God that it
*must* be because Job is a sinner that he is afflicted, having no facts of his
own to go upon, he proceeds to invent them, and enumerates the crimes
of which he considers Job to have been guilty.  He thus so far forgets
himself as to accuse his friend of wholesale cruelty and oppression, as well
as of an entire disregard of God.  But he has scarcely brought his
accusations before he seems to feel his own harshness, for his words
almost immediately take a gentler tone, and in a passage of great beauty
he exhorts Job to repentance, his last utterance ending (like his earliest
one) with an exquisite picture of the bright future that may yet be in store
for Job if he will only make his peace with God and put away his evil from
him.

The whole speech falls naturally into four divisions :

(1)  *The proof of Job's wickedness.*  1—5.

(2)  *Description of it in detail.*  6—11.

(3)  *Warning against the careless security of the wicked.*  12—20.

(4)  *Earnest appeal to Job to reconcile himself with God.*  21—30.

**XXII.**  1 Then answered Eliphaz the Temanite, and
said,

2 Can a man be profitable unto God?
Surely he that is wise is profitable unto himself.

3 Is it any pleasure to the Almighty, that thou art righteous?
Or is it gain *to him,* that thou makest thy ways perfect?

1—5.  **The proof of Job's wickedness.**  Eliphaz starts by asking
whether God has anything to gain
from Job, or whether his righteousness would bring God any profit?
He cannot be inflicting suffering
upon him simply on His own account, as if He would be advantaged
by it (1—3).  It is absurd to suppose
that He is chastising him because of

his piety (4).  Consequently the
only inference which remains is that
it is as a punishment for great sins
on his part (5).

2.  *Can a man be profitable
unto God?  Surely he that is wise
is profitable unto himself.*  Eliphaz
means to say that God is not really
affected by man's conduct.  He has
nothing to gain from his righteous-

4 Is it ¹for thy fear *of him* that he reproveth thee,
  That he entereth with thee into judgement?
5 Is not thy wickedness great?
  Neither is there any end to thine iniquities.
6 For thou hast taken pledges of thy brother for nought,
  And stripped the naked of their clothing.
7 Thou hast not given water to the weary to drink,
  And thou hast withholden bread from the hungry.
8 But as for ²the mighty man, he had the ³earth;
  And ⁴the honourable man, he dwelt in it.

¹ Or, *for fear of thee*     ² Heb. *the man of arm.*     ³ Or, *land*
⁴ Heb. *he whose person is accepted.*

ness, and nothing to lose by his sinfulness. A man's wisdom only affects and profits himself. Hence God's treatment of Job cannot possibly be affected by *personal* considerations of His own pleasure or advantage.

4. *Is it for thy fear* of him *that he reproveth thee?* The A.V. *'for fear of thee'* gives a wrong turn to the words. *Fear* here as often in the O.T. means piety or reverence. Cf. iv. 6, where as here 'thy fear *of God'* signifies 'thy religion.'

5. Job's sufferings must be due to his sins, and from the greatness of his sufferings the greatness of his wickedness may be inferred.

6—11. **Description of Job's wickedness in detail.** Eliphaz now proceeds to enumerate the kind of offences of which Job *must* have been guilty. Without a shadow of proof for his assertions he tells him to his face that he has oppressed the helpless (6) and refused to show the commonest humanity to those who were starving (7). He has treated the whole land as belonging to him alone (8), and has despised and ill-treated the widow and the

orphan (9). It is for such sins as these that he is overwhelmed by terrors and calamities, and immersed in darkness and affliction (10, 11).

6. *for nought,* i.e. without cause, or undeservedly. See what Job himself says of the violent on this subject in his reply, xxiv. 3, 'they take the widow's ox for a pledge,' and 9, 'they take a pledge of the poor.' For the provisions of the law which regulated the taking of pledges see Exod. xxii. 26, 27; Deut. xxiv. 6, 17. It was expressly laid down that the widow's raiment was not to be taken in pledge; and in any case if a neighbour's garment was thus taken it was to be restored before sundown. In clause *b* Eliphaz probably means to suggest that Job has disregarded such merciful provisions as these. *Thou hast stripped the naked of their clothing.* Job answers this outrageous charge in xxxi. 19, 20.

7. Cf. Isaiah lviii. 7, 10, and see Job's answer in xxxi. 17.

8. Eliphaz apparently means to charge Job with adding house to house, and laying field to field (cf. Isaiah v. 8), and selfishly taking

9 Thou hast sent widows away empty,
  And the arms of the fatherless have been broken.
10 Therefore snares are round about thee,
  And sudden fear troubleth thee,
11 ¹Or darkness, that thou canst not see,
  And abundance of waters cover thee.
12 Is not God in the height of heaven?
  And behold the ²height of the stars, how high they are!
13 And thou sayest, What doth God know?
  Can he judge through the thick darkness?

¹ Or, *Or dost thou not see the darkness, and the flood of waters that covereth thee?*
² Heb. *head.*

possession of the whole land. 'The mighty man' (literally *the man of arm*) and 'the honourable man' (literally *he whose person is accepted*) are evidently intended to apply to Job himself.

9. 'The widow and the orphan' are frequently given as examples of those who have no power to help themselves, in whose case therefore oppression becomes peculiarly hard-hearted. Cf. Deut. xxvii. 19; Jer. vii. 6; xxii. 3.

*the arms of the fatherless have been broken.* 'The arms' here stand as a symbol of their strength, or resources. With this charge of Eliphaz contrast Job's own description of his treatment of such persons, xxix. 12, 13; xxxi. 16—18.

10. It is for such conduct as this that Job's calamities have over-whelmed him.

*snares.* The word is used in the same way in Ps. xi. 6, 'Upon the ungodly he shall rain snares'; and for the combination of 'snares' (Heb. *pachim*) and 'fear' (*pachad*) see Isaiah xxiv. 17.

11. The margin of the R.V. should probably be followed: *Or*

*dost thou not see the darkness, and the flood of waters that covereth thee? Dost thou not see,* i.e. 'dost thou not comprehend,' or 'under-stand the meaning of.' Darkness and waterfloods are common images of calamity. Cf. xxvii. 20. The last clause of this verse occurs again in xxxviii. 34.

12—20. **Warning against the careless security of the wicked.** Does Job imagine that since God dwells in the height of heaven He is too far removed to take cognizance of the affairs of men, and that He cannot see through the thick clouds beneath His feet (12—14)? Let him not copy the example of those wicked men of old who argued in this fashion, and who were pre-maturely swept away in the Deluge (15, 16), men who had bidden good-bye to God altogether in spite of all the blessings He had showered upon them (17, 18 *a*). For himself Eliphaz will repudiate such thoughts and counsels, counting himself among the righteous who exult when their oppressors are destroyed (18 *b*—20).

13. *What doth God know?* Cf.

14 Thick clouds are a covering to him, that he seeth not ;
   And he walketh ¹in the circuit of heaven.
15 ²Wilt thou keep the old way
   Which wicked men have trodden ?
16 Who were snatched away before their time,
   Whose foundation was poured out as a stream :
17 Who said unto God, Depart from us ;
   And, What can the Almighty do ³for ⁴us ?
18 Yet he filled their houses with good things :
   But the counsel of the wicked is far from me.
19 The righteous see it, and are glad ;
   And the innocent laugh them to scorn :
20 *Saying*, Surely they that did rise up against us are cut off,
   And ⁵the remnant of them the fire hath consumed.

¹ Or, *on the vault*      ² Or, *Dost thou mark*      ³ Or, *to*      ⁴ Heb. *them*.
    ⁵ Or, *that which remained to them*  Or, *their abundance*

Ps. xciv. 7, 'And they say, The Lord shall not see, neither shall the God of Jacob consider.' It is just the same kind of unbelief which Eliphaz here attributes to Job.

*thick darkness.* The word is the same that is used of the 'thick darkness where God was' at Sinai, Exod. xx. 21. Cf. Deut. iv. 11; 1 Kings viii. 12; Ps. xviii. 9.

14. *in the circuit of heaven*: perhaps, with R.V. marg. *on the vault of heaven*. The word for 'circuit' or 'vault' is only found again in Prov. viii. 27, and Is. xl. 22.

16. To his rebuke of Job's supposed disregard of God Eliphaz adds a warning reminding him of the fate of the antediluvians. Cf. 2 Pet. iii. 4. The allusion in this and the following verses is probably to the sinners before the Flood rather than to the destruction of the cities of the plain, as Ewald supposes.

17. *Who said unto God, Depart from us.* Cf. xxi. 14.

*And, What can the Almighty do for us?* Better (as R.V. marg.) *to us*. The Hebrew has *them* instead of *us*. But this is probably a clerical error. The LXX. reads ἡμῖν, *us*.

18. *But the counsel of the wicked is far from me.* In repudiating all sympathy with such sinners Eliphaz adopts the words already used by Job in xxi. 16, where see note.

19. The exultation of the righteous at the fate of sinners is a thought which meets us frequently in the Old Testament, e.g. Pss. lii. 6; lviii. 10. It belongs to an early stage in the development of moral character.

20. *the remnant of them.* Rather *that which remained to them* or *their abundance*, i.e. their possessions, as in Ps. xvii. 14, where the word occurs again. So R.V. marg. The A.V. entirely misses the meaning of the whole verse.

21 Acquaint now thyself with him, and be at peace :
[1]Thereby good shall come unto thee.

22 Receive, I pray thee, [2]the law from his mouth,
And lay up his words in thine heart.

23 If thou return to the Almighty, thou shalt be built up ;
[3]If thou put away unrighteousness far from thy tents.

24 And lay thou *thy* [4]treasure [5]in the dust,
And *the gold of* Ophir among the stones of the brooks ;

---

[1] Or, as otherwise read, *Thereby shall thine increase be good.*
[2] Or, *instruction*     [3] Or, *Thou shalt put away...and shalt lay up*
[4] Heb. *ore.*     [5] Or, *on the earth*

**21—30. Earnest appeal to Job to reconcile himself with God.** In these verses Eliphaz finally takes leave of his friend with an earnest exhortation to him to make his peace with God (21), making a threefold appeal to Job, i. that he should receive God's teaching (22); ii. that he should turn to God and put away his evil from him (23); and iii. that he should set his heart on no earthly thing (24). If he will do this, then God will prove Himself to be his richest treasure (25), for all Job's prayers shall be heard and granted (26, 27): his purpose shall be established, and he shall walk in the light of God's favour (28). Should he be momentarily cast down, he shall be raised up again, and his pious intercessions shall avail mightily for others, even for sinners (29, 30).

21. *Thereby good shall come unto thee.* The form of the word for *shall come unto thee* is irregular, and is probably due to corruption of the text. A very slight change of pointing gives *thereby thine increase shall be good.* So the margin of the R.V. after the LXX.

22. *Receive, I pray thee, the law from his mouth.* Interesting as being the only occurrence of the word *law* (tôrah) in the whole book, though there can be no possible allusion to the Mosaic law in it. It is simply divine instruction of which Eliphaz speaks.

23. *thou shalt be built up,* i.e. *restored,* or *established.* Cf. the use of the same word in Jer. xii. 16, 'If they will diligently learn the ways of my people...then *shall they be built up* in the midst of my people.'

24. *treasure.* The word is only found in this and the following verse (unless it should also be read in Ps. lxviii. 30). Apparently it properly means *precious ore.* The versions give no help.

*And* the gold of *Ophir among the stones of the brooks.* The italics in the English versions show that there is no word in the original for *the gold. Ophir,* the name of the place (probably in Arabia), is here used for the fine gold which was brought thence to Palestine. Cf. xxviii. 16; 1 Kings ix. 28; Isaiah xiii. 12; Ps. xlv. 9.

The whole verse is an exhortation to Job to cast away his earthly treasures as things of no value.

25 And the Almighty shall be thy [1]treasure,
   And [2]precious silver unto thee.
26 For then shalt thou delight thyself in the Almighty,
   And shalt lift up thy face unto God.
27 Thou shalt make thy prayer unto him, and he shall hear
      thee ;
   And thou shalt pay thy vows.
28 Thou shalt also decree a thing, and it shall be established
      unto thee ;
   And light shall shine upon thy ways.
29 When they [3]cast *thee* down, thou shalt say, *There is* lifting
      up ;
   And [4]the humble person he shall save.
30 He shall deliver [5]*even* him that is not innocent :

[1] Heb. *ore.*　　[2] Or, *precious silver shall be thine*
[3] Or, *are made low*　　[4] Heb. *him that is lowly of eyes.*
[5] Many ancient versions read, *him that is innocent.*

25. If he does so, *then* (better than *and*) *the Almighty shall be thy treasure, and precious silver unto thee.* The word rendered *precious* is of very doubtful meaning. It is only found again in Numb. xxiii. 22; xxiv. 8, where R.V. has '*strength* (marg. *horns*) of the wild ox'; and Ps. xcv. 4, '*the heights* (marg. *strength*) of the mountains are his also.' Possibly in the passage before us the word means *heaps* or *bars* (=ingots).

26. *And shalt lift up thy face unto God*; the phrase denotes the glad confident look of conscious rectitude, as in xi. 15; cf. 2 Sam. ii. 22.

27. *And thou shalt pay thy vows.* Cf. Ps. l. 14.

28. *Thou shalt also decree a thing.* The verb is found nowhere else with the meaning of *decree.* It is apparently one of the Aramaisms of the book which may point to a comparatively late date

for its composition. See the Introduction, p. xxi.

29. A difficult verse. The Hebrew word for *lifting up* occurs again only in xxxiii. 17 and Jer. xiii. 17, in both which passages it means *pride.* Hence it may be given the same meaning here. So Driver, after Hitzig, would render *When they have humbled thee, and thou sayest* (i.e. complainest), *Pride, He will save him that is lowly of eyes* (i.e. Job himself); as much as to say, 'If thou art humble, God will defend thee, when the proud seek to bring thee down.'

30. Even sinners shall be delivered through the intercession of the penitent and now upright Job. An unconscious prophecy of what actually happened in the end. Cf. xlii. 8. The curious rendering of the A.V. *the island of the innocent* is easily explained, for the negative particle here used is a most unusual one in Biblical Hebrew (occurring

Yea, he shall be delivered through the cleanness of thine hands.

again only in 1 Sam. iv. 21 in the name *Ichabod,* i.e. no glory or inglorious), and is identical in form with the word for *island.* With this utterance we take leave of Eliphaz, who never speaks again. There is something pathetic in the picture of this good man, so earnest in his endeavour to help his friend, so sure of his own position, and capable of uttering such real truths in language of great beauty, and yet so utterly unable to conceive of any truths beyond those contained in his own Shibboleths, and the formulæ in the use of which he has grown up. It is pleasant to feel that he ends his last speech, like his first, in a tone of gentleness.

**XXIII., XXIV.**   Job's answer to Eliphaz.

Eliphaz had urged Job to 'acquaint himself with God' and thus find peace (xxii. 21). To this Job replies by a pathetic complaint of the impossibility of 'finding' God. He renews his former lamentation, and declares that there is no possibility for him to approach God since God has determined to destroy him. He can trace no moral rule in God's dealings with him, and when (xxiv.) he looks out from himself on the world at large there too there is nothing but confusion and disorder; no rule of righteous retribution, such as the friends had spoken of, is discernible. They may talk of the short-lived prosperity of the wicked, and of the swift fate that overtakes him, but facts, stubborn facts, give the lie to their contention.

The speech as a whole may be divided as follows:

(1) *Job's answer to the appeal of Eliphaz: his longing to find God.* xxiii. 1—7.

(2) *The ~~hopeless~~ impossibility of finding Him.*   8—12.

(3) *The reason for this: God's determination to destroy him.* 13—17.

(4) *Proof from facts that no moral rule is discernible in the government of the world at large.* xxiv.

**XXIII.**   1 Then Job answered and said,

**XXIII.** 1—7. **Job's answer to the appeal of Eliphaz: his longing to find God.** Job begins by complaining that his complaint is counted as rebellion, and that God's hand weighs heavy upon him (1, 2). He longs to find Him, and plead his cause before Him and argue it out with Him (3—5); for he is sure that if only he could come face to face with Him, God would not overwhelm him with His might but would listen to his vindication, and suffer him to establish his innocence (6, 7).

The thought in these verses is much the same as that which we have met with before, especially in ix. and xiii., but it is here expressed with far less passion and bitterness of feeling. Thus the effect of the assured position reached in xix. is clearly manifested. See p. 102.

2 Even to-day is my complaint ¹rebellious :
  ²My stroke is heavier than my groaning.
3 Oh that I knew where I might find him,
  That I might come even to his seat !
4 I would order my cause before him,
  And fill my mouth with arguments.
5 I would know the words which he would answer me,
  And understand what he would say unto me.
6 Would he contend with me in the greatness of his power?
  Nay ; ³but he would give heed unto me.
7 There the upright might reason with him ;
  So should I be delivered for ever from my judge.

¹ Or, *bitter*  Or, accounted *rebellion*
² Or, *My hand is heavy upon* (or *because of*)  The Sept. and Syr. read, *His hand.*
³ Or, *he would only give heed*

2. *Even to-day is my complaint rebellious.* If the text is correct this is the only possible translation ; and the words must mean that his expostulations with God are counted as rebellion against Him. But a very slight change would enable us to read *bitter* for *rebellious*, with the A.V. and R.V. marg. after the Vulgate. Cf. vii. 11, 'I will complain in the bitterness of my soul.'

*My stroke is heavier than my groaning.* This translation is hardly possible. The word rendered *stroke* means properly *hand* ; and the translators of the English versions have taken it as meaning *a blow from the hand* ; thus '*my stroke*' means *the blow from God's hand upon me.* But there is little doubt that the text is faulty, and that instead of *my hand* we should read *his hand* with the LXX. and Syriac ; and render the whole clause *his hand is heavy upon* (or *because of*) *my groaning.* For God's hand as 'heavy upon' someone see Ps. xxxii. 4, and cf. 1 Sam. v. 6, 11.

3. *seat.* The word is found here only in this sense. It appears to mean *fixed dwelling-place.*

6. *Would he contend with me in the greatness of his power?* Cf. ix. 19, 34; xiii. 21. Job here repeats the thought to which he has more than once given expression, and urges that God should not crush him by His irresistible power, but listen patiently while he pleads his cause.

*Nay; but he would give heed unto me.* For the use of the verb in this sense see iv. 20. The A.V. (*put* strength *in me*) is quite incorrect.

7. *There the upright might reason with him. There,* i.e. in that case (if God would give heed) an upright man would be disputing with him (the 'upright man' being of course Job himself), and the result would be what Job has all along been convinced would follow, viz. *so should I be delivered for ever from my judge.*

8  Behold, I go forward, but he is not *there*;
   And backward, but I cannot perceive him:
9  On the left hand, when he doth work, but I cannot behold
   him:
   He ¹hideth himself on the right hand, that I cannot see
   him.
10 ²But he knoweth ³the way that I take;
   When he hath tried me, I shall come forth as gold.
11 My foot hath held fast to his steps;
   His way have I kept, and turned not aside.
12 I have not gone back from the commandment of his lips;
   I have treasured up the words of his mouth ⁴more than
   my ⁵necessary food.

¹ Or, *turneth himself to...him, but*        ² Or, *For*        ³ Heb. *the way* that is
*with me.*        ⁴ Or, *more than my own law*  The Sept. and Vulgate have, *in my*
*bosom.*        ⁵ Or, *portion*  See Prov. xxx. 8.

**8—12. The hopeless impossibility of finding God.** Job has expressed his longing to find God and plead his cause with him, but he is at once overcome by the thought of the impossibility of doing so. He may search in one direction or another, North, South, East, or West, but wherever it may be, God hides Himself from him (8, 9). And yet God Himself knows perfectly well that Job is innocent, that he has not turned aside from the right way (10, 11), nor forsaken God's commandments, but rather has treasured up His words (12).

8. *Behold, I go forward...and backward.* Cf. Ps. cxxxix. 5, 'Thou hast beset me behind and before,' where the words for 'behind' and 'before' are the same as those used here. But since the word for *forward* is often used for *the East*, which the Hebrews regularly regarded as in front of them, it is possible that the four words here rendered *forward, backward, on*

the *left hand, on the right hand*, may refer to East and West, North and South. For *the right hand* as signifying the South see Ps. lxxxix. 12; and cf. Ezek. xvi. 46, where on the left and right hands are respectively the North and South.

10. *When he hath tried me, I shall come forth as gold.* Perhaps, as Davidson, *If he tried me, I should come forth as gold.* The words are almost parenthetical, as if Job felt that God refused him access to Him, because He knew that if He tried him, he would come forth as gold. See Davidson's note.

11, 12. These verses describe *the way* which Job takes and which God knows so well.

12. *I have treasured up the words of his mouth more than my necessary food.* The last words of this clause are difficult. *More than my necessary food* represent a single word in Hebrew made up of a preposition, a substantive and

13 But ¹he is in one *mind*, and who can turn him?
   And what his soul desireth, even that he doeth.
14 For he performeth that which is appointed for me :
   And many such things are with him.
15 Therefore am I troubled at his presence ;
   When I consider, I am afraid of him.
16 For God hath made my heart faint,
   And the Almighty hath troubled me :
17 ²Because I was not cut off before the darkness,
   Neither did he cover the thick darkness from my face.

¹ Or, *he is one*     ² Or, *For I am not dismayed because of the darkness,*
*nor because thick darkness covereth my face*

a pronoun. The substantive is used for a *prescribed portion* or *allowance of food* in Gen. xlvii. 22; Prov. xxxi. 15 (cf. xxx. 8); Ezek. xvi. 27. Hence A.V. and R.V. Its commoner meaning is *statute* or *enactment*. Hence the margin of the R.V. *more than my own law.* Neither meaning, however, seems quite natural here. A very slight change would enable us to follow the LXX. (ἐν δὲ κόλπῳ μου) and Vulgate (in sinu meo) and render 'I have treasured up the words of his mouth *in my bosom*' (cf. xix. 27). This gives an excellent sense and is adopted by many moderns.

**13—17. The reason why he cannot find God is that God has determined to destroy him.** When God has made up His mind there is no turning Him from His purpose ; and this persecution of him to the death is only one instance of His performing what He has determined (13, 14). Therefore Job is disturbed and affrighted, because it is *God* Who is troubling him and making him faint (15, 16). It is this rather than the calamity itself and his own suffering, which tries him so sorely (17).

13. *But he is in one* mind, *and who can turn him?* The general sense is clear but the actual translation of the first words is doubtful. The R.V. margin has 'He is one': and the clause may mean that God is alone and unapproachable (Vulg. Ipse enim solus est), and therefore acts as He pleases uninfluenced by men. For the expression *Who can turn him?* see ix. 12.

14. *For he performeth that which is appointed for me*, i.e. in bringing these calamities upon Job God is simply carrying out a predestined decree.

*And many such things are with him*, i.e. it is only one instance out of many of God's arbitrary and inscrutable action.

16. The emphasis rests on God. It is because *God* is the author of his calamities that Job is so disturbed and distressed.

17. *Because I was not cut off before the darkness, neither did he cover the thick darkness from my face.* Better with the margin of the R.V. *For I am not dismayed because of the darkness, nor because thick darkness covereth my face.* Job means to say that it is not the

**XXIV.** 1 ¹Why are times not laid up by the Almighty?
And why do not they which know him see his days?
2 There are that remove the landmarks;
They violently take away flocks, and feed them.
3 They drive away the ass of the fatherless,
They take the widow's ox for a pledge.

¹ Or, *Why is it, seeing times are not hidden from the Almighty, that they which know him see not his days?*

darkness of his present lot which in itself disturbs him so : but rather the fact that it is *God* Who brings it upon him. *Darkness* as so often in this book is a figure for calamity. Cf. v. 14; xii. 25; xix. 8; xxii. 11.

**XXIV. The proof from facts that no moral rule is discernible in the government of the world at large.** The proof which Job now proceeds to give that the government of the world is not carried on in accordance with the moral rule which his friends claimed for it is given with great fulness and elaborateness of detail. The stages of it are clearly marked, as follows.

(*a*) *description of the evil doings of the tyrants.* 1—4.

(*b*) *the miserable plight of the poor.* 5—8.

(*c*) *renewed description of the oppressors and oppressed.* 9—12.

(*d*) *description of other kinds of sinners.* 13—17.

(*e*) *the fate of these men is nothing different from the fate of others.* 18—25.

**1—4. Description of the evil doings of the tyrants.** Why is it, asks Job, that God does not appoint a set time for the manifestation of His judgment upon sinners, and thus exercise His righteous rule (1)?

The wickedness of men cries out for such a judgment, for oppressors are everywhere riding rough-shod over the rights of the poor and helpless. They seize their flocks and herds, and compel them to seek a refuge in the recesses of the land (2—4).

1. *Why are times not laid up by the Almighty? and why do not they which know him see his days?* (The A.V. in this verse is quite wrong.) The *times* are the set times for judgment, as the *days* are those of God's manifesting Himself to right the wrong; and Job's complaint is that there is no sign that these are appointed by God.

2. *There are that remove the landmarks* : a sin forbidden in the Mosaic law (see Deut. xix. 14; xxvii. 17) but evidently common in ancient Israel. Cf. Hos. v. 10; Prov. xxii. 28.

*They violently take away flocks, and feed them,* i.e. adding insult to injury, when they have forcibly carried off the flocks of the poor, they proceed to pasture them openly in the sight of their true owners. The A.V. *feed thereof* gives a wrong turn to the clause.

3. *They drive away the ass of the fatherless, they take the widow's ox for a pledge.* Cf. the question of Samuel, 'Whose ox have I taken? or whose ass have I taken?'

4 They turn the needy out of the way :
   The ¹poor of the earth hide themselves together.
5 Behold, as wild asses in the desert
   They go forth to their work, seeking diligently for ²meat ;
   The wilderness *yieldeth* them food for their children.
6 They cut ³their provender in the field ;
   And they glean the vintage of the wicked.
7 They lie all night naked without clothing,
   And have no covering in the cold.

¹ Or, *meek*     ² Heb. *prey*.     ³ Or, *his*

1 Sam. xii. 3.  For the 'fatherless'
and the 'widow' see on xxii. 9 ; and
for 'pledge' see xxii. 6.

   **4.**  *They turn the needy out of
the way.*  See Amos v. 12, where a
similar phrase occurs : 'that turn
aside the needy in the gate from
their right,' and cf. Is. x. 2.

   *The poor of the earth hide them-
selves together.*  For the *poor of the
earth* cf. Amos viii. 4 ; Zeph. ii. 3 ;
Is. xi. 4 ; Ps. lxxvi. 9.  They *hide
themselves* from these oppressors in
dens and caves of the earth ; cf.
xxx. 6.

   **5—8.  The miserable plight of
the poor.**  These hapless 'poor of
the earth' are driven forth like wild
asses to seek their food in the
desert (5), content with a provender
fit only for beasts, and with the
gleanings of the rich oppressor's
vintage (6).  The poor wretches
with little or no clothing are exposed by night to the cold, and to
the drenching rain ; and forced to
huddle up against the rock for
shelter from the fury of the storm
(7, 8).

   It seems tolerably clear that in
this passage, and again in xxx. 1—8,
we have a description of the Aborigines who had been dispossessed
by a race of conquerors, who drove

them into caves and holes of the
earth, where they dragged out a
miserable existence, scarcely able to
support themselves or to provide
the barest necessities of life.  There
are traces of the existence of such
races in various parts of the Old
Testament ; see especially the reference to the Horites (probably 'cave-
dwellers'), the original inhabitants
of Seir who were dispossessed by
the Edomites, in Deut. ii. 12, 22,
and cf. 1 Sam. xiii. 6, which shows
the plight to which the Israelites
themselves were reduced during the
oppression of the Philistines.

   **5.**  *They go forth to their work* :
what the *work* is, is explained in
the following words, *seeking diligently for meat.*

   **6.**  *They cut their provender in
the field*, cf. xxx. 4.  The word
for *provender* is only found elsewhere in vi. 5 ; Is. xxx. 24 ; in each
case of the *fodder* for cattle.  It is
probably designedly used here to
indicate the character of the food
with which these miserable creatures
had to be content.

   *they glean the vintage of the
wicked.*  The words probably mean
nothing more than that they get
what they can from the neglected
gleanings of the oppressor's vin-

8 They are wet with the showers of the mountains,
And embrace the rock for want of a shelter.
9 There are that pluck the fatherless from the breast,
And ¹take a pledge of the poor :
10 *So that* they go about naked without clothing,
And being an-hungred they carry the sheaves ;
11 They make oil within the walls of these men ;
They tread *their* winepresses, and suffer thirst.
12 From out of the ²populous city men groan,
And the soul of the wounded crieth out :
Yet God imputeth it not for folly.

¹ Or, *take in pledge that which is on the poor*     ² Heb. *city of men.*

tage ; though from the verb used (lit. *to gather late fruit*) Delitzsch argues that 'the rich man prudently hesitates to employ these poor people as vintagers ; but makes use of their labour to gather the straggling grapes which ripen late, and were therefore left at the vintage season.'

8. *the showers of the mountains.* The word is a strong one, and would be better rendered by *storms.*

*And embrace the rock for want of a shelter* : a forcible description of the way in which they huddle up against the rock to escape the fury of the storm to which they are exposed.

**9—12. Renewed description of the oppressors and oppressed.** The cruel oppressors pluck the orphan from the widow's breast, and take in pledge the poor man's clothing, so that he is reduced to go about his work naked and starving (9, 10): and thus he has to labour in the tyrant's wine and oil presses (11). The cry of the sufferers goes up to heaven, but God gives no sign of caring (12).

The allusion in these verses appears to be to the state of some who were reduced to a condition of serfdom and enforced labour, like the Gibeonites ; cf. Josh. ix. 27.

9. The R.V. makes it clear that another set of persons from those just described is spoken of here. *There are that pluck the fatherless from the breast.* Correct the A.V. which fails to indicate this.

*And take a pledge of the poor.* The construction is difficult on account of the preposition *upon* which stands in the original before *the poor.* The words may mean either (1) *they take pledges* (and so get power) *over the poor,* or (2) *they take in pledge* (that which is) *on the poor,* i.e. his clothing. So R.V. marg. This suits best with the following clause, 'so that *they go about naked without clothing,*' and see the note on xxii. 6.

10. *And being an-hungred they carry the sheaves.* Correct the A.V. 'The point lies in the antithesis between *hungry* and *carry sheaves* ; though labouring amidst the abundant harvest of their masters they are faint with hunger themselves.' Davidson.

12. *From out of the populous*

13 These are of them that rebel against the light ;
  They know not the ways thereof,
  Nor abide in the paths thereof.
14 The murderer riseth with the light, he killeth the poor
      and needy ;
  And in the night he is as a thief.
15 The eye also of the adulterer waiteth for the twilight,
  Saying, No eye shall see me :
  And he ¹disguiseth his face.
16 In the dark they dig through houses :
  ²They shut themselves up in the day-time ;
  They know not the light.

  ¹ Or, *putteth a covering on his face*
  ² Or, Which *they had marked for themselves*

*city men groan.* The Hebrew has *from out of the city of men.* But in Deut. ii. 34; iii. 6, and (prob.) Judg. xx. 48, where the same phrase *city of men* occurs, it means the male population (the city so far as it consisted of men, see Driver on Deuteronomy, p. 44), a meaning which is not suitable here: and it is best to read with some Hebrew MSS. and the Syriac, *from out of the city dying men groan,* which furnishes an exact parallel to *the soul of the wounded crieth out* in the next clause.

*Yet God imputeth it not for folly.* See the note on i. 22 for the meaning of the word *folly.*

**13—17. A description of other kinds of sinners.** There are also sinners who hate the light and shun it (13), as the murderer (14), the adulterer (15), and the housebreaker (16). All these love darkness, and fear the light as the gloom of death (17).

**13.** *These are of them that rebel against the light.* The words introduce the description of a new class of sinners. *The light* is the light of the sun, but there is undoubtedly a reference to spiritual light as well. They 'love darkness rather than light because their deeds are evil.'

**14.** *The murderer riseth with the light,* i.e. in the earliest dawn, while it is still half dark.

*he is as a thief,* i.e. he acts the thief.

**15.** *he disguiseth his face.* Rather (as R.V. marg.) *he putteth a covering on his face.* With this verse cf. Prov. vii. 9.

**16.** *In the dark they dig through houses.* This verse refers to another sin, viz. that of house-breaking and burglary. In the East where whole villages consist of houses built entirely of unburned brick, made by tramping up the soil into thick mud mixed with straw, to 'dig through the wall' is not a difficult process. Cf. Ezek. viii. 8; xii. 3; and S. Matthew vi. 19, 'where thieves break through (lit. *dig through*) and steal.' See Thomson, *The Land and the Book,* p. 544.

*They shut themselves up in the*

17 For the morning is to all of them as the shadow of death ;
  For they know the terrors of the shadow of death.

*daytime* : literally *by day they seal
up for themselves* ; i.e. according to
most (as R.V.) the burglars shut
themselves up by day ; so in the
parallel clause 'they know not the
light.' Some however render the
clause as the A.V. and R.V. marg.
*Which they have marked* (lit. *sealed*)
*for themselves in the daytime*; while
the rendering of the LXX. ἡμέρας
ἐσφράγισαν ἑαυτοῖς (so C, but B and
others ἑαυτούς) has suggested to
Siegfried to read *days* for *by day*
which would give the meaning *they
seal up days to themselves*, i.e. the
daytime is to them as it were sealed
up and disused.

17. To these men morning brings
terrors, and inward darkness like the
shadow of death.   Cox aptly quotes
from Shakespeare the lines

'Then thieves and robbers range
   abroad unseen
In murders and in outrage...
But when from under this terrestrial
   ball
He fires the proud tops of the
   Eastern pines,
And darts his light through every
   guilty hole,
Then murders, treason, and detested
   sins,
The cloak of night being pluck'd
   from off their backs,
Stand bare and naked, trembling at
   themselves.'
   *Richard II.* Act III. Scene II.

18—25.  The fate of these men
is nothing different from the fate
of others.  The friends may urge
that the sinner is speedily swept
away like a straw on the face of the
stream, that his fields are under
God's curse so that he can no longer

visit them with pleasure (18), they
may quote the proverb that the
sinner is consumed in Hades as the
snow vanishes in summer (19); they
may maintain that his fate is to be
destroyed by worms, while he is forgotten on earth even by the mother
who bare him, and that the oppress-
or and his sin are destroyed together
(20, 21); but as a matter of fact God
upholds these mighty men, and even
when they have thought that their
end was coming, they rise up as strong
as ever (22).  God makes them to be
secure and at ease, as He watches
over their ways (23).   They are exalted—and if the friends maintain
that it is only for a moment and
that they are soon cut off, the
answer is that they are only brought
low just as all others are, sharing
the common lot of men, and that
they are only cut off like ripe ears
of corn and not prematurely (24):
and, says Job in conclusion, prove
me a liar, if you can (25)!

There is a difficulty about this
passage because verses 18—21 and
22—25 appear to give two entirely
different accounts of the fate of
the wicked.  In the first part it is
maintained that a righteous retribution speedily overtakes them, which
is the very point which the friends
have all along urged, and which Job
has directly traversed in chapter
xxi, while in the latter part (22—25)
it is shown that their fate is no
worse than that of others, or rather
that they are exceptionally prosperous in life.  It is impossible to
think that *both* explanations are Job's
own, and so there can be little doubt
that in the first part (18—21) he

18 ¹He is swift upon the face of the waters ;
　　Their portion is cursed in the earth :
　　He turneth not by the way of the vineyards.
19 Drought and heat ²consume the snow waters :
　　*So doth* ³Sheol *those which* have sinned.
20 The womb shall forget him ; the worm shall feed sweetly
　　　on him ;
　　He shall be no more remembered :
　　And unrighteousness shall be broken ⁴as a tree.
21 He devoureth the barren that beareth not ;
　　And doeth not good to the widow.

---

¹ Or, Ye say, *He is &c.*　　　² Heb. *violently take away.*
³ Or, *the grave*　　　⁴ Or, *as a tree ; even he that devoureth &c.*

---

is quoting a sort of summary of the arguments of the friends and giving the popular view (so the margin of the R.V.); and then in verses 22—25 he turns round upon them and gives his own view of the matter. Cf. xxi. 16, where a somewhat similar instance of a quotation of the friends' arguments is found with nothing to indicate that it is a quotation, and see below on xxvii. 7.

18. In order to make it clear that Job is quoting the opinion of others it is necessary either to put these verses (18—21) within inverted commas, or to render with the margin of the R.V. 'Ye say, *He is swift &c.*'

*upon the face of the waters.* The sinner is compared to a straw or twig carried rapidly down the stream. A similar comparison is found in Hos. x. 7, 'As for Samaria, her king is cut off as foam (*or* twigs) upon the water.' Cf. also xx. 28.

*He turneth not by the way of the vineyards.* His 'portion,' i.e. his estate or property being cursed by God, he no longer visits and contemplates with pleasure the smiling vineyards. 'The general meaning of the phrase is the converse of that expressed by "Sitting under his vine and figtree," 1 Kings iv. 25 ; Micah iv. 4.' Davidson.

19. This verse evidently contains some popular proverb illustrating from the melting of the snow in summer, the fate of the sinner, who disappears in Hades.

20. Even the mother that bare him shall forget him.

*as a tree.* Cf. xix. 10, 'He hath broken me down on every side, and I am gone : and mine hope hath he plucked up as a tree.'

21. Render, with the margin of the R.V., in close connexion with the previous verse : *even he that devoureth the barren that beareth not, and doeth not good to the widow.* The *barren that beareth not*, as in Isaiah liv. 1, is the representative of the lonely and helpless, along with the widow, for whom cf. xxii. 9.

22 ¹He draweth away the mighty also by his power :
   He riseth up, and no man is sure of life.
23 *God* giveth them to be in security, and they rest thereon ;
   ²And his eyes are upon their ways.
24 They are exalted ; yet a little while, and they are gone ;
   ³Yea, they are brought low, they are ⁴taken out of the
      way as all other,
   And are cut off as the tops of the ears of corn.
25 And if it be not so now, who will prove me a liar,
   And make my speech nothing worth ?

¹ Or, *Yet God by his power maketh the mighty to continue : they rise up,
when they believed not that they should live*
     ² Or, *But*     ³ Or, *And when they are &c.*     ⁴ Or, *gathered in*

22. *He draweth away the mighty also by his power: he riseth up, and no man is sure of life.* This, which is the translation of both A.V. and R.V., takes the verse as continuing the description of the wicked man from 21. But it is far better to take it with the margin of the R.V. as the commencement of a fresh description of his fate, and to render, *Yet God by his power maketh the mighty to continue; they rise up when they believed not that they should live.* This describes the sinner as exceptionally prosperous, and as flourishing again, even though he had despaired of life.

23. *And his eyes are upon their ways,* i.e. He regards them with favour and kindness, which is the general meaning of the expression to 'set the eyes on' someone. See Deut. xi. 12 ; Pss. xxxiii. 18 ; xxxiv. 15.

24. *They are exalted; yet a*

*little while, and they are gone* : Job seems here once more to quote the popular view almost as if, after saying that *they are exalted,* he was interrupted by one of the friends with the objection that after all it was only for a moment, *Yet a little while and they are gone,* (cf. Ps. xxxvii. 10), to which he retorts *Yea, they are brought low, they are gathered in* (R.V. marg.) *as all other* ; i.e. it is only the common lot of men which they share (cf. xxi. 26) : indeed they may be regarded as exceptionally blessed, for they are not cut off prematurely, but only *as the tops of the ears of corn,* i.e. in a ripe old age (cf. the description given by Eliphaz of a good man's end 'like as a shock of corn cometh in in its season' in v. 26).

25. A final challenge to the friends to prove him wrong.

**XXV.**   Third speech of Bildad.
   The brevity of this last speech of Bildad indicates very clearly that the friends have exhausted their arguments, and that they are incapable of answering Job's disproof of their theory of suffering. Bildad makes no attempt to deny the fact of the confusions existing in the world to which

Job has pointed in his arraignment of the doctrine of Divine Providence, and of the government of the world by rewards and punishments of the good and evil respectively.  They are too plain to be denied : and having nothing fresh to bring forward he is forced to content himself with a final protest against the *spirit* of Job's remarks, and an endeavour to subdue his friend's seeming arrogance by contrasting the majesty and purity of God with the littleness and impurity of man, as if to ask, How can Job, a mere worm as he is, dare to imagine that he can be counted innocent before the all holy God ?  There is nothing new in the suggestion implied in these words.  Bildad is merely borrowing from Eliphaz who has already said the same thing twice over (see iv. 17, and xv. 14), and indeed Job himself has more than once admitted its truth (see ix. 2, and xiv. 4).

The chapter is too short to allow of detailed analysis : but its substance may be paraphrased as follows.  Look, says Bildad, at the greatness, and absolute rule of God in the heavens above.  There all things obey His will and tremble before Him.  If He say Peace, there is stillness.  Thousands at His bidding wait.  His light shines on all (1—3).  What presumption, then, is it for weak frail man to think that he can be justified before Him (4)!  If even the heavenly bodies are not spotless in His sight, what folly for man to imagine that *he* can be (5, 6)!

**XXV.**   1 Then answered Bildad the Shuhite, and said,
2 Dominion and fear are with him ;
He maketh peace in his high places.
3 Is there any number of his armies ?
And upon whom doth not his light arise ?

2.  *Dominion and fear are with him,* i.e. God rules over all things, and His rule inspires awe and terror.

*He maketh peace in his high places.* The *high places* are the heavens above, as in xvi. 19.  The 'making peace' may refer to the stilling of the storm, or, as Davidson supposes, the words may 'include a reference to traditional discords among the heavenly hosts.  Cf. xxi. 22; xl. 10 seq.; Is. xxiv. 21; Rev. xii. 7.'

3.  *Is there any number of his armies ?* The word for *armies* is not the usual one for His 'hosts,'
whether used of the stars, or of the angels.  It is the same word which has been employed in xix. 12 of the *troops* of God, by whom Job complains that he is assaulted, and is ordinarily used of bands or troops as making inroads.  It may possibly here be applied to the stars (cf. Judg. v. 20, 'the stars in their courses fought against Sisera'), or again, it may be referred to the angels.  Cf. Rev. xii. 7.

*And upon whom doth not his light arise ?* The radiance which proceeds from God illuminates all things, and none can escape from its searching light.

4 How then can man be just ¹with God?
  Or how can he be clean that is born of a woman?
5 Behold, even the moon hath no brightness,
  And the stars are not pure in his sight:
6 How much less man, that is a worm!
  And the son of man, which is a worm!

¹ Or, *before*

4—6. Imitated from the words of Eliphaz in iv. 17, and xv. 14.

5, 6. Cf. Ps. viii. 3, 4. Even the moon appears dark before the light of God, and the very stars of heaven are seen to be dim and dull: how much more must this be the case with man, who is but a worm of the earth! Two different words for worm are here used, the second being also used of a weak and despised man in Ps. xxii. 6. Cf. Is. xli. 14.

**XXVI.** Job's answer to Bildad.

Job evidently feels that there is very little to reply to in the speech to which he has just listened. He has heard it all before, and has already given his assent to it: only it does not help forward the discussion in any way or afford any solution of the problem that is perplexing him. Accordingly he begins with a few words of scornful introduction pointing this out (1—4); after which he takes up the subject of God's greatness where Bildad left it, and shows how God's power is acknowledged and manifested in the underworld (5, 6) and displayed in the earth and the heavens above (7—14). This description of God's power, it must be admitted, contributes nothing fresh to the discussion, the reason being that there was nothing fresh to reply to; but it is obviously intended to show that Job himself knows it all quite as well as his friend who has so kindly taken upon himself the task of instructing him.

The chapter falls into two parts:

(1) *Scornful words of introduction.* 1—4.

(2) *Description of the greatness of God as manifested in Sheol, the earth, and the heavens.* 5—14.

**XXVI.** 1 Then Job answered and said,
2 How hast thou helped him that is without power!
  How hast thou saved the arm that hath no strength!

1—4. **Scornful words of introduction.** Job here sarcastically enlarges on the wonderful help and strength his friend has proved to a weak and feeble creature like himself (1, 2). What wise counsel, what sound knowledge he has brought him (3)! Where did it all come from? and for whose benefit was it really meant (4)?

2. *him that is without power,* viz. Job himself, who is referred to all through these verses as admittedly weak and feeble.

3 How hast thou counselled him that hath no wisdom,
  And plentifully declared sound knowledge!
4 To whom hast thou uttered words?
  And whose ¹spirit came forth from thee?
5 ²They that are deceased tremble
  Beneath the waters and the inhabitants thereof.

¹ Heb. *breath*.     ² Or, *The shades*  Heb. *The Rephaim*.

**3.** *sound knowledge*, the same word as in v. 12, where see note.

**4.** *To whom hast thou uttered words?* The question is a pertinent one because Bildad's remarks had been so utterly irrelevant, that Job scornfully suggests that they cannot have been meant for *him*.

*And whose spirit came forth from thee?* i.e. whence didst thou draw thine inspiration? Surely it did not need God's inspiration to teach him what he had uttered. Eliphaz had already twice given expression to the thought on which his speech is based. Thus Job here 'charges him with having dressed himself in borrowed robes, and inquires from whose wardrobe they have been stolen' (S. Cox).

**5—14. Description of the greatness of God as manifested in Sheol, the earth, and the heavens.** Before God even the weak and motionless inhabitants of the shadowy underworld tremble, for to *Him* those gloomy regions lie bare and open (5, 6). He it is by whom the earth was first poised in midspace (7). By Him the waters are gathered into clouds, which only burst and discharge their contents at His bidding, and which enshroud His throne (8, 9). By Him the bounds of the horizon are fixed, and limits set to light and darkness (10).

Even the solid pillars upon which the vault of heaven rests tremble at His word (11). He it is who not only creates the storm and the raging of the sea, but also quells and calms it, and banishes the night-wrack from the sky (12, 13). And yet, great as these marvels of His power are, after all they show us but the fringes of His ways. To their innermost essence who can penetrate (14)?

**5.** *They that are deceased tremble.* The word rendered *they that are deceased* (the 'Rephaim,' see R.V. marg.) is used for the shades of the departed here and in Ps. lxxxviii. 10; Prov. ii. 18; xxi. 16; Is. xiv. 9; xxvi. 14. It probably means originally weak and flaccid. The same word (whatever its origin in this sense may be) is also used for an extinct race of reputed giants in Gen. xiv. 5; xv. 20; Deut. ii. 11, and elsewhere. Hence the curious renderings of the ancient versions in the passage before us. LXX. γίγαντες, Symmachus θεομάχοι, Vulg. *gigantes*, so the Targum and the Syriac.

*tremble*, and not *are formed* (A.V.), is certainly correct.

*Beneath the waters and the inhabitants thereof.* The words embody the conception that Sheol, the abode of 'the shades,' is beneath the earth.

6 ¹Sheol is naked before him,
   And ²Abaddon hath no covering.
7 He stretcheth out the north over empty space,
   And hangeth the earth ³upon nothing.
8 He bindeth up the waters in his thick clouds ;
   And the cloud is not rent under them.
9 He closeth in the face of his throne,
   And spreadeth his cloud upon it.
10 He hath described a boundary upon the face of the
      waters,
   Unto the confines of light and darkness.

¹ Or, *The grave*       ² Or, *Destruction*       ³ Or, *over*

6.   *Abaddon hath no covering.* The word *Abaddon,* which means *destruction,* is found together with Sheol in Prov. xv. 11, and (in a slightly different form) xxvii. 20. It occurs together with *death* in Job xxviii. 22, and as parallel to *the grave* in Ps. lxxxviii. 11. It is the place of destruction or ruin : and it is a gain to have the original word retained in the English translation here because of its recurrence in the New Testament as the title of the 'angel of the abyss,' whose 'name in Hebrew is Abaddon, and in the Greek tongue he hath the name Apollyon' Rev. ix. 11.

7.   *He stretcheth out the north over empty space.* If, as seems probable, the *empty space* represents the atmosphere above the earth, then *the north* will mean the northern sky round the pole star. This as the beholder looks upward by night might well seem to be *stretched out* over vacancy. Elsewhere (Ps. civ. 2) God is said to '*stretch out* (the same word) the heavens like a curtain,' cf. Isaiah li. 13.

*And hangeth the earth upon nothing.* It is absurd to read into these words the discoveries of modern astronomy. The whole conception is that of the ancients. The heavens stretched out like a curtain above—then the vacant space of the atmosphere, and beneath this the solid earth resting upon nothing.

8, 9.   The marvels of the formation of the clouds, in which God binds up the waters, so that they do not burst except at His command. Elsewhere (xxxviii. 37) the clouds are called 'the bottles of heaven,' i.e. skin-bottles, which explains the language here.

9.   *He closeth in the face of his throne,* i.e. the seat of God is regarded as above the clouds, and shrouded by them. Cf. Ps. civ. 3, 13 ; Amos ix. 6.

10.   *He hath described a boundary upon the face of the waters, unto the confines of light and darkness.* The idea of this verse seems to be that God has drawn as a circle a line round upon the face of the waters, i.e. He has marked out the horizon, which is the borderline between light and darkness. All is bright within it, but beyond it all is conceived as dark.

11 The pillars of heaven tremble
And are astonished at his rebuke.
12 He ¹stirreth up the sea with his power,
And by his understanding he smiteth through ²Rahab.
13 By his spirit the heavens are ³garnished ;
His hand hath pierced the ⁴swift serpent.

¹ Or, *stilleth*          ² See ch. ix. 13.
³ Heb. *beauty*.     ⁴ Or, *fleeing* Or, *gliding*

11.  *The pillars of heaven*—may be the lofty mountains, on whose summits the sky seems to rest. These *tremble*, either in earthquakes, or when the thunder peals forth. Cf. Ps. xxix. 6, 8; civ. 32.

12.  *He stirreth up the sea with his power*.  Almost the same words are found in Isaiah li. 15, and Jer. xxxi. 35; but the meaning of the verb is uncertain.  It properly means to move violently backwards and forwards, to throw into a state of trembling, hence to terrify, and so possibly as the margin of the R.V. *He stilleth* (after the LXX. κατέπαυσεν).  In this case the whole verse will refer to the quelling of the storm (see below).  But it is more probable that, in accordance with its original meaning, it signifies 'to throw into a state of commotion,' as R.V. *He stirreth up* the sea, and, if taken in this way, this first clause will attribute the *rising* of the storm to the action of God, while the second clause tells us that the same power can *quell* it (the rendering of the A.V., *He divideth the sea*, comes from the Targum, but is certainly incorrect; nor can there be any allusion to the passage of the Red Sea.  It is the wonders of *nature* of which Job is speaking).

*And by his understanding he smiteth through Rahab.*  Correct the A.V. *the proud*, and on *Rahab*

see the note on ix. 13.  Rahab here, as there, is probably the mythical dragon which stands as the personification of the sea ; so that to *smite through Rahab* is to calm the waves of the sea and to quell the storm.  There appears to be a clear connexion between this whole passage and Isaiah li. 9—15.  The coincidence between the previous clause and verse 15 has been already noted : and in Is. li. 9, we read 'art thou not it that hath cut Rahab in pieces and pierced the dragon ?' where not only is there a similar reference to Rahab, but the word for *cut in pieces* is apparently the same that is used here for *smite through*, and *pierced* occurs in the next verse in the passage before us, as well as in Isaiah.

13.  *By his spirit the heavens are garnished*.  Literally *are beauty*.  The words must refer to the clearing of the sky after the storm, the same thing being figuratively described in the next clause in the allusion to the nature myth of Leviathan.  See the following note.

*His hand hath pierced the swift serpent.*  (Correct the A.V. *formed*.) The same words *the swift serpent* occur again in Isaiah xxvii. 1, where they are descriptive of Leviathan ; and there can be no doubt that in the verse before us there is an allusion to the myth already referred to in iii. 8, and the belief that darkness

14 Lo, these are but the outskirts of his ways :
   And ¹how small a whisper ²do we hear of him !
   But the thunder of his ³power who can understand ?

¹ Or, *how little a portion*        ² Or, *is heard*        ³ Or, *mighty deeds*

was caused by the dragon swallowing up the sun.  The piercing or wounding this swift serpent would cause him to abandon his prey, and once more the light would shine.

14.  All these wonders of nature are wrought by the Almighty power of God, but marvellous as they seem to us they are after all only the edges, the fringes of His ways, and the sound of His voice is scarcely heard in them.  If He were to raise it, and manifest Himself as He is in reality, who could stand ?

**XXVII., XXVIII.**   Job's first monologue.

Surprise has often been felt that Job's last speech in answer to Bildad is not followed, as in the earlier circles of speeches, by one from Zophar, with a further reply from Job; but that the friends appear to retire, and are no more mentioned (except in xxxii. 1—5 and xlii. 7 seq.), while Job continues his speech in the form of a twofold monologue (xxvii., xxviii., and xxix.—xxxi.), introduced in each case by a formula which occurs nowhere else in the whole book, 'And Job again took up his parable and said' (xxvi. 1; xxix. 1).   And the difficulty is increased by these two facts: (1) in a considerable part of his first monologue, beginning with xxvii., verse 7, Job apparently deserts the position which he has all along maintained, and goes over to that taken by the friends, describing the fate which overtakes the ungodly in very much the same terms as those which they have already employed; and (2) beautiful and impressive as chapter xxviii. is, it is not easy to see its connexion with the speech in which it occurs, or indeed with the poem as a whole.   In consequence of these difficulties a considerable number of critics have held that there has been some dislocation of the text, that the passage which causes the difficulty in chapter xxvii. (7—23) is really the missing speech of Zophar (so Kennicott in the last century), and that chapter xxviii. is a later interpolation.   Accordingly various attempts have been made to rearrange the text, so as to make this third circle correspond exactly with the two earlier ones : but it has generally been felt that any such attempt cannot be so limited as merely to assign to Zophar the verses in question, and to cut out chapter xxviii., for obviously there would be a great lack of *proportion* in the various speeches as so arranged.   Hence, a considerable number of further alterations are found to be necessitated before anything like a satisfactory result is obtained ; and even so, what is satisfactory to one critic is not so to another, for scarcely any two critics are agreed in their rearrangement, as is shown in the note below¹.   What

¹ Thus Bickell (who is followed by Dillon, *The Sceptics of the Old Testament*) rearranges the text as follows: *Bildad*, xxv. 1—3 ; xxvi. 12—14; xxv. 4—6. *Job's reply*, xxvi. 1—2, 4 ; xxvii. 2, 4—6, 11, 12 ; xxviii. 1—3, 9—11, 20—28. *Zophar*, xxvii. 7—10, 14—20.  *Job's reply*, xxix. 1—4, 6—9, 11—17, 21, 22 ;

commends itself to one writer is summarily rejected by another; and to the present writer it certainly appears that the difficulties involved in the acceptance of the text as it has come down to us are less than those which are created by the attempts at reconstruction proposed in some modern Commentaries. It is admitted that xxvii. 7—23 is a real difficulty, but on the whole it seems better to accept it as part of Job's speech, even if no thoroughly satisfactory explanation of it can be offered, rather than to venture on a wholesale manipulation of the text, for which there is no external evidence, and which, in the face of so much disagreement among the critics themselves, must be pronounced extremely precarious and uncertain; while in regard to chapter xxvi<sup>ii</sup>, as Dr Driver justly remarks, 'it is scarcely possible that such a noble and characteristic passage can have been inserted in the poem by a later hand.'

Accepting then the arrangement of the text which has come down to us in our Hebrew Bibles as correct, and regarding xxviii. as an integral part of the original poem, the two chapters before us (xxvii., xxviii.) are here treated as Job's first monologue. Job has now completely silenced his friends. He has appealed to facts which give the lie to the major premiss of their syllogism, and establish the seeming inequality of God's ways. He is consequently left as victor, not as having solved the problem, or offered any explanation of the mystery of pain, but simply as having demolished their 'short and easy method' of accounting for suffering. Whatever be the true account of it, the old doctrine of retribution has hopelessly broken down; and it appears as if this monologue was meant to point out that since the problem is insoluble by man his true wisdom is to acquiesce in his ignorance, and, leaving speculation, to devote himself to practical works of goodness: much in the same spirit as the writer of Ecclesiastes gives 'the conclusion of the whole matter' at the close of his dreary reflections on things in general. 'Fear God and keep his commandments, for this is the whole duty of man' (Eccl. xii. 13). We may, then, suppose a pause to occur at the close of Job's answer to Bildad in xxvi.; and then, after an interval, when Zophar fails to come forward, he 'takes up his parable' and recommences, beginning, after his usual style,

xxx. 1, 2, 8—11, 13—15, 17—31; xxxi. 5—14, 23, 15—17, 19—22, 24—27, 29—37.

Cheyne assigns to *Bildad* xxv., xxvi. 5—14; to *Job* xxvi. 1—4; xxvii. 1—7; to *Zophar* xxvii. 8—10, 13—23; and to *Job* xxvii. 11, 12; xxix.—xxxi.; taking xxviii. as a later addition.

Duhm gives to *Bildad* xxvi. 1—4; xxv. 2—6; xxvi. 5—14; to *Job* xxvii. 1—6, 12; to *Zophar* xxvii. 7—11, 13—23; and to *Job* xxix.—xxxi., taking xxviii. by itself.

According to Siegfried, *Bildad's* speech is contained in xxv., xxvi. 5—14; while xxvi. 1—4, xxvii. 2—6 belong to *Job*. xxvii. 7—23 are a 'correcting interpolation' conforming the speeches of Job to the orthodox doctrine of retribution; while xxviii. is a 'polemical interpolation' directed against the tendency of the poem! No third speech is assigned to *Zophar*, but xxix.—xxxi. are regarded as the continuation of Job's utterance.

with a protestation of his innocence, and determination to hold fast his integrity (xxvii. 1—6); then follows the passage, of which it is so hard to give a satisfactory explanation (xxvii. 7—23), and which contains a graphic description of the terrible fate which awaits the sinner, his dreary and hopeless condition as abandoned by God, and the swift and complete retribution which overtakes him for his wrong-doing; and lastly in chapter xxviii. we have a marvellous panegyric on the divine wisdom, in which it is shown that, clever and cunning as man is, and able to find out many inventions, yet he can never attain to the true wisdom, which belongs to God only as the Creator of all things. Man is utterly unable to understand the principles that rule in the world. He has his wisdom indeed, which is to 'fear the Lord and to depart from evil,' but to comprehend the world is quite beyond him. Thus in analysing the speech, we may mark out the main divisions as follows:

(1)  *Introductory protestation of integrity.*  xxvii. 1—6.

(2)  *Description of the fate of the sinner.*  7—23.

(3)  *Man is very clever, and able to discover silver, gold, and precious stones of all kinds.*  xxviii. 1—11.

(4)  *But wisdom can nowhere be discovered by him, nor purchased with his precious stones.*  12—19.

(5)  *Wisdom is not found even in the world below. God alone knoweth the way to it, as the Creator of all things. The only wisdom for man is to fear Him.*  20—28.

**XXVII.**  1 And Job again took up his parable, and said,

2 As God liveth, who hath taken away my right;
And the Almighty, who hath ¹vexed my soul;

¹ Heb. *made my soul bitter.*

**XXVII. 1—6. Introductory protestation of integrity.** Job begins with an oath by the God who has made his soul bitter (1, 2) —for he is still able to breathe and speak (3)—and protests that he will not be guilty of insincerity or untruthfulness (4). He will neither admit his friends to be right, nor deny his own integrity (5). He will cling to his righteousness which he has all along maintained, for he has nothing to reproach himself with (6).

1. *And Job again took up his parable.* The expression is found again more than once in the narrative of Balaam (Numb. xxiii. 7 seq.) but occurs nowhere else.

2. *As God liveth.* Cf. 2 Sam. ii. 27, where the form of the oath is almost the same (*Elohim* instead of *El* being the only difference). Elsewhere the form is almost always 'As the LORD liveth,' which occurs more than thirty times in the course of the Old Testament, from Judg. viii. 19 onwards.

THE BOOK OF JOB [XXVII. 3–7

3 ¹(For my life is yet whole in me,
   And the spirit of God is in my nostrils ;)
4 Surely my lips ²shall not speak unrighteousness,
   Neither ³shall my tongue utter deceit.
5 God forbid that I should justify you :
   Till I die I will not put away mine integrity from me.
6 My righteousness I hold fast, and will not let it go :
   My heart ⁴shall not reproach *me* so long as I live.
7 Let mine enemy be as the wicked,
   And let him that riseth up against me be as the un-
      righteous.

¹ Or, *All the while my breath is in me...nostrils ; surely*    ² Or, *do*
³ Or, *doth*    ⁴ Or, *doth not reproach* me for *any of my days*

**3.** *For my life is yet whole in me &c.*: The R.V. rightly takes this verse as parenthetical. The Hebrew of the first clause is peculiar, but almost the same phrase is found in 2 Sam. i. 9, which fixes its meaning, and shows that the clause is correctly rendered in the R.V. (as against the A.V. and R.V. marg.).
*spirit of God*, better *breath of God*. Contrast xxvi. 4.

**4.** Here we have the substance of the oath begun in verse 1. The first word of the verse is the regular form in an adjuration for expressing an emphatic negative *Surely...not*. It literally means *if* : the full form being ' God do so to me and more also *if*,' sometimes expressed, as in 1 Sam. iii. 17, but more often implied, as here.

**5.** *God forbid.* The word is properly a substantive meaning something profane; used as an exclamation *ad profanum !* i.e. *far be it from me.*
*justify you*, i.e. admit you to be right.

**6.** *My heart shall not reproach me so long as I live*, better, as R.V.

marg., *doth not reproach me for any of my days.* The LXX. in this clause is noteworthy, οὐ γὰρ σύνοιδα ἐμαυτῷ ἄτοπα πράξας, as containing the remarkable phrase used by S. Paul in 1 Cor. iv. 4, ' I know nothing by myself' A.V. or as it is more accurately rendered in R.V. '*against myself*,' οὐδὲν γὰρ ἐμαυτῷ σύνοιδα. Is the coincidence accidental, or may we see in the phrase an unconscious reminiscence of the language of Job ?

**7—23. Description of the fate of the sinner.** Here follows a wish that the speaker's enemy may meet with the fate that befalls the sinner (7), whose condition when God cuts him off is described as hopeless (8). He may cry to God when trouble falls upon him, but there is no answer (9): he has no pleasure in God so that he should naturally turn to Him (10). The speaker next proceeds to offer to instruct his hearers concerning God's dealings with men—for, though they have opportunities enough of knowing it, they yet seem insensible of it (11, 12). This, then, is the fate of the sinner (13). His family may increase, but it will be only to be cut off by the sword, the famine, and the pestilence (14, 15). He may amass his treasures of silver and costly raiment—they are only stored up to be enjoyed by better men than he (16, 17). His house is flimsy and easily destroyed (18). One day he is in full possession of his wealth : the next morning finds him dead and gone (19). Sudden terrors fall upon him : the storm sweeps him away (20, 21). God's wrath overtakes him as he flees, and men drive him with contumely from their midst (22, 23).

There is no difficulty about the meaning of the words here used. The translation of the whole passage is simple enough, and it is only here and there that a phrase occurs of which the rendering is doubtful. The only difficulty is to understand how the words can be regarded as appropriate in the mouth of Job, and this, as was indicated above, is a real problem. Various theories have been proposed, but none of them seems entirely satisfactory. The common view among those who uphold the integrity of the text is that Job has at last found his way to a position of assured trust in God, and that in this description of the fate of a sinner he is modifying his former extravagant utterances. There are, however, grave objections to this view; (1) in chapters xxix.—xxxi. he distinctly maintains his former position, and still speaks of God as his 'adversary' (xxxi. 35). (2) The description of the fate of a sinner is no 'modification' of his earlier view, but an absolute and sweeping contradiction of it. Formerly he had maintained that no

moral rule was discernible in the government of the world : now (on the view that these verses contain his own sentiments) he roundly accepts the orthodox doctrine of retribution which the friends had all along maintained, and yet reproaches them with folly (12) ! As Davidson drily remarks : 'To appropriate their sentiments and cover the operation by calling them foolish persons was not generous.' Another view is that Job is here not giving his own views at all, but simply repeating with bitter scorn the kind of language used by his friends and almost parodying it, before proceeding in xxviii. to give up the problem altogether as insoluble, and fall back on the *practical* wisdom of a life of *duty*. In favour of this it may be noticed (1) that he has already in a somewhat similar way cited in scorn their description of the fate of the wicked in xxiv. 18—21, and placed side by side with it what he holds to be the true state of the case, and (2) that verse 13 is drawn almost word for word from the conclusion of Zophar's speech in xx. 29, in which he had so strongly insisted on the very points here urged. This looks very much as if the passage was intended to be a citation of the friends' words. And if it be said that 'there is nothing in the passage to suggest that the sentiments are not those of the speaker himself,' it may be replied that this is often the case with the dramatic poetry of the ancients. When it was *recited*, emphasis and tone and gesture were all brought into play, and indicated how it was to be understood. But as the ancients made no use of inverted commas and exclamation stops, by

8 For what is the hope of the godless, ¹though he get him
  gain,
  When God taketh away his soul?
9 Will God hear his cry,
  When trouble cometh upon him?
10 Will he delight himself in the Almighty,
  And call upon God at all times?
11 I will teach you concerning the hand of God;
  That which is with the Almighty will I not conceal.
12 Behold, all ye yourselves have seen it;
  Why then are ye become altogether vain?
13 This is the portion of a wicked man with God,
  And the heritage of oppressors, which they receive from
  the Almighty.

¹ Or, *when God cutteth him off, when he taketh &c.*

the help of which a modern writer can often convey his meaning to his reader, the *written* poem must often be obscure. Dr Davidson raises a further objection that when the speaker 'undertakes to teach concerning the hand of God, it cannot be doubted that the following verses contain the lesson, namely, God's way of dealing with the wicked. If verses 11, 12 be connected with xxviii. the teaching must be sought in that chapter. But there is really no teaching regarding the "hand" of God in xxviii., though much regarding the ingenuity of man. The intermediate passage, xxvii. 13—23, hides the incongruity of this view; but if these verses be removed and xxviii. read in connexion with xxvii. 11, 12, what Job says to his friends is this: "I will teach you concerning the hand of God!—It is simply incomprehensible!"' Some weight undoubtedly is due to this objection, but it does not appear conclusive. Why, after all, should not Job say

this to his friends? He quotes a summary of their words, he tells them that man is marvellously clever, *but* that with all his wisdom he cannot discover the principles that rule in the world, for they are incomprehensible. That is his teaching concerning 'the hand of God.' On the whole this explanation appears to the present writer the most probable one that has yet been proposed. He is free to confess that he is not entirely satisfied with it: but the alternative seems to lie between accepting this explanation, and confessing that the difficulty is insurmountable, and readers must make the choice for themselves.

8. *what is the hope of the godless, though he get him gain.* Better, with R.V., marg. *when God cutteth him off.*

13. Cf. xx. 29, a great part of which is verbally quoted here: '*This is the portion of a wicked man from God, and the heritage* appointed unto him by God.'

14 If his children be multiplied, it is for the sword ;
   And his offspring shall not be satisfied with bread.
15 Those that remain of him shall be buried in death,
   And his widows shall make no lamentation.
16 Though he heap up silver as the dust,
   And prepare raiment as the clay ;
17 He may prepare it, but the just shall put it on,
   And the innocent shall divide the silver.
18 He buildeth his house as the ¹moth,
   And as a booth which the keeper maketh.
19 He lieth down rich, but he ²shall not be gathered ;
   He openeth his eyes, and he is not.

¹ Some ancient versions have, *spider*.
² Some ancient versions have, *shall do so no more*.

15. *Those that remain of him shall be buried in death.* As 'the sword' and famine have been mentioned in the previous verse it is well to take *death* here as signifying *the pestilence*, as in Jer. xv. 2; xviii. 21 (see R.V.); xliii. 11, and cf. the use of θάνατος in the New Testament, Rev. vi. 8; xviii. 8.

*And his widows shall make no lamentation.* The same words are found in Ps. lxxviii. 64.

16. *Though he heap up silver as the dust,* the clause occurs also in Zech. ix. 3.

*And prepare raiment as the clay.* With this clause again cf. Zech. ix. 3, where the 'clay' or 'mire of the streets,' as well as the 'dust,' is similarly used as an emblem of great abundance. Costly raiment was a common form of Eastern wealth. Cf. the allusions in the N.T., S. Matt. vi. 19; S. James v. 2.

18. *He buildeth his house as the moth,* i.e. it is frail and easily crushed. Cf. the allusion in iv. 19.

*And as a booth which the keeper maketh.* The word for *booth* is the same which occurs in Isaiah i. 8 for a booth (A.V. *cottage*) *in a vineyard.* It is a poor, perishable structure, easily overthrown, consisting of little more than four poles covered with boughs. See the picture of one in Thomson's *Land and the Book,* p. 361. The 'keeper' is the watchman set to guard the vineyard.

19. *He lieth down rich, but he shall not be gathered.* The thought of this verse may well be illustrated by our Lord's parable of the rich fool in S. Luke xii. 16 seq. The word for *gathered* is often used of a man being gathered to his fathers in death ; but it is also used of the body being composed or arrayed for burial, see Jer. viii. 2; xxv. 33; Ezek. xxix. 5, and possibly this is the meaning here. In the parable of Dives and Lazarus we have 'the rich man died *and was buried,*' S. Luke xvi. 22. The words before us may point to some indignity in the absence of the burial. Or possibly the Massoretic punctuation is incorrect, and we should render the clause *but he shall do so no more.* So LXX. and many moderns. See R.V. marg.

10—2

20 Terrors overtake him like waters ;
   A tempest stealeth him away in the night.
21 The east wind carrieth him away, and he departeth ;
   And it sweepeth him out of his place.
22 For *God* shall hurl at him, and not spare :
   He would fain flee out of his hand.
23 Men shall clap their hands at him,
   And shall hiss him out of his place.

**XXVIII.**    1 ¹Surely there is a mine for silver,
   And a place for gold which they refine.

¹ Or, *For*

20. *Terrors overtake him like waters.* Cf. Bildad's words in xviii. 11, ' *Terrors* shall make him afraid on every side,' and for the *waters* cf. the words of Eliphaz in xxii. 11, ' and abundance of waters cover thee.'
*A tempest stealeth him away.* In the original the words are the same as those found in xxi. 18, ' as chaff that *the storm carrieth away*,' where Job is similarly summarizing the statements of his friends.
21. *The east wind carrieth him away.* Cf. the allusions to the east wind, the most violent in Western Asia, in Ps. xlviii. 7 ; Is. xxvii. 8 ; Jer. xviii. 17 ; Ezek. xxvii. 26.
22. *For* God *shall hurl at him, and not spare.* The object of the verb is not expressed. The R.V. apparently takes it to be such missiles as javelins or great stones, rather than arrows, which would be shot, and not *hurled.* A similar use of the verb without the object expressed is found in Numb. xxxv. 20.
23. *Men shall clap their hands at him.* For clapping the hands as a sign of derision cf. xxxiv. 37, and Lam. ii. 15 ; and for *hissing* in mockery see 1 Kings ix. 8 ; Lam. ii. 15, 16 ; Jer. xix. 8 ; xlix. 17.

**XXVIII.** According to the explanation of xxvii. 7—23, adopted (not without much hesitation) above, this chapter follows naturally enough with the design of showing how hopeless it is for man to expect to understand God's method of ruling the world ; and the method by which the writer seeks to enforce this upon us is this. He sets before us in sharpest contrast (1) the wonderful skill and ingenuity of man in compelling nature to yield up her secrets to him, and (2) his entire failure in the search after 'wisdom,' i.e. an intellectual apprehension of the principles of God's government. This is one of the secrets of God, known only to the Creator of all things ; and for man the only ' wisdom' is of a practical rather than an intellectual nature, viz. to fear God, and to depart from evil. Thus the solution of the problem which has so perplexed Job is given up in despair. It is incomprehensible, and man had better cease thinking about it. This may seem to adopt a position not very far removed from Agnosticism, and it is one which no Christian teacher could consent to adopt as a permanent one, for it amounts to a recommendation to *cease thinking.* But as a *temporary* relief there are probably times in the life of most persons when it will appear to be the best course for them to follow. Voltaire's 'travailler sans raisonner, c'est le seul moyen de rendre la vie supportable' may sometimes be the rule even for a Christian. For a man who is endowed by God with powers of reason and intellect, deliberately to abstain from using them, and to turn away from any endeavour to find an answer to perplexing questions concerning the Divine government of the world, cannot be right *as a permanent condition.* But, as Dr Newman has pointed out in a famous sermon, there are some trials of faith which are best met by simple *obedience,* which is 'the remedy for religious perplexity'; and when men are bewildered and puzzled, and doubtful about the very foundations of religion, they will often by leaving speculation and turning to active work in the course of plain duty find that in time their perplexities disappear, and the difficulties solve themselves. See Newman's *Parochial and Plain Sermons,* Vol. I. Sermon xviii. 'Obedience the remedy for religious perplexity.'

The analysis of this chapter has already been given on p. 143. It is therefore not repeated here.

1—11. **Man is very clever, and able to discover silver, gold, and precious stones of all kinds.** Silver, gold, iron and brass—these treasures are all yielded up to man (1, 2), who can search out the very darkest recesses of the earth (3). He sinks the shafts of his mines and men descend into the bowels of the earth, far from the haunts of men (4). On the earth's surface he grows his corn, which supplies him with food, while far down below he is ransacking its treasures, its gold and precious stones, and searching it as by fire (5, 6). No falcon's eye is keen enough to spy out those hidden recesses, and no beast of prey can make his way thither (7, 8). Man alone has the skill to dig down to the very roots of the mountains (9), and hew out his passages in the solid rocks, binding up the streams so that they shall not flood his mines, and bringing out the hidden treasures to the light of day (10, 11).

There are few passages in the Old Testament in which the gain to the English reader from the possession of the Revised Version is greater than this. For the first time the verses are made intelligible to him, and the changes of translation (especially those in verses 3 and 4) make it clear that the whole passage is a wonderfully vivid and graphic description of mining operations as carried on in the ancient world. In very early days copper mines were worked in the Sinaitic peninsula; gold mines in Nubia; and from Idumæa between Petra and Zoar copper (and possibly also both gold and silver) could be procured; while in Lebanon there were iron works and iron mines (cf. Deut. viii. 9, where they are alluded to). With some, if not all, of these the writer of the Book of Job must have been familiar, for his picture of the miners descending in their cages, 'swinging to and fro' as they are let down to the bottom of the shaft, is evidently drawn from life, and there are even possible traces of familiarity on his part with the technical vocabulary of the industry (see the notes on 4, 10, 11).

2 Iron is taken out of the ¹earth,
   And brass is molten out of the stone.
3 *Man* setteth an end to darkness,
   And searcheth out to the furthest bound
   The stones of thick darkness and of the shadow of death.
4 ²He breaketh open a shaft away from where men sojourn ;
   They are forgotten of the foot *that passeth by* ;
   They hang afar from men, they ³swing to and fro.

---

¹ Or, *dust*
² Or, *The flood breaketh out from where men sojourn ;* even the waters *forgotten
of the foot : they are minished, they are gone away from man*     ³ Or, *flit*

---

1. *Surely* (or better, with the margin of R.V., *For*) *there is a mine for silver.* The word for *mine* (lit. place of going forth, or source) is only found here in this particular sense, but there can be no doubt as to its meaning. The rendering *vein* in the A.V. is suggested by the Vulgate, *venarum suarum principia.*

*And a place for gold which they refine* (better than A.V. *where they fine it*). The allusion is not to the place where the process of refining is carried on, but rather to the gold mine itself from which the precious metal is procured. For other allusions to refining gold and silver see Ps. xii. 6 ; 1 Chr. xxviii. 18 ; xxix. 4 ; Mal. iii. 3, in all of which the same word occurs.

2. *And brass is molten out of the stone.* Brass should be *copper.* The clause might literally be rendered *and stone one melteth into copper.*

3. Man *setteth an end to darkness.* It is quite clear that man is the subject spoken of, so the R.V. is quite justified in inserting the word in italics in order to make the meaning clear to the English reader. The verse is, of course, descriptive

of man's power of penetrating and bringing light into the dark underground passages in his mines. The word rendered in the R.V. *the furthest bound* (better than A.V. *all perfection*) is that used in xxvi. 10, '*the boundary* of light and darkness.'

4. *He breaketh open a shaft away from where men sojourn.* Man is still the subject. The word for *shaft* is commonly used for a winter torrent and the valley through which it flows. Hence the marginal reading of R.V. *the flood breaketh out &c.* But there is a general agreement among commentators that in this passage it must be taken of the 'shaft' of the mine. Possibly it was a technical term (correct the A.V. accordingly).

*They are forgotten of the foot that passeth by*, i.e. men walk about the earth over the heads of the miners, utterly oblivious of what is going on beneath their feet.

*They hang afar from men, they swing to and fro*, viz. as they descend the shaft either in cages or let down by ropes. Instead of *swing* the R.V. marg. suggests 'they *flit* to and fro,' but the rendering given in the text is preferable.

5  As for the earth, out of it cometh bread :
   And underneath it is turned up as it were by fire.
6  The stones thereof are the place of sapphires,
   ¹And it hath dust of gold.
7  That path no bird of prey knoweth,
   Neither hath the falcon's eye seen it :
8  The ²proud beasts have not trodden it,
   Nor hath the fierce lion passed thereby.
9  He putteth forth his hand upon the flinty rock ;
   He overturneth the mountains by the roots.
10 He cutteth out ³channels among the rocks ;
   And his eye seeth every precious thing.

---

¹ Or, *And he winneth lumps of gold*      ² Heb. *sons of pride.*      ³ Or, *passages*

5.  This verse brings out the contrast suggested by the peaceful look and condition of the earth above with its cornfields, and the restless energy of man burrowing underground, and 'overturning' everything in his search for hidden treasures, *as by fire.* The reference is probably not to blasting (though that was practised by the ancients, see Pliny, *H. N.* XXXIII. 4, 21), which would require *by fire* alone. '*As* by fire' points rather to a comparison of the destruction wrought by man with that worked by the destroying element.

6 mentions some of the treasures which man carries off, *sapphires* and *lumps of gold* (R.V. marg.).

7  *Neither hath the falcon's eye seen it.* The Hebrew word *Ayyah* is probably *the kite* rather than the falcon (cf. Lev. xi. 14 ; Deut. xiv. 13). It affords 'the strongest instance of that keenness of sight for which all birds of prey are remarkable,' see Tristram, *Nat. Hist. of the Bible,* p. 187. Even the keen-eyed bird of prey, says Job, which 'can detect the path of a wounded deer from a

height, where it can itself be descried by no human eye,' cannot discern the path along which the miner passes in the bowels of the earth.

8.  *The proud beasts,* lit. *the sons of pride* (LXX. υἱοὶ ἀλαζόνων). The same phrase is used in xli. 34 (Heb. 26) and nowhere else. The Targum takes it here, in accordance with the parallelism, of lions, and it must refer to beasts of prey generally. These with all their strength cannot penetrate to the depths where man is working.

9—11 are descriptive of the operations of the miner. Verse 9 is general in its terms, introducing the subject, and describing how man *puts forth his hand upon the flinty rock.* Verse 10 tells how he cuts out his passages in the depth of the mine, and exposes to view the coveted treasures, while verse 11 describes the measures taken to save the mine from being flooded.

10.  *He cutteth out channels among the rocks.* The word rendered *channels* is properly used in the singular of the river Nile, and in the plural of its arms or canals. Here, how-

11 He bindeth the streams [1] that they trickle not;
   And the thing that is hid bringeth he forth to light.
12 But where shall wisdom be found?
   And where is the place of understanding?
13 Man knoweth not the price thereof;
   Neither is it found in the land of the living.
14 The deep saith, It is not in me:
   And the sea saith, It is not with me.

---

[1] Heb. *from weeping.*

---

ever, there can be no allusion to these. The *channels* of which Job is speaking are cut out of the solid rock, and must refer to the passages formed for working the mine. Probably the word was a technical one in this sense.

11. *He bindeth the streams that they trickle not,* literally *that they weep not* (see R.V. marg.). Here again the term is probably a technical one, and it is interesting to find that in the present day 'our colliers name the action of the water that percolates through and into their workings *weeping*' (S. Cox).

12—19. **Wisdom can nowhere be discerned by man, nor purchased with his precious stones.** The only thing that baffles man in his search after it is wisdom. This he can neither purchase nor discover (12, 13). He will search for it in the depths and in the sea in vain (14). He may offer for it all the treasures of Arabia and India, but its price is far above them all (15—19).

12. *But where shall wisdom be found?* On *wisdom* (Khochmah) see the Introduction, p. ix. Here it is specially a knowledge of the principles in accordance with which God rules and governs the world.

13. *Man knoweth not the price thereof.* For *price thereof* the LXX.

reads *way thereof*, ὁδὸν αὐτῆς, which only involves the change of a single letter, and is adopted by some moderns. But the Massoretic text yields an excellent sense, and has the support of the other ancient Greek versions, Aquila, Symmachus, Theodotion, as well as the Targ., Syriac, and Vulgate.

*the land of the living,* a phrase which occurs several times in the religious poetry of the Hebrews, and which always refers to life here on earth as distinct from anything beyond the grave, see Ps. xxvii. 13; lii. 5; cxvi. 9; cxlii. 5; and Is. xxxviii. 11. So here, when Job says that wisdom cannot be found in the land of the living, the meaning is that it cannot be found anywhere on the earth, and then he proceeds in the next verse to show that neither in the sea nor the depths beneath the earth is it to be discovered.

14. *The deep saith, It is not in me.* The *deep* and the *sea* are not exactly convertible terms, though the former is sometimes used for the waters of the sea, see xxxviii. 30, and xli. 32 (Heb. 24). Here it is rather the great abyss lying under the earth, 'out of which perhaps the sea is fed' (Davidson), cf. Gen. i. 2; vii. 11; viii. 2.

15  It cannot be gotten for <sup>1</sup>gold,
    Neither shall silver be weighed for the price thereof.
16  It cannot be valued with the gold of Ophir,
    With the precious <sup>2</sup>onyx, or the sapphire.
17  Gold and glass cannot equal it :
    Neither shall the exchange thereof be <sup>3</sup>jewels of fine gold.
18  No mention shall be made of coral or of crystal :
    Yea, the price of wisdom is above <sup>4</sup>rubies.
19  The topaz of Ethiopia shall not equal it,
    Neither shall it be valued with pure gold.

---

<sup>1</sup> Or, *treasure*       <sup>2</sup> Or, *beryl*       <sup>3</sup> Or, *vessels*
            <sup>4</sup> Or, *red coral*   Or, *pearls*

15.  *It cannot be gotten for gold.* The word for *gold* is peculiar, but is probably connected with the expression used for *pure gold* in 1 Kings vi. 20, 21; vii. 49, 50; x. 21; 2 Chr. iv. 20, 22; ix. 20.

*Neither shall silver be weighed for the price thereof.* For the practice of *weighing* rather than *counting* the silver given as a price see Gen. xxiii. 16; Zech. xi. 12.

16.  *the gold of Ophir*, see the note on xxii. 24.

17.  *glass.* The word occurs nowhere else, but the rendering of the R.V. is probably correct. So the Targum, LXX. ὕαλος, and Vulg. *vitrum*, though there is some ancient authority for the A.V. *crystal.* Glass, however, was regarded as a great rarity and as most precious by the ancients.

*fine gold*, the word is the same as that which occurs in Ps. xix. 10; xxi. 3; cxix. 127; Cant. v. 11, 15; Prov. viii. 19; Is. xiii. 12; Lam. iv. 2.

18.  *coral.* The word occurs again only in Ezek. xxvii. 16. It is certainly the name of some precious stone or treasure, but the ancient

versions give no help towards its meaning as they take it from a root meaning *to be high,* and translate vaguely, LXX. μετέωρα, Sym. ὑψηλά, Vulg. *excelsa. Coral* of the English versions is probably correct.

*crystal.* The word is only found here. The LXX. translators did not recognize it, and simply put the Hebrew word into Greek letters γαβείς. The R.V. is more probable than the A.V. *pearls*, which according to Jewish tradition is the meaning of the next term used, where A.V. and R.V. both have *rubies.* The Hebrew word occurs several times in Proverbs iii. 15; viii. 11; xx. 15; xxxi. 10, and once besides in Lamentations iv. 7. *Red coral*, an alternative suggested in the margin of R.V., was proposed by Michaelis as being favoured by a possible etymology of the word. Neither LXX. nor Vulg. gives any help, as in both cases the translators have confused the word or followed a different reading (LXX. ἐσώτατα, Vulg. *occultis*).

19.  *The topaz of Ethiopia.* So LXX. and Vulgate.

20 Whence then cometh wisdom?
   And where is the place of understanding?
21 Seeing it is hid from the eyes of all living,
   And kept close from the fowls of the air.
22 ¹Destruction and Death say,
   We have heard a rumour thereof with our ears.
23 God understandeth the way thereof,
   And he knoweth the place thereof.
24 For he looketh to the ends of the earth,
   And seeth under the whole heaven;

¹ Heb. *Abaddon.*

*pure gold.* The word for *gold* is the same as that used in verse 16 for the *gold* of Ophir. It is a rare and late word—possibly a loan-word in Hebrew, but there is no doubt about its meaning, cf. xxxi. 24; Ps. xlv. 9; Prov. xxv. 12 etc.

**20—28. Wisdom is not found even in the world below. God alone knoweth the way to it, as the Creator of all things. The only wisdom for man is to fear Him.** If then wisdom cannot be thus acquired, if neither man nor beast nor bird can descry it, where is it to be found (20, 21)? Neither death nor destruction can help to its discovery, since they know nothing but a rumour of it (22). None but God possesses any true knowledge of it. He knows it and can descry it, for His eye ranges over all things (23, 24). He it is Who at Creation weighed the winds and measured out the waters (25); He it is Who has ordered the laws which govern the rain, and created the thunder and the lightning (26). And when He thus ordered creation, Wisdom was present to Him, He declared it, gave it existence, and contemplated it in all its fulness

with Divine approval (27). But for man the only wisdom that He has appointed is of a *practical* character, viz. to fear Him, and to forsake wrongdoing (28).

20. Repeated almost verbally from verse 12.

22. *Destruction,* i.e. in Hebrew *Abaddon,* which is here personified together with Death. See the note on xxvi. 6, and cf. the personification of Death and Sheol in Rev. vi. 8.

*We have heard a rumour thereof with our ears.* Death and Destruction only know it by report. They have not seen it, and have no personal knowledge of it. Cf. the contrast between the hearing of the ear and seeing with the eye in xlii. 5.

24—26. The writer's thoughts pass from the *government* to the *creation* of the world, and it is not easy to say exactly where the transition is made. In verse 25 he is clearly thinking of God's all-seeing eye surveying His creation, and of the *present* regulation of all things by Him. But the opening words of verse 27 ' *Then* did He see it' show that he has gone back in thought to

25 ¹To make a weight for the wind ;
    Yea, he meteth out the waters by measure.
26 When he made a decree for the rain,
    And a way for the lightning of the thunder :
27 Then did he see it, and ²declare it ;
    He established it, yea, and searched it out.
28 And unto man he said,
    Behold, the fear of the Lord, that is wisdom ;
    And to depart from evil is understanding.

¹ Or, *When he maketh*                    ² Or, *recount*

the time of the Creation; and it is most natural to take verse 26 'When He made a decree etc.' of the original fixing of the laws which govern the elements, though it is doubtful whether the verbs in verse 25 should be translated as in the *present* tense (A.V. and R.V.) or (as by Davidson) in the past.

26. *When he made a decree for the rain.* Cf. the allusion to the former and the latter rain in Jer. v. 24.

*a way for the lightning of the thunder,* the whole phrase is repeated in xxxviii. 25. The word for *lightning* is not the common one, and occurs elsewhere only in Zech. x. 1.

27. *Then,* i.e. at the time when God created the world, and appointed the laws which regulate it, Wisdom was visible to Him. He could *see it,* and *declare* it, i.e. either (1) *count* it, enumerate its various parts and powers, or (2) utter its name, and so call it into being.

*He established it,* i.e. He fashioned and created it (for this use of the word see Is. xl. 20). Cf. Prov. viii. 22 seq., where Wisdom is personified

and introduced as saying, 'The LORD possessed (or *formed,* R.V. marg.) me in the beginning of His way.' The whole passage should be compared with that before us, as illustrating the thoughts to which Job gives expression.

28. See Prov. i. 7, 'The fear of the LORD is the beginning of knowledge'; iii. 7, 'Fear the LORD and depart from evil'; xvi. 6, 'By the fear of the LORD men depart from evil'; and cf. the description of Job given in i. 1, 'one that feared God, and eschewed (the same word in the original as that used here for *depart from*) evil.'

The reading in this verse is not certain, as a large number of MSS. and some editions of the Hebrew text have 'the LORD' (i.e. Jehovah) instead of 'the Lord' (i.e. Adonay). The latter word *Adonay* occurs nowhere else in this book, whereas, as we have already seen, *Jehovah* occasionally escapes from the lips of Job (see the note on i. 21), and if the passage before us is a reminiscence of the language of the book of Proverbs cited above, its occurrence would easily and naturally be accounted for here.

**XXIX.—XXXI.**  Job's second monologue.

This second monologue, which gives the last words of Job in the discussion, is entirely free from the perplexing difficulties which have met us in the earlier one. Here and there the text and meaning of the words may be most uncertain, but the general drift and purpose of the whole section is perfectly clear. Job now returns from the general subject to the consideration of his own case. His thoughts go back to the days of old, and he begins with a beautiful description of his former prosperity when God was with him and he was respected and honoured of all men. He then describes in touching and pathetic terms the miseries of the present, and after repudiating all offences against the moral law, which (on the orthodox theory of retribution) would naturally account for such suffering, he ends with an appeal to God to meet him and bring a definite accusation against him. Thus in this monologue taken as a whole Job is simply reasserting in calmer language and with greater elaborateness of detail (consistently with the less passionate tone adopted since xix.) the position which he has all along maintained with regard to the purely *personal* part of the question. God formerly was his friend. Now He is his enemy : he knows of no reason that can account for this change, but yet is sure that, if he could only meet God face to face, hear what He has to say, and plead his cause before Him, somehow or other all would be well.

Of the whole section, Cox truly says that ' from a purely literary point of view the second monologue is even more beautiful than the first. It has, indeed, no passage of such sustained grandeur, none so rich in instruction or so profoundly suggestive, as the disquisition on Wisdom and Understanding in Chapter xxviii. ; but for grace, and pathos, in charm of picturesque narrative, and pensive, tender, yet self-controlled emotion richly and variously expressed, it may be doubted whether Chapters xxix. and xxxi. have ever been surpassed, while even their singular power is enhanced by the contrasts supplied in Chapter xxx. He must be dull and hard indeed who can read these Chapters without being touched to the very heart.'

From what has been already said it will be seen that the monologue falls into three main divisions, which may be thus summarized :

(1)  '*A sorrow's crown of sorrows is remembering happier things.*' xxix.

(2)  ' *The lowness of the present state
that sets the past in this relief.*'  xxx.

(3)  *Solemn repudiation of all offences that might account for the change in God's treatment, and final cry for God to meet him.*  xxxi.

**XXIX.  A sorrow's crown of sorrows is remembering happier things.**

The chapter may be further subdivided as follows :

(*a*)  *Description of Job's state when God was with him in the days of old.*  1—10.

(b) *The reason for the respect and honour in which he was then held.* 11—17.

(c) *Description of his former feelings.* 18—20.

(d) *Renewed description of the respect then paid to him.* 21—25.

**XXIX.** 1 And Job again took up his parable, and said,
2 Oh that I were as in the months of old,
As in the days when God watched over me;
3 When his lamp shined ¹upon my head,
And by his light I walked through darkness;
4 As I was in ²the ripeness of my days,
When the ³secret of God was upon my tent;
5 When the Almighty was yet with me,
And my children were about me;

¹ Or, *above*  ² Heb. *my days of autumn.*  ³ Or, *counsel* Or, *friendship*

**1—10. Description of Job's state when God was with him in the days of old.** Job here gives expression to a great longing for a return of the old bright days when God was with him, and His light shone round about him (1—3), when he enjoyed God's friendship, and was blessed with the companionship of his children (4, 5). All things combined to minister to his prosperity (6), while, if he took his seat 'in the gate' for judgment, all men, great and small, young and old, united to show him respect and esteem (7—10).

1. *And Job again took up his parable.* See the note on xxvii. 1.

3. *When his lamp shined upon my head.* God's *lamp*, like 'the light of His countenance' (Ps. lxxx. 3), is a natural figure for the gracious loving-kindness of God.

4. *As I was in the ripeness of my days.* Better than A.V. *the days of my youth* (after the Vulgate), for the phrase is literally (as noted in R.V. marg.) *my days of autumn.* There is no thought of his days being in 'the sere and yellow leaf,' but the expression refers to the time when he was in his prime; or possibly, as Davidson thinks, he may only mean to 'compare his former time of prosperity to the *season* of the year, the autumn, the time of fruit-gathering and plenty and joy.' (This however would rather require the rendering *days of my autumn,* instead of *my days of autumn;* but will the Hebrew allow of this?)

*When the secret of God was upon my tent.* The word for *secret* has already occurred twice in this book, viz. in xv. 8, 'Hast thou heard the *secret counsel* of God?' and in xix. 19, 'All my inward friends (lit. 'the men of my *council*') abhor me,' and for God's *secret* cf. Amos iii. 7; Ps. xxv. 14; Prov. iii. 32. The word seems here to mean *friendship* rather than *counsel.*

6 When my steps were washed with butter,
  And the rock poured me out rivers of oil !
7 When I went forth to the gate unto the city,
  When I prepared my seat in the ¹street,
8 The young men saw me and hid themselves,
  And the aged rose up and stood ;
9 The princes refrained talking,
  And laid their hand on their mouth ;
10 The voice of the nobles was ²hushed,
   And their tongue cleaved to the roof of their mouth.
11 For when the ear heard *me*, then it blessed me ;
   And when the eye saw *me*, it gave witness unto me :

---

¹ Or, *broad place*        ² Heb. *hid.*

6. *When my steps were washed with butter, and the rock poured me out rivers of oil!* The figures here used are natural ones to express plenty and prosperity. For *butter* cf. xx. 17, where it is similarly used, 'He shall not look upon the rivers, the flowing streams of honey and *butter.*' Oil is frequently used to represent plenty and fertility, e.g. 2 Kings xviii. 32. The steps being *washed with butter* indicates the overflowing abundance in the midst of which he walked, while the hard rock *pouring out rivers of oil* suggests that the most surprising and unexpected blessings were showered upon him.

7. *When I went forth to the gate unto the city, when I prepared my seat in the street.* The *gate* and the street or rather *broad place* (R.V. marg.) denote the place where justice was administered : the broad, open square inside the city gate. For *the gate* see the note on v. 4, and for the *broad place* within it used as a place of assembly cf. 2 Chr. xxxii. 6 ; Nehem. viii. 1. The words of the verse before us *unto the city* seem to imply that Job's own dwelling was in the country, and that he came in to the city in the morning as a magistrate to administer justice. Cf. a similar allusion in xxxi. 21. [The LXX. translators must have read שַׁחַר *early*, ὄρθριος, instead of שַׁעַר, *to the gate.*]

8. *and hid themselves,* i.e. withdrew out of respect and reverence.

9, 10. *The princes...the nobles.* The use of these terms brings out the character of the society in which Job is supposed to have lived.

*and laid their hand on their mouth,* cf. xxi. 5 ; xl. 4.

11—17. **The reason for the respect and honour in which Job was formerly held.** The reason for this was the estimation in which he was held by all men. All who saw him, or even heard of him, followed him with benedictions (11), because he was the champion of the distressed and helpless (12, 13). His integrity was wrapped round him like a garment, and his uprightness was a crown of glory to him (14). All who were unable to help themselves, whether previously

12  Because I delivered the poor that cried,
    The fatherless also, [1]that had none to help him.
13  The blessing of him that was ready to perish came upon
      me :
    And I caused the widow's heart to sing for joy.
14  I put on righteousness, and it [2]clothed me :
    My justice was as a robe and a [3]diadem.
15  I was eyes to the blind,
    And feet was I to the lame.
16  I was a father to the needy :
    And [4]the cause of him that I knew not I searched out.
17  And I brake the [5]jaws of the unrighteous,
    And plucked the prey out of his teeth.
18  Then I said, I shall die [6]in my nest,
    And I shall multiply my days as [7]the sand :

[1] Or, and him that had &c.
[2] Or, clothed itself with me     [3] Or, turban     [4] Or, the cause which I knew not
[5] Heb. great teeth.     [6] Or, beside  Heb. with.     [7] Or, the phœnix

known to him or not, looked to him for help, and found the succour they needed, and were delivered from their oppressors (15—17).

12. Cf. Ps. lxxii. 12, where the language is very similar. On the *fatherless* and the *widow* (ver. 13) see the note on xxii. 9.

14. *I put on righteousness, and it clothed me*, or more accurately, *it clothed itself with me* (R.V. marg.), as if he was the very incarnation of righteousness. Cf. the phrase used in Judg. vi. 34, 'the spirit of the LORD clothed itself with Gideon,' and see 1 Chr. xii. 18; 2 Chr. xxiv. 20.

*a diadem* : the word is that used of the tiara or turban of the high priest in Zech. iii. 5.

17. *the jaws*, or rather *the great teeth*. The word is the same as that which occurs in Ps. lviii. 6, 'Break out *the great teeth* of the

young lions, O Lord.' Cf. also Prov. xxx. 14 ; Joel i. 6.

18—20. **Description of Job's former feelings.** Job here describes how in these happy days he had felt secure of the continuance of his prosperity, and reckoned on a long and prosperous life, crowned by a peaceful death in his bed (18), for his prosperity seemed firmly rooted, and ministered to by gracious influences of all kinds (19). He had been proud that his honour was untarnished, and that his vigour was always fresh (20).

18. *Then I said.* The R.V. is probably right in taking the whole passage to the end of verse 20 as what Job 'said,' and so translates the verbs in verses 19 and 20 in the *present*, and not (as A.V.) in the *past*.

*And I shall multiply my days as the sand.* The comparison of the

19 My root is ¹spread out ²to the waters,
     And the dew lieth all night upon my branch :
20 My glory is fresh in me,
     And my bow is renewed in my hand.
21 Unto me men gave ear, and waited,
     And kept silence for my counsel.

¹ Heb. *opened.*        ² Or, *by*

multitude of his days to the count-less grains of sand is certainly an unexpected one, but perhaps not more surprising than the comparison of Solomon's 'largeness of heart' to 'the sand that is on the sea shore,' 1 Kings iv. 29 (Heb. v. 9). There is, however, something very attractive in the alternative rendering suggested in the margin of the R.V., *as the phœnix*, which of course takes the words as containing an allusion to the fabled bird of antiquity referred to by Hesiod (*Fragm.* 50) and Herodotus (II. 73). In favour of this interpretation we have (1) a widespread Jewish tradition, the story being frequently referred to in Rabbinical writers and directly connected with this passage (see Buxtorf, Lexicon Chald. and Rabb. s.v. חול), (2) the rendering of the LXX. ὥσπερ στέλεχος φοίνικος, which is perhaps a gloss, or an alteration of the original reading ὥσπερ φοίνιξ, (3) the ren-dering of the Vulgate, *sicut palma*, 'like a palm tree' (cf. Ps. xcii. 12), 'phœnix' being the name for both the bird and the tree, (4) the con-text, as this rendering makes the parallelism very complete :
'I said, I shall die in my nest,
 I shall multiply my days as the phœnix.'
It may be added that a mytho-logical allusion of this kind would be perfectly natural in the mouth

of Job. Cf. iii. 8 ; ix. 13 ; xxvi. 12, 13. But as the word חול everywhere else means *sand*, and is so translated here by the Targum, Syriac, and Arabic, the alternative suggested above cannot be considered certain, and though it deserves a place in the margin it is perhaps well that the Revisers did not admit it to a place in the text. On the fable of the phœnix see further Bp. Lightfoot on Clem. Rom. I. xxv.

19. *My root is spread out to the waters.* Cf. the similar illustration in Ps. i. 3, of the righteous man, 'he shall be like a tree planted by the streams of water'; and Numb. xxiv. 6, 'As cedar trees beside the waters.'

*And the dew lieth all night upon my branch.* For the dew as an emblem of refreshment and gracious influence see Deut. xxxii. 2; Ps. cxxxiii. 3; Prov. xix. 12 ; Hos. xiv. 6.

20. *My glory is fresh in me.* Glory here seems to signify honour or reputation. This, Job says, was untarnished. *My bow* in the next clause is (as frequently) a symbol of strength. To 'break the bow' is to destroy anyone's strength, see Jer. xlix. 35 ; Hos. i. 5. So for the bow to be *renewed* is for the strength to remain vigorous and lusty.

21—25. **Renewed description of the respect formerly paid to him.** In those days, if a debate arose, men waited and listened for

22 After my words they spake not again ;
　And my speech dropped upon them.
23 And they waited for me as for the rain ;
　And they opened their mouth wide *as* for the latter rain.
24 [1]If I laughed on them, they [2]believed *it* not ;
　And the light of my countenance they cast not down.
25 I chose out their way, and sat *as* chief,
　And dwelt as a king in the army,
　As one that comforteth the mourners.

[1] Or, *I smiled on them when they had no confidence*　　[2] Or, *were not confident*

his opinion, and the last word in the discussion rested with him (21, 22). A word from him revived the drooping spirits of others, and he could confidently smile when they were perplexed or despairing (23, 24). He was like a king among them all, or as one who could comfort the hearts of the mourners (25).

22, 23. For the illustration here given cf. Deut. xxxii. 2, 'My doctrine shall drop as the rain, my speech shall distil as the dew, as the small rain upon the tender herb, and as the showers upon the grass.' For *the latter rain*, i.e. the showers of spring in March and April, and its specially *refreshing* character, see Prov. xvi. 15, and Hosea vi. 3.

24. *If I laughed on them, they believed* it *not*, i.e. it seemed too good to be true that he should smile on them. But it is better to follow the margin of the R.V. and read *I smiled on them when they had no confidence*. When they were downcast and despondent he cheered them up by his brightness.

*And the light of my countenance they cast not down*, i.e. no hopelessness on their part could make him depressed.

25. *I chose out their way.* Either (1) I selected the course for them to follow, or more probably (2) I gladly frequented their society.

**XXX.** Job now turns from the thought of his past happiness and lets his mind dwell upon the wretchedness of the present, describing in pathetic terms his condition of abject misery as a despised outcast, and one who suffers from a loathsome disease inflicted by the hand of God. The whole chapter shows very clearly how it is

'The haze of grief
Makes former gladness loom so great,
The lowness of the present state
That sets the past in this relief.'

The detailed analysis may be given as follows :

(1) *Description of the outcasts who now mock him.* 1—8.
(2) *The indignities which he has to suffer at their hands.* 9—15.
(3) *His hapless plight and the description of his disease.* 16—23.
(4) *Despairing cry, suggested by the contrast between the brightness of the past and his present abject misery.* 24—31.

**XXX.**  1 But now they that are younger than I have
me in derision,
Whose fathers I disdained to set with the dogs of my flock.
2 Yea, the strength of their hands, whereto should it profit
me?
Men in whom ¹ripe age is perished.
3 They are gaunt with want and famine ;
²They gnaw the dry ground, ³in the gloom of wasteness
and desolation.

¹ Or, *vigour*          ² Or, *They flee into the wilderness, into &c.*
³ Or, which *yesternight* was   Or, *on the eve of*

**1—8. Description of the out-
casts who now mock him.** All
is changed now, for those whom he
had formerly despised now make a
mockery of him, feeble, half-starved
creatures who prowl round in the
desert, sustaining themselves on
such leaves and roots as they can
find there (1—4); men after whom
a hue and cry is raised if they
appear in civilized society (5), poor
creatures who are forced to live
in dens and caves (6), who creep
about in the bush, as outcasts driven
out from the land (7, 8). The whole
description should be compared
with that given in xxiv. 5—8 (where
see note). Both passages obviously
refer to the same race of aborigines,
driven out by some stronger con-
quering power.

1. *But now they that are younger
than I have me in derision.* Formerly when he came into the
assembly 'the young men saw' him,
'and hid themselves,' see xxix. 8.
*Whose fathers I disdained to set
with the dogs of my flock.* Dogs
were used in the East, not for
driving the sheep, but simply for
protecting them from the attacks
of wolves and jackals by night.
Cf. Tristram, *Nat. Hist. of the*

*Bible*, p. 141, ' The shepherd's dog
of Syria is not the intelligent
companion and henchman of his
master; he is simply the guardian
of the flock at night from wild
beasts.' Job means to say that formerly he had considered the race of
men who now mock him as unfit to
be regarded as the equals of even
such creatures as these.

2. *Yea, the strength of their
hands &c.* So feeble were they that
he could look for no profit from
their labour.

*ripe age.* The word occurs again
only in v. 26. The R.V. is better than
the A.V. *old age;* but the margin of
the R.V. is better still, *vigour*.

3. *They are gaunt with want
and famine.* The words used in
this clause are all rare ones. *Gaunt*
is, literally, hard or barren, and
probably here means wizened. It
is used again only in iii. 7, and
Is. xlix. 21. *want* occurs elsewhere
only in Prov. xxviii. 22; *famine*
only in v. 22.

*They gnaw the dry ground.* The
word for *gnaw* is only found again
in ver. 17 of this chapter. The
R.V. is probably correct (so the
Vulgate), but there is some authority
for the rendering of the A.V. (and

4 They pluck salt-wort by the bushes ;
   And the roots of the broom *are* [1]their meat.
5 They are driven forth from the midst *of men* ;
   They cry after them as after a thief.
6 [2]In the clefts of the valleys must they dwell,
   In holes of the earth and of the rocks.
7 Among the bushes they bray ;
   Under the [3]nettles they [4]are gathered together.

---

[1] Or, *to warm them*          [2] Or, *In the most gloomy valleys*
[3] Or, *wild vetches*          [4] Or, *stretch themselves*

---

R.V. marg.) *fleeing into* (so LXX. and Targ.). Taking the R.V. as right the reference will be to the attempt of these poor creatures to secure a scanty sustenance from the desert.

*in the gloom.* The meaning of the Hebrew word is very doubtful : elsewhere it means *yesterday* or *recently*. See Gen. xix. 34; xxxi. 29, 42; 2 Kings ix. 26. If this meaning be retained here the clause must be translated, *which formerly was desolate and waste;* so substantially R.V. marg. as well as A.V. But the thought is hardly a natural or appropriate one, and on the whole it is best to retain the rendering of R.V. though possibly the text may be corrupt.

4. *They pluck salt-wort by the bushes.* The plant is mentioned nowhere else, but is thought to be not (as A.V.) *mallows*, but a species of sea purslaine, which 'grows abundantly on the shores of the Mediterranean, in salt marshes, and also on the shores of the Dead Sea still more luxuriantly...It has small, thick, sour-tasting leaves which could be eaten, but it would be very miserable food.' Tristram, *Nat. Hist. of the Bible*, p. 466.

*And the roots of the broom* (rather than *juniper*, A.V.). See Tristram, *op. cit.* p. 360, where it is noted that 'its roots are very bitter, but its softer portions might doubtless, like many other leguminous plants, sustain life in extremity.' It is possible, however, that instead of *are their meat* we should translate the last word of the verse *to warm them,* in which case the allusion would be to the use of the roots of the broom as fuel. 'It is ruthlessly uprooted by the Arabs, who collect it wherever it is tolerably abundant for the manufacture of charcoal.' Tristram, *ut supr.*, and cf. Ps. cxx. 4, 'coals of broom.'

6. *In the clefts of the valleys must they dwell. Clifts* in the modern text of the A.V. is a misprint for *clifts* and is first found in 1762.

*In holes of the earth and of the rocks.* The word for *rocks* occurs only here and in Jer. iv. 29, of the rocks as a place of refuge. For *holes* as hiding-places see 1 Sam. xiv. 11, and cf. xiii. 6.

7. *nettles.* The plant alluded to (mentioned also in Prov. xxiv. 31; Zeph. ii. 9) can hardly be our stinging-nettle, because it was of sufficient size for these outcasts to shelter under it. According to Tristram it is probably the prickly

11—2

8  *They are* children of fools, yea, children of ¹base men ;
   They ²were scourged out of the land.
9  And now I am become their song,
   Yea, I am a byword unto them.
10 They abhor me, they stand aloof from me,
   And spare not to spit ³in my face.
11 For he hath loosed ⁴his cord, and afflicted me,
   And they have cast off the bridle before me.
12 Upon my right hand rise the ⁵rabble ;
   They thrust aside my feet,
   And they cast up against me their ways of destruction.
13 They ⁶mar my path,
   They set forward my calamity,
   *Even* men that have no helper.

---

¹ Heb. men of *no name.*     ² Or, *are outcasts from the land*
³ Or, *at the sight of me*     ⁴ According to another reading, *my cord* (or
*bowstring*).          ⁵ Or, *brood*          ⁶ Or, *break up*

---

acanthus, a very common and
troublesome weed in Palestine, often
reaching a height of six feet. See
*Nat. Hist. of the Bible,* p. 475.

*they are gathered together,* or
rather (as R.V. marg.) *they stretch
themselves.*

**9—15. The indignities which
he has to suffer at their hands.**
And these are the men who now
make Job a laughing-stock and
pour contempt upon him (9, 10).
God has turned against him, and so
these men cast off all restraint
(11), and, helpless outcasts though
they are, rise up against him and
attack him, adding insult to injury
in their treatment of him (12—14)
until his reputation and honour are
swept away altogether (15).

9. *And now I am become their
song.* Cf. Lam. iii. 14, 'I am become a derision to all my people;
and their song all the day,' and Ps.
lxix. 12.

10. *And spare not to spit in my
face.* Cf. xvii. 6, and Is. l. 6.

11. *For he hath loosed his cord.*
If the reading is correct the reference might be to the uncovering the
bowstring in order to shoot, as in
Hab. iii. 9, 'Thy bow was made quite
bare.' So apparently the LXX. ἀνοί-
ξας γὰρ φαρέτραν αὐτοῦ, which is
followed by the Vulgate. Or the
words might be better taken of the
cord or rein, wherewith God had
controlled Job's assailants : this is
now *loosed,* so they *cast off the
bridle before* him. But the marginal reading of the Hebrew is '*my*
cord,' in which case the word must
be taken of the string of Job's bow
(symbolic of strength) which is now
relaxed. Contrast what he said in
xxix. 20 of the days of his prosperity : 'my bow is renewed in my
hand.'

12. *they cast up against me
their ways of destruction.* The

14 ¹As through a wide breach they come :
   In the midst of the ruin they roll themselves *upon me.*
15 Terrors are turned upon me,
   ²They chase ³mine honour as the wind ;
   And my welfare is passed away as a cloud.
16 And now my soul is poured out ⁴within me ;
   Days of affliction have taken hold upon me.
17 In the night season my bones are ⁵pierced ⁶in me,
   And ⁷the *pains* that gnaw me take no rest.

---

¹ Or, *As a wide breaking in* of waters       ² Or, *Thou chasest*
³ Or, *my nobility*          ⁴ Heb. *upon.*        ⁵ Or, *corroded* and drop
*away from me*       ⁶ Heb. *from off.*       ⁷ Or, *my sinews take &c.*

---

figure is seemingly taken from an assault upon a city, the besieging army casting up their mounts against it. Cf. xix. 12.

14. The figure is still that of the storming of a city. The breach is made in the walls, and through it the enemy pours in *in the midst of the ruin.*

15. *Terrors are turned upon me.* The word for 'terrors' is that used by Bildad in xviii. 11, ' *Terrors* shall make him afraid on every side.'

16—23. His hapless plight and the description of his disease. Added to this cruel treatment from the very abjects, there is the misery brought about by the disease from which he suffers; days and nights of acute, gnawing pains are his (16, 17): God has seized him and cast him down to the lowest depths (18, 19). The sufferer appeals to Him in vain for help (20). He has become a cruel persecutor to him (21); He whirls him away in the storm of His wrath, and is rapidly bringing him to death, the 'meeting-place' for all living (22, 23).

16. *And now.* Each of the first three sections in this chapter begins with the same words. Cf. ver. 1 and 9.

*my soul is poured out within me* (lit. *upon me*), cf. Ps. xlii. 4, ' I pour out my soul *within* (lit. *upon*) me.'

17. *In the night season my bones are pierced in me,* or possibly, as R.V. marg., *are corroded* and drop *away from me.* The Hebrew is difficult, but the general sense is clear; the reference being to the sufferings caused by the painful disease from which he suffered, and its effect upon his bones. Leprosy has been called by an Arabian historian *the disease which devours the limbs.*

*And the* pains *that gnaw me.* Literally *my gnawers,* the word being the same that is used in ver. 3, ' They *gnaw* the ground.' The Vulgate has *qui me comedunt.* But the LXX. τὰ δὲ νεῦρά μου, with several Rabbinic authorities, takes the word as referring to the *sinews.* So A.V. and R.V. marg.

18. A verse which is the despair of commentators. As it stands it seems impossible to extract any intelligible sense out of it : and none of the

18 ¹By the great force *of my disease* is my garment dis-
   figured :
   It bindeth me about as the collar of my coat.
19 He hath cast me into the mire,
   And I am become like dust and ashes.
20 I cry unto thee, and thou dost not answer me :
   I stand up, and thou lookest at me.
21 Thou art turned to be cruel to me :
   With the might of thy hand thou persecutest me.
22 Thou liftest me up to the wind, thou causest me to ride
   *upon it* ;
   And thou dissolvest me in the storm.
23 For I know that thou wilt bring me to death,
   And to ²the house appointed for all living.

---

¹ Or, *By* his *great force is &c.*        ² Or, *the house of meeting for &c.*

---

emendations that have been suggested can be regarded as entirely
satisfactory. The best, perhaps, is
that of Siegfried, suggested by
the LXX., ἐπελάβετό μου τῆς στολῆς,
'By His great force He hath laid
hold of my garment.' The underlying image is that of pursuit by an
enemy; the pursuer seizes him by
the garment in which he is closely
enveloped, and throws him down.
But even then the next clause
remains a difficulty, and it is best to
admit that the text is corrupt and
the true meaning of the verse lost
beyond recovery.

19. *He hath cast me into the
mire.* For the figure cf. Ps. xl. 2;
lxix. 2.

*I am become like dust and ashes,*
i.e. he is like the dunghill upon
which he is seated. Cf. ii. 8.

20. *I stand up, and thou lookest
at me,* i.e. God regards him with
indifference, looks at him, but does
nothing to help him. This must

be the meaning of the words if
the text is correct. But there is
some slight authority for the insertion of the negative before the verb:
*and thou regardest me not.* So the
Vulg. and one Hebrew MS. Hence
A.V.

21. *thou persecutest me.* The
same word as that used in xvi. 9,
'He hath torn me in his wrath, and
*persecuted me.'*

22. *thou dissolvest me in the
storm.* This is probably correct,
the word rendered *storm* being
apparently the same as that found
in xxxvi. 29, '*the thunderings* of his
pavilion'; and xxxix. 7, '*the shoutings* of the driver.'

23. *the house appointed for all
living* : better as R.V. marg. *the
house of meeting for all living.*
The word is the same as that in the
phrase so frequently used of the
tabernacle, the tent of *meeting* (*sc.*
of God with His people); Exod.
xxvii. 21, &c.

24 ¹Surely against a ruinous heap he will not put forth his
  hand;
  Though *it be* in his destruction, *one may utter* a cry
  because of these things.
25 Did not I weep for him that was in trouble?
  Was not my soul grieved for the needy?
26 When I looked for good, then evil came;
  And when I waited for light, there came darkness.
27 My bowels boil, and rest not;
  Days of affliction are come upon me.
28 I go ²mourning without the sun:
  I stand up in the assembly, and cry for help.

¹ Or, *Howbeit doth not one stretch out the hand in his fall? or in his calamity
  therefore cry for help?*    ² Or, *blackened, but not by the sun*

24—31. **Despairing cry, suggested by the contrast between the brightness of the past and his present abject misery.** Since, then, he is so utterly ruined, is it not natural that he should stretch out his hand and cry for help (24)? In former days he had brought sympathy to cheer others, but now when he looks for blessings for himself there is nothing but misery and unrest (25—27). He is dried up, helpless, fit only to keep company with the beasts of the desert (28, 29); his skin is shrivelled up and his bones consumed by a raging fire within (30). What wonder then that all the music of his life has become a mournful dirge (31)?

24. *Surely against a ruinous heap he will not put forth his hand &c.* One of the most difficult verses in the poem. The ancient versions are quite unintelligible, and it must be admitted that it is very difficult to extract any satisfactory sense from the Hebrew text. Of the various renderings proposed that in the margin of the R.V. is perhaps the most satisfactory: *Howbeit doth not one stretch out the hand in his fall? or in his calamity therefore cry for help?* But the probability is that there is some deep-seated corruption of the text and that the true reading cannot now be recovered.

27. *My bowels boil, and rest not.* In this and the following verses Job is describing the effects of the loathsome disease from which he suffered. The *bowels* are regarded as the seat of the emotions and feelings. Cf. Lam. i. 20, 'I am in distress, my bowels are troubled.' Cant. v. 4 (see R.V. marg.); Is. xvi. 11. The word for *boil* is found again in xli. 31 (Heb. 23): elsewhere only in Ezek. xxiv. 5.

28. *I go mourning without the sun.* For the first words cf. Ps. xlii. 9. But the clause is best translated here: *I am blackened, but not by the sun*; referring, of course, to the effect of the disease.

*I stand up in the assembly.* The *assembly* is the court in which he conceives himself as pleading.

29 I am a brother to jackals,
   And a companion to ostriches.
30 My skin is black, *and falleth* from me,
   And my bones are burned with heat.
31 Therefore is my harp *turned* to mourning,
   And my pipe into the voice of them that weep.

29. *I am a brother to jackals.* The A.V. regularly translates the word *tannim*, which is here used, by *dragons* after the Vulgate, but *jackals* is 'the only translation which will harmonize all the passages,' Tristram, *Nat. Hist. of the Bible*, p. 110. See Is. xiii. 22; xxxiv. 13; xliii. 20; Jer. ix. 11; x. 22; Mic. i. 8, &c. The wailing cry of the jackal is frequently alluded to, and it is probably this as well as its association with the desert that makes Job claim kinship with it.

*And a companion to ostriches. owls* of the A.V. follows the Vulgate; but there is no doubt that the ostrich is alluded to. It is frequently mentioned together with jackals, as inhabiting desolate and lonely places, and its cry, says Tristram, is 'like the hoarse lowing of an ox in pain,' *op. cit.* p. 234.

30. The effect of the disease upon his bodily frame. Cf. ver. 17.

31. *my pipe.* See the note on xxi. 12.

**XXXI.** In this third part of the second monologue Job solemnly repudiates all offences, the commission of which might conceivably account for the change in God's treatment of him; after which he ends with a final expression of his longing to meet God. The detailed analysis may be given as follows:

(1) *Repudiation of all sins of sensuality.* 1—12.

(2) *Repudiation of abuse of his power.* 13—23.

(3) *Repudiation of covetousness, idolatry and dishonourable thoughts.* 24—34.

(4) *Final cry, and longing to meet God.* 35—40.

**XXXI.**  1 I made a covenant with mine eyes;
   How then should I look upon a maid?

1—12. **Repudiation of all sins of sensuality.** He begins by describing how he had 'made a covenant' with his eyes, bargaining with them that they should not look upon a woman to lust after her (1), influenced by the love of God, whom he had taken as his portion, and the

fear lest evil should overtake him, as the eye of God was upon him (2—4). If then he has acted deceitfully (and he only asks to be fairly weighed), or if his eyes have enticed him to sin, or if his hands have been polluted, then indeed may all his labours be in vain (5—8).

2 ¹For what *is* the portion of God from above,
　And the heritage of the Almighty from on high?
3 Is it not calamity to the unrighteous,
　And disaster to the workers of iniquity?
4 Doth not he see my ways,
　And number all my steps?
5 If I have walked with vanity,
　And my foot hath hasted to deceit;
6 (Let me be weighed in an even balance,
　That God may know mine integrity;)
7 If my step hath turned out of the way,
　And mine heart walked after mine eyes,
　And if any spot hath cleaved to mine hands:
8 Then let me sow, and let another eat;
　Yea, let ²the produce of my field be rooted out.

¹ Or, *For what portion* should I have *of God...and what heritage &c.? Is there not calamity &c.?*
² Or, *my offspring*　Heb. *my produce.*

Again, if he has sinned with the wife of another, then may he pay the penalty by the dishonour of his own wife, for he would richly deserve it (9—12).

1. *How then should I look upon a maid?* An anticipation of our Lord's words in S. Matt. v. 28.

2—4. These verses indicate the considerations which restrained him from sin: he is flinging himself back into his former feelings and describing them. He was restrained (*a*) by the thought that the sin would cut him off from God. Render with the margin of the R.V. *For what portion* should I have *of God, and what heritage of the Almighty?* (*b*) by the fear of the punishment of wrong-doing, *Is there not calamity to the unrighteous &c.?* (R.V. marg.); and (*c*) by the thought that God's all-seeing eye was on him (4).

5—7 contain the protestation, repudiating any sin of hypocrisy or the slightest deviation from the right course; ver. 6 being parenthetical; and then ver. 8 contains the imprecation on himself, if he has been guilty of any of the sins he has repudiated.

8. *Then let me sow, and let another eat.* Cf. the denunciations in Lev. xxvi. 16; Deut. xxviii. 33.

*the produce of my field.* [Heb. *my produce.*] It is doubtful whether the word should be taken in this sense or (as in A.V. and R.V. marg.) *my offspring* (Vulg. *progenies mea,* after Symmachus τὰ ἔκγονά μου). In both the other passages in which it occurs in Job (v. 25; xxvii. 14) it is used of *offspring*, as it is in Is. xlviii. 19; lxi. 9; lxv. 23; but in Is. xxxiv. 1; xlii. 5, it must be taken of the *produce of the earth*, and this seems to suit the parallelism best here.

9 If mine heart have been enticed unto a woman,
   And I have laid wait at my neighbour's door:
10 Then let my wife grind unto another,
   And let others bow down upon her.
11 For that were an heinous crime;
   Yea, it were an iniquity to be punished by the judges:
12 For it is a fire that consumeth unto ¹Destruction,
   And would root out all mine increase.
13 If I did despise the cause of my manservant or of my
     maidservant,
   When they contended with me:
14 What then shall I do when God riseth up?
   And when he visiteth, what shall I answer him?
15 Did not he that made me in the womb make him?
   And did not one fashion us in the womb?

---

¹ Heb. *Abaddon.*    See ch. xxvi. 6.

---

**9.** A further protestation, followed, as before, by an imprecation upon himself in ver. 10, *grind unto another,* i.e. serve him as his slave—the slave being also generally the concubine of the master. For women grinding cf. S. Matt. xxiv. 41.

**11.** *For that*—viz. to dishonour his neighbour's wife—*were an heinous crime.* The last word is specially used in the 'law of holiness' in Leviticus, of unchastity and licentiousness. See Lev. xviii. 17; xix. 29; xx. 14.

**12.** *For it*—viz. the sin—*is a fire that consumeth unto Destruction.* The Hebrew word is *Abaddon,* on which see the note on xxvi. 6. For the complete ruin which this sin entailed Davidson aptly refers to Proverbs v. 8—14; vi. 24—35; vii. 26, 27.

**13—23. Repudiation of abuse of his power.** Had he dealt unfairly by his household servants, he would be dumbfoundered in the presence of God, for all are equally subject to Him as His creation (13—15). Had he oppressed the poor, or failed in kindness to the widow and the fatherless (16, 17)—nay he has watched over and protected them (18)—had he turned the naked from his door unclothed and unwarmed (19, 20), had he meanly raised his hand against those who had no power of remonstrance (21), then gladly would he suffer the penalty of seeing his arm fall powerless by his side (22); for he was restrained from such sins by the thought of God's majesty and judgment (23).

**14.** *when God riseth up, sc.* to judgment.

**15.** The thought is similar to that expressed by S. Paul in Eph. vi. 9, 'And, ye masters, do the same things unto them, and forbear threatening: knowing that both

16  If I have withheld ¹the poor from *their* desire,
    Or have caused the eyes of the widow to fail ;
17  Or have eaten my morsel alone,
    And the fatherless hath not eaten thereof ;
18  (Nay, from my youth he grew up with me as with a
        father,
    And I have been her guide from my mother's womb ;)
19  If I have seen any perish for want of clothing,
    Or that the needy had no covering ;
20  If his loins have not blessed me,
    And if he were not warmed with the fleece of my sheep ;
21  If I have lifted up my hand against the fatherless,
    Because I saw my help in the gate :
22  Then let my shoulder fall from the shoulder blade,
    And mine arm be broken from the bone.
23  For calamity from God was a terror to me,
    And by reason of his excellency I could do nothing.
24  If I have made gold my hope,
    And have said to the fine gold, *Thou art* my confidence ;

---

¹ Or, *aught that the poor desired*

---

their Master and yours is in heaven, and there is no respect of persons with Him.'

16, 17.  Cf. xxii. 6, 7, 9, and xxix. 11—17, where see notes.

18 is parenthetical like ver. 6.

20.  *the fleece of my sheep.* Cf. Prov. xxvii. 26, 'the lambs are for thy clothing.'

21.  *Because I saw my help in the gate,* i.e. because I saw that I could obtain a favourable verdict in court.  *the gate* as in v. 4 ; xxix. 7.

22.  The imprecation, suggested by the 'lifting up the hand' of the previous verse. *Chanelbone* (in the margin of the A.V.) is an old term for the collar-bone. The Hebrew word only occurs in this sense here.

23.  The considerations which restrained him from these sins of oppression, just as in ver. 2—4 he stated those which kept him from indulging in sensual sins.

*calamity from God was a terror to me,* i.e. he was restrained by the fear of God's judgment.  *calamity* as in ver. 3.

*And by reason of his excellency* ; or rather *Majesty,* as Davidson renders it.

24—34.  **Repudiation of covetousness, idolatry, and dishonourable thoughts.**  If he had put his trust in his riches (24, 25), or had been led astray to worship the heavenly bodies (26, 27), that would indeed have been a sin deserving of punishment as a virtual denial of God (28).  If he had exulted in the misfortunes of others (29)—as a matter of fact he had been careful

25 If I rejoiced because my wealth was great,
   And because mine hand had gotten much ;
26 If I beheld ¹the sun when it shined,
   Or the moon walking in brightness ;
27 And my heart hath been secretly enticed,
   And ²my mouth hath kissed my hand :
28 This also were an iniquity to be punished by the judges :
   For I should have ³lied to God that is above.
29 If I rejoiced at the destruction of him that hated me,
   Or lifted up myself when evil found him ;
30 (Yea, I suffered not my ⁴mouth to sin
   By asking his life with a curse ;)
31 If the men of my tent said not,
   ⁵Who can find one that hath not been satisfied with his
   flesh ?

¹ Heb. *the light.*      ² Heb. *my hand hath kissed my mouth.*
³ Or, *denied God*      ⁴ Heb. *palate.*
⁵ Or, *Oh that we had of his flesh ! we cannot be satisfied.*

never to invoke evil upon his enemy (30)—if his companions could not bear testimony to his generosity and ready hospitality (31, 32), if he had tried to conceal his guilt (as Adam tried to conceal his in the garden) from fear of men, and if in dread of their contempt he had hidden himself (33, 34).

24. *fine gold.* See on xxviii. 16.

26. *If I beheld the sun when it shined &c.* : the allusion is to the worship of the heavenly bodies, a sin to which Israel was much drawn during the later years of the kingdom. See the references to it in 2 Kings xvii. 16; xxi. 3, 5 ; xxiii. 4, 5, 12 ; Zeph. i. 5 ; Jer. vii. 18 ; viii. 2; xix. 13; xliv. 17; Ezek. viii. 16, as well as the warning against it in Deut. iv. 19 ; xvii. 3.

27. *And my mouth hath kissed my hand.* For the kiss as symbolizing worship, and offered to idols

see 1 Kings xix. 18 ; Hos. xiii. 2 ; and cf. Pliny, *Hist. Nat.* xxviii. 2, ' Inter adorandum dexteram ad osculum referimus et totum corpus circumagimus.'

28. *This also were an iniquity to be punished by the judges.* Substantially repeated from verse 11.

*For I should have lied to God.* Better perhaps with R.V. marg. *denied God.*

30 is parenthetical, like verses 6 and 18.

31. *If the men of my tent said not &c.* The A.V. (with which the margin of the R.V. agrees) is quite defensible as a translation of the Hebrew, but it does not suit well with the context; and it is far more natural to render as is done in R.V., *Who can find one that hath not been satisfied with his flesh?* though the rendering has no support from antiquity; and *meat* might have seemed more natural than *flesh* in

32 The stranger did not lodge in the street ;
　　But I opened my doors to ¹the traveller ;
33 If ²like Adam I covered my transgressions,
　　By hiding mine iniquity in my bosom ;
34 Because I feared the great multitude,
　　And the contempt of families terrified me,
　　So that I kept silence, and went not out of the door—
35 Oh that I had one to hear me !

¹ Heb. *the way*.　　　² Or, *after the manner of men*

this connexion. *Flesh* may, however, perhaps be accounted for as pointing to the sumptuous character of the entertainment he provided : flesh-meat being in most cases reserved for great occasions.

32. *The stranger did not lodge in the street.* This verse may be illustrated from, and possibly contains a reminiscence of the story of Lot and the two angels in Gen. xix. ; and cf. Judg. xix. 19, 20.

33. *If like Adam I covered my transgressions.* Cf. Hos. vi. 7, 'But they, *like Adam*, have transgressed the covenant.' In both these passages it is hard to decide which is the right translation, *like Adam*, or *after the manner of men*, R.V. marg. The historical allusion would be quite in place here, and in harmony with verse 32, and other such possible allusions in the book; and on the whole it seems preferable to the marginal rendering, for to say baldly that it is 'after the manner of men' to 'hide iniquity in their bosom,' and to 'cover their transgression' is rather sweeping. Why should Job attribute hypocrisy to the race, rather than the other sins of which he had been speaking? Whereas to cover his transgression was exactly what Adam attempted to do. (The versions give very

little help. The LXX. misses the meaning altogether, or may have had a different reading. The Vulgate, however, has *sicut homo*.)

34. *Because I feared the great multitude*, influenced, as we should say, by public opinion, and the dread of being despised and looked down on.

*So that I kept silence, and went not of the door*—the idea is that had he been conscious of sins, he would have shut himself up for fear of exposure. How contrary this was to his real course of conduct is shown by xxix. 7 seq. and 25.

35—40. **Final cry, and longing to meet God.** Here Job suddenly breaks off, omitting the imprecation which would naturally have followed as in verses 10 and 22; and gives expression to his longing for God to hear him—he is ready, he says, to sign his name to his protestations of innocence and would give much to have the indictment which his adversary has drawn against him (35). If only he had this, he would, not indeed confess to the sins with which it charged him, but would rather boldly pin it upon his breast like some decoration of honour, and would advance in royal fashion to meet the charge (36, 37). Finally, if his broad acres can tell of op-

(Lo, here is my [1]signature, let the Almighty answer me ;)
And *that I had* the [2]indictment which mine adversary
    hath written !

36 Surely I would carry it upon my shoulder ;
    I would bind it unto me as a crown.

37 I would declare unto him the number of my steps ;
    As a prince would I [3]go near unto him.

38 If my land cry out against me,
    And the furrows thereof weep together ;

[1] Heb. *mark*.    [2] Heb. *book*.    [3] Or, *present it* to him

pression, or injustice on his part, then he wishes nothing better than that they should drop out of cultivation altogether (38—40).

35. *Oh that I had one to hear me !* The *one* is, as appears from what follows, God Himself.

*Lo, here is my signature, let the Almighty answer me.* The word for *signature*, is *tav*, the name of the letter *t*, the ancient form of which was a cross. Hence some have thought of Job as making his 'mark' instead of signing his name at the foot of his protestations of innocence. This however is precarious : it probably merely means his sign or signature. The only other occurrence of the word is in Ezek. ix. 4, where it is used of the '*mark* upon the foreheads of the men that sigh and cry' for the abominations in Jerusalem. The rendering of the A.V. *My desire is that the Almighty would answer me,* comes from the Targum, but confuses *mark* (וְתָו *tav*) with the similar word for 'desire' (תַּאֲוָה).

*And* that I had *the indictment which mine adversary hath written !* (This rendering and not that of the A.V. is correct.) The *adversary* is, of course, God. The expressions in this clause are taken

from legal procedure. The 'Adversary' being the opponent in a suit or controversy (cf. for the phraseology Judg. xii. 2 ; Is. xli. 11 ; Jer. xv. 10). The *indictment* is literally *book* (hence A.V.), i.e. the written accusation.

36. If only he had this *indictment* he would not regard it as something to be ashamed of, but would treat it as some precious treasure, to be laid upon the shoulder, or bound like a crown round his brow. For the binding of ornaments on the person cf. Is. xlix. 18.

37. *I would declare unto him the number of my steps,* i.e. there is nothing in his past life or actions which he has to conceal.

*As a prince would I go near unto him,* i.e. confidently and proudly, not like one with the consciousness of guilt.

38—40. Job here takes up the series of imprecations once more. Many commentators have concluded that these verses are out of place, and would insert them earlier in the chapter, before the expression of the longing to meet God, placing them between verses 23 and 24. But this change seems unnecessary, and, as Davidson says, 'if the verses belong to the passage at all, which there is

39 If I have eaten the ¹fruits thereof without money,
    Or have caused the owners thereof to lose their life :
40 Let ²thistles grow instead of wheat,
    And ³cockle instead of barley.

     The words of Job are ended.

¹ Heb. *strength.*      ² Or, *thorns*      ³ Or, *noisome weeds*

no reason to doubt, they seem to stand in the only place suitable for them.'

38. *If my land cry out against me &c.* The language is very forcible and expressive—the land itself being regarded as wronged, and hence crying out, and even weeping, the wrong supposed being, as is shown by verse 39, the robbery of the land, or the forcible seizing of it from the rightful owners, who are in some way or other done to death, made to *lose their life.* Cf. the story of Naboth's vineyard in 1 Kings xxi.

40. *Let thistles grow instead of wheat.* Rather *thorns* or *brambles* than *thistles.* Cf. Hos. ix. 6 ; Is. xxxiv. 13. *cockle,* mentioned here only. From the derivation the word must mean some offensively smelling plant, but what is not certain. See Tristram, *Natural History of the Bible,* p. 439.

*The words of Job are ended.* Probably an editorial note, similar to that found at the close of the second book of the Psalms (Ps. lxxii.), ' The prayers of David the son of Jesse are ended.'

## PART III.   THE SPEECHES OF ELIHU.
## CHAPTERS XXXII.—XXXVII.

We have now come to the close of the debate between Job and his friends, and with the termination of this it must be admitted that the interest of the book begins to wane. We crossed the watershed (so to speak) in the second circle of speeches. Since then we have seen how the friends were gradually silenced and Job left master of the field, having demolished their position, but having started no theory of his own to account for suffering. *Negatively* he has broken down an inadequate theory ; but *positively* all that he has accomplished is to advance certain considerations (the doctrine of a future life and of God as his vindicator) which enable him to acquiesce, though as his parting words show, not without difficulty, in his present ignorance. The close of the last chapter manifests how keenly he felt the unsatisfactoriness of his present position, even though the soreness of feeling has largely passed away. He still longs for light · " Give light and let me die " (ἐν δὲ φάει καὶ ὄλεσσον) might almost be taken as the expression of his feelings. And now quite suddenly a new character appears on the scene, who has never been previously introduced or even mentioned earlier in the book ; and, as was shown in the Introduction, it is more than doubtful whether this section of the work, which contains his speeches (xxxii.—xxxvii.), comes from the same hand as the rest of the poem. For the arguments on either side see the Introd. p. xxv. It was there shown that probable motives for the introduction of these chapters might be found in the desire to rebuke the lack of reverence towards God which Job had frequently manifested, and also to give fuller expression to a view of the purpose of suffering which is almost overlooked in the original poem, viz. that it is, to use Butler's expression, 'designed for moral discipline and improvement.' Of this there is no trace in the Prologue, which very forcibly indicates how suffering tests a man, i.e. is designed for his *probation* but gives no hint of its effect on character, or of the *improvement* which it is intended to work. Faint indications of this thought may be detected here and there in the debate between Job and his friends (see especially v. 8, 17), but it is nowhere put prominently forward, nor does it appear that the author attached any special importance to it. Hence it is not improbable that when its great value as an element in the solution of the problem of suffering had been fully realized, some later poet introduced this section with the design of giving it its true position and emphasizing its importance. If this is so he deserves a tribute of admiration for the skill with which he has effected the addition to the poem without destroying the unity of the book. He has linked on the speeches to the earlier part by frequent quotations from Job's speeches, and has thus made it appear that Elihu has been a silent listener to the whole argument, and he has connected it naturally with what follows by making the last speech of Elihu appear to be influenced by the gathering storm, out of which the Lord answers Job immediately afterwards.

Altogether Elihu's utterances are made to consist of four distinct speeches contained respectively in (1) xxxii. and xxxiii., (2) xxxiv., (3) xxxv., and (4) xxxvi. and xxxvii. In the first and fourth of these he gives his theory of the purpose of suffering, while in the second and third his main thought is that God's greatness should have prevented Job from charging Him with arbitrariness, and he thus rebukes the temper and spirit of the sufferer, which has evidently deeply shocked him.

**XXXII.**   1 So these three men ceased to answer Job, 2 because he was righteous in his own eyes. Then was kindled the wrath of Elihu the son of Barachel the Buzite, of the family of Ram : against Job was his wrath kindled,

XXXII. 1—5. The friends are silenced, and the new speaker, *Elihu the son of Barachel the Buzite, of the family of Ram*, is introduced.

2. *Elihu* (meaning *He is my God*) occurs elsewhere as the name of Samuel's great-grandfather, 1 Sam. i. 1; of one of David's brethren,

1 Chr. xxvii. 18; of a Manassite, 1 Chr. xii. 20; and of a Korahite, 1 Chr. xxvi. 7. *Barachel* (*God doth bless*) occurs nowhere else. *Buziie*, i.e. descended from Buz the second son of Nahor, Abraham's brother, Gen. xxii. 21; cf. Jer. xxv. 23; *the family of Ram* is mentioned no-

3 because he justified himself rather than God.  Also against
   his three friends was his wrath kindled, because they had
4 found no answer, and yet had condemned Job.  Now
   Elihu had ¹waited to speak unto Job, because they were
5 elder than he.  And when Elihu saw that there was no
   answer in the mouth of these three men, his wrath was
   kindled.
6 And Elihu the son of Barachel the Buzite answered and
   said,
   I am young, and ye are very old ;
   Wherefore I held back, and durst not shew you mine
   opinion.

¹ Heb. *waited for Job with words.*

where else unless Ram be taken as
a shortened form of *Aram* (= Syria),
so Symmachus, Συρίας.

*against Job was his wrath kin-
dled, because he justified himself
rather than God,* i.e. in maintaining
his own righteousness he had im-
pugned God's justice, charging Him
directly with cruelty and unfairness.

3. *because they had found no
answer, and yet had condemned
Job.* Rather, *because they did not
find an answer and condemn* (i.e.
so as to condemn) *Job.* The con-

struction seems to suggest this
rendering.  See Davidson's *Hebrew
Syntax,* § 48 *a.*

The clause is noteworthy as being
according to tradition one of the
*tikkunê Sopherim,* or corrections
of the scribes (see above, p. 38).
The original reading is supposed to
have been *condemned God,* which
was altered by the scribes out of
reverence.  It is probable, however,
that the tradition is erroneous and
that the Massoretic text is correct.

**XXXII. 6—XXXIII. 33.**   The First Speech of Elihu.
This first speech is very largely taken up by the speaker's apology for
intervening ; but after a lengthy and rather pompous introduction he at
last comes to the point, and after summarizing Job's charges and complaints
against God, maintains that Job is wrong in asserting that God will not
answer him, for as a matter of fact, he says, God really does answer men,
and that in various ways.  The speech, then, may be analysed as follows :

(1) *The speaker's apology for interfering : addressed to Job's
friends.* xxxii. 6—22.

(2) *Introductory remarks addressed to Job.*  xxxiii. 1—7.

(3) *Summary of Job's charges against God and complaints that
God will not answer.* 8—13.

(4) *God does answer man, and that in various ways.* 14—28.

(5) *Conclusion, bringing home to Job the object of God's dealings
with men.* 29—33.

7 I said, Days should speak,
   And multitude of years should teach wisdom.

8 But there is a spirit in man,
   And the breath of the Almighty giveth them understanding.

9 It is not the great that are wise,
   Nor the aged that understand judgement.

10 Therefore I ¹said, Hearken to me ;
   I also will shew mine opinion.

11 Behold, I waited for your words,
   I listened for your reasons,
   Whilst ye searched out what to say.

¹ Or, *say*

**XXXII. 6—22. The speaker's apology for interfering : addressed to Job's friends.** Elihu begins by explaining why he has not inter-vened earlier in the debate : he was restrained by the natural modesty of youth in the presence of older and wiser persons (6, 7). But, after all, wisdom is not the exclusive property of the aged, but is a Divine gift, and therefore he will venture to give his opinion (8—10). He has been waiting and listening while they framed their arguments, and has noted how they were utterly unable to convince Job or to answer him (11, 12). It is no excuse to say that he was a greater master of wisdom than they had expected to find him, and that none but God could convince him (13). His de-fence has not touched the position which Elihu himself would take up, for he certainly would not use the friends' arguments (14). He sees how completely they are silenced, and fails to see why he should be required to wait any longer before speaking ; and therefore he will now have his say (15—17), for he is full of matter, and burning with the eager desire to speak and unburthen himself of his thoughts (18—20). He will, then, give his opinion with-out flattery or respect of persons, but simply as a plain blunt man, governed by the fear of God (21, 22).

8. *But there is a spirit in man, &c.*, cf. xxxiii. 4, ' The *spirit* of God hath made me, and the *breath* of the Almighty giveth me life' ; and see the account of the creation of man in Gen. ii. 7, 'The LORD God...breathed into his nostrils the *breath* of life.' This, says Elihu, is the true source of wisdom. The translation of the A.V. *the inspira-tion of the Almighty* comes from the Vulgate (*inspiratio Omnipotentis*), and is interesting as being the sole use of the word *inspiration* in the Old Testament.

10. *Therefore I said, Hearken to me.* The verb in the Hebrew is in the singular, which would suggest that the exhortation is addressed to Job. But the LXX., Syriac, and Vulgate all have the plural, which is probably correct, as the whole of this section appears to be spoken to the friends.

12 Yea, I attended unto you,
　　And, behold, there was none that convinced Job,
　　Or that answered his words, among you.
13 [1]Beware lest ye say, We have found wisdom ;
　　God may vanquish him, not man :
14 For he hath not directed his words against me ;
　　Neither will I answer him with your speeches.
15 They are amazed, they answer no more :
　　They have not a word to say.
16 And shall I wait, because they speak not,
　　Because they stand still, and answer no more ?
17 I also will answer my part,
　　I also will shew mine opinion.
18 For I am full of words ;
　　The spirit [2]within me constraineth me.
19 Behold, my belly is as wine which hath no vent ;
　　Like new [3]bottles [4]it is ready to burst.
20 I will speak, that I may [5]be refreshed ;
　　I will open my lips and answer.
21 Let me not, I pray you, respect any man's person ;
　　Neither will I give flattering titles unto any man.
22 For I know not to give flattering titles ;
　　*Else* would my Maker soon take me away.

[1] Or, *Lest ye should say, We have found out wisdom ; God thrusteth him down, not man : now he &c.*　　　[2] Heb. *of my belly.*　　　[3] Or, *wineskins*
[4] Or, *which are ready*　　　[5] Or, *find relief*

13, 14. *Beware lest ye say &c.* Taking the R.V. as correct, these verses may be regarded as a warning to the friends not to make the excuse that they have met with deeper 'wisdom' than they expected in Job, and that it was beyond the power of man to convict him, a task which must therefore be left to God.

15, 16. Elihu continues half to himself, and half to the bystanders (cf. xxxiv. 10), commenting on the attitude of the friends, and the manner in which they are silenced.

19. *new bottles*, or rather *wineskins*. Cf. S. Matt. ix. 17.

20. *that I may be refreshed*, or rather (as R.V. marg.) *find relief*. Cf. 1 Sam. xvi. 23, where the same phrase is employed of the *relief* which Saul obtained from David's playing, when he was troubled by an evil spirit from God. For the thought of this verse see Wordsworth's *Ode on Intimations of Immortality*:

'A timely utterance gave that thought relief,
　And I again am strong.'

21, 22. A disclaimer of any intention to flatter or to 'respect persons.' That is not his line, for he

**XXXIII.** 1 Howbeit, Job, I pray thee, hear my speech,
And hearken to all my words.

2 Behold now, I have opened my mouth,
My tongue hath spoken in my ¹mouth.

3 My words *shall utter* the uprightness of my heart :
And that which my lips know they shall speak sincerely.

4 The spirit of God hath made me,
And the breath of the Almighty giveth me life.

5 If thou canst, answer thou me ;
Set *thy words* in order before me, stand forth.

6 Behold, ²I am toward God even as thou art :
I also am formed out of the clay.

7 Behold, my terror shall not make thee afraid,
Neither shall my pressure be heavy upon thee.

8 Surely thou hast spoken in mine hearing,
And I have heard the voice of *thy* words, *saying,*

---

¹ Heb. *palate.*     ² Or, *I am according to thy wish in God's stead*

---

knows that if he were guilty of regarding the persons of men, God's judgment would soon and deservedly fall upon him.

**XXXIII. 1—7. Introductory remarks addressed to Job.** Elihu now turns to Job, and addressing him by name asks his attention (1), while he proceeds to speak out his thoughts candidly and sincerely (2, 3), as God who created him enables him (4); and then let Job answer him if he can (5), for both alike are God's creation, and thus equals, and it is not for him, a mere man, to overwhelm his opponent with terror, as God might do (6, 7).

4. Cf. xxxii. 8, where see note.

6, 7. *Behold, I am toward God even as thou art,* i.e., I stand in the same relation towards Him as thou dost ; explained by the parallel clause, *I also am formed out of the clay.* And since Elihu is thus a mere man like Job himself, they can meet on equal terms, and there is no

fear of his overwhelming him with his terror, as Job had always felt that God would do. The rendering of the A.V. (with which the R.V. marg. agrees) suggests that Elihu regards himself as God's representative, who has appeared in accordance with the wish so often expressed by Job for a Divine Manifestation. But the R.V. is to be preferred.

7 is drawn (with the necessary changes) direct from xiii. 21, where Job says to God, *Let not thy terror make me afraid;* and cf. ix. 34, where almost identical words occur. The allusion to these passages is very clear.

*Neither shall my pressure be heavy upon thee.* This rendering is probably correct, the word for *pressure* (which occurs nowhere else) being formed from a verb found in Prov. xvi. 26. But the A.V. *my hand* has the support of the LXX.; and some probability is given to this (which involves a slight change of

9 I am clean, without transgression ;
   I am innocent, neither is there iniquity in me :
10 Behold, he findeth ¹occasions against me,
   He counteth me for his enemy ;
11 He putteth my feet in the stocks,
   He marketh all my paths.
12 ²Behold, I will answer thee, in this thou art not just ;
   For God is greater than man.
13 ³Why dost thou strive against him?
   For he giveth not account of any of his matters.
14 For God speaketh ⁴once,
   Yea twice, *though man* regardeth it not.

¹ Or, *causes of alienation*
² Or, *Behold, in this thou art not just; I will answer thee : for &c.*
³ Or, *Why dost thou strive against him, for that he…matters?*
⁴ Or, *in one way, yea, in two*

text) by a comparison of xiii. 21, *Withdraw thy hand from me*, as this verse is certainly alluded to in the previous clause.

**8–13. Summary of Job's charges against God and complaints that God will not answer.** He has heard Job's words, and has noted his professions of innocence (8, 9), together with his complaints that God is treating him cruelly and punishing him undeservedly (10, 11); and he feels impelled to reprove him for his unjustifiable and unreasonable murmuring, because God, who is so great, gives no explanation of His treatment of men (12, 13).

9. *I am clean &c.* Elihu here refers to such utterances of Job as those in ix. 21; xii. 4; xvi. 17, in all of which passages he has maintained his innocence.

10. *Behold, he findeth occasions against me.* The word rendered *occasions* occurs nowhere else except in Numb. xiv. 34, where it is rendered *alienation*. So here the margin of the R.V. *causes of*

*alienation.* Cf. for the thought xiii. 24; xix. 11.

*He counteth me for his enemy* : the words are quoted verbally from xiii. 24.

11. *He putteth my feet in the stocks &c.* The whole of this verse is cited from xiii. 27.

12, 13. Job, says Elihu, is not right in making these charges against God, Who is too great to be thus called to account, and cannot be expected to vindicate His ways to man. In ver. 13 it is best to follow the margin of the R.V. and translate : '*Why dost thou strive against him, for that he giveth not account of any of his matters?*' The last clause is intended to give the ground of Job's complaint, rather than (as A.V. and R.V.) Elihu's explanation of its unreasonableness.

**14—28. God does answer man, and that in various ways.** Job had complained that God would not answer : but, says Elihu, as a matter of fact God *does* answer, and that in various ways often disregarded by

15  In a dream, in a vision of the night,
    When deep sleep falleth upon men,
    In slumberings upon the bed ;
16  Then he ¹openeth the ears of men,
    And sealeth their instruction,
17  ²That he may withdraw man *from his* purpose,
    And hide pride from man ;
18  ³He keepeth back his soul from the pit,
    And his life from perishing by the ⁴sword.
19  He is chastened also with pain upon his bed,
    ⁵And with continual strife in his bones :

¹ Heb. *uncovereth.*
² Or, *That man may put away* his *purpose, and that he may hide*
³ Or, *That he may keep back*          ⁴ Or, *weapons*
⁵ Another reading is, *While all his bones are firm.*

men (14); e.g. He speaks to man in dreams and visions, through which He communicates His will to him and confirms it, in order to wean him from his sin and save him from perishing (15—18). He disciplines him also by means of pain and suffering, through which man is brought low and comes very near to death (19—22). By means also of His holy angels He interprets to man the meaning of this chastisement and shows him what is right, and then pardons him and redeems him from the power of the grave (23, 24), so that the sufferer is restored to health and vigour (25); his prayer is heard ; once more he sees God's face with joy (26); and confesses before men how he had sinned and gone wrong in the past, but has now been redeemed and saved from death by the gracious mercy of God (27, 28).

14.  *For God speaketh once, yea twice.* Cf. ver. 29, *twice, yea thrice.* These are simply examples of the 'ascending enumeration,' adopted for the sake of emphasis. See the note on v. 19.

15.  *In a dream,* as He spoke to Abimelech, and saved him from sin when he had taken Sarah, Gen. xx. 3, and cf. the account which Eliphaz gives of his vision in iv. 12 seq.

16.  *Then he openeth* (Heb. *uncovereth*) *the ears of men.* To 'uncover the ear of anyone' is in Hebrew a regular expression for *revealing* something to him. See 1 Sam. ix. 15 ; xx. 2, 12 ; xxii. 8, 17 ; 2 Sam. vii. 27, &c. and cf. Ps. xl. 6.

*And sealeth their instruction,* i.e. stamps it upon their minds.

17, 18.  The beneficent purposes of this revelation. It is made in order to *withdraw man* from any evil purpose that he may have, and to *hide pride* from him; lit. to 'cover' it, i.e. to conceal it, and so to withdraw him from it. In verse 18 follow the margin of the R.V. and render : *that he may keep back &c.* The *sword* is literally *javelin,* as in xxxvi. 12. In both passages it merely stands for God's judgment.

19.  Here Elihu's theory of suffering comes out very clearly : it is intended by God to be a merciful

20 So that his life abhorreth bread,
   And his soul dainty meat.
21 His flesh is consumed away, that it cannot be seen ;
   And his bones that were not seen stick out.
22 Yea, his soul draweth near unto the pit,
   And his life to the destroyers.
23 If there be with him ¹an angel,
   An interpreter, one ²among a thousand,
   To shew unto man ³what is right for him ;
24 ⁴Then he is gracious unto him, and saith,
   Deliver him from going down to the pit,
   I have found a ransom.

---

¹ Or, *a messenger*   ² Or, *of the thousand*   ³ Or, *his uprightness*
⁴ Or, *And he be gracious...and say...ransom : his flesh &c.*

---

chastisement, designed for man's 'moral discipline and improvement.'

*And with continual strife in his bones* (literally, *and the strife of his bones is constant*). The text of this clause is somewhat uncertain. The R.V. follows the reading found in the Hebrew text. But the margin of the Hebrew has another reading, found also in the Targ., Syriac, Theodotion and the Vulgate, which gives the meaning adopted in R.V. marg. *While all his bones* (literally, *the multitude of his bones*) *are firm*, i.e. while he is still young and lusty, cf. xx. 11.

The description of the sickness in this and the following verses seems to be suggested by the disease from which Job was suffering. 'No one can well doubt whence all these details were drawn who remembers how Job had sighed, "I *waste* away!" "My *limbs* are a shadow!" "My *leanness* beareth witness against me!" "*My bones burn* with heat!" "*I loathe my life!*" "*My breath is spent! My days are extinct! For me the tomb.*" (S. Cox.)

22. *the destroyers*, i.e. the 'angels of evil,' Ps. lxxviii. 49; cf. 2 Sam. xxiv. 16; 1 Chr. xxi. 15, 'the destroying angel,' and 1 Cor. x. 10.

23. *If there be with him an angel, an interpreter, one among a thousand.* The thought is that God sends one of the thousands of angels who are His ministers (cf. Ps. ciii. 20, 21) to interpret the meaning of the sickness, to show to the sufferer why it is sent, *and what is right for him*, i.e. what his duty is. It is, perhaps, not surprising that commentators have found in this passage a presage of the mediation of Christ, and have taken the angel as 'the angel of the Covenant,' who is 'superior to the thousands.' But such a method of interpretation is forced and unnatural, and there can be little doubt that the explanation given above is the correct one.

24. *Then he is gracious unto him*, i.e. *God* is gracious to the sufferer, and gives the word to deliver him from death, from the power of which he is 'redeemed.' The word for *ransom* occurs again

25  His flesh shall be fresher than a child's ;
    He returneth to the days of his youth :
26  He prayeth unto God, and he is favourable unto him ;
    So that he seeth his face with joy :
    And he restoreth unto man his righteousness.
27  [1]He singeth before men, and saith,
    I have sinned, and perverted that which was right,
    And [2]it profited me not :
28  He hath redeemed my soul from going into the pit,
    And my life shall behold the light.
29  Lo, all these things doth God work,
    Twice, *yea* thrice, with a man,
30  To bring back his soul from the pit,
    That he may be enlightened with the light of [3]the living.

---

[1] Or, *He looketh upon men*
[2] Or, *it was not requited unto me*  Or, *it was not meet for me*        [3] Or, *life*

in xxxvi. 18, where it appears to
refer to Job's sufferings.  Probably
something of the same kind is intended here.  The sinner's suffering
is accepted as sufficient.  Cf. Is. xl.
2.  It is possible, however, to refer
it to the man's penitence, or, as
Davidson says, ' the woɪds may mean
nothing more than that God is
pleased of His goodness to hold the
sinner as ransomed and delivered
from the consequences of his sin.'

25.  The sinner's restoration to
health.  Cf. the description of Naa-
man's cleansing from his leprosy :
' his flesh came again like unto the
flesh of a little child.'  2 Kings v.
14.

26—28.  His restored communion
with God, and thankfulness publicly
expressed before men.

27.  *And it profited me not.*
The exact meaning of the clause is
uncertain : perhaps the first marginal rendering of the R.V. is the
best, *It was not requited unto me.*

28.  *And my life shall behold the*

*light,* i.e. the light of the sun, cf.
ver. 30.  There is no thought of
spiritual 'light' here.  The A.V. in
this verse follows the marginal reading of the Hebrew, *his soul,...his
life;* which is also adopted in the
Targum and Vulgate.  But the
reading of the Hebrew text which
has the first person, *my soul...my
life* is supported by the Syriac and
Theodotion, and appears to be more
natural.

29—33.  **Conclusion, bringing
home to Job the object of God's
dealings with men.**  This, says
Elihu, is God's method of disciplin-
ing men, and thus saving them from
death (29, 30).  Job should attend
to it and listen (31).  If he has
anything to say in answer, let him
say on (32) : if not, let him hearken
while Elihu will further instruct
him (33).

29.  *Twice,* yea *thrice,* see above
on verse 14.

30.  *the light of the living* : the
same phrase occurs in Ps. lvi. 13.

31 Mark well, O Job, hearken unto me :
   Hold thy peace, and I will speak.
32 If thou hast any thing to say, answer me :
   Speak, for I desire to justify thee.
33 If not, hearken thou unto me :
   Hold thy peace, and I will teach thee wisdom.

**XXXIV.** The Second Speech of Elihu.

Elihu has now brought forward his theory of suffering as disciplinary, and has thus introduced what is practically a new thought into the poem. But it was not only because this truth had been almost entirely overlooked by both Job and his friends that he had intervened. He had been much shocked and pained by the irreverence of Job's language, and the charge which he had repeatedly brought against God of treating him unjustly. To this point Elihu now turns his attention in his second discourse, the main object of which is to show that anything like injustice is inconsistent with the very idea of God and with all that we know of Him, whether we consider His position as that of supreme ruler of the world, or whether we look at His action in history. The main divisions of the speech, which occupies but a single chapter, are these :

(1) *Introductory appeal to his hearers.* 1—4.

(2) *Recapitulation of Job's charges against God.* 5—9.

(3) *Refutation of them :*

    (*a*) *They are inconsistent with the idea of God, and with His character as Almighty.* 10—15.

    (*b*) *It is not only absurd but also inconsistent with facts to suppose that the All-Sovereign and Omniscient can do wrong.* 16—28.

    (*c*) *Therefore man has no right to murmur against God.* 29—33.

(4) *Conclusion, condemning Job for his ill-considered utterances.* 34—37.

**XXXIV.** 1 Moreover Elihu answered and said,
2 Hear my words, ye wise men ;
   And give ear unto me, ye that have knowledge.

1—4. **Introductory appeal to his hearers.** Elihu now turns to the bystanders and asks their attention (1, 2): let them discriminate, and exercise their moral sense in deciding where the right lies (3, 4).

2. *ye wise men...ye that have knowledge.* Cf. 10, *ye men of understanding*, and 34. In all these passages the reference is evidently not to the three friends, but rather to the bystanders, who have listened to the

3 For the ear trieth words,
  As the palate tasteth meat.
4 Let us choose for us that which is right :
  Let us know among ourselves what is good.
5 For Job hath said, I am righteous,
  And God hath taken away my right :
6 ¹Notwithstanding my right I am *accounted* a liar ;
  ²My wound is incurable, *though I am* without transgression.
7 What man is like Job,
  Who drinketh up scorning like water ?
8 Which goeth in company with the workers of iniquity,
  And walketh with wicked men.
9 For he hath said, It profiteth a man nothing
  That he should ³delight himself with God.

¹ Or, *Should I lie against my right ?*    ² Heb. *Mine arrow.*
³ Or, *consent with*    See Ps. l. 18.

debate and are invited to judge of the argument.

3. Quoted direct from xii. 11.

**5—9. Recapitulation of Job's charges against God.** Once more Elihu summarizes Job's impatient utterances, his assertions of his own rectitude, and complaints of the cruel treatment he has received and the hardships which, in spite of his innocence, he is made to endure (5, 6). Where can such another be found, so greedy of scoffing, and so ready to join with sinners and to maintain that it is idle for a man to serve God (7—9)?

5. *I am righteous.* Cf. xiii. 18, where Job says, 'I know that I am righteous.' *And God hath taken away my right,* quoted from xxvii. 2.

6. *Notwithstanding my right I am* accounted *a liar.* These words occur nowhere among Job's utterances; but their general sense is similar to that of ix. 20, 'Though I

be righteous, mine own mouth shall condemn me : though I be perfect, it shall prove me perverse.' *My right* signifies 'the justice of my cause.'

*My wound,* literally *my arrow,* as in vi. 4, 'the arrows of the Almighty,' cf. xvi. 13.

7. *Who drinketh up scorning like water.* Cf. the similar expression in xv. 16, 'a man that drinketh iniquity like water,' and on the naturalness of such an idiom in the mouth of an Oriental see Thomson, *The Land and the Book,* p. 319.

9. '*It profiteth a man nothing &c.*' Elihu here puts into Job's mouth words which he had never used, though the sentiments might perhaps be fairly inferred to be his from chapters xxi. and xxiv., in which he drew attention to the inequalities of this life, the misfortunes of the righteous and the exceptional prosperity of the ungodly. Cf. xxxv. 2,

10 Therefore hearken unto me, ye men of understanding :
   Far be it from God, that he should do wickedness ;
   And from the Almighty, that he should commit iniquity.
11 For the work of a man shall he render unto him,
   And cause every man to find according to his ways.
12 Yea, of a surety, God will not do wickedly,
   Neither will the Almighty pervert judgement.
13 Who gave him a charge over the earth ?
   Or who hath ¹disposed the whole world ?
14 ²If he set his heart ³upon ⁴man,
   *If* he gather unto himself his spirit and his breath ;

---

¹ Or, *laid* upon him        ² According to another reading, *If he cause his heart*
to *return unto himself.*        ³ Or, *upon himself*        ⁴ Heb. *him.*

---

3, where similar sentiments are ascribed to Job by Elihu.

**10—33. Refutation of these charges.**

(*a*) **They are inconsistent with the idea of God, and with His character as Almighty.** 10—15. Listen, says Elihu to the bystanders : it is impossible to entertain the idea that Almighty God will act unfairly (10). He will strictly requite every man according to his work (11). It cannot be thought that He will give an unjust judgment (12), for is He not the Omnipotent ruler of the universe (13)? Should He withdraw His care and sustaining control over it, its inhabitants must perish at once (14, 15).

The idea of these verses is that since God is 'All-Sovereign' He can have no motive for injustice, and that the fact of His sustaining the world is a practical proof of His goodness and lovingkindness.

10. *Far be it from God.* See the note on xxvii. 5.

13. Cf. xxxvi. 23, where a similar question is asked in almost the same terms.

14. *If he set his heart upon man* : better with R.V. marg. *upon himself.* The thought is that if God withdraw His attention from man, and fix it on Himself alone, man must forthwith perish, for it is only God's loving and sustaining care that keeps him alive. There is a doubt about the reading in this verse, as the texts vary between *set his heart* and *cause his heart to return* : the difference between the two is, however, of no great importance.

If *he gather unto himself his spirit and his breath* : i.e. the *spirit* and *breath* which God hath breathed into man, see Gen. ii. 7. If God *gathers* this *to himself*, man must die. Cf. Ps. civ. 29, 30, ' *Thou gatherest in their breath, they die, and return to their dust.* Thou sendest forth *thy spirit,* and they are created.' The personal pronoun '*his* spirit...*his* breath,' may thus refer either to man or to God.

15  All flesh shall perish together,
And man shall turn again unto dust.
16  [1]If now *thou hast* understanding, hear this :
Hearken to the voice of my words.
17  Shall even one that hateth right govern ?
And wilt thou condemn him that is just *and* mighty ?
18  [2]Is it *fit* to say to a king, *Thou art* vile ?
*Or* to nobles, *Ye are* wicked ?
19  *How much less to* him that respecteth not the persons of
princes,
Nor regardeth the rich more than the poor ?
For they all are the work of his hands.
20  In a moment they die, [3]even at midnight ;
The people are shaken and pass away,
And the mighty are taken away without hand.

[1] Or, *Only understand*    [2] Or, as read by some ancient versions, *Who saith to..*
vile, and to...wicked ; that respecteth &c.    [3] Or, *and at midnight the people &c.*

15.  *man shall turn again unto dust.*  See the primary passage in Gen. iii. 19, ' Dust thou art, and *unto dust shalt thou return.*'

(*b*)  It is not only absurd, but also inconsistent with facts, to suppose that the All-Sovereign and Omniscient can do wrong. 16—28. Turning now to Job, Elihu bids him attend, and repeats the thought. Surely the ruler of all must be just (16, 17). Is it seemly for the subject to charge the king with unbecoming conduct ? Still less should the creature dare to arraign the Creator, who regards no man's person, and to whom rich and poor are alike, as the work of His hands (18, 19). The mighty perish suddenly without the intervention of man, for His eyes are upon them (20, 21). No darkness can conceal them from Him, and He needs no long inquiry in order to give His sentence (22, 23). He brings down

the mighty and sets up others in their place (24). He notes their evil deeds, and destroys them by striking them down publicly like common criminals (25, 26), because they sinned against Him, and wronged the poor, to whose cry His ear is ever open (27, 28).

16.  The singular number is here used, marking that Elihu is no longer appealing to the bystanders (as in verses 2 and 10), but directly to Job himself.

18.  *Is it* fit *to say to a king,* Thou art *vile ?* lit. *worthless* ! The word being *Belial,* which is properly a substantive meaning worthlessness; a ' man of Belial' being a worthless, good-for-nothing fellow ; cf. 1 Sam. xxv. 25 ; 2 Sam. xvi. 7; xx. 1, &c.

20.  *In a moment they die, even at midnight,* cf. ver. 25, ' He overturneth them *in the night.*' The thought is merely that of *sudden* destruction.

21 For his eyes are upon the ways of a man,
   And he seeth all his goings.
22 There is no darkness, nor shadow of death,
   Where the workers of iniquity may hide themselves.
23 For he needeth not further to consider a man,
   That he should go before God in judgement.
24 He breaketh in pieces mighty men ¹*in ways* past finding out,
   And setteth others in their stead.
25 Therefore he taketh knowledge of their works ;
   And he overturneth them in the night, so that they are
      ²destroyed.
26 He striketh them as wicked men
   ³In the open sight of others ;
27 Because they turned aside from following him,
   And would not have regard to any of his ways :
28 ⁴So that they caused the cry of the poor to come unto
   him,
   And he heard the cry of the afflicted.

¹ Or, *without inquisition*   ² Heb. *crushed.*   ³ Heb. *In the place of beholders.*
⁴ Or, *That they might cause...and that he might hear*

*And the mighty are taken away without hand,* i.e. by no human hand or agency.

21. *For his eyes,* viz. God's eyes.

23. *For he needeth not further to consider a man.* God needs no long and anxious inquiry before giving judgment, since He is omniscient.

24. in ways *past finding out.* The same phrase occurs again in xxxvi. 26, where it must be translated in some such way as 'past finding out,' or 'unsearchable.' Here, however, it probably means (as R.V. marg.), *without inquisition.* (The A.V. *without number* comes from the Vulgate *et innumerabilis,* but is certainly incorrect.)

26. *as wicked men.* The phrase is a difficult one. It seems properly to mean *instead* of wicked men and

so 'like common criminals.'

(*c*) **Therefore man has no right to murmur against God.** 29—33. It is, then, vain to find fault with what God does, whether He speaks peace to a troubled soul, or whether He hides His face—whether He deals thus with a nation, or with a single individual, in order to prevent evil from gaining the mastery (29, 30). Who could dare to say to God, 'Thou hast made me suffer, though I was innocent,' or who could speak as if it were doubtful whether he had sinned, and ask for an explanation from God on such a matter (31, 32)? Is it reasonable for man to dictate to God how He is to treat him? To such a claim Elihu himself will have nothing to say, whatever Job may think (33).

29 When he giveth quietness, who then can condemn?
   And when he hideth his face, who then can behold him?
   Whether *it be done* unto a nation, or unto a man, alike:
30 That the godless man reign not,
   That there be none to ensnare the people.
31 For hath any said unto God,
   I have borne *chastisement,* [1] I will not offend *any more*:
32 That which I see not teach thou me:
   If I have done iniquity, I will do it no more?
33 Shall his recompence be as thou wilt, that thou refusest it?
   For thou must choose, and not I:
   Therefore speak what thou knowest.
34 Men of understanding will say unto me,
   Yea, every wise man that heareth me:
35 Job speaketh without knowledge,
   And his words are without wisdom.
36 Would that Job were tried unto the end,
   Because of his answering like wicked men.
37 For he addeth rebellion unto his sin,
   He clappeth his hands among us,
   And multiplieth his words against God.

[1] Or, *though I offend not*

29. *when he hideth his face*: a frequent figure for God's displeasure, see Ps. xxx. 7; civ. 29, &c.: and thus the opposite idea of *beholding Him* denotes the enjoyment of His favour.

31. Render with R.V. marg., *I have borne chastisement, though I offend not.*

33. *Shall his recompence be as thou wilt, that thou refusest it?* The whole passage is difficult, but these words appear to mean: Are you to dictate to God how He is to requite you, since you appear to object to His present treatment of you?

34—37. **Conclusion, condemning Job for his ill-considered utterances.** All thoughtful and unprejudiced persons must agree that Job's words were not marked by wisdom (34, 35). It were well if he could be thoroughly tried by God, because his answers were such as only wicked men could give, and he was proceeding to what approaches very near to blasphemy against God (36, 37). As Davidson says: 'the language exceeds in harshness almost anything that the three friends had said.'

34. Again the reference to the bystanders. Cf. ver. 2 and 10.

37. *For he addeth rebellion unto his sin.* It was his *sin* which, Elihu supposes, had called down God's judgment. His *rebellion* is his defiant attitude towards God.

*He clappeth his hands.* For this as an act of derision see xxvii. 23.

**XXXV.** The Third Speech of Elihu.

The train of thought running through this third speech is difficult to trace, and in places the language is very obscure. But it appears to be intended as a kind of supplement to the foregoing speech. In his summary of Job's words in xxxiv. 9, Elihu had represented him as saying, 'It profiteth a man nothing that he should delight himself with God,' but in his answer he had nowhere dealt with this complaint. He therefore takes it up now, and in this third utterance of his gives his reply to it, maintaining that God's greatness is such that He is in no way affected by man's righteousness or wickedness. These can only affect man himself. Hence he apparently means Job to infer that since there is a real and admitted distinction between good and evil, it must matter what his conduct is; and, since it cannot matter to God, it must matter to himself. Having somewhat obscurely established this, Elihu proceeds to admit that there are cases in which innocent persons, when suffering, are apparently disregarded by God (and therefore their righteousness may seem not to profit them); but he explains these by maintaining that their cry to God is only the shriek of physical pain, no real heartfelt appeal to God; and that is why it is not heard. Thus Job's complaints against God are shown to be utterly unreasonable.

The speech may be divided as follows:

(1) *Recapitulation of Job's complaints against God.* 1—3.

(2) *The answer to them.* 4—8.

(3) *Exceptions accounted for, in which men cry to God and are not heard.* 9—13.

(4) *Concluding rebuke of Job.* 14—16.

**XXXV.** 1 Moreover Elihu answered and said,

2 Thinkest thou this to be *thy* right,

*Or* sayest thou, My righteousness is more than God's,

3 That thou sayest, What advantage will it be unto thee?

*And*, What profit shall I have, more than if I had sinned?

**1—3. Recapitulation of Job's complaints against God.** Elihu begins by once more summing up the substance of Job's charges: Does he really imagine that his cause is just, and that he is righteous, when he urges that his righteousness has been of no avail or profit to him (1—3)?

**2, 3.** Job has nowhere used the actual words which Elihu here attributes to him any more than he had those which were put into his mouth in xxxiv. 9, where see the note. It is difficult to attach any very clear meaning to the words of verse 2, which afford a good instance of the obscurity which is often complained of in Elihu's utterance. Every word in the verse is common enough, and the meaning of each taken separately is perfectly familiar, and yet it is hard to say precisely what we are intended to understand by the sentence as a whole. Probably the English versions are right, though Davidson

4 I will answer thee,
And thy companions with thee.
5 Look unto the heavens, and see ;
And behold the skies, which are higher than thou.
6 If thou hast sinned, what doest thou against him ?
And if thy transgressions be multiplied, what doest thou
unto him ?
7 If thou be righteous, what givest thou him ?
Or what receiveth he of thine hand ?
8 Thy wickedness *may hurt* a man as thou art ;
And thy righteousness *may profit* a son of man.
9 By reason of the multitude of oppressions they cry out ;
They cry for help by reason of the arm of the mighty.

would render the second clause thus : 'And callest thou it, my just cause against God.' The word *this* must in any case refer to what follows in verse 3.

3. The R.V. here is clearly right (as against the A.V.) in the rendering *more than if I had sinned?*

4—8. **The answer to Job's complaints.** Elihu now states that he is prepared to answer Job and others like him (4). Let them look at the height of heaven, and can they imagine that any amount of earthly sin can really affect one whose dwelling is so high, or that man's goodness can be of any profit to Him (5—7)? Man's conduct, whether good or evil, can only affect himself (8).

4. *thy companions*; not the three friends, but Job's fellows in sin, i.e. others like him.

6—8. These verses do little more than repeat the thoughts to which Eliphaz had already given expression in xxii. 2, 3, that man's conduct cannot really affect the great and lofty God in any way, but that 'he that is wise is profitable to himself.'

8. A literal translation of this verse would be, *Thy wickedness hath regard to a man like thee; and thy righteousness to a son of man*, i.e. thy conduct affects *thyself*, and not God, *son of man* being a common Hebrew idiom for *a man*, see on xvi. 21.

9—13. **Exceptions accounted for, in which men cry to God and are not heard.** True that, when oppressed, men are ready enough to make their voice heard ; but it is no real appeal to the gracious God Who would have them show themselves superior to the brute creation (9—11). They cry out when brought low, but are not answered, because it is but a vain cry, which God cannot be expected to regard (12, 13).

9. *By reason of the multitude of oppressions they cry out.* The R.V. is probably correct (as against the A.V.) but the Hebrew is somewhat unusual. The meaning apparently is that though men do cry out under suffering, yet they are not heard by God because their cry is only a scream wrung from them by

10 But none saith, Where is God my Maker,
   Who giveth songs in the night ;
11 Who teacheth us more than the beasts of the earth,
   And maketh us wiser than the fowls of heaven?
12 There they cry, ¹but none giveth answer,
   Because of the pride of evil men.
13 Surely God will not hear vanity,
   Neither will the Almighty regard it.
14 How much less when thou sayest ²thou beholdest him
     not,
   The cause is before him, and thou waitest for him !
15 But now, because he hath not visited in his anger,
   ³Neither doth he greatly regard arrogance ;

---

¹ Or, *but he answereth not*  ² Or, *thou beholdest him not! The cause is before*
*him ; therefore wait thou for him*  ³ Or, *Thou sayest, He doth not greatly*
*regard arrogance.  Thus doth &c.*

---

physical pain, as it might be from
the brute creation : and not the
devout appeal for help which should
be sent up by rational beings to
their loving Creator.

10.  *Who giveth songs in the*
*night,* i.e. who when all things are
dark and gloomy suddenly makes
the heart to sing for joy. Cf. Ps.
xxxii. 7, 'Thou art my hiding place;
thou wilt preserve me from trouble;
thou wilt compass me about with
songs of deliverance,' and see Acts
xvi. 25.

12.  *There they cry, but none*
*giveth answer, because of the pride*
*of evil men.* The last words *be-*
*cause &c.* are to be taken in close
connexion with the opening of the
sentence, as giving the reason for
the cry.

14—16.  **Concluding rebuke of**
**Job.** Still less can God be expected
to regard Job's complaint that he
cannot find Him, that the cause is
before Him, and that he (Job) is

waiting for Him to answer, when,
just because God is slow to wrath,
he complains that He takes no
notice of man's overbearing conduct
(14, 15).  This, says Elihu in conclusion, is but a specimen of Job's
ignorance and folly (16).

Again the passage is very obscure,
but on the whole the paraphrase
above seems to give the sense.

14.  *How much less when &c.,*
possibly this should simply be rendered *yea, when.*

15.  The margin of the R.V.
seems to give the most probable
sense : *But now, because he hath*
*not visited in his anger,* thou sayest,
*He doth not greatly regard arro-*
*gance,* i.e. because God is slow in
visiting their iniquities upon sinners
in His righteous indignation Job
complains that He cares nothing
for the wrong that is being done by
the haughty oppressors.  The word
for *arrogance* (פשׁ) is very uncertain ; it is found nowhere else, and

16 Therefore doth Job open his mouth in vanity ;
　He multiplieth words without knowledge.

may be merely a clerical error for the common word for *transgression* (פֶּ֫שַׁע), which was possibly read by the translators of the LXX. (or rather by Theodotion) and Symmachus, παράπτωμα. So Vulg. *scelus.*

16. *Therefore* (or *Thus*, R.V. marg.) *doth Job open his mouth in vanity.* The word for *vanity* is a different one from that found in verse 13: that suggested the idea of something unreal or untrue: in this the thought is rather of what is fruitless and to no purpose.

**XXXVI., XXXVII.** The Fourth Speech of Elihu.

Elihu has now rebuked Job sufficiently for his arrogance and the want of reverence displayed in his complaints against God ; but he feels that he still has something to say ; and accordingly his last speech (in which the *hortatory* element is much more prominent than in the earlier ones) is devoted to two objects : (1) It is designed to impress upon Job still more strongly the theory already expounded in xxxiii. 19 seq., viz. that suffering is *disciplinary,* and to apply it directly to Job's own case ; and (2) it is intended also to enforce with additional illustrations the thought of the *greatness* of God, and consequently of the unreasonable character of Job's demand to comprehend all His ways. In enforcing this in the latter part of his speech Elihu anticipates to some extent the thought of the next section of the book, where the Almighty answers Job out of the whirlwind ; and it would almost appear as if the author intended us to think that his utterances were influenced by the storm which from xxxvi. 29 we feel to be rising.

The speech is best analysed as follows :

(1) *Introductory apology for speaking.* xxxvi. 1—4.

(2) *God's providential ordering of the affairs of men is designed for their moral discipline and improvement.* xxxvi. 5—15.

(3) *Application of this to the case of Job.* xxxvi. 16—25.

(4) *The marvels of nature testify to God's greatness and to the mystery which shrouds His ways.* xxxvi. 26—xxxvii. 13.

(5) *Closing appeal to Job to lay it to heart and acquiesce.* xxxvii. 14—24.

**XXXVI.** 1 Elihu also proceeded, and said,
2 ¹Suffer me a little, and I will shew thee ;
　For ²I have yet somewhat to say on God's behalf.

¹ Heb. *Wait for.*　　²　Heb. there are *yet words for God.*

**XXXVI.** 1—4. **Introductory apology for speaking.** Elihu begins by apologizing for taxing Job's patience, but has still something to say on God's behalf to vindicate His righteousness, and is confident

3 I will fetch my knowledge from afar,
  And will ascribe righteousness to my Maker.
4 For truly my words are not false :
  One that is perfect in knowledge is with thee.
5 Behold, God is mighty, and despiseth not any :
  He is mighty in strength of ¹understanding.
6 He preserveth not the life of the wicked :
  But giveth to the afflicted *their* right.
7 He withdraweth not his eyes from the righteous :
  But with kings upon the throne
  He setteth them for ever, and they are exalted.
8 And if they be bound in fetters,
  And be taken in the cords of affliction ;
9 Then he sheweth them their work,
  And their transgressions, that they have behaved them-
    selves proudly.

¹ Heb. *heart.*

in his own ability to teach as well as in his sincerity (1—4).

4. *One that is perfect in know-ledge.* It is impossible to acquit Elihu of overweening arrogance when he makes this claim for himself, for he is assuming that which in the very next chapter he ascribes to God, see xxxvii. 16, where the expression is almost identical with that in this verse.

5—15. **God's providential ordering of the affairs of men is designed for their moral discipline and improvement.** God is all-powerful, but never despises men, but rather gives to all their due (5), punishing the wicked, and exalting the suffering righteous (6, 7). If these last are permitted to suffer, it is that He may show them where they are wrong, and bring them to a better mind (8—10). If they take heed, they are restored to life and prosperity. If they fail to regard it, they are doomed to perish miserably (11, 12). If the ungodly are rendered bitter instead of being drawn to God by their afflictions, what wonder that they are cut off when still young, while the righteous are delivered by means of their sufferings (13—15) ?

7. *But with kings upon the throne &c.* Cf. 1 Sam. ii. 8, 'He raiseth the poor out of the dust...to set them among princes, and to make them inherit the throne of glory'; see also Ps. cxiii. 8, 9.

8. *And if they be bound in fetters.* The parallel expression, *taken in the bonds of affliction*, shows that this is to be understood figuratively, of chastisement generally. Elihu's theory of the *disciplinary* value of suffering is here brought out very forcibly.

13—2

10  He openeth also their ear to instruction,
    And commandeth that they return from iniquity.
11  If they hearken and serve *him*,
    They shall spend their days in prosperity,
    And their years in ¹pleasures.
12  But if they hearken not, they shall perish by ²the sword,
    And they shall die without knowledge.
13  But they that are godless in heart lay up anger:
    They cry not for help when he bindeth them.
14  ³They die in youth,
    And their life *perisheth* ⁴among the ⁵unclean.
15  He delivereth the afflicted ⁶by his affliction,
    And openeth their ear ⁷in oppression.
16  Yea, he would have ⁸led thee away ⁹out of distress
    Into a broad place, where there is no straitness ;
    And that which is set on thy table should be full of
    fatness.
17  But thou ¹⁰art full of the judgement of the wicked :
    Judgement and justice take hold *on thee*.

¹ Or, *pleasantness*     ² Or, *weapons*     ³ Heb. *Their soul dieth*.     ⁴ Or, *like*
⁵ Or, *sodomites*  See Deut. xxiii. 17.     ⁶ Or, *in*     ⁷ Or, *by adversity*
⁸ Or, *allured thee*     ⁹ Heb. *out of the mouth of*.     ¹⁰ Or, *hast filled up*

12.  *they shall perish by the sword*.  See the note on xxxiii. 18.

13.  *But they that are godless in heart lay up anger*.  The *anger* is apparently not to be taken of God's wrath (as if the passage was parallel to Rom. ii. 5) but rather of the impatience and resentment which the sinners cherish at God's dealings with them.  So Delitzsch and Davidson, and cf. Rev. xvi. 9.

14.  *They die in youth*.  Cf. the words of Zophar in xx. 11, 'His bones are full of his youth, but it shall lie down with him in the dust.'
*And their life* perisheth *among the unclean* (Vulg. *inter effeminatos*).  The word for *unclean* (qedêshim) literally means ' sacred,' but it is the technical name for those who

practised immorality in the worship of a deity and in the immediate precincts of a temple.  Such persons are frequently referred to in the Old Testament, ' especially in the period of the monarchy, when rites of foreign origin made their way into both Israel and Judah.'  See 1 Kings xiv. 24 ; xv. 12 ; xxii. 46 ; 2 Kings xxiii. 7 ; and Deut. xxiii. 17, with Driver's note.  The allusion here must be to their habits of life leading to a premature and miserable death.

15.  *And openeth their ear*, cf. verse 10, and see note on xxxiii. 16.

16—25.  **Application of this to the case of Job.**  And as for Job himself, God would have delivered him from his distress, and heaped

18 ¹Because there is wrath, beware lest thou be ²led away by
   *thy* sufficiency ;
   Neither let the greatness of the ransom turn thee aside.

¹ Or, *For beware lest wrath lead thee away into mockery*
² Or, *allured*

His favours upon him (16), only Job
had joined the sinners in their judgment of God, and therefore God's
judgment must keep its hold upon
him (17). Let him, however, beware lest his resentment at it lead
him into the sin of the scorner, and
lest the greatness of the 'ransom'
demanded from him lead him to
despair, for no material wealth can
avail to redeem him (18, 19). It
is not for him to desire God's
judgments (20); rather let him be
warned against encouraging a rebellious mind under his afflictions
(21), for there is none like God in
power and wisdom, and man cannot
call Him to account for His doings
(22, 23). Therefore Job should submit to Him and glorify His works,
which are the theme of the praise
of others (24, 25).

The whole passage is one of the
most obscure to be found anywhere
in the book, but it is thought that
the above may indicate the general
line of thought, so far as it can be
discovered. Siegfried marks verses
19 and 20 as 'unintelligible,' and
Davidson says of verses 16—19 that
' the general sense as expressed by
the A.V. is probably correct, *unless
probability be considered too strong
a term to employ of any rendering.*'
The R.V., however, which has been
published since Davidson wrote,
gives a better sense in several
places.

16.  The figures in this verse are

frequent ones for enlargement and
prosperity. For the *broad place*
cf. Pss. iv. 1 ; xviii. 36 ; and for the
plentiful table see Ps. xxiii. 5.

17.  *But thou art full of the
judgement of the wicked.* The *judgement* in this clause is probably not
the sentence of condemnation passed
by God upon the wicked, but the
*judgement passed by the wicked*
upon God's dealings with him ; and
because Job has identified himself
with them, and accepted this 'judgement,' therefore God's *judgement and
justice take hold of him.*

18.  A most obscure passage. On
the whole it is best to follow the
margin of the R.V. and render, *For
beware lest wrath lead thee away
into mockery*, taking the words as
a charge to Job not to suffer his
anger and excitement to lead him
to greater lengths and a worse sin.
Cf. xxxiv. 37.

*Neither let the greatness of the
ransom turn thee aside.* The *ransom* here, as probably in xxxiii. 24,
is to be taken of Job's afflictions, to
which a disciplinary power is attached. 'Elihu admonishes Job not
to allow himself to be drawn by the
heat of passion into derision, nor to
be allured from the right way by
the ransom which is required of
him as the price of restoration to
happiness, viz. humble submission
to the divine chastisement, as though
this ransom were exceeding great.'
Delitzsch.

19 ¹Will thy riches suffice, ²*that thou be* not in distress,
  Or all the forces of *thy* strength?

20 Desire not the night,
  When peoples ³are cut off in their place.

21 Take heed, regard not iniquity :
  For this hast thou chosen rather than affliction.

22 Behold, God doeth loftily in his power :
  Who is a teacher like unto him?

23 Who hath enjoined him his way?
  Or who can say, Thou hast wrought unrighteousness?

24 Remember that thou magnify his work,
  Whereof men have sung.

25 All men have looked thereon ;
  Man beholdeth it afar off.

26 Behold, God is great, and we know him not ;
  The number of his years is unsearchable.

---

¹ Or, *Will thy cry avail*    ² Or, *that are without stint*    ³ Heb. *go up.*

19. *Will thy riches suffice,* that thou be *not in distress, or all the forces of* thy *strength ?* No amount of wealth can buy exemption from suffering, or prove a 'ransom.' Cf. Ps. xlix. 6—8. But the margin of the R.V. is possible : *Will thy cry avail*: as a word of the same form means both *riches*, and *a cry*, cf. xxx. 24. *That thou be not in distress* is perhaps better taken as by the margin of the R.V. of the riches *that are without stint.* (The A.V. *no, not gold* takes the form בֶּצֶר as a variant form of בֶּצֶר the word for *precious ore* used in xxii. 24.)

20. *Desire not the night,* i.e. the night of judgment, when God's vengeance falls, for if it overtakes whole nations (*peoples*) how can the individual hope to escape?

22. Once more Elihu dwells on the thought of God's greatness, and the impossibility of man calling him to account, cf. xxxiv.

24. *Whereof men have sung* (Vulg. *de quo cecinerunt homines*). This is a preferable rendering to that of the A.V. *which men behold.*

**XXXVI. 26—XXXVII. 13. The marvels of nature testify to God's greatness and to the mystery which shrouds His ways.** Elihu now develops the thought of God's mysterious greatness, and illustrates it from the raindrops which He draws together and discharges from the skies (26—28). So also the mysteries of the clouds and thunder are beyond the power of man to comprehend (29), as is the light with which God clothes Himself (30). All these are His ministers both of judgment and of mercy (31). He too controls the lightning, and the thunder tells of His presence (32, 33). Man trembles before Him, when the sound of His voice is heard, and the lightnings flash forth at His direction (xxxvii. 1—5). He too

27 For he draweth up the drops of water,
Which distil in rain ¹from ²his vapour:
28 Which the skies pour down
And drop upon man abundantly.
29 Yea, can any understand the spreadings of the clouds,
The thunderings of his pavilion?
30 Behold, he spreadeth his light ³around him ;
And he ⁴covereth the bottom of the sea.
31 For by these he judgeth the peoples ;
He giveth meat in abundance.

¹ Heb. *belonging to.*    ² Or, *the vapour thereof*    ³ Or, *thereon*
⁴ Or, *covereth it with the depths of the sea*

gives a charge to the snow, and the rains of winter when man's work is stayed, and the beasts of the earth seek the shelter of their lairs (6—8). At His bidding the storm arises, and the frost comes, which congeals the waters (9, 10). He it is who fills the clouds with moisture, and controls their motions, guiding them as He will, to do His bidding, either to chastise man or to help him (11—13).

26. *The number of his years is unsearchable.* God's eternity enhances the thought of His greatness.

27. *For he draweth up the drops of water.* The verb properly means to diminish (hence A.V. *maketh small*), and then to restrain, withdraw. It possibly denotes here the withdrawal of the drops from the cloud when its contents are discharged on the earth. The R.V. seems to suggest that the first clause of the verse refers to the evaporation through which moisture is *drawn up* from the surface of the earth, and the second to the downpour of the cloud in rain; but as Davidson says, 'this is rather scien-

tific and complex; neither does the word mean to *draw up.*'

29. *The thunderings of his pavilion.* Cf. Ps. xviii. 11, 'He made darkness his hiding-place, his *pavilion* round about him; darkness of waters, thick clouds of the skies.' For the word rendered *thunderings* cf. xxx. 22 with the note.

30. *Behold, he spreadeth his light around him.* Cf. Ps. civ. 2, 'Who coverest thyself with light as with a garment.'

*And he covereth the bottom of the sea.* It is very uncertain what the allusion here refers to and no really satisfactory explanation of the words has been suggested. The *roots of the sea* is hardly an expression that can be applied to the 'waters above the firmament,' and yet no reason can be given why the fact that God 'covers the bottom of the sea' should be mentioned here. Nor is the marginal rendering of the R.V., *He covereth it with the depths of the sea,* easier to account for.

31. *For by these he judgeth the peoples: he giveth meat in abundance.* *These* referring to the phenomena of the storm, which may be

32 He covereth his hands with the ¹lightning ;
    And giveth it a charge ²that it strike the mark.
33 The noise thereof telleth concerning ³him,
    The cattle also concerning ⁴*the storm* that cometh up.

---

¹ Heb. *light.*      ² Or, *against the assailant*      ³ Or, *it*      ⁴ Or, him

---

sent either in judgment, or as a gracious rain upon God's inheritance, refreshing it when it was weary. Cf. Ps. lxviii. 9.

32. *He covereth his hands with the lightning ;* literally *light,* but the word appears to be rightly rendered *lightning* here and in xxxvii. 3, 11, and 15. Cf. Hab. iii. 11, where the 'light of thine arrows' refers to the lightning.

*that it strike the mark,* a phrase of doubtful import. The A.V. is entirely wrong; but the margin of R.V. *against the assailant* may possibly be correct.

33. *The noise thereof telleth concerning him,* i.e. the thunder announces the approach of God.

*The cattle also concerning* the storm *that cometh up* (or, as R.V. marg., *him that cometh up*). Certainly the natural rendering of the clause is that which takes 'the cattle' as the subject, and supplies the verb 'tell' from the previous line. In this case the reference will be to the restlessness and uneasy motions of the cattle which seem like dim forebodings of the approaching storm. But it is possible to take it as the accusative used here instead of the dative after the verb : 'the noise thereof telleth...*to the cattle also*' &c., as if it meant 'even the cattle hear with terror His mighty voice.' Whichever way it be taken, however, it must be admitted that the reference to the cattle is unexpected and seems somewhat out of place ; and there is possibly some deep-seated corruption of the text, so that the true sense is lost beyond recovery. Siegfried omits the words altogether as 'in this connexion entirely without sense.'

**XXXVII.** 1—5. The description of the thunderstorm is continued. It is described as present, and it is most natural to suppose that the poet intended us to think of the storm as already gathering, out of which the Almighty answered Job.

**XXXVII.**  1 At this also my heart trembleth,
    And is moved out of its place.
2 Hearken ye unto the noise of his voice,
    And the ¹sound that goeth out of his mouth.
3 He sendeth it forth under the whole heaven,
    And his ²lightning unto the ³ends of the earth.

---

¹ Or, *muttering*      ² Heb. *light.*      ³ Heb. *skirts.*

4 After it a voice roareth ;
  He thundereth with the voice of his majesty :
  And he stayeth them not when his voice is heard.
5 God thundereth marvellously with his voice ;
  Great things doeth he, which we cannot comprehend.
6 For he saith to the snow, Fall thou on the earth ;
  Likewise to the shower of rain,
  And to the showers of his mighty rain.
7 He sealeth up the hand of every man ;
  That all men whom he hath made may know *it*.
8 Then the beasts go into coverts,
  And remain in their dens.
9 Out of ¹the chamber *of the south* cometh the storm :
  And cold out of the ²north.

---

¹ See ch. ix. 9.      ² Heb. *scattering* winds.

**4.** *he stayeth them not*, viz. the lightnings, which are His ministers and go forth at His bidding. Cf. xxxvi. 32.

**6—10.** Snow, rain and ice.

**6.** *the shower of rain......the showers of his mighty rain.* The words seem to refer to the heavy rains (not as A.V. *small rain*) of the winter.

**7.** *He sealeth up the hand of every man*, i.e. probably *seals it up* so that he cannot work with it in winter.

*That all men whom he hath made may know* it. This is the only possible rendering of the Hebrew text as it stands. But the rendering of the A.V. *that all men may know his work*, which is based on the Vulgate (*ut noverint singuli opera sua*, so the Targ. and substantially the Syriac), requires a very slight change in the Hebrew (אנשים מעשהו for אנשי מעשהו), and receives some support from the parallel in xxxiii. 17, *that man may put away his purpose.* The meaning in either case

is that God's dealings with men through nature are intended to teach them lessons of His Almighty power, cf. Rom. i. 20.

**9.** *Out of the chamber* of the south *cometh the storm.* The italics in the R.V. show that there is nothing in the original about *the south ;* the expression is simply *out of the chamber.* But the word is the same as that used in ix. 9, where the south is mentioned : 'the chambers of the south.' Hence the insertion in the R.V. here, and the overbold rendering *out of the south* of the A.V. There is, however, no reason to connect the two passages together : and probably the phrase merely means that God brings the storm out of its chamber where it has been stored up, as elsewhere He is said to 'bring forth the winds out of his treasuries,' Ps. cxxxv. 7.

*And cold out of the north.* 'The north' is a highly doubtful rendering. The word appears properly to mean *the scatterers*, and to be used of the winds, that scatter the

10 By the breath of God ice is given :
  And the breadth of the waters is ¹straitened.
11 Yea, he ladeth the thick cloud with moisture ;
  He spreadeth abroad the cloud of his ²lightning :
12 And it is turned round about by his guidance,
  That they may do whatsoever he commandeth them
  Upon the face of the habitable world :
13 Whether it be for correction, or for his ³land,
  Or for mercy, that he cause it to come.
14 Hearken unto this, O Job :
  Stand still, and consider the wondrous works of God.

¹ Or, *congealed*    ² Heb. *light.*    ³ Or, *earth*

clouds and clear the sky when the frost comes (a similar phrase is quoted from the Qoran, li. 1). See R.V. marg.

11—13. The movements of the clouds.

11. The A.V. is hopelessly wrong here, but the R.V. gives the sense quite clearly. It is God who fills the clouds with moisture, and spreads abroad the cloud whence issues the lightning.

12. He too controls its motions to do His bidding.

*by his guidance.* The word except for its occurrence here is peculiar to the book of Proverbs, where it is found in i. 5; xi. 14; xii. 5; xx. 18; xxiv. 6. The phrase *the habitable world*, also finds its only parallel in Proverbs; see viii. 31.

13. *Whether it be for correction, or for his land, or for mercy.* It seems pretty clear that the second *or* has been accidentally inserted, and that only two alternatives are suggested, *correction for his land* on the one hand, and *mercy* on the other.

14—24. **Closing appeal to Job to lay it to heart and acquiesce.** Let Job listen to this and consider (14): can he explain the mysteries of God's working with the lightning and the clouds, or the warmth of which he is conscious when the south wind blows (15—17)? Can he spread out the expanse of the firmament as God does (18)? If so, let him instruct his companions who make no pretence to understand such mysteries (19). Job may do as he pleases, but no one should ever tell God that *he* (Elihu) would claim to speak with Him, for that would be the same thing as to wish for destruction (20). Why, if man cannot bear to gaze on the glorious light of the sun when the wind has swept the clouds from the sky, how can he expect to look on the glory of the terrible Majesty of God Himself (21, 22)? No, it is impossible for man to discover the Almighty, who can only be trusted to deal justly, and before whom men must bow with fear, for He regards not those who are wise in their own understanding (23, 24).

15 Dost thou know how God layeth *his charge* upon them,
   And causeth the [1]lightning of his cloud to shine?

16 Dost thou know the balancings of the clouds,
   The wondrous works of him which is perfect in knowledge?

17 [2]How thy garments are warm,
   [3]When the earth is still by reason of the south *wind*?

18 Canst thou with him spread out the sky,
   Which is strong as a molten mirror?

19 Teach us what we shall say unto him ;
   *For* we cannot order *our speech* by reason of darkness.

20 Shall it be told him that I would speak?
   [4]Or should a man wish that he were swallowed up?

---

[1] Heb. *light*.        [2] Or, *Thou whose garments are &c.*
[3] Or, *When he quieteth the earth by the south* wind
[4] Or, *If a man speak, surely he shall be swallowed up*

---

16. *the balancings of the clouds.* The word for *balancings* occurs nowhere else : and it is possible that it originated in a miswriting of a word which occurs in xxxvi. 29, where we have *the spreadings of the clouds* (מפרשי עב ; here מפלשי עב).

*him which is perfect in knowledge.* Cf. the note on xxxvi. 4.

17. *How thy garments are warm.* Better, with R.V. marg., *Thou whose garments are warm.* The reference is to the effect of the sirocco ' of the quiet kind,' without wind, as described by Thomson in *The Land and the Book*, p. 537, ' This sensation of dry hot clothes is only experienced during the siroccos,' and of its effect in quieting the earth, he says, ' There is no living thing abroad to make a noise. The birds hide in thickest shades ; the fowls pant under the walls with open mouth and drooping wings ; the flocks and herds take shelter in caves and under great rocks ; the labourers retire from the fields, and close the windows and doors of their houses ; and travellers hasten to take shelter in the first cool place they can find. No one has energy enough to make a noise, and the very air is too weak and languid to stir the pendent leaves even of the tall poplars. Such a south wind with the heat of a cloud does indeed bring down the noise and quiet the earth.'

18. *Canst thou with him spread out the sky, which is strong as a molten mirror?* The word for *spread out* is that from which the word for *firmament* in Gen. i. 6 is derived.

19. *we cannot order* our speech *by reason of darkness.* The **darkness** here, as in Eccl. ii. 14, **is the** darkness of ignorance.

20. *Shall it be told him that* **I** *would speak?* Apparently the question is merely Elihu's method **of**

21 And now men ¹see not the light which is bright in the
   skies :
   But the wind passeth, and cleanseth them.
22 Out of the north cometh ²golden splendour :
   God hath upon him terrible majesty.

¹ Or, *cannot look on the light when it is bright in the skies, when the wind hath
passed, and cleansed them*    ² Heb. *gold.*

disclaiming any desire or intention
on his own part of addressing complaints to God, whatever Job may
say.

*Or should a man wish that he
were swallowed up?* Again the
question, which might be rendered
*or did a man ever say* ( = intend)
*that he should be annihilated* (see
Driver's *Hebrew Tenses*, § 9), is designed to bring out the absurdity of
the supposition that Elihu would
wish to challenge God for His
government of the world—to do
this would be to court destruction.

21, 22 are most obscure and
perplexing, and no explanation
hitherto proposed seems entirely
satisfactory. On the whole it is
best to take the rendering of the
R.V. marg., *And now men cannot
look on the light when it is bright
in the skies, when the wind hath
passed, and cleansed them,* i.e. even
as it is, men cannot endure to gaze
at the light in its brightness.

22. *Out of the north cometh
golden splendour.* The words furnish another good illustration of the
obscurity of Elihu's style. There is
no doubt about the meaning of any
one of the three words of which the
sentence consists : *out-of-the-north
cometh gold :* but it is almost if not
quite impossible to extract any
satisfactory sense out of the sentence
as a whole. Some, as Delitzsch and
Ewald, take the word *gold* (Vulg.

*aurum*) literally, and suppose that
the passage contains a condensed
picture of what is pourtrayed at
length in xxviii., as if Elihu intended
to say, 'From the north cometh gold,
which man wrests from the darkness
of the gloomy unknown region of the
north : upon God on the contrary
is terrible majesty, i.e. it covers Him
like a garment, making Him inac-
cessible.' This appears very forced
and unnatural ; and it is more
probable that *gold* is not to be taken
strictly, but, as it is by the LXX.
(νέφη χρυσαυγοῦντα), and the R.V., of
*golden splendour,* or *golden light.*
So Davidson, who thinks that it
refers to the brightness of the
sunlight when the clouds are dis-
persed by the north wind (hence
*from the north*), and holds that the
clause continues the thought of the
previous verse, while the antithesis
is contained in what follows : *God
hath upon him terrible majesty,* i.e.
if men cannot look upon the light
when it shines in the cloudless heaven,
how much less shall they bear to
look upon the majesty of God, sur-
rounded with terrible glory. There
is however a difficulty about this,
because, according to Proverbs xxv.
23, the north wind must be regarded
as *bringing forth rain* (see R.V.),
rather than as dispersing the clouds ;
and when it is borne in mind that in
Ezek. i. 4, the manifestation of God in
the whirlwind and fire, a brightness

23 *Touching* the Almighty, we cannot find him out ; he is
  excellent in power :
  And ¹in judgement and plenteous justice he will not
  afflict.
24 Men do therefore fear him :
  He regardeth not any that are wise of heart.

¹ Or, *to judgement...he doeth no violence*

comes out of the north it seems best to take the clause before us not as continuing the thought of the previous verses, but as the commencement of the antithesis, *From the north cometh golden splendour* (i.e. the glorious light with which God is covered, Ps. civ. 2), *God hath upon him terrible majesty.* This appears to ·be the most plausible explanation of the passage that is forthcoming; but it is hard to feel completely satisfied with it, and one cannot help suspecting that the text is corrupt.

23.    *And in judgement and plenteous justice he will not afflict.* If this rendering be adopted it must mean that he will not *afflict unjustly,* but as there is nothing in the text to suggest this limitation it is perhaps better to translate with the margin of the R.V., *To judgement and plenteous justice he doeth no violence,* which furnishes the thought of God's perfect justice to balance that of His *power* in the previous clause.

## PART IV. THE ANSWER OF THE ALMIGHTY OUT OF THE WHIRLWIND. CHAPTERS XXXVIII.— XLII. 6.

A sense of surprise and disappointment is not seldom felt by readers of this fourth section of the book.    While its wondrous beauty cannot fail to impress the reader, yet he looks for deeper teaching on the mystery of suffering and is perplexed at not finding it.    Job has cried passionately for God to appear and suffer him to plead his cause before Him.    And now, when God takes him at his word, and manifests Himself in answer to his appeal, it is neither to listen to his complaints, nor to justify His ways and explain the principles of His government of the world.    Rather it is to overwhelm Job with questions which are intended to bring home to him the impossibility of his arguing with God or understanding the method of Divine Providence.    This is not what we should have expected ; and hence the sense of disappointment.    But we must bear in mind (1) the early date, if not of the *book*, yet of the narrative contained in it.    The scene is laid in patriarchal times, and the special character in which God revealed Himself to the patriarchs was that of God *Almighty (El Shaddai),* see Gen. xvii. 1 ; (2) the *Eastern* character of the book.    The religious thought of the East has always tended to dwell on the Almighty power and universal sovereignty of God more than Western minds have done.   Further, with regard to such questions as those discussed in the debate between Job and his friends, God's method all through the history of the world has been not to solve them for man by the direct teaching of revelation, and thus free him from the responsibility of inquiry, but rather to lead him to work out the answers for himself by patient thought and observation of the teachings of nature and history.   The purpose of His revelation is to discipline the heart rather than to satisfy the intellect, and this purpose the manifestation here granted to Job completely fulfils.   All through Job's speeches there had been visible a sense of *injustice* on the part of God.   It is to rebuke this and to bring him back to a right frame of mind towards God that the revelation is made.   Job had not failed under the trial imposed upon him.   He had never bidden farewell to God, as Satan had suggested that he would do. Moreover as compared with the friends he had spoken that which was right of God (see xlii. 8).   He had been true to facts.   The friends by their theory of retributive justice had dishonoured the Divine administration ; and Job by holding up the inequalities and perplexities of life had at least kept free from false and unfair inferences as regards others.   But all the same he had said many blameworthy things ; and to this point the answer is directed. The speculative question of the purpose of suffering is nowhere dealt with or even touched upon : but the condemnation of the friends in the epilogue gives the Divine verdict in Job's favour on this issue.   The speeches of the Almighty are directed to another point, viz., to that attitude of *soreness* and feeling of *injustice* which can never be justifiable *unless the whole case is known ;* and by means of this wonderful panorama of creation there is brought home to Job the conviction that the whole case is *not* known.   He therefore feels that he was wrong in his charges against God, and the vision finally brings home to him, as the vision of God brought home to Isaiah, to S. Peter, and to hundreds of others after them, the sense of *personal sin.*   ' I had heard of thee by the hearing of the ear ; but now mine eye seeth thee.   Wherefore I abhor myself, and repent in dust and ashes.'

The answer of the Almighty is comprised in two distinct speeches. The first (xxxviii. 1—xl. 2) sets before Job the wonders of nature, both inanimate and animate ; and by a series of rapid questions as to his share in the work of creation and his knowledge of the secrets of nature convinces him of the absurdity of his challenge of God (xl. 3—5).   But Job had not only challenged God to explain His conduct, he had further deliberately questioned the principles of His rule, and accused Him of injustice ; and therefore in the second speech (xl. 6—xli. 34) he is 'ironically invited to assume the Divine attributes, and rule the world himself : and as a test of his capabilities, two formidable creatures, the work of God's hand like himself, are described at some length, and he is asked whether he can subdue *them*' (Driver).

**XXXVIII. 1—XL. 2.**   The first speech of the Almighty.
Almost all commentators on the book dwell on the marvellous power and beauty of the whole passage   As Driver says, it 'transcends all other

descriptions of the wonders of creation or the greatness of the Creator which are to be found either in the Bible or elsewhere.' 'For descriptive power,' says Cheyne, it is 'without a parallel.' Reference may also be made to the remarks of Humboldt on the 'many questions here proposed, which the natural philosophy of the present day enables us to propound more formally, and to clothe in more scientific language, but cannot satisfactorily solve' (*Cosmos*, vol. II. p. 46).

The speech after the introductory challenge (ver. 1—3) falls into two main divisions, and may be analysed as follows :

(1) *The wonders of inanimate nature.* xxxviii. 4—38.

　(*a*) The creation of the earth. 4—7.

　(*b*) The government of the sea. 8—11.

　(*c*) The mysteries of light and darkness. 12—21.

　(*d*) Snow and hail, rain and frost. 22—30.

　(*e*) The stars, the lightning and clouds. 31—38.

(2) *The wonders of animate nature.* xxxviii. 39—xxxix. 30.

　(*a*) Introductory allusion to birds and beasts of prey. xxxviii. 39—41.

　(*b*) The wild goats. xxxix. 1—4.

　(*c*) The wild ass. 5—8.

　(*d*) The wild ox. 9—12.

　(*e*) The ostrich. 13—18.

　(*f*) The war-horse. 19—25.

　(*g*) The hawk and eagle. 26—30.

**XXXVIII.** 1 Then the LORD answered Job out of the whirlwind, and said,

2 Who is this that darkeneth counsel
By words without knowledge ?

**XXXVIII. 1—3. Introductory challenge to Job.** God now answers Job out of the whirlwind (1), and, rebuking him for confusing matters by his ignorant words, bids him stand up to Him and answer His challenge (2, 3).

1. *Then the LORD answered Job out of the whirlwind.* The storm, here as elsewhere in the O.T., is 'the forerunner of God's self-manifestation' (Delitzsch); cf. Exod. xix. 16 ;

1 Kings xix. 11 ; Ezek. i. 4.

2. *Who is this that darkeneth counsel by words without knowledge ?* The reference is of course to the utterances of Job, and not to those of Elihu, and the form of the question in the original seems to suggest that Job's words have scarcely died away before the intervention takes place. (Cf. Introd. p. xxv.)

3 Gird up now thy loins like a man ;
　For I will demand of thee, and declare thou unto me.
4 Where wast thou when I laid the foundations of the
　　earth ?
　Declare, ¹if thou hast understanding.
5 Who determined the measures thereof, ²if thou knowest ?
　Or who stretched the line upon it ?
6 Whereupon were the ³foundations thereof ⁴fastened ?
　Or who laid the corner stone thereof ;
7 When the morning stars sang together,
　And all the sons of God shouted for joy ?

---

¹ Heb. *if thou knowest understanding.*
² Or, *seeing*　　³ Heb. *sockets.*　　⁴ Heb. *made to sink.*

---

**3.** *I will demand of thee, and declare thou unto me.* This is the answer to those appeals of Job in which he had passionately cried to the Almighty to meet him, and had declared his readiness either to answer to God's charges whatever they might be, or, if God so desired, to state his own case first for God to answer. See ix. 35 ; xiii. 22 ; xxxi. 35.

**4—38. The wonders of inanimate nature.**

(*a*) **The creation of the earth.** 4—7. Was Job present at the creation of the world, or had he any share in fashioning it (4, 5)? What does *he* know of the laying of the foundations or of the corner-stone of it, in that age of dim antiquity when there were none but angels to sing their hymns of praise at God's creative work (6, 7) ?

**5.** *Who determined the measures thereof.* All the figures here employed, the *measures*, or dimensions, the measuring line, the sinking of the foundation, and the laying of the corner-stone, are of course taken from the building of a house, the world being regarded as some mighty edifice reared by the heavenly architect.

**7.** *When the morning stars sang together.* Stars and angels are mentioned together in Ps. cxlviii. 3, 4, and possibly the stars are included in the 'hosts' of God in Ps. ciii. 21, as well as the angels. For the *sons of God* (= the angels) cf. i. 6, and note. Davidson aptly quotes from Milton's Hymn *On the Nativity,*

　' Such music, as 'tis said,
　　Before was never made,
　But when of old the sons of morning
　　sung,
　While the Creator great
　　His constellations set,
　And the well-balanced world on
　　hinges hung,
　And cast the dark foundations deep,
　And bid the weltering waves their
　　oozy channel keep.'

The passage has also influenced Tennyson, who speaks of

　' the matin songs, that woke
　　The darkness of our planet.'
　　　*In Memoriam,* lxxvi.

(*b*) **The government of the sea.** 8—11. Had Job any share in

8 Or *who* shut up the sea with doors,
　When it brake forth, ¹*as if* it had issued out of the
　　womb ;
9 When I made the cloud the garment thereof,
　And thick darkness a swaddlingband for it,
10 And ²prescribed for it my ³decree,
　And set bars and doors,
11 And said, Hitherto shalt thou come, but no further ;
　And here shall thy proud waves be stayed ?
12 Hast thou commanded the morning since thy days *began*,
　*And* caused the dayspring to know its place ;
13 That it might take hold of the ends of the earth,
　And the wicked be shaken out of it ?
14 It is changed as clay under the seal ;
　And *all things* stand forth ⁴as a garment :

---

¹ Or, *and issued*　² Heb. *brake.*　³ Or, *boundary*　⁴ Or, *as in a garment*

controlling the sea, when it first broke forth as from the womb (8), when God swaddled it with mist and darkness (9), when He fixed its barriers, and imprisoned it within its bounds (10, 11)?

The sea is here compared to a new-born child, breaking forth (for the Hebrew word in this connexion see Ps. xxii. 10) from the womb, and then wrapped in swaddling clothes.

10. *And prescribed for it my decree.* Better, with the margin of R.V., *brake for it my boundary.* The same substantive is used for the boundary of the sea in xxvi. 10, as well as in Jer. v. 22 and Prov. viii. 29 ; and the verb *break* may refer to the rugged, precipitous and broken shores of the sea.

(*c*) **The mysteries of light and darkness.** 12—21. Can Job summon at will the morning light and bid it shine in the dark places of the earth, shaming those who love

deeds of darkness, and revealing the world in its form and beauty (12—15)? or what does he know of the depths of ocean, and of the dim world beneath (16, 17)? or what of the breadth of earth's surface (18)? or of the sources of light and darkness (19, 20)? only if his days went back to the time of creation could he explain such mysteries as these (21).

12. *since thy days* began. Cf. ver. 21.

13. *the ends of the earth,* lit. the *wings* of the earth : the same phrase as in xxxvii. 3.

*And the wicked be shaken out of it.* The dawn is poetically conceived as seizing by the corners the covering of darkness that lay like a pall over the earth, and shaking out the wicked from it.

14. *It is changed as clay under the seal.* Another striking figure. As the dawn spreads over the earth, its face seems to take shape

15 And from the wicked their light is withholden,
   And the high arm is broken.
16 Hast thou entered into the springs of the sea?
   Or hast thou walked in the ¹recesses of the deep?
17 Have the gates of death been revealed unto thee?
   Or hast thou seen the gates of the shadow of death?
18 Hast thou comprehended the breadth of the earth?
   Declare, if thou knowest it all.
19 Where is the way to the dwelling of light,
   And as for darkness, where is the place thereof;
20 That thou shouldest take it to the bound thereof,
   And that thou shouldest discern the paths to the house
      thereof?
21 *Doubtless*, thou knowest, for thou wast then born,
   And the number of thy days is great!
22 Hast thou entered the treasuries of the snow,
   Or hast thou seen the treasuries of the hail,
23 Which I have reserved against the time of trouble,
   Against the day of battle and war?

¹ Or, *search*

and form beneath it as its outline is revealed, as clay takes shape under the impress of the seal.

15. *And from the wicked their light is withholden.* Cf. xxiv. 17, the *light* of the wicked is the darkness, for the 'morning is to them as the shadow of death.'

17. *Have the gates of death been revealed unto thee...the gates of the shadow of death?* The realm of death or Hades here, as elsewhere, is conceived as a strong place with gates and bolts and bars, situated beneath the depths of the sea. Cf. xvii. 16, where see note.

(*d*) **Snow and hail, rain and frost.** 22—30. Has Job inspected the storehouses where God keeps the snow and the hail which He sends in His wrath upon the earth (22, 23)? What does he know of

the laws according to which the light is diffused, and the east wind spread abroad (24)? Has he had anything to do with clearing a track for the storm of rain, or for the lightning, when God brings the rain on the waste deserts and clothes them with verdure (25—27)? Can he produce at will the rain, or the dew, or the ice, or the frost which congeals the face of the deep (28—30)?

22. *Hast thou entered the treasuries of the snow?* For the same idea, viz. of God's storehouses for the forces of nature, cf. Deut. xxviii. 12; Ps. cxxxv. 7; Jer. x. 13; li. 16.

23. *Which I have reserved against the time of trouble.* The thought of this verse may be illustrated from Josh. x. 11; Ps. xviii. 13, 14; lxviii. 14.

24 ¹By what way is the light parted,
   Or the east wind scattered upon the earth?
25 Who hath cleft a channel for the waterflood,
   Or a way for the lightning of the thunder;
26 To cause it to rain on a land where no man is;
   On the wilderness, wherein there is no man;
27 To satisfy the waste and desolate *ground*;
   And to cause the ²tender grass to spring forth?
28 Hath the rain a father?
   Or who hath begotten the drops of dew?
29 Out of whose womb came the ice?
   And the hoary frost of heaven, who hath ³gendered it?
30 The waters ⁴are hidden as *with* stone,
   And the face of the deep ⁵is frozen.

¹ Or, *Which is the way* to the place where *the light is &c.*    ² Or, *greensward*
³ Or, *given it birth*     ⁴ Or, *are congealed like stone*     ⁵ Heb. *cohereth.*

**24.** *By what way is the light parted.* Except for the verb the clause is identical with that in ver. 19, and after the question put there it seems scarcely likely that the one here should run in almost identical terms, *which is the way to the place where the light is parted?* Either then we must take the question as in A.V. and R.V. and suppose *way* to refer to the *manner* in which the light is parted (so Delitzsch), or we must suppose that there is a textual error. The LXX. instead of *light* give *hoar-frost* (πάχνη).

**25.** *Who hath cleft a channel for the waterflood?* The next clause seems to indicate that the *waterflood* is not a river, but rather a downpour of rain, for which a *channel* is supposed to be made in the skies.
*Or a way for the lightning of the thunder*, repeated from xxviii. 26.

**26.** 'Not merely for the purposes of His rule among men does God direct the changes of the weather contrary to human foresight; His care extends also to regions where no human habitations are found.' Delitzsch.

**28.** *Hath the rain a father?* i.e. a *human* father. Can a mere man like Job produce it?

**30.** *The waters are hidden as with stone.* Better, with the margin of the R.V., *The waters are congealed like stone.*

(*e*) **The stars, the lightning and clouds.** 31—38. What power has Job to control the movements of the constellations (31, 32), or what does he know of the laws that govern the heavens (33)? Can he summon the clouds at will, or send forth the lightnings to do his bidding (34, 35)? Can he supply the masses of clouds, and the meteors of heaven with intelligence to carry out his behests (36)? Or can he regulate the clouds, and bring rain at will in torrents upon the earth (37, 38)?

31 Canst thou bind the ¹cluster of the Pleiades,
   Or loose the bands of Orion?
32 Canst thou lead forth ²the Mazzaroth in their season?
   Or canst thou guide the Bear with her ³train?
33 Knowest thou the ordinances of the heavens?
   Canst thou establish the dominion thereof in the earth?
34 Canst thou lift up thy voice to the clouds,
   That abundance of waters may cover thee?
35 Canst thou send forth lightnings, that they may go,
   And say unto thee, Here we are?
36 Who hath put wisdom in the ⁴inward parts?
   Or who hath given understanding to the ⁵mind?
37 Who can number the clouds by wisdom?
   Or who can ⁶pour out the bottles of heaven,

---

¹ Or, *chain*  Or, *sweet influences*      ² Or, *the signs of the Zodiac*
³ Heb. *sons*.      ⁴ Or, *dark clouds*      ⁵ Or, *meteor*      ⁶ Heb. *cause to lie down*.

---

**31.** *Canst thou bind the cluster of the Pleiades.* Of the four names mentioned in this and the following verse, *three*, viz. *Kîmah* (the Pleiades), *K'sil* (Orion), and *Ash* or *Ayish* (the Bear), have been already mentioned in ix. 9, where see note. The fourth, viz. *the Mazzaroth*, is of uncertain meaning (the LXX., like the English versions, leaves it untranslated, Μαζουρώθ. The Vulg. has *Lucifer*, the Targum *the planets*). A word of similar sound, *Mazzaloth*, occurs in 2 Kings xxiii. 5, with the meaning of *the planets*, or *the signs of the zodiac* (hence R.V. marg. here), and some have thought that the word before us is only another form of this. It appears, however, impossible to determine the meaning precisely. Another word of uncertain import is that translated in the R.V. *cluster*. The A.V. *sweet influences* (as if it referred to the supposed influence of the stars on the lives of men) is

certainly wrong. *Bands* or *chain* is more probably the meaning (so LXX. δεσμόν, and Targ.).

**36.** *Who hath put wisdom in the inward parts? or who hath given understanding to the mind?* The verse is obscure, but the English versions can hardly be correct, as it is inconceivable that the reference can be to the heart of man, for the subject of the heavenly forces is continued in the next verse. The context then imperatively demands some reference to it here. The word rendered *inward parts* only occurs again in Ps. li. 6, where it certainly has this meaning; but here it is best to take it of the *layers of cloud* (the root signifying to overspread, or overlay), so R.V. marg. *dark clouds*. The word translated *mind* is found nowhere else, and its meaning must be conjectural. *Meteor* of the R.V. marg. is perhaps as likely as any of the renderings suggested.

**37.** *Who can number the clouds*

38 When the dust runneth into a mass,
   And the clods cleave fast together?
39 Wilt thou hunt the prey for the lioness?
   Or satisfy the appetite of the young lions,
40 When they couch in their dens,
   *And* abide in the covert to lie in wait?
41 Who provideth for the raven his food,
   When his young ones cry unto God,
   *And* wander for lack of meat?

**XXXIX.**   1 Knowest thou the time when the wild goats
   of the rock bring forth?
   *Or* canst thou mark when the hinds do calve?
2 Canst thou number the months that they fulfil?
   Or knowest thou the time when they bring forth?

---

*by wisdom?* i.e. who can count them, so as to dispense them in due proportion.

*Or who can pour out the bottles of heaven?* The verb literally means *cause to lie down*, which the A.V. takes as equivalent to *stay*. The R.V. *pour out* is however correct.

**XXXVIII. 39—XXXIX. 30. The wonders of animate nature.**

(*a*) **Introductory allusion to birds and beasts of prey,** xxxviii. 39—41. Can Job undertake to provide the ravenous beasts of prey with food, or to satisfy the wants of the ravens (39—41)?

39, 40. The lion, cf. Ps. civ. 21. On the various names for *lion* in Hebrew see the note on iv. 10.

41. *the raven.* 'The raven is repeatedly cited as manifesting the goodness and care of God for His lower creatures. Not only is its home in desolate places, but its food is scanty and precarious, and must be sought out over a wide extent of country, as may be seen by its habit of flying restlessly about in constant

search of food.' Tristram, *Nat. Hist. of the Bible*, p. 199. Cf. the allusions in Ps. cxlvii. 9; S. Luke xii. 24.

(*b*) **The wild goats,** xxxix. 1—4. What does Job know of the mysteries connected with the birth of the wild goat or of the fawn (1, 2)? The young are brought forth without the help or observation of man: they thrive, and presently leave their dams, needing their care no longer (3, 4).

1. *the wild goats of the rock,* cf. Ps. civ. 18. The creature referred to is a species of ibex, and though familiar with the animal, the Jews 'knew but little of its habits owing to its extreme wariness and wildness' (Tristram, p. 95). Hence the mention of it here.

*canst thou mark when the hinds do calve?* The shyness and timidity of the deer was evidently proverbial. Cf. Ps. xxix. 9.

3. *They cast out their sorrows.* The parallelism makes it clear, that their 'sorrows' refer to their off-

3 They bow themselves, they bring forth their young,
They cast out their sorrows.
4 Their young ones are in good liking, they grow up in the
open field ;
They go forth, and [1]return not again.
5 Who hath sent out the wild ass free?
Or who hath loosed the bands of the wild ass?
6 Whose house I have made the wilderness,
And the salt land his dwelling place.
7 He scorneth the tumult of the city,
Neither heareth he the shoutings of the [2]driver.
8 The range of the mountains is his pasture,
And he searcheth after every green thing.
9 Will the [3]wild-ox be content to serve thee?
Or will he abide by thy crib?

---

[1] Or, *return not unto them*    [2] Or, *taskmaster*    [3] See Num. xxiii. 22.

spring. The figure is found elsewhere in poetry. Cf. Euripides, *Ion*, l. 45, ὠδῖνα ῥῖψαι.

4. *they grow up in the open field.* This rendering is decidedly to be preferred to that of the A.V., *with corn.*

(*c*) **The wild ass**, 5—8. Was it Job who sent forth the wild ass to claim his liberty in the wilderness (5, 6)? Is it his doing that this creature shuns the habitations of men, and is untamed by man, ranging the mountains at will in search of his pasture (7, 8)?

5. *Who hath sent out the wild ass free?* There are various allusions in different parts of the O.T. to the 'wild and untameable nature of this animal; to its extreme shyness and wariness, its fleetness, and its abode in the most desolate and barren deserts.' See xxiv. 5; Is. xxxii. 14; Jer. ii. 24; xiv. 6; Hos. viii. 9; Dan. v. 21; and cf. Tristram, p. 41.

7, 8. There seems to be an implied contrast in these verses between the habits of the wild ass and those of his domesticated brother.

(*d*) **The wild ox**, 9—12. Will the wild ox obey Job or do his bidding (9)? Can Job yoke him to his plough or harrow (10)? and will he trust him to labour for him with the docility of the domesticated ox (11, 12)?

9. *Will the wild-ox be content to serve thee?* The unfortunate rendering of the A.V. *the unicorn* comes from the LXX. μονόκερως. Aquila has *rhinoceros*, 'the nearest approach to a unicorn that exists in the world of reality' (Davidson). So also Jerome in the Vulgate, and the Targum: but allusions elsewhere, e.g. Deut. xxxiii. 17; Ps. xxii. 21, make it clear that a two-horned animal is intended, and there is now a general consent among expositors that the *reem* of the O.T. is the wild ox. See the interesting

10 Canst thou bind the wild-ox with his band in the furrow?
   Or will he harrow the valleys after thee?
11 Wilt thou trust him, because his strength is great?
   Or wilt thou leave to him thy labour?
12 Wilt thou confide in him, that he will bring home thy
      seed,
   And gather *the corn of* thy threshing-floor?
13   The wing of the ostrich rejoiceth ;
   *But* are her pinions and feathers [1]kindly?
14 For she leaveth her eggs on the earth,
   And warmeth them in the dust,

---

[1] Or, like *the stork's*

discussion in Tristram, p. 146 seq.

*Or will he abide by thy crib?* the *crib* as in Prov. xiv. 4 and Is. i. 3 is simply the manger.

(*e*) **The ostrich, 13—18.** The ostrich may proudly rear herself aloft, but what of her disposition (13)? Her eggs are left in the dust in heedlessness of what may happen to them (14, 15). She is lacking in the instincts of motherhood because God has never imparted them to her (16, 17). But in other qualities she excels, and when she rouses herself to flight she can outstrip the fleetest horse and his rider (18).

13. *The wing of the ostrich rejoiceth ; but are her pinions and feathers kindly?* The A.V. Gavest thou *the goodly wings unto the peacocks? or wings and feathers unto the ostrich?* is certainly wrong. The Hebrew word for peacocks is quite different from that which occurs here, and it is clear that the *renânim* mentioned here are ostriches. In the second clause the word rendered *kindly* may also be translated 'like *the stork's*' (so R.V. marg.), the stork being proverbial

for its kindly, affectionate nature (cf. Tristram, p. 244), so different from that of the ostrich as here described in accordance with popular belief.

14. *For she leaveth her eggs on the earth, and warmeth them in the dust.* Dr Tristram writes on this as follows: 'The ostrich is polygamous, and several hens deposit their eggs in one place—a hole in the sand. The eggs are then covered over, and left during the heat of the day, but in the colder regions at any rate, as in the Sahara, the birds sit regularly during the night, and until the sun has full power, the male also incubating. But the ostrich lays an immense number of eggs, far more than are ever hatched, and round the covered eggs are to be found many dropped carelessly, as if she forgot that the frost might crack them, or the wild beast might break them. But most naturalists confirm the statement of the natives, that the eggs on the surface are left in order to afford sustenance to the newly-hatched chicks, which could not otherwise find food at first in these arid regions,' p. 237. This

15 And forgetteth that the foot may crush them,
   Or that the wild beast may trample them.
16 She ¹is hardened against her young ones, as if they were
   not hers :
   Though her labour be in vain, *she is* without fear ;
17 Because God hath ²deprived her of wisdom,
   Neither hath he imparted to her understanding.
18 What time she ³lifteth up herself on high,
   She scorneth the horse and his rider.
19  Hast thou given the horse *his* might ?
   Hast thou clothed his neck with ⁴the quivering mane ?

---

¹ Or, *dealeth hardly with*        ² Heb. *made her to forget wisdom.*
    ³ Or, *rouseth herself up to flight*        ⁴ Heb. *shaking.*

passage may show how natural was the popular belief in the cruelty and folly of the ostrich to which reference is here made. Cf. a similar allusion to her cruelty in Lam. iv. 3, 'Even the jackals draw out the breast, they give suck to their young ones : the daughter of my people is become cruel, like the ostriches in the wilderness.'

18. *What time she lifteth up herself on high,* referring of course to the movement of the ostrich, 'half running, half flying,' by which it covers the ground with incredible speed, calculated by Dr Livingstone at twenty-six miles an hour.

*She scorneth the horse and his rider.* This verse forms the natural transition to the next subject.

(*f*) **The war-horse,** 19—25. Does the horse owe to Job his might, and his tossing mane (19)? Is Job the creator of this glorious creature, who bounds forward, and snorts and paws the ground in his fury (20, 21), fearlessly eager for the fray, rejoicing in the battle in spite of the missiles that are flashing and hurtling around (22, 23) and excited by the sound of the trumpet (24, 25)?

As illustrating this famous description both Delitzsch and Davidson quote from Layard's *Discoveries,* p. 330, the following: 'Although docile as a lamb, and requiring no other guide than the halter, when the Arab mare hears the war-cry of the tribe (cf. verse 25) and sees the quivering spear of her rider (cf. verse 23), her eyes glitter with fire, her blood-red nostrils open wide, her neck is nobly arched, and her tail and mane are raised and spread out to the wind (cf. verse 19). A Bedouin proverb says that a high-bred mare when at full speed should hide her rider between her neck and her tail.' Reference should also be made to the spirited description in Virgil, *Georgics,* III. ll. 77—88.

19. *Hast thou clothed his neck with the quivering mane ?* This translation is probably correct, but the single word rendered *quivering mane* literally means *shaking.* *Thunder* of the A.V. is a not unnatural mistake, as the word is almost identical with that so rendered in verse 25.

20 Hast thou made him to leap as a locust ?
  The glory of his snorting is terrible.
21 ¹He paweth in the valley, and rejoiceth in his strength :
  He goeth out to meet ²the armed men.
22 He mocketh at fear, and is not dismayed ;
  Neither turneth he back from the sword.
23 The quiver rattleth ³against him,
  The flashing spear and the javelin.
24 He swalloweth the ground with fierceness and rage ;
  ⁴Neither believeth he that it is the voice of the trumpet.
25 As oft as the trumpet *soundeth* he saith, Aha !
  And he smelleth the battle afar off,
  The thunder of the captains, and the shouting.
26  Doth the hawk soar by thy wisdom,
  *And* stretch her wings toward the south ?
27 Doth the eagle mount up at thy command,
  And make her nest on high ?

---

¹ Heb. *They paw.*    ² Or, *the weapons*    ³ Or, *upon*
⁴ Or, *Neither standeth he still at &c.*

20. *Hast thou made him to leap as a locust?* Much to be preferred to the rendering of the A.V., *Canst thou make him afraid as a grasshopper ?* For the comparison of locusts to horses, see Joel ii. 4; Rev. ix. 7.

24. *Neither believeth he that it is the voice of the trumpet.* If this rendering is correct it must mean that 'he hardly trusts his ears for gladness' (Davidson), cf. xxix. 24, but it is better to translate (with R.V. marg.) *neither standeth he still at the sound of the trumpet,* and refer it to the impatience of the war-horse for the fray, and the impossibility of holding him in. Cf. Virgil: 'Tum si qua sonum procul arma dedere, *Stare loco nescit,* micat auribus, et tremit artus.' *Georg.* III. l. 82.

(*g*) **The hawk and eagle,** 26—30. Is it by Job's wisdom and direction that the hawk spreads its wings and migrates southwards (26)? or that the eagle soars aloft to her eyrie in the crags (27, 28)? whence she spies out the far-off prey, and swoops down on it (29, 30).

26. *Doth the hawk soar by thy wisdom?* The hawk is a general term for smaller birds of prey, cf. Lev. xi. 16 ; Deut. xiv. 15 ; and see Tristram, p. 189.

And *stretch her wings toward the south,* referring to the migratory habits of such birds.

27. *Doth the eagle mount up at thy command ?* The eagle of Scripture (cf. ix. 26) is, as Tristram shows, properly the griffon-vulture (to be carefully distinguished from the disgusting Egyptian vulture), and ' so

28 She dwelleth on the rock, and hath her lodging *there,*
Upon the crag of the rock, and the strong hold.
29 From thence she spieth out the prey ;
Her eyes behold it afar off.
30 Her young ones also suck up blood :
And where the slain are, there is she.

**XL.** 1 Moreover the LORD answered Job, and said,
2 Shall he that cavilleth contend with the Almighty ?
He that argueth with God, let him answer it.

3 Then Job answered the LORD, and said,

far from conveying the idea of a repulsive bird to the Oriental mind, has been universally adopted as the type of the lordly and noble,' p. 172.

29. *From thence she spieth out the prey; her eyes behold it afar off.* 'The power of vision in the eagle is amazing, almost incredible. No sooner does a kid fall in the wilderness among the thick bushes, than some of these keen-sighted hunters after prey notice it from their pathway in mid-heaven, and circling round and round, they pounce down upon it and bear it away to their nest. This appears to be done purely by sight.' Thomson, *The Land and the Book,* p. 175. Cf. Tristram, p. 169.

30. *Her young ones also suck up blood.* Cf. Prov. xxx. 17, 'The eye that mocketh at his father, and despiseth to obey his mother, the ravens of the valley shall pick it out, and the young eagles shall eat it.'

*And where the slain are, there is she.* 'Although this is a habit it shares with the eagle, yet no eagles congregate like the griffon ; and while the latter may be seen by hundreds, the less conspicuous eagles are only to be counted by a few individuals here and there.' Tristram,

p. 175. This verse may well have been in our Lord's mind when He said, 'Wheresoever the carcase is, there will the eagles be gathered together,' S. Matt. xxiv. 28, cf. Rev. xix. 17, 18.

**XL. 1—5. Conclusion and result of the speech.**

1, 2. The speech now at the close reverts to the point at which it began, cf. xxxviii. 1—3, and Job 'the caviller' is asked whether he really wishes to contend with God ; if so, *let him answer it.*

3—5. But the panorama of creation, and the pointed question addressed to him have done their work. Job acknowledges his littleness, and confesses his inability to answer. 'The God who sets bounds to the sea, who refreshes the desert, who feeds the ravens, who cares for the gazelle in the wilderness and the eagle in its eyrie, is the same God Who now causes him seemingly thus unjustly to suffer. But if the former is worthy of adoration, the latter will also be so. Therefore Job confesses that he will henceforth keep silence, and solemnly promises that he will now no longer contend with Him.' Delitzsch.

4 Behold, I am of small account ; what shall I answer thee ?
  I lay mine hand upon my mouth.
5 Once have I spoken, and I will not answer ;
  Yea twice, but I will proceed no further.

5. *Once have I spoken...yea*　note on v. 19.
*twice;* i.e. *repeatedly.* See the

**XL. 6—XLI.** 34. Second speech of the Almighty.
On the purpose of this speech see above, p. 206. It may be analysed
thus :

(1) *Introductory challenge to Job to undertake the rule of the
world.* 6—14.

(2) *Description of Behemoth.* 15—24.

(3) *Description of Leviathan.* ch. xli.

The elaborate descriptions of these two Egyptian monsters are introduced to show Job how little capable he is of governing the world. If he
could not even draw a cord through the nose of Behemoth, or touch
Leviathan with impunity, how could he expect to stand before God ?

6 Then the LORD answered Job out of the whirlwind, and
  said,
7 Gird up thy loins now like a man :
  I will demand of thee, and declare thou unto me.
8 Wilt thou even disannul my judgement ?
  Wilt thou condemn me, that thou mayest be justified ?
9 Or hast thou an arm like God ?
  And canst thou thunder with a voice like him ?

6—14. **Introductory challenge
to Job to undertake the rule of
the world.** Again the Almighty
begins by bidding Job stand up to
Him and answer His challenge (6,
7). Is he prepared to dispute God's
justice, and to pronounce Him wrong
in order to justify himself (8) ? Can
he really claim the strength of God,
or speak with the same mighty
power (9) ? Let him then assume
the prerogatives of God, put on all
the majesty he can, and pour forth

his wrath, and see if he is able to
bring low the proud and haughty,
or destroy the wicked (10—13).
Then will God be ready to acknowledge him, and admit his power to
save himself (14).

7. Repeated from xxxviii. 3.

8. *Wilt thou even disannul my
judgement ?* The question seems to
refer to the tendency which Job had
shown all along to dispute God's
justice, to *break* or deny His rectitude.

10 Deck thyself now with excellency and dignity ;
   And array thyself with honour and majesty.
11 Pour forth the overflowings of thine anger :
   And look upon every one that is proud, and abase him.
12 Look on every one that is proud, *and* bring him low ;
   And tread down the wicked where they stand.
13 Hide them in the dust together ;
   Bind their faces in the hidden *place*.
14 Then will I also confess of thee
   That thine own right hand can save thee.
15  Behold now [1]behemoth, which I made with thee ;
   He eateth grass as an ox.

---

[1] That is, *the hippopotamus*.

---

10. *array thyself with honour and majesty.* The very same words are used of God in Ps. civ. 1, 'Thou art clothed with honour and majesty,' and cf. Ps. xcvi. 6, where honour and majesty are similarly spoken of as attributes of God. These parallels show that the verse before us is intended as a challenge to Job to assume the prerogatives of God.

11. *look upon every one that is proud, and abase him.* Cf. Is. ii. 11—17.

13. *Hide them in the dust together.* Cf. Is. ii. 10, 'Hide thee in the dust.'

*Bind their faces in the hidden* place. The *hidden place* is probably the darkness of Sheol. Thus the verse means destroy them body and soul in death.

14. *That thine own right hand can save thee.* Cf. the similar language used of God Himself in Ps. xcviii. 1 ; Is. lix. 16 ; lxiii. 5.

15—24. **Description of behemoth.** Let Job regard the great Egyptian monster the hippopotamus,

which is the creation of God exactly as he is (15). Let him mark well his extraordinary strength, his iron frame and huge limbs (16—18). This great beast is the mightiest of God's creation, and God has provided him with teeth like a great sword wherewith he sweeps the hillsides for his food (19, 20), though his favourite resort is to be found in the marshes and the bed of the river, where he lies under the shadow of the lotus trees and willows (21, 22) heedless of the rising and overflowing of the river (23). What man is there that can take him when he is on the alert, or lead him captive with his nose pierced with a hook (24) ?

15. *Behold now behemoth.* The ancient versions either leave the name untranslated (as the Vulgate and Syriac), or render by some general term for beasts (as the LXX. θηρία, and Aquila and Theodotion κτήνη). Older expositors for the most part thought of the elephant : but it has been generally agreed since the days of Bochart that the

16 Lo now, his strength is in his loins,
　And his force is in the muscles of his belly.
17 He moveth his tail like a cedar :
　The sinews of his thighs are knit together.
18 His bones are *as* tubes of brass ;
　His [1]limbs are like bars of iron.
19 He is the chief of the ways of God :
　[2]He *only* that made him can make his sword to approach
　*unto him.*

---

[1] Or, *ribs*　　[2] Or, *He that made him hath furnished* him with *his sword*

hippopotamus is intended, and the description corresponds so closely with the reality that there can be little doubt that this is correct (see however the note at the end of xli.). The name *behemoth* is in form the plural of the word for 'beasts,' but it has been widely thought that here it is really a Hebraized form of an Egyptian name for the hippopotamus, *p-ehe-mou, the ox of the water* (so Ewald, Delitzsch, Dillmann, and Davidson). This is, however, questioned apparently with good reason by Cheyne (see the *Expositor* for July 1897, p. 30). But whether the name be Egyptian, or whether as is more probable it is an *intensive* plural, the beast *par excellence*, it evidently stands here as the proper name of the brute described. It is possible also that in Ps. lxxiii. 22, 'I was as a beast before thee,' we should render, 'A behemoth was I with thee'; and it has been suggested (though the suggestion has not commended itself to most commentators) that a similar reference may be found in Is. xxx. 6.

*which I made with thee*, i.e. it is God's creation like Job himself.

*He eateth grass as an ox.* 'The hippopotamus is strictly herbivorous

and makes sad havoc among the rice fields and cultivated grounds when at night he issues forth from the reedy fens.' Tristram, p. 52.

17. *He moveth his tail like a cedar.* It has been objected to the identification of behemoth with the hippopotamus that the tail of the last-mentioned beast 'would surely not have been compared to a cedar by a truthful though poetic observer like the author of chapters xxxviii. xxxix' (Cheyne, *Job and Solomon*, p. 56). But the comparison of the short, stiff, muscular tail, to the strong and elastic cedar branch (which is probably intended) seems really to be perfectly natural, and need cause no difficulty.

19. *He is the chief of the ways of God.* 'Chief' is literally *first*, not of course in time, but in magnitude and power, as one of the hugest of creatures.

*He* only *that made him can make his sword to approach* unto him. A clause of very doubtful meaning, the A.V. and R.V. follow the Targum and Vulgate *qui fecit eum applicabit gladium ejus.* But this seems out of place and unnatural. It is difficult to think that the text is correct, but taking it as it stands the best rendering is that of R.V.

20 Surely the mountains bring him forth food ;
   Where all the beasts of the field do play.
21 He lieth under the lotus trees,
   In the covert of the reed, and the fen.
22 The lotus trees cover him with their shadow ;
   The willows of the brook compass him about.
23 Behold, if a river ¹overflow, he trembleth not :
   He is confident, though Jordan swell even to his mouth.
24 Shall any take him when he is on the watch,
   Or pierce through his nose with a snare ?

---

¹ Or, *be violent*

marg., *He that made him hath furnished* him with *his sword.* The 'sword' in this case must be taken to refer to the formidable teeth with which the hippopotamus is furnished, with which the creature can 'cut the grass as neatly as if it were mown with the scythe, and is able to sever, as if with shears, a tolerably stout and thick stem.' Wood's *Mammalia* as quoted in Tristram, p. 52.

20. *Surely the mountains bring him forth food.* Again it is objected that it is 'difficult to see how the hippopotamus could get upon the mountains' (Siegfried). But he is said to search the rising grounds near the river for his sustenance in company with the animals of the land (Tristram), and this is probably what is intended.

23. *Behold, if a river overflow, he trembleth not.* This (and not the rendering of the A.V.) is correct. The rising of the water does not disturb the creature, as it 'lies in the long reaches of rivers, often sinking to the bottom for a considerable time, and then rising to the surface, where it lies motionless, with only its eyes

and nostrils above water' (Tristram).

*He is confident, though Jordan swell even to his mouth.* The clause evidently means the same as the previous one, but the mention of *Jordan* is unexpected, as there is no trace of the hippopotamus ever having been found there. Probably the name is introduced as a typical specimen of a rushing river—'though a Jordan swell' &c.

24. *Shall any take him when he is on the watch, or pierce through his nose with a snare ?* Here again it has been said that the hippopotamus was 'habitually hunted by the Egyptians with lance and harpoon and was therefore no fit symbol of indomitable pride.' But is it as a symbol of pride that it is introduced? It is rather as a symbol of strength and might; and though the beast undoubtedly *was* hunted and taken, yet the question 'shall any take him *when he is on the watch*' is pertinent enough. Cf. Prov. i. 17 for the phrase rendered *on the watch. Snare* apparently stands here for the hook or cords which might be supposed to be put through its nose after its capture.

**XLI. Description of Leviathan.** The chapter falls into two parts:

(1) The impossibility of capturing and taming Leviathan, and the moral to be drawn from it. 1—11.

(2) Description of the creature in detail. 12—34.

¹**XLI.** 1 Canst thou draw out ²leviathan with a fish hook?
    Or press down his tongue with a cord?
2 Canst thou put ³a rope into his nose?
    Or pierce his jaw through with a ⁴hook?
3 Will he make many supplications unto thee?
    Or will he speak soft words unto thee?
4 Will he make a covenant with thee,
    That thou shouldest take him for a servant for ever?

---

¹ [Ch. xl. 25 in Heb.]
² That is, *the crocodile*.    ³ Heb. *a rope of rushes*.    ⁴ Or, *spike*

---

1—11. **The impossibility of capturing and taming leviathan, and the moral to be drawn from it.** Can Job take the crocodile with a hook and cord (1, 2)? Will the creature come fawning on him, or make an agreement to serve him like a domestic animal (3, 4)? Can Job tame him and take him for a pet (5)? Can fishermen bargain over him as they do over their fish (6)? or can he be speared as fish can (7)? Should any man venture to attack him, he will have good cause to remember it, and is not likely to repeat the operation (8, 9). And if man thus dare not arouse him, what folly is it for him to expect to stand before his Creator (10, 11)!

1. *Canst thou draw out leviathan with a fish hook?* There can be no doubt that here *leviathan* means the crocodile. The name

stands fitly as a symbol of Egypt in Ps. lxxiv. 14. Elsewhere it is used as symbolical of the power of Babylon, Is. xxvii. 1; in Ps. civ. 26 it is apparently used of the whale; and in Job iii. 8 it has stood as the name of a mythical dragon (see note on the passage). The word properly means *twisted* or *coiled*. The versions for the most part leave it untranslated, though the LXX. has δράκων.

2. As verse 1 referred to the impossibility of taking this huge creature with a hook and line, so this verse appears to allude to the practice of passing a rope of rushes through the gills of the fish when taken. Job is ironically asked whether he can do this with leviathan, or hold him suspended with a hook in his nose. The word for *rope* is properly *rush*, and refers to a line made of twisted rushes.

5 Wilt thou play with him as with a bird?
  Or wilt thou bind him for thy maidens?
6 Shall the bands *of fishermen* make traffic of him?
  Shall they part him among the merchants?
7 Canst thou fill his skin with barbed irons,
  Or his head with fish spears?
8 Lay thine hand upon him;
  Remember the battle, and do so no more.
¹9 Behold, the hope of him is in vain:
  Shall not one be cast down even at the sight of him?
10 None is so fierce that he dare stir him up:
  Who then is he that can stand before me?

¹ [Ch. xli. 1 in Heb.]

**5.** *Wilt thou play with him as with a bird?* Most commentators quote in illustration of this from Catullus, *Passer deliciæ meæ puellæ.* A similar phrase to the opening words *Wilt thou play with him* is found in Ps. civ. 26, 'There is leviathan whom thou hast formed *to take his pastime therein*' (R.V. marg. *to play with him*), but it is doubtful whether the meaning is the same.

**6.** *Shall the bands* of fishermen *make traffic of him?* The word translated *bands* means *associates* or *partners* in a trade or calling, cf. S. Luke v. 7. The word for *make traffic* is the same that is translated *make merchandise* in vi. 27. It is a rare word, only occurring elsewhere in Deut. ii. 6; Hos. iii. 2.

*Shall they part him among the merchants?* literally *the Canaanites*, i.e. Phœnicians, who were the great traders of antiquity. Cf. Prov. xxxi. 24; Zech. xiv. 21.

**7.** *Canst thou fill his skin with barbed irons, or his head with fish spears?* The words for *barbed irons* and *spears* used in this verse are

found nowhere else, but there is no doubt about their meaning. The fish spear is said to be much used in the smaller streams and northern rivers of the Lebanon. (Tristram, p. 292.) It is obvious that it would be useless against the crocodile.

**8.** *Lay thine hand upon him.* The charge is of course ironical. Let Job dare to touch him! Such a commotion will be raised, that he will have good cause to *remember the battle,* i.e. the struggle, and the best advice that can be given him is to *do so no more,* i.e. not to attempt to repeat the operation.

**9.** *Behold, the hope of him is in vain.* The pronoun here apparently refers not to leviathan but to his assailant. *His hope,* i.e. the assailant's hope of getting the better of him, *is in vain,* has turned out deceptive.

**10, 11.** The moral of this. As Delitzsch says: 'one sees from these concluding inferences, thus applied, what is the design, in the connexion of this second speech of Jehovah, of the reference to behemoth and leviathan, which some-

11  Who hath first given unto me, that I should repay him?
     *Whatsoever is* under the whole heaven is mine.
12  I will not keep silence concerning his limbs,
     Nor his mighty strength, nor his comely proportion.
13  Who can ¹strip off his outer garment?
     Who shall come within his double bridle?
14  Who can open the doors of his face?
     ²Round about his teeth is terror.
15  *His* ³strong scales are *his* pride,
     Shut up together *as with* a close seal.

---

¹ Heb. *uncover the face of his garment.*          ² Or, *His teeth are terrible
round about*          ³ Or, *courses of scales*  Heb. *channels of shields.*

what abruptly began in xl. 15. If
even the strength of one of God's
creatures admits no thought of
being able to attack it, how much
more should the greatness of the
Creator deter man from all resistance! For no one has any claim
on God, so that he should have the
right of appearing before Him with
a rude challenge. Every creature
under heaven is God's; man therefore possesses nothing that was not
God's gift, and he must humbly
yield, whatever God gives or takes
away.'

*Who hath first given unto me,
that I should repay him?* Apparently this is the origin of S.
Paul's words in Rom. xi. 35, τίς
προέδωκεν αὐτῷ, καὶ ἀνταποδοθήσεται
αὐτῷ; and it is worth noticing that
both here and in 1 Cor. iii. 19
where he quotes Job v. 13 his
citations are taken from the Hebrew,
and not from the LXX., which has
here τίς ἀντιστήσεταί μοι καὶ ὑπο-
μενεῖ;

12—34. **Description of leviathan in detail.** Job is now called
on to admire the various parts and

features of the crocodile: his terrible
jaws and teeth (13, 14); his strong
scales (15—17); the terror of his
breath (18—21); his lusty strength
(22—24); the dread which he inspires (25); the futility of man's
weapons against him (26—29); his
belly and its impression on the
mud where he lies (30); the dis-
turbance he creates in the deep
(31, 32); and his preeminence
among God's creatures (33, 34).

13. *Who can strip off his outer
garment?* literally *who can uncover
the face of his garment?* The
*garment* must refer to his scaly
coat, the question being a general
preliminary one, before the details
are touched upon in turn.

*Who shall come within his double
bridle?* The *double bridle* evidently signifies the upper and lower
jaws armed with powerful teeth.

15. His *strong scales are* his
*pride.* The expression in the
original for *his strong scales* is a
strange one, *the channels of his
shields.* It refers perhaps to the
furrows or indentations between
the scales of the crocodile.

J.

16 One is so near to another,
   That no air can come between them.
17 They are joined one to another ;
   They stick together, that they cannot be sundered.
18 His neesings flash forth light,
   And his eyes are like the eyelids of the morning.
19 Out of his mouth go burning torches,
   And sparks of fire leap forth.
20 Out of his nostrils a smoke goeth,
   As of a seething pot and *burning* rushes.
21 His breath kindleth coals,
   And a flame goeth forth from his mouth.
22 In his neck abideth strength,
   And terror danceth before him.
23 The flakes of his flesh are joined together :
   They are firm upon him ; they cannot be moved.

18. *His neesings flash forth light.* The picture in these verses is hyperbolical and is intended to describe his gleaming eyes and violent snorting. When the creature sneezes, as it basks in the sunshine, the hot breath appears like a stream of light. *Neesing* is merely the old form of sneezing. Cf. Shakespeare,

And waxen in their mirth and
   *neeze* and swear
A merrier hour was never wasted
   there.
*Midsummer Night's Dream*, ii. 1. 56.

*neesed* was originally read in the A.V. in 2 Kings iv. 35, though modern editions since 1762 read *sneezed.*

*the eyelids of the morning*, the same expression as in iii. 9.

20. *Out of his nostrils a smoke goeth.* Cox aptly quotes the following from Bertram's *Travels in North and South Carolina.* ' I perceived a crocodile rush from a small lake, whose banks were covered with reeds. It puffed out its enormous body, and reared its tail in the air. *Thick smoke came with a thundering sound from his nostrils.* At the same time an immense rival rose from the deep on the opposite bank. They darted at one another, and *the water boiled beneath them.*' For the last phrase cf. ver. 31.

*As of a seething pot and* burning *rushes.* The A.V. here *seething pot or caldron* is quite wrong though supported by Rabbinic authority. The R.V. gives the true meaning, inserting however the word *burning* (which has no equivalent in the original) to indicate that the rushes are used as fuel.

22. *terror danceth before him.* A very vivid phrase and better than the rendering of the A.V. The word for *danceth* occurs nowhere else, but there is no doubt as to its meaning.

24  His heart is as firm as a stone ;
    Yea, firm as the nether millstone.
25  When he raiseth himself up, the mighty are afraid :
    By reason of consternation they are beside themselves.
26  If one lay at him with the sword, it cannot avail ;
    Nor the spear, the dart, nor the ¹pointed shaft.
27  He counteth iron as straw,
    *And* brass as rotten wood.
28  The ²arrow cannot make him flee :
    Slingstones are turned with him into stubble.
29  Clubs are counted as stubble :
    He laugheth at the rushing of the javelin.

---

¹ Or, *coat of mail*      ² Heb. *son of the bow.*

24.  *firm as the nether millstone*, which would naturally be the harder and even more solid than the upper stone which lay upon it.

25.  *By reason of consternation they are beside themselves*. The verb here used is employed in the Levitical law in the sense of *purify oneself from uncleanness*, Numb. viii. 21 ; xix. 12, 13, 20 ; xxxi. 19, 20, 23.  Hence the Vulgate *purgabuntur*, and the A.V. *purify themselves* in this verse.  But there can be no thought of the ceremonies of the Law here, and the R.V. is right.

26—29.  The futility of weapons against him.  ' His whole head, back, and tail are covered with horny, quadrangular plates, or scales, set so closely together that the sharpest spear can seldom find its way through them, and even a rifle ball glances off them if it strike obliquely' (Cox).  It has been objected to the identification of leviathan with the crocodile that the latter was attacked and killed by the Egyptians, while in these verses leviathan is said to laugh at his assailants (Cheyne, *Job and Solomon*,

p. 57).  The objection does not seem worth much, for even if harpooning the crocodile *was* practised in ancient days, yet the broad fact as stated above in the citation from Cox is literally true, and is amply sufficient to account for the poet's language.

26.  *the pointed shaft*. The Hebrew word *Shiryah* occurs nowhere else. The A.V. like the ancient versions (LXX. or rather Theodot. θώραξ, Vulg. *thorax*, so Targ.) takes it as a cognate form of the word *Shiryon* found in 1 Kings xxii. 34 ; Is. lix. 17, for *coat of mail* (*habergeon*, which occurs also in the A.V. in Exod. xxviii. 32 ; xxxix. 23 ; 2 Chr. xxvi. 14 ; Neh. iv. 16, is properly a little coat of mail covering the head and shoulders).  But this seems out of place here, as the writer is evidently speaking of the weapons with which leviathan is attacked.  The word is probably the equivalent of a similar Arabic word, and means (as R.V.) a *pointed shaft* or harpoon.

29.  *Clubs*, better than *darts* of the A.V. Aquila and Theodotion σφῦραι, Symmachus σφῦρα, Vulg. *malleus*.

30 His underparts are *like* sharp potsherds :
He spreadeth *as it were* a threshing wain upon the mire.

31 He maketh the deep to boil like a pot :
He maketh the sea like ointment.

32 He maketh a path to shine after him ;
One would think the deep to be hoary.

33 Upon earth there is not his like,
That is made without fear.

34 He beholdeth every thing that is high :
He is king over all the [1]sons of pride.

---

[1] See ch. xxviii. 8.

30. *His underparts are* like *sharp potsherds.* Though the scales of the belly are tolerably smooth, yet those of the underside of the huge tail are sufficiently sharp to make the comparison apt; and where the creature has been lying in the morass, they leave an impression which may well be compared to the marks of a *threshing wain upon the mire.* For the threshing wain cf. Amos i. 3, where see Driver's note *in loc. (Cambridge Bible for Schools and Colleges)* with the illustration in the additional note on p. 227.

31, 32. The description in these verses is very vivid. It speaks for itself, and scarcely needs any commentary beyond the quotation from Bertram's *Travels* given above on ver. 20. The *path* which he *maketh to shine after him* is the track which he leaves as he propels himself by his huge tail, and *one would think the deep to be hoary* because of the trail of foam upon it.

34. *He beholdeth every thing that is high,* i.e. he regards such things without fear.

*the sons of pride.* Cf. xxviii. 8, where the same expression occurs.

Two questions which have been raised concerning these descriptions of behemoth and leviathan require a brief notice. (1) Is the common interpretation given above, which identifies them with the hippopotamus and crocodile, correct? Cheyne in his *Job and Solomon* in 1887 styled them 'fancy sketches,' and declared that 'neither behemoth nor leviathan corresponds strictly to any known animal,' but that they seemed to him 'to claim a kinship with the dragon and other imaginary monsters of the Swiss topographers of the sixteenth century' (p. 55 seq.). He now (1897) admits that they 'may, up to a certain extent, be identified with the hippopotamus and the crocodile,' and confesses that in 1887 he 'slightly underestimated the element of actuality in the poet's description,' but he still maintains that 'the descriptions are hyperbolical and unpleasing if referred to the real monsters of the Nile,' and takes them as 'mythic monsters' (*Expositor* for July 1897, p. 32 seq.). The difficulties, however, in the way of regarding them as poetical descriptions of the hippopotamus and crocodile seem very slight. As far as behemoth is concerned, apart from the name,

**XLII.** 1 Then Job answered the LORD, and said,
2 I know that thou canst do all things,
And that no purpose of thine can be restrained.

they are chiefly to be found in verses 17, 20, and 24, where they have been considered, and it is thought satisfactorily answered, in the notes; and as to the name, to say that if the writer had meant the hippopotamus he would probably have called it 'the swine of the Nile' is pure assumption. So far as is known neither the hippopotamus nor the crocodile has any proper descriptive name in Hebrew that the writer could have used. With regard to the crocodile there is really no feature in the description which does not appear to be substantially accurate. It must be remembered that the descriptions are poetical, and when we bear in mind Herder's remark (cited by Delitzsch) that the writer does not 'mean to furnish any contributions to Pennant's *Zoologie* or to Linnæus's *Animal Kingdom*,' we may safely conclude that the traditional interpretation is correct, and that they are no mythical creatures which are here described, but the actual monsters of the Nile as they exist, and as the poet had probably seen them.

(2) The second question is concerned with the authorship of this section. It has appeared to some critics (as Ewald, Dillmann, Cheyne, and Siegfried) that the descriptions are prolix and laboured, and out of harmony with the rest of Jehovah's utterances, and thus that it is improbable that they come from the same hand as the marvellous descriptions in the first speech of the Almighty. It is, however, hard to cut them out without further

alteration and rearrangement of the text. Their removal would leave the two speeches of Jehovah very ill-balanced, and it cannot be conceded that they are out of place where they stand. Their purpose (as indicated above on p. 206) is obvious and natural enough, and has appeared so to the great majority of commentators. Moreover, the argument from *style*, if it stand alone, is very precarious, and to the present writer it does not appear that the difference is sufficient to warrant any hesitation in accepting this section as a part of the original poem.

**XLII.** 1—6. **The effect of Jehovah's second speech.** The effect of this speech is that Job is completely broken down. The first speech had silenced him: this has shown to him himself, for in the light of God's greatness he sees his own littleness together with his folly and presumption in having challenged God, and seeing this he is humbled to the dust.

He begins by acknowledging God's Almighty power and wisdom (1, 2), and then, quoting God's reproach to him, admits that he had spoken without knowledge (3); and finally, again quoting God's challenge to him (4), confesses humbly that now that he *sees* God, he knows himself, and repents of his sin towards God (5, 6).

2. The confession is not simply of God's abstract might (i.e. ability to *do all things*) but rather of power directed by wisdom (that *no purpose* of God *can be restrained*), for the

3 ¹Who is this that hideth counsel without knowledge?
　Therefore have I uttered that which I understood not,
　Things too wonderful for me, which I knew not.
4 Hear, I beseech thee, and I will speak;
　²I will demand of thee, and declare thou unto me.
5 I had heard of thee by the hearing of the ear;
　But now mine eye seeth thee,
6 Wherefore I ³abhor *myself*, and repent
　In dust and ashes.

¹ See ch. xxxviii. 2.　　² See ch. xxxviii. 3, xl. 7.　　³ Or, *loathe* my words

speeches of the Almighty have illustrated His wisdom and goodness in the government of the world, as well as His power.

3. *Who is this that hideth counsel without knowledge?* Job here quotes the words of the Almighty in xxxviii. 2. He cites, as it were, the charge that had been made against him, and then pleads guilty. He *has* committed the folly of pronouncing an opinion on things that were far beyond his comprehension, when he charged God with injustice, and declared that there was no moral rule in the government of the world.

4. *Hear, I beseech thee, and I will speak; I will demand of thee, and declare thou unto me.* The second clause of this verse is another direct citation of Jehovah's words, and is taken from xxxviii. 3 and xl. 7, but it is difficult to know whether in the first clause Job is himself appealing to the Almighty to listen while he completes his answer, or whether, like the second clause, the first is intended to summarize Jehovah's address to him. Davidson takes this latter view, rendering *Hear now* (instead of *I beseech thee*) as more appropriate in the mouth of God. But the particle here used certainly generally denotes the intreaty of an inferior, and the words of this clause (unlike those of the following one) are nowhere found in the speeches of Jehovah. It seems best, then, to take them as Job's intreaty to Him.

6. *Wherefore I abhor* myself. As the italics of the English versions show, there is no object of the verb stated in the original. It may be left indefinite. *I abhor it*, i.e. *I loathe my words*, as R.V. marg.

## PART V. THE EPILOGUE. CHAPTER XLII. 7—17.

The drama has now reached its conclusion, and for the sake of completeness it only remains that the narrative should be satisfactorily wound up. This is done in xlii. 7—17, where the writer drops the poetical form and reverts to the plain prose of the prologue. In this epilogue Jehovah first pronounces His verdict, condemning the friends and bidding them offer a sacrifice, promising to pardon them at Job's intercession (7—9). Job is accepted and restored to all, and more than all, his former prosperity (10). His friends come to congratulate him (11). His flocks and herds are increased (12). Children are born to him; and a long and prosperous life is granted to him before his death (13—17).

It has been noticed that a sense of disappointment is sometimes felt with regard to the speeches of the Almighty from the whirlwind. A still deeper feeling of the same character is experienced by some persons on reading the epilogue. That Job should be restored to earthly prosperity and receive twice as much of this world's goods as he had before enjoyed, while the cause of his suffering remains as great an enigma to him as ever, may seem a tame ending to a work of such extraordinary force, and we can hardly doubt that a modern poet would have brought the book to a 'more inward and spiritual conclusion' (Cox). But we must bear in mind the limitations under which the poet worked. He wrote under the conditions of Hebrew thought, and of his own day, and we have no right to expect modern and Christian ideas from him. Moreover the Epilogue *has* its teaching for us, which we cannot afford to lose. It indicates that even in this life God is on the side of virtue; and the use which S. James makes of it in reminding his hearers of 'the end of the Lord,' i.e. *the end appointed by the Lord* (see Mayor on James v. 11) in connexion with *the patience of Job*, in order to point the general moral of his Epistle, viz. that 'patient endurance of affliction leads to wisdom and final happiness,' may serve to show us that the teaching of the book would have been incomplete without it.

7  And it was so, that after the LORD had spoken these words unto Job, the LORD said to Eliphaz the Temanite, My wrath is kindled against thee, and against thy two friends: for ye have not spoken of me the thing that is
8  right, as my servant Job hath. Now therefore, take unto

7. *ye have not spoken of me the thing that is right, as my servant Job hath.* Job had in his agony said many blameworthy things, but he had at least kept from false inferences with regard to God's providential government of the world which the friends had not done. 'The *right* in Job's speeches consisted of his having denied that affliction is always a punishment of sin, and in his holding fast the consciousness of his innocence, without suffering himself to be persuaded

of the opposite. That denial was right; and this truthfulness was more precious to God than the untruthfulness of the friends who were zealous for the honour of God.' Delitzsch.

*my servant Job*, as in the prologue, i. 8.

8. *Now therefore, take unto you seven bullocks and seven rams... and offer up for yourselves a burnt offering.* As in the prologue the writer makes the offering for sin a *burnt offering*, and not the technical

you seven bullocks and seven rams, and go to my servant
Job, and offer up for yourselves a burnt offering ; and my
servant Job shall pray for you ; for him will I accept, that
I deal not with you after your folly ; for ye have not
spoken of me the thing that is right, as my servant Job
9 hath. So Eliphaz the Temanite and Bildad the Shuhite
and Zophar the Naamathite went, and did according as
the LORD commanded them : and the LORD accepted Job.
10 And the LORD turned the captivity of Job, when he
prayed for his friends : and the LORD gave Job twice as
11 much as he had before. Then came there unto him all
his brethren, and all his sisters, and all they that had
been of his acquaintance before, and did eat bread with
him in his house : and they bemoaned him, and comforted
him concerning all the evil that the LORD had brought
upon him : every man also gave him a ¹piece of money,

¹ Heb. *kesitah.*

*sin offering* of the Law, because the
scene is laid in patriarchal times, cf.
i. 5, and see the Introd. p. xix.
*Seven* is the sacred number.

*my servant Job shall pray for
you ; for him will I accept.* Cf.
Gen. xx. 7, 'Restore the man's
wife ; for he is a prophet, and he
shall pray for thee, and thou shalt
live.'

10. *And the Lord turned the
captivity of Job.* The phrase is
sometimes appealed to as if it indicated that the book belonged to
the time of the Babylonian captivity,
and that Job was intended to be a
sort of representative of the nation
of Israel. Such an inference is,
however, highly precarious, for (1)
the rendering *turn the captivity* is
uncertain. Many moderns would
translate *turn the fortunes* (taking
the word שְׁבוּת or שְׁבִית as akin to
the verb שׁוּב, lit. *turn the turning,*—and not as from שָׁבָה, to lead

captive) ; and (2) the phrase occurs
in places where there can be no
possible reference to a literal *captivity,* as in Ezek. xvi. 53, 'I will
turn again their captivity, the captivity of Sodom and her daughters,'
where it is explained immediately
afterwards by the parallel expression
'Sodom and her daughters *shall
return to their former estate.*' Moreover (3) it is used in Amos ix. 14
and Hosea vi. 11 long before the
Babylonian captivity.

11. *every man also gave him a
piece of money.* As is noted in the
margin of the R.V. the Hebrew word
is *kesitah,* which only occurs elsewhere in Gen. xxxiii. 19 ; Josh. xxiv.
32, of the hundred *pieces of money*
which Jacob gave for the parcel of
ground at Shechem (cf. the Introd.
p. xix.). The ancient versions as a
rule render it by 'lambs' (so LXX.
Syr. Vulg. and Targ.) ; but this is
certainly wrong. Symmachus has

12 and every one a ring of gold. So the LORD blessed the
   latter end of Job more than his beginning : and he had
   fourteen thousand sheep, and six thousand camels, and a
13 thousand yoke of oxen, and a thousand she-asses. He
14 had also seven sons and three daughters. And he called
   the name of the first, Jemimah ; and the name of the
   second, Keziah ; and the name of the third, Keren-happuch.
15 And in all the land were no women found so fair as the
   daughters of Job : and their father gave them inheritance
16 among their brethren. And after this Job lived an hundred
   and forty years, and saw his sons, and his sons' sons, *even*
17 four generations. So Job died, being old and full of days.

rightly νόμισμα, and it seems to denote properly something weighed out, and so may be used for an uncoined piece of money, which would fit in well with the early date of the transactions in connexion with which the word occurs.

12. *fourteen thousand sheep, and six thousand camels, and a thousand yoke of oxen, and a thousand she-asses.* The numbers are exactly double those given in c. i. 3.

13. *He had also seven sons and three daughters.* The numbers here are the same as those of his children before his calamities, see i. 2. And yet it is said that 'the Lord gave Job *twice as much* as he had before.' Is it, as Delitzsch holds, that this is intended to be so far a doubling, because his deceased children were not really lost to him (cf. 2 Sam. xii. 23)? 'The author of this book, in everything to the most minute thing consistent, here gives

us to understand that with men who die and depart from us the relation is different from that with things which we have lost' (Delitzsch).

14. *Jemimah*, possibly = a dove *Keziah* = cassia (cf. Ps. xlv. 8 ; Cant. i. 3) ; *Keren-happuch* = horn of eye paint.

15. *their father gave them inheritance among their brethren.* According to the Mosaic law the daughters only inherited when there were no sons. See Numb. xxvii. 8.

16. *And Job lived an hundred and forty years.* Another indication that the scene is laid in patriarchal times.

17. *So Job died, being old and full of days.* Cf. the accounts of the deaths of the patriarchs, Abraham, Gen. xxv. 8 ; Isaac, Gen. xxxv. 29 (where the exact phrase *old and full of days* occurs) ; and Joseph, Gen. l. 23, 26.

# INDEX.

[1] In the case of commentaries and works on Job frequently referred to it has not been thought necessary to indicate more than the first reference in this index.

CAMBRIDGE : PRINTED BY J. AND C. F. CLAY, AT THE UNIVERSITY PRESS.

## 1983-84 TITLES

| 0104 | MacDonald, Donald | Biblical Doctrine of Creation and the Fall: Genesis 1-3 | 18.95 |
| 1401 | Bennett, William H. | An Exposition of the Books of Chronicles | 17.50 |
| 1903 | Cox, Samuel | The Pilgrim Psalms: An Exposition of the Songs of Degrees | 9.50 |
| 2703 | Wright, Charles H. H. | Studies in Daniel's Prophecy | 13.95 |
| 3202 | Kirk, Thomas | Jonah: His Life and Mission | 12.95 |
| 4503 | Olshausen, Hermann | Studies in the Epistle to the Romans | 16.50 |
| 8803 | Westcott, Frederick B. | The Biblical Doctrine of Justification | 15.25 |
| 8804 | Salmond, S. D. F. | The Biblical Doctrine of Immortality | 26.95 |
| 9516 | Harris, John | The Teaching Methods of Christ: Characteristics of Our Lord's Ministry | 16.75 |
| 9517 | Blaikie, William G. | The Public Ministry of Christ | 13.25 |
| 9518 | Laidlaw, John | Studies in the Miracles of Our Lord | 14.75 |

## TITLES CURRENTLY AVAILABLE

| 0101 | Delitzsch, Franz | A New Commentary on Genesis ( 2 vol.) | 30.50 |
| 0102 | Blaikie, W. G. | Heroes of Israel | 19.50 |
| 0103 | Bush, George | Genesis (2 vol.) | 29.95 |
| 0201 | Murphy, James G. | Commentary on the Book of Exodus | 12.75 |
| 0202 | Bush, George | Exodus | 22.50 |
| 0203 | Dolman, D. & Rainsford, M. | The Tabernacle (2 vol. in 1) | 19.75 |
| 0301 | Kellogg, Samuel H. | The Book of Leviticus | 21.00 |
| 0302 | Bush, George | Leviticus | 10.50 |
| 0401 | Bush, George | Numbers | 17.95 |
| 0501 | Cumming, John | The Book of Deuteronomy | 16.00 |
| 0601 | Blaikie, William G. | The Book of Joshua | 15.75 |
| 0602 | Bush, George | Joshua & Judges (2 vol. in 1) | 17.95 |
| 0603 | Kirk, Thomas & Lang, John | Studies in the Book of Judges (2 vol. in 1) | 17.75 |
| 0701 | Cox, S. & Fuller, T. | The Book of Ruth (2 vol. in 1) | 14.75 |
| 0901 | Blaikie, William G. | First Book of Samuel | 16.50 |
| 0902 | Deane, W. J. & Kirk, T. | Studies in the First Book of Samuel (2 vol. in 1) | 19.00 |
| 0903 | Blaikie, William G. | Second Book of Samuel | 15.00 |
| 1101 | Farrar, F. W. | The First Book of Kings | 19.00 |
| 1201 | Farrar, F. W. | The Second Book of Kings | 19.00 |
| 1301 | Kirk, T. & Rawlinson, G. | Studies in the Books of Kings (2 vol. in 1) | 20.75 |
| 1701 | Raleigh, Alexander | The Book of Esther | 9.75 |
| 1801 | Gibson, Edgar Charles | The Book of Job (available December) | 10.00 |
| 1802 | Green, William H. | The Argument of the Book of Job Unfolded | 13.50 |
| 1901 | Dickson, David | A Commentary on the Psalms (2 vol.) | 32.50 |
| 1902 | MacLaren, Alexander | The Psalms (3 vol.) | 45.00 |
| 2001 | Wardlaw, Ralph | Book of Proverbs (3 vol.) | 45.00 |
| 2101 | MacDonald, James M. | The Book of Ecclesiastes | 15.50 |
| 2102 | Wardlaw, Ralph | Exposition of Ecclesiastes | 16.25 |
| 2201 | Durham, James | An Exposition on the Song of Solomon | 17.25 |
| 2301 | Kelly, William | An Exposition of the Book of Isaiah | 15.25 |
| 2302 | Alexander, Joseph | Isaiah (2 vol.) | 29.95 |
| 2401 | Orelli, Hans C. von | The Prophecies of Jeremiah | 15.25 |
| 2601 | Fairbairn, Patrick | An Exposition of Ezekiel | 18.50 |
| 2701 | Pusey, Edward B. | Daniel the Prophet | 19.50 |
| 2702 | Tatford, Frederick Albert | Daniel and His Prophecy | 9.25 |
| 3001 | Cripps, Richard S. | A Commentary on the Book of Amos | 13.50 |
| 3201 | Burns, Samuel C. | The Prophet Jonah | 11.25 |
| 3801 | Wright, Charles H. H. | Zechariah and His Prophecies | 24.95 |
| 4001 | Morison, James | The Gospel According to Matthew | 24.95 |
| 4101 | Alexander, Joseph | Commentary on the Gospel of Mark | 16.75 |
| 4102 | Morison, James | The Gospel According to Mark | 21.00 |
| 4201 | Kelly, William | The Gospel of Luke | 18.50 |
| 4301 | Brown, John | The Intercessory Prayer of Our Lord Jesus Christ | 11.50 |
| 4302 | Hengstenberg, E. W. | Commentary on the Gospel of John (2 vol.) | 34.95 |
| 4401 | Alexander, Joseph | Commentary on the Acts of the Apostles (2 vol.) | 27.50 |
| 4402 | Gloag, Paton J. | A Critical and Exegetical Commentary on the Acts of the Apostles (2 vol.) | 29.95 |
| 4403 | Stier, Rudolf E. | Words of the Apostles | 18.75 |
| 4502 | Moule, H. C. G. | The Epistle to the Romans | 16.25 |
| 4601 | Brown, John | The Resurrection of Life | 15.50 |
| 4602 | Edwards, Thomas C. | A Commentary on the First Epistle to the Corinthians | 18.00 |
| 4603 | Jones, John Daniel | Exposition of First Corinthians 13 | 9.50 |
| 4801 | Ramsey, William | Historical Commenatry on the Epistle to the Galatians | 17.75 |
| 4802 | Brown, John | An Exposition of the Epistle of Paul to the Galatians | 16.00 |
| 4901 | Westcott, Brooke F. | St. Paul's Epistle to the Ephesians (available December) | 10.50 |
| 4902 | Pattison, R. & Moule, H. | Exposition of Ephesians: Lessons in Grace and Godliness (2 vol. in 1) | 14.75 |
| 5001 | Johnstone, Robert | Lectures on the Book of Philippians | 18.25 |
| 5102 | Westcott, F. B. | The Epistle to the Colossians | 7.50 |
| 5103 | Eadie, John | Colossians | 10.50 |
| 5104 | Daille, Jean | Exposition of Colossians | 24.95 |
| 5401 | Liddon, H. P. | The First Epistle to Timothy | 6.00 |
| 5601 | Taylor, Thomas | An Exposition of Titus | 20.75 |
| 5801 | Delitzsch, Franz | Commentary on the Epistle to the Hebrews (2 vol.) | 31.50 |
| 5802 | Bruce, A. B. | The Epistle to the Hebrews | 17.25 |
| 5803 | Edwards, Thomas C. | The Epistle to the Hebrews | 13.00 |
| 5901 | Johnstone, Robert | Lectures on the Epistle of James | 16.50 |
| 5902 | Mayor, Joseph B. | The Epistle of St. James | 20.25 |
| 5903 | Stier, Rudolf E. | Commentary on the Epistle of James | 10.25 |
| 6201 | Lias, John J. | The First Epistle of John | 15.75 |
| 6202 | Morgan, J. & Cox S. | The Epistles of John (2 vol. in 1) | 22.95 |
| 6501 | Manton, Thomas | An Exposition of the Epistle of Jude (available December) | 14.00 |
| 6601 | Trench, Richard C. | Commentary on the Epistles to the Seven Churches | 8.50 |
| 7000 | Tatford, Frederick Albert | The Minor Prophets (3 vol.) | 44.95 |
| 7001 | Orelli, Hans C. von | The Twelve Minor Prophets | 15.50 |
| 7002 | Alford, Dean Henry | The Book of Genesis and Part of the Book of Exodus | 12.50 |
| 7003 | Marbury, Edward | Obadiah and Habakkuk | 23.95 |
| 7004 | Adeney, Walter | The Books of Ezra and Nehemiah | 13.00 |
| 7101 | Mayor, Joseph B. | The Epistle of St. Jude & The Second Epistle of Peter | 16.30 |
| 7102 | Lillie, John | Lectures on the First and Second Epistles of Peter | 19.75 |
| 7103 | Hort, F. J. A. & Hort, A. F. | Expository and Exegetical Studies | 29.50 |
| 7104 | Milligan, George | St. Paul's Epistles to the Thessalonians | 12.00 |
| 7105 | Stanley, Arthur P. | Epistles of Paul to the Corinthians | 20.95 |
| 7106 | Moule, H. C. G. | Colossian and Philemon Studies | 12.00 |
| 7107 | Fairbairn, Patrick | The Pastoral Epistles | 17.25 |
| 7108 | Cox, S. & Drysdale, A. H. | The Epistle to Philemon (2 vol. in 1) | 9.25 |

## TITLES CURRENTLY AVAILABLE